The British tradition of minority government

MANCHESTER
1824

Manchester University Press

The British tradition of minority government

Timothy Noël Peacock

Manchester University Press

Published by Manchester University Press
Altrincham Street, Manchester M1 7JA

www.manchesteruniversitypress.co.uk

British Library Cataloguing-in-Publication Data
A catalogue record for this book is available from the British Library

ISBN 978 1 5261 2326 8 hardback

First published 2018

Typeset in Minion Pro by
Servis Filmsetting Ltd, Stockport, Cheshire
Printed in Great Britain by
CPI Group (UK) Ltd, Croydon, CR0 4YY

Contents

Preface

One of the most significant phenomena in British political history since the 1970s has been the formation of minority governments by prime ministers, including Edward Heath, Harold Wilson, Jim Callaghan, John Major and, most recently, Theresa May in June 2017. Steeped in the majoritarian culture of the 'Westminster system', dominated by single-party adversarial majority governments, historians and commentators have not given the phenomenon of minority government the attention it has deserved, which has led to a number of pervasive 'myths'. These myths may be, on the one hand, widely held beliefs explicitly articulated (such as there being a binary choice in election dates between 1978 and 1979). On the other hand, myths may arise through an implicit acceptance of, or a failure to question, the inevitability of certain events (such as the Government formed in April 1976 continuing as a minority without holding an election or forming a coalition).

Consequently, minority governance has been dismissed as an aberration, an interlude between 'normal' and 'victorious' administrations, which have commanded the interest of politicians, political analysts and the general public. This study seeks to challenge these myths and established perceptions of minority government in the 1970s through a reading of declassified internal government and party files, and to demonstrate that there is a distinctive 'British tradition of minority government' that provides a new perspective on the existing corpus of international theory regarding the subject.

To support the concept of this hitherto unrecognised tradition, the study incorporates comparisons with British minority administrations from the 1920s to the Conservative Minority Government elected in June 2017. Comparisons are also made with minority governments globally to distinguish the unique and distinctive contribution of Britain's tradition. There is not the scope here to conduct detailed comparisons across the full range of British minority governments historically. A further study of other administrations will be needed to trace the impact and evolution of this tradition.

Acknowledgements

I would like to express my warmest gratitude to the Arts and Humanities Research Council (AHRC) who funded my initial investigations into the subject; those who gave permission to access unpublished party files; to the staff of the various libraries that I have visited, in particular at the Churchill Archives Centre, Cambridge, the Bodleian Library, Oxford, The National Archives, London, the London School of Economics (LSE) Archives, the Parliamentary Archives, Westminster, the Labour History Archive Study Centre, Manchester, the National Library of Wales, Aberystwyth, and the University of Glasgow Library; the staff of Manchester University Press, for their support in preparing the manuscript; my friends, for their kind words and interest in my work; Professors Phillips O'Brien, Simon Ball and Andrew Thorpe for their advice and encouragement; and last, but not least, my parents, Noël and Sandra Peacock, whose inspiration, unfailing support and encouragement mean more than words can say.

1

Myths, methods and minorities

New perspectives

[On 7 February 1978, Prime Minister James Callaghan] said that it was quite conceivable the outcome of the election would, as he had indicated to Mr Steel, be a close run thing with the Tories being the largest party without an overall majority [...] he would resign in those circumstances [...] in his judgement Mrs Thatcher would certainly try to remain as Prime Minister for as long as possible, even if only for a fortnight – he would do the same in her shoes.[1]

This previously classified Labour Government minute from February 1978 records a candid discussion between Labour Prime Minister James Callaghan and his Principal Private Secretary Sir Kenneth Stowe. At a time when the Government had no overall majority, and a sudden election followed by another 'hung parliament' was considered to be a serious possibility, Callaghan was weighing up whether to resign immediately and allow Conservative Opposition leader Margaret Thatcher to form a minority government, or to attempt to stay in office himself by making further deals with other political parties. On 9 June 2017, the unexpected loss of the Conservative Government's majority in a snap general election led senior Conservatives to weigh up in the early hours of the morning whether or not Prime Minister Theresa May should resign. As it became clearer that the Conservatives would be the largest party and not far short of a majority, the decision taken was that May should remain as leader for the immediate future, and the Government should attempt to remain in office by forming a minority government with the Democratic Unionist Party (DUP).[2]

Conservative plans for a coalition government, a snap general election, prime ministers considering whether to stay in office after an electoral or a referendum defeat, and the contemplation of both Labour and Conservative deals with parties including, among others, the Liberals, Scottish National Party (SNP) and Northern Ireland Unionist parties, are all aspects readily identifiable in British politics since 2010, particularly following the indecisive result in June 2017.[3] However, plans for all these different scenarios, drawn up by political leaders and their advisers in the 1970s, were contained in previously classified files, released in the years up to and after 2015. These documents challenge the mythology that dominates historical accounts, documentary films and television news programmes, in particular the contention that the minority governments of this era were weak, unthinking aberrations, alien to Britain's otherwise strong majoritarian political traditions.

Using these newly available sources, including Labour and Conservative strategy papers, this study provides fresh perspective on 1970s Britain and on the country's contemporary politics. The work examines different aspects that had to be confronted by political leaders, including, *inter alia*, forming governments, handling parliamentary defeats, electoral timing, negotiating with other parties and making post-electoral plans for a minority or coalition government. At one level, by bringing to light hidden narratives, it aims to demythologise the widespread academic and popular understanding of this era, showing that both main parties were far more strategically proactive than has previously been assumed. At another level, it demonstrates the British exceptionalism in minority government against an international backcloth, and provides a methodological foundation for examining contemporary challenges of new forms of government in democracies around the world.

The focus in this study is on events during the 1970s which have not been fully explored, but which were of great importance to contemporary actors in their day-to-day work in Parliament. While some of these events might seem comparatively trivial, they were of critical importance to the *modus operandi* of the Government and Opposition. This means that the study will not give as much attention to some of the issues which have been more widely debated, such as the postwar consensus (a more obvious manifestation of which was the aim of maintaining full employment through state intervention in the economy) and the International Monetary Fund (IMF) crisis in 1976.

Definitional issues: what is a minority government?

Minority government is a concept which has become more commonly articulated in response to the changing landscape of British politics in the twenty-first century. Indecisive opinion-polling led to significant talk of a 'hung parliament' and prospective minority government prior to the 2010 and 2015 general elections, and, following devolved elections in 2016, the administrations in both the Scottish Parliament and Welsh Assembly were minority governments. The June 2017 Westminster election led to a Conservative Minority Government and has provoked much popular and scholarly commentary on the subject. However, the meaning of this term is often not clearly defined and has changed over time.

Minority government in its modern form occurs in a parliamentary democracy when a political party forms a government, but does not itself have a majority of the seats in the main legislative chamber. Such a government has to rely on the cooperation or abstention of other parties for it successfully to enact or repeal legislation, and for its day-to-day survival in votes of confidence.

In the eighteenth and early nineteenth centuries, many, if not all, British administrations, could be regarded more loosely as 'minority' governments. Some did have 'majorities' of MPs in Parliament who aligned with them on particular issues, but such support was not automatically guaranteed. In cases where parliamentary approval was required for a Budget or for legislation, it often resulted in the assembly of ad hoc agreements with individuals or groups of MPs, or else relied on the absence of any unified opposition. A number of governments collapsed in cases when these arrangements failed and ministers were defeated in Parliament on a significant issue.[4]

A number of developments in the mid- to late nineteenth century increased the potential challenges for running governments based on these ad hoc groupings: extension of the voting franchise; the emergence of disciplined political parties; the increased responsibilities of administrations and their need to pass significant parliamentary legislation; and the fact that governments were decided by winning national elections rather than having their leaders selected by the monarch. The increasing 'norm' in Westminster since the Second World War (and even earlier) has been perceived to be that of a single-party majority governance, achieved by the victors at general elections.

The term 'minority government' has sometimes led to confusion when referring to British politics as a class-based conflict between the citizenry and a 'minority' elite in political institutions. Others have taken it as a reference to inequalities in the electoral system, and the ability of parties to win elections on a 'minority', for example, the Labour Government of 2005 and Conservative Government of 2015 winning a majority of parliamentary seats on less than 36.9 per cent of the total votes cast.[5] The term 'minority government' has also been misapplied to presidential or semi-presidential systems, including that in France, in which a separately appointed executive, usually a president, does not hold a corresponding majority in the country's legislature. However, these executives are not totally dependent on their position in a parliament for the continuation of their office. While alternative terms such as 'minority Presidential Government' may serve as clarification, these are not currently widely used. For the purpose of this book, such a 'minority' state will be identified using the conventional label of 'cohabitation', in which a president and legislature are elected separately and controlled by opposing political parties.[6]

The term for describing the state of a parliament without a majority has been subject to some debate. The commonly accepted lexicon of 'hung parliament', first widely used in response to the 1970s experience of minority governments in Britain, has, particularly in advance of and following the 2010 election, been challenged by commentators because of its negative connotations; alternative terms advanced have included 'no overall control' and that of 'a balanced parliament'.[7] However, these labels are themselves indicative of a normative approach to politics, 'balanced' implying the absence of a single-party majority as more favourable. There is also potential confusion with the term 'balanced parliament' being used by commentators to describe constitutional concepts such as the 'balance of powers' between different parts of the legislature, referring to long-standing treatises on parliamentary democracy like Walter Bagehot's *The English Constitution*.[8] The phrases 'minority government' or 'hung parliament', which have been common parlance since the 1970s, will primarily be used here as factual descriptors of the institution.

British tradition of minority government

What is this tradition?

It is our contention that these minority government experiences in the 1970s are indicative of a concept which we shall refer to hereafter as the 'British tradition of minority government'. This 'tradition' consists primarily of the following four aspects:

1) *Preference for minority government when there is no majority*: The main political parties in Britain have historically, when faced with no single-party parliamentary majority in the House of Commons, preferred to form minority governments rather than coalitions. The few exceptions to this are in wartime emergencies or, as in 1931 and 2010, when the country was faced with a perceived significant economic crisis. This is in contrast to the many minority administrations since the late nineteenth century. The Wilson and Callaghan Governments rejected potential plans for coalition or fresh elections, as we shall see in Chapters 3 and 8.
2) *Continued desire for majoritarian rule*: Minority governments in Britain, or main parties faced with the prospect of minority rule, will try, wherever possible, to return to single-party majority rule, rather than accepting political or institutional changes (such as electoral reform) which might lead to future minority or coalition governments. In the 1970s, governments and oppositions blocked a number of proposals that could have brought Britain more into line with minority or coalition-oriented European countries, discussed in greater detail in Chapters 4–6.
3) *Pragmatic adaptation*: Minority governments in Britain have been willing to innovate where necessary to ensure their own political survival and legislative success, while still endeavouring to fulfil their 'continued desire for majoritarian rule'. An example of this in the 1970s would be the negotiation of the limited interparty agreement in the form of the Lib–Lab Pact, often misidentified by commentators as 'confidence and supply'.

4) Self-referencing: Minority governments in Britain have adopted or justified strategies primarily through reference to British political history and the contemporary British political system, rather than by drawing inspiration from other countries with their own established traditions of minority government. Strategy papers from the 1970s provide strong indication of this self-referencing, even of administrations far removed from contemporary experience, such as Conservative Minority Governments from the nineteenth century.

Methodological issues: our model for rereading minority governments

Our work employs a new critical model for the study of minority governments, which, in the first instance, provides fresh scholarly insights into 1970s Britain, but which also may act as a foundation for the re-examination of other historic British minority administrations and those in other countries.

The first distinctive feature of this approach is that the study is structured around an interparty comparison of Minority Labour Governments with the Conservative Oppositions that they were facing. This framework goes beyond existing histories of minority governments, which are often non-comparative or else usually compare administrations from different time periods or from different countries. A parallel study of both parties in the same time period shows how the same historical national political situation conditioned the different responses through their different roles.

Arising from this comparison is the exploration of the Opposition's role in this process. There are as yet no studies concentrating on how opposition parties respond to minority government, the specific challenges faced by them often acting merely as a corollary to those faced by governments. Examination of this underappreciated area demonstrates how significant a problem minority government could be for an opposition party, in terms of parliamentary strategy and the need to avoid appearing irresponsible.

The third aspect of the model is that of combining a rereading of existing theoretical models with a comprehensive historical case study. Many works on minority government are primarily concerned either with revising theoretical models, illustrated through brief references to particular examples, or with non-theorised but nevertheless valuable discussion of the case history of those minority governments. By studying the life cycle of particular minority governments from their formation to dissolution, we are able to investigate areas that have been neglected in minority government theory, including electoral timing and planning for future minority or coalition administrations.

Although there have been a number of works on 1970s British history, these do not devote significant attention to several important areas that will be addressed here, including, amongst others, the 1974 Labour Government, the parliamentary strategies of Callaghan and Thatcher, and Labour/Conservative pre-electoral plans for minority or coalition governments. Even detailed political histories that seek to address some of these areas, including seminal works such as David Butler and Dennis Kavanagh's consideration of the 1974 Government in *The British General Election of October 1974*, were written without access to classified sources.[9] The few works that consider the history of the 1970s in the context of British minority government, including Butler's *Dilemmas of a Hung Parliament* and the relevant chapter of Peter Hennessy's *Distilling the Frenzy*, are necessarily constrained by their particular overarching focus, concentrating on constitutional rather than political aspects, and only able to devote limited space to detailed consideration of any one period.[10]

The essays contained in Anthony Seldon and Kevin Hickson's *New Labour, Old Labour*, published on the thirtieth anniversary of Wilson's return to office in 1974, offer a particularly thorough reappraisal of the Wilson and Callaghan Governments, from policies they enacted to their minority position in Parliament. However, this revisionist work, by the editors' own admission, was intended to provide a state of knowledge prior to release of the secret government and opposition documents that will form the basis of this study.[11]

An important rereading of politics during the 1970s, which draws upon both declassified internal party sources and scholarship, may be found in Andrew Thorpe's *A History of the Labour Party*.[12] However, given the overarching nature of the work, which takes in the entire history of the Labour Party, there is, understandably, not scope within a single chapter to consider the Wilson and Callaghan Governments' parliamentary situation in any significant detail.

More popular histories similarly do not focus on the minority status of these governments. For example, Dominic Sandbrook's *Seasons in the Sun*, while providing some very interesting insights through declassified sources, and acting as a foundation for part of his BBC documentary series *The 1970s*, comments more on the broader socioeconomic and global background of life in Britain during the period.[13]

The international historical and political science corpus of works considering minority government lacks any serious examination of Britain. One of the best indications of this is Kaare Strøm's seminal work *Minority Government and Majority Rule*, in which Wilson's 1974 Minority Labour Government is cited as the principal introductory example, but is given no more consideration throughout the entire book. The only references to British politics in further chapters of the work consist of comments on the majoritarian political culture of Westminster, and the likelihood that this would produce minority as opposed to coalition governments.[14] Thomas Bergman's 1993 work similarly emphasises that Britain and Canada are exceptions to these political science models, as both countries have had fewer minority administrations than other Western Hemisphere countries.[15]

In the run-up to the British general election of 2010, when a hung parliament seemed the most likely outcome, a number of publications sought to address the potential problems of minority government.[16] These studies cited a range of different historical examples of hung parliaments, both from Britain and abroad, with notable contributions being the collaborative works of *No Overall Control*, edited by Alex Brazier and Susanna Kalitowski, on behalf of the Hansard Society, and *Making Minority Government Work*, edited by Roger Hazell and Akash Paun, who were, at the time, both serving at University College London's Constitution Unit.[17] However, the major concern in these works was to inform and influence decision-makers in the event of no party gaining a majority in 2010 and subsequent elections, rather than to provide a more in-depth historical analysis of the experience, political approach or strategy of any past British minority government, which will be the focus in this book.

International minority government theory

As highlighted, the study of minority governments around the world has, comparatively speaking, received less attention from historians and political scientists as opposed to that afforded to coalitions or single-party majority governments. It is only since the beginning of the twenty-first century that this field has begun to provoke greater scholarly interest in countries facing fresh experiences with minority administrations, including pioneering studies on minority governments in Spain and Australia that seek to redefine our understanding of the field as a whole.[18]

Theoretical appraisals from the 1950s onwards, rather than studying minority government as a phenomenon in itself, examined such governments as 'deviant cases' of unfulfilled potential coalitions. Later works since the 1970s have sought to redress this imbalance, looking at minority administrations as the product of rational actors and not inherently weaker than other forms of democratic government. The most detailed studies of minority government have been produced in countries with relatively commonplace experiences of such administrations, including, amongst others, Denmark and Canada. While there are similarities between minority governments in different countries, there are also significant variations and distinct national political cultures and institutions. Increased occurrences of minority governments around the world after the 2008 financial crisis have promoted greater scholarly interest. However, as indicated, the UK has been curiously neglected. Minority governments in Britain have received even less consideration in their own right than their counterparts in other countries, whether by scholars of political history or those working in the political science aspects of minority government.[19]

By looking at some of the developments in minority government theory, it is possible to glimpse a particularly confusing picture. Orthodox theories have never fully been discredited, while revisionist and other subsequent theoretical considerations often provide only unsteady foundations that continue to be much contested by scholars. While it would be impractical to consider all the different aspects of this theoretical development, a brief overview will chart something of the debates, as well as highlighting aspects that will be relevant for consideration of the Wilson and Callaghan Governments and their Conservative opponents in subsequent chapters.

Early theorised approaches used game-theory models to analyse political leaders as rational actors, including the pioneering work of William Riker in the 1950s, *The Theory of Political Coalitions*, which established important foundations for coalition theory and what would become the orthodox view of minority governments.[20] This orthodoxy, developed in subsequent studies, characterised minority governments in an almost completely negative light, in effect representing 'failed' coalitions. They are seen as rare deviations from the 'norm' of majority governments, arising from crises, fractionalisation of existing party systems, increased political polarisation or unresolvable conflicts between parties and as inherently weak and short-lived. Furthermore, such political actors, it is argued, are primarily driven to seek office rather than other goals such as enactment of policies, while, as with coalition formation more generally, any attempts to construct coalitions will always favour the smallest number of MPs/parties needed to get a majority (or 'minimal-winning coalition'). While 'minimal winning' has been much criticised or modified, not least to include the general preference for coalitions of ideologically similar parties, it continues to act as a powerful starting point for explaining the political behaviour of what are still perceived to be 'rational actors'.

Revisionist scholarship, led by Strøm's articles in the 1980s and his seminal work *Minority Government and Majority Rule*, has largely accepted the game-theory approach, but challenged the cited causes and conclusions about minority governments, suggesting that: such governments are far more common across different European countries; they may be the product of rational behaviour by political actors; they are not necessarily weaker or more short-lived than majority or coalition governments; and parties may pursue alternative goals to seeking office – including maximising votes or enactment of certain policies.[21]

Following Strøm's work, scholars have reinterpreted the previously listed causes of minority government, as well as looking to other factors that may influence the government-formation process, a particularly important debate being over the effect of institutions on constraining or facilitating particular types of government formation. Some of these ideas were widely accepted, including the notion that minority governments were more likely to form in cases where this is a 'negative' framing of parliamentary rules, supposedly the case in Britain; that is, a new government did not have to win a parliamentary vote to establish itself, and could exist if tolerated by opposition parties. Even this idea has not gone unchallenged, however – an alternative suggestion by Lanny Martin and Randolph Stevenson in 2010 being that the probability of a minority government forming does not depend on the presence or absence of a formal investiture rule, based upon a new data sample of different governments.[22] Furthermore, this study, with its focus on highlighting the importance of parties working together in the past as a guide to future cooperation, also serves to reflect the employment of other non-institutional factors, including decision-making by individual party leaders and local political history.

Uncertainty over what constitutes a minority government in practice has led to theorists debating the boundaries between minority and majority governments, and how these governments should be defined. Taylor and Laver, amongst others,[23] have argued that minority governments which 'almost' pass the majority threshold are more likely to be able to stay in power by relying on the votes of one or two parliamentarians from other parties, and even, in some cases, to function similarly to a majority government. There have been a number of developments since the 1980s aiming to understand the greater complexity of political actors that shape minority government and coalition formation. Thomas Bergman's model of 'multiple goals in multiple arenas', for example, suggests that different branches of the same party may seek different outcomes at a local or national level in terms of forming a minority or coalition government.[24]

Studies have also sought further to challenge well-established notions that would, on the face of it, appear to be long-held self-evident truths of minority government, such as their desirability. One such example may be seen in Yannick Dufresne and Neil Nevitte's study of public perceptions of minority government in Canada, suggesting that, contrary to 'conventional wisdom', 'substantial proportions of the Canadian public actually prefer minority rather than majority governments'. Undoubtedly this is an area of investigation which may well be much explored and debated by scholars in the years ahead.[25]

Some theoretical observations of minority government behaviour also would initially appear rather paradoxical, such as those of Christoffer Green-Pedersen; he argues that particularly contentious legislation in 1980s Denmark, including significant welfare reform and tax changes, could only be passed as a result of a minority rather than majority government, given the need for elements in different parties to cooperate with one another against legislators within their own parties and external pressure groups who would have otherwise blocked the measures.[26] Regardless of which perspective is adopted, the absence of a guaranteed legislative majority undoubtedly presents the most significant set of strategic challenges which the leadership of a minority government has to overcome on a day-to-day basis.

Demythologising minority government

It is sometimes difficult to identify the distinct 'myths' that have been formed around the 1970s minority governments. Reflection on this period through the prism of subsequent events has dominated the popular discourse so much that these myths are not always clearly articulated.

Labour's eighteen years in opposition after being defeated in 1979 reinforced notions of failure and also conditioned the extra-parliamentary focus of Wilson and Callaghan's legacy. The Thatcher Governments, facing bitter conflicts against trade union power in the 1980s, sought to buttress their position through raising the spectre of their predecessors' failures, particularly in the 'Winter of Discontent'. Politicians and activists on the left wing of Labour, and those who later supported the modernising agenda of 'New Labour', also frequently criticised their political forebears, emphasising policy failures to add intellectual credence to their own political agendas to reshape the party, and to reposition it ideologically further to the left or right.[27]

One of the best examples of how these perceptions have been shaped may be seen in the BBC news tribute to Callaghan after his death in 2005, prepared and narrated by Political Editor Andrew Marr, using archival footage.[28] The opening lines of the report immediately framed his time in office as part of these greater meta-narratives: 'Jim Callaghan was Old Labour's last Prime Minister, and the only man to have held all four Great Offices of State. He was also the man toppled after the "Winter of Discontent", by the very trade unions he had courted all his life.' Some of the most dominant and stark footage in the report consisted of picket lines and strikes, or of Callaghan being interviewed about being unable to recover from the adverse economic situation. The closing bucolic image of the former Prime Minister retiring to his farm, surrounded by sheep, was a poignant metaphor of the loss of political stature. While Callaghan was naturally the focus of such a report, Parliament was barely even mentioned, with no reference to Callaghan not having a majority or the loss of votes which eventually brought down the Government.

In part, the 'myths' of these news reports and documentaries, concentrating on extra-parliamentary events, have been conditioned by the availability of film material. Coverage of prime ministers from the 1990s onwards has often included clips of significant events from the House of Commons, such as Geoffrey Howe's resignation speech which helped to bring down Thatcher, or David Cameron's charge of 'he was the future once' to Tony Blair at Prime Minister's Questions in 2005. This footage does not exist for the Wilson and Callaghan years. Television recording of the House of Commons did not begin until November 1989, and radio coverage had only begun sporadically from 1975. As such, the importance of events that were filmed outside Parliament during this earlier period are all the more magnified in television media coverage, and in the documentaries and programmes on the period.[29]

Efforts to cover parliamentary events in greater detail have been limited and have relied on fresh interviews with contemporary participants.[30] However, even these interviews, along with the preponderance of biographies or personal reflections in the form of political diaries and memoirs, do not have an overall specific focus on minority government, principally aiming to put into the public domain the interviewee's/author's recollections of the events, with the view sometimes being to revise popular perceptions of the author or that of her or his biographical subject.[31]

One of the single greatest myths arising from these sources of coverage is that outside events superseded those in Parliament, the main parties in the 1970s concentrating more on policy and external socioeconomic pressures, and not thinking strategically about the state of minority government beyond merely reacting to events on a day-to-day basis. Chapter 2 will question this myth and will show that the strategy-making processes in the Labour and the Conservative Parties were geared towards minority government. While political 'strategies' pursued by parties, internal conflicts over strategy or approaches to individual pieces of legislation have received significant consideration, studies have not often examined the underlying strategy-making processes in detail, along with the relative importance of the particular bodies and individuals involved.[32]

The first section will lay the foundation for subsequent chapters by ana-lysing these strategy-making processes, demonstrating how groups that have been traditionally ignored were, in fact, both influenced by, and influential in, internal discussions. Papers from Conservative leader Edward Heath's 'Party Strategy Group', for example, indicate that its creation in 1974 was primarily a response to the then recently formed Wilson Minority Government. The remit of this group included the study of minority government and different strategies, including considering plans to establish a formal Conservative–Liberal electoral pact. Although significant work was done to promote this latter possibility, the disbanding of the group for largely political reasons in 1975 temporarily curtailed further planning in this area.[33]

While no new separate units were created thereafter during the 1970s solely to deal with minority government, papers and correspondence from the existing government and opposition groups demonstrate that their procedures for strat-egy formation were often modified, and that some new institutions were created to consider different aspects relating to minority government, such as periodic meetings between Callaghan and all the Government whips.

The chapter will also highlight the role of individuals in the different parties who advised the party leadership on minority government, whether leaders of research departments for the Government and Opposition, such as Bernard Donoughue or Chris Patten, or those who served in other important roles, including, among others, Michael Foot, Tom McNally, David Lipsey, Keith Joseph and Lord Thorneycroft.

It has often been assumed that the formation of the Wilson and Callaghan Minority Governments were inevitable, histories mainly concentrating on changes in personnel and policy. Chapter 3 will challenge this long-standing myth by examining the prospect of alternative possibilities that were considered but not adopted, including early elections or interparty coalitions.

The effects of the 1975 European referendum will also be examined in this and subsequent chapters as part of the internal strategic dialogue. While conducted under a majority government, the referendum prompted further planning related to minority and coalition administrations, including the Conservatives' active consideration of forming a national unity government as a response to Labour's internal difficulties in the aftermath of the result.

A particular focus of existing studies and televised histories is that of extra-parliamentary events during this period, such as the IMF crisis.[34] Wilson's experience of taking office in 1974 without a majority is often largely ignored, being subsumed within discussion of his other administrations, or tied more into the defeat of the Heath Government and its failure to form a coalition. When considering Callaghan, his accession to the premiership is normally recorded in a few lines, noting the transition, emphasising his personal qualities, his choice of personnel and/or the tasks and limitations faced by his new administration.[35] While Peter Hennessy's *Distilling the Frenzy*, provides some interesting historico-political insights into changes in the processes of forming British minority governments since the 1970s, the constitutional scope of this work limits any detailed exploration of parliamentary strategy.[36]

The chapter will begin by considering alternatives to Labour Minority Governments that were explored by contemporary policymakers from both parties. One such alternative, for example, may be seen in the prime ministerial minutes, which record the previously unrecognised complexity of the Heath Government's failed efforts to remain in office during March 1974, examining the possibility of forming a Conservative Minority Government through deals with other parties, including the SNP.[37] Another example includes internal correspondence and discussions between Callaghan and Cabinet ministers following his appointment as Prime Minister, showing that the Government was considering a formal interparty deal with the Northern Ireland Social Democratic and Labour Party (SDLP) in order to retain a parliamentary majority.[38]

The final part of the chapter will consider the often overlooked role of the Conservative Opposition, and their internal debates on how to respond to the 'new' state of minority government. Different options were considered, including calls for the potential restructuring of parliamentary committees and how relations were conducted between the Government and Opposition. The internal dialogue shows that, in spite of changes in the leadership of the party, the opposition approach to Callaghan linked back to precedents and discussions initiated in response to Wilson's Government.

Parliamentary defeats are often cited as evidence of the weakness of governments, even more so those without a majority. Chapter 4 will question the myths of 1970s minority governments' inability to pass significant legislation without the cooperation of opposition parties. In addition, it will challenge the contrary myth, that of the powerlessness of the Opposition to engineer parliamentary defeats.[39] These reassessments will look at the evolution of Labour and Conservative political management of parliamentary defeats, including more radical options that were considered to pass parliamentary bills, such as pre-legislative referenda. There is no single work concentrating on either Wilson or Callaghan's relations with Parliament. Philip Norton's valuable examination of MP rebellions during the 1970s addresses parliamentary relations more from a statistical than strategic perspective.[40]

The first part of this chapter will consider often overlooked early conflicts for both administrations. Internal party files show the importance of these events in establishing the legislative *modus operandi* for the new minority governments. Confrontations considered will include the Wilson Government's Queen's Speech in 1974 and the Callaghan Government's dispute over the Aircraft and Shipbuilding Bill in 1976. The internal strategic dialogues that will be explored here include some of the proposed methods for circumventing the state of minority government, such as assigning seats to committees considering legislation on the basis of a bill's majority, rather than on the political composition of Parliament. The Opposition's withdrawal from cooperation with the Government during a legislative dispute in 1976 led to internal Conservative debates which questioned how long this obstruction of parliamentary business could be maintained, and whether this reactive measure could be employed as a deliberate future tactic.

The second part of this chapter will consider in greater depth the Government's proposed but often unimplemented procedural and institutional reforms for dealing with minority government. Some of these potential innovations included reform of the House of Lords, the introduction of proxy or electronic voting in the Commons and the use of pre-legislative UK-wide referenda to enable passage of the Devolution Bill in 1976–77.

Thereafter, the chapter will look at other radical approaches which were considered, such as both governments actively contemplating or seeking their own defeat in Parliament on certain issues. The first defeat of the Wilson Minority Administration, for example, on the issue of tax and trade union funding, was actually celebrated by government MPs and seen by Labour's strategy-makers as an important step towards any future election campaign.

The Conservative–Liberal Democrat Coalition Government at Westminster in 2010–15 represented a historic first in postwar British politics, but its antecedents were a very different kind of interparty agreement – the Pact between the Liberals and Labour during the 1970s. Chapter 5 will explore the myths surrounding the inevitability and form of this 1977–78 Lib–Lab Pact, and how both main parties actively considered other forms of formal interparty cooperation during this period.

As of 2017, only three books have been published which focus solely on the Pact, one of which was written prior to the 1979 election, while another was authored by the Liberal leader, David Steel, an architect of and major participant in the Pact.[41] A long overdue and particularly scholarly contribution has been Jonathan Kirkup's 2016 book, although, given his specialism, the focus of the work is, understandably, on the Liberals, rather than on the Labour and Conservative strategies that we shall be examining.[42] Mark Oaten's 2007 work *Coalition* revisits and rereads the Lib–Lab Pact using papers declassified in 2006–7, but, as an overarching study of the phenomenon of 'Coalition', it devotes limited space to the 1970s.[43]

A particular focus of this chapter will be the often overlooked renegotiation of the Pact, showing the alternative options that were explored by the Government. Declassified records that were originally not supposed to be retained provide especially interesting insights into the internal debates, including a record of a special Strategy Cabinet at Chequers in the summer of 1977. Other papers provide a further basis for demythologising the operation and end of the Pact. Suggestions of any official record of Callaghan and Steel's meetings were firmly denied at the time. However, such records were, in fact, kept, providing a particularly useful source and containing sometimes very open and detailed discussions between the two leaders about aspects of minority government that do not appear in their autobiographical accounts or television interviews.

While it has often been assumed that the Opposition were staunchly against coalitions and pacts, the latter part of this chapter examines the Conservatives' response to the Pact and their exploration of potential interparty deals during the Callaghan Government.

The emphasis on the Pact has often been relegated to a few lines or soundbites about other interparty initiatives during this period. The only detailed considerations have been reserved for the most important instances, such as the no confidence vote in 1979, which will be examined in Chapter 9. Chapter 6 will explore the myths concerning the avoidance of informal interparty cooperation during the Pact, and the belief that any informal agreements were the exclusive purview of the Government. This chapter will include consideration of how the Government and Opposition responded to the prospect of informal cooperation with the Liberals, Scottish and Welsh Nationalist Parties, and Unionist and Republican Parties from Northern Ireland.[44]

This chapter will focus particularly on hitherto unrecognised internal debates on interparty cooperation: how such interactions should be conducted; the extent to which the main parties were willing to compromise; and day-to-day legislative battles that were important but which are usually neglected in favour of headline-grabbing bills. These discussions included the Government's consideration of alternative ad hoc legislative deals with the Ulster Unionists and

SNP during the Pact, at times when Liberal cooperation was not considered to be forthcoming. These strategic dialogues also reveal the Government's active avoidance of approaches employed by minority governments overseas, such as the co-authoring of legislation by different parties and official sponsoring of bills by individual MPs.

The few works that consider these smaller parties in their own right during this period have not, by the nature of their holistic approach and source availability, been able to give as much consideration to such parties' strategies pertaining to minority government. While evidence of parliamentary strategies within these smaller parties is often limited or inaccessible, it has been possible to locate some of this material through alternative channels. One such example has been that of internal strategy papers contained in the archives of Enoch Powell, Ulster Unionist MP, not subject to the fifty-year rule of the Ulster Unionist Party's (UUP's) archives. This consideration of the parliamentary contribution of these newer parties to minority government, at a time when they first gained significant levels of representation in Westminster during the 1970s, is particularly relevant as a foundation for further studies of such parties in their own right through the optics of parliamentary affairs and minority government.[45]

The latter section of this chapter will re-examine the Opposition's approach to informal interparty cooperation, including the greater complexity of their relations with the Liberals, and efforts to gain support from smaller parties including the UUP.

In addition to studying the meetings and correspondence involving the party leaders, this chapter will incorporate papers from the party organisations, including from Labour's National Executive Committee (NEC), which will highlight the existence, but also significant limitations, of wider cross-party cooperation during this period.

Prime Minister Theresa May's shock announcement in April 2017 of a general election provides a clear example of the continued, and often overlooked, importance of electoral timing. Electoral timing could be of even greater significance for minority governments. Chapter 7 will address several of the most persistent myths about 1970s elections: that there was a fixed binary choice in the electoral timing for the different governments; that the actual choice of an election date was inevitable; and that these dates were the product of political gambling, rather than serious and detailed strategic consideration. The myth that the Opposition was purely a reactive observer to this process of timing will also be looked at in detail. This chapter seeks, in addition, to address the lack of detailed consideration of electoral timing as a subject in its own right, as it is normally confined to brief discussions within overarching political histories or books on election campaigns. An exception to this omission is Alastair Smith's *Election Timing*, although this is primarily an overarching comparative political science work, rather than a detailed historical case study.[46]

As a direct result of the state of minority government, both main parties in 1970s Britain actually conducted extensive planning for an election being called across a range of different dates. The 1974 Wilson Government considered whether to call a general election within weeks of taking office in March, alternative dates to the actual October 1974 poll ranging from June 1974 through to early 1975. Rather than the autumn 1978/spring 1979 dichotomy that is usually presented by historians and political analysts for the Callaghan Government, a general election was considered at various points during 1976, 1977, 1978 and 1979.[47]

The chapter will go on to discuss the considerable efforts of government and opposition strategy-makers to forecast possible election dates, as well as prepare for contingencies that took into account a number of different factors. Internal papers, including briefings prepared for Wilson and Callaghan, records of meetings and correspondence between advisers, allow for a re-examination of the strategic motivations behind the Government's timing. Callaghan's consultations were far more wide-ranging than is evident in his autobiography, and the state of minority government was even more central to the decision over timing than has previously been recognised. These papers also reveal an evolving strategic dialogue, including Callaghan's order for the preparation of contingency plans in the event of an unexpected major legislative defeat and forced election.[48]

The final section will discuss Conservative efforts to anticipate a possible election date, including such sources as calendars, minutes of meetings and hypothetical wargames. Forecasting sometimes compelled strategy-makers to question the very basis of their assumptions and rationality of their opponents. At one point, leading Conservative Research Department (CRD) members trying to understand the Government's decisions over electoral timing wondered if Callaghan was not seeking electoral victory, but rather another minority government or coalition.

The uncertainty of the result in the 2015 election, following the existing coalition government prompted much speculation and interest in what plans the different parties had for post-electoral government formation. Their 1970s counterparts were similarly engaged in such preparations, albeit in some cases more embryonic. Chapter 8 will deal with the myth that Labour and Conservative post-electoral plans were only geared towards outright victory. This section will examine Labour's, and especially the Conservatives', secret plans for future minority or coalition governments.

Even those studies which recognise contemporary fears of another hung parliament do not consider internal Labour and Conservative planning for future minority or coalition governments.[49] Those few works which have examined the history of coalition and national unity governments in Britain were either written prior to the release of the internal documents, or else do not use them to discuss this pre-electoral planning.[50] Some of these sources include the record of Callaghan's personal reflections on post-electoral strategy following one of his meetings with Steel in 1978, and papers from his political advisers setting out starting points for how to approach prospective post-electoral coalition negotiations.

The Conservatives' campaign for a government of national unity in October 1974 has often been regarded as merely an electoral tactic. However, internal debates over the shape of any such prospective coalition show that great attention was given to this proposal. Papers detailing the Opposition's approach to an indecisive 1978–79 election show even more evidence than the Government of plans for coalition. Members of the CRD were tasked to produce at least three different plans in 1977–78 concerning the possibilities of minority and coalition government following a general election. Although Thatcher disliked public admission of anything other than outright victory, she facilitated internal discussion of these papers by a special committee that she had established, chaired by her close ally Keith Joseph, to examine plans for a future Conservative Government. These blueprints, with titles such as 'The Hung Parliament Contingency', were part of an internal opposition strategic dialogue, containing such insights as an exploration of the conditions under which the Conservatives would seek to form a minority government or coalition following an election. These papers also examined more radical possibilities, including the unthinkable prospect of the Conservatives making a coalition deal with the SNP, or even a grand coalition with Labour.

Many governments in Britain and abroad, both minority and majority, have been brought down by votes of no confidence, although the absence of a majority increases this possibility significantly. The penultimate chapter will re-examine three myths regarding the demise of the Callaghan Government, following defeat in a no confidence vote on 28 March 1979: that the calling of the no confidence vote was a forgone conclusion; that the result of this no confidence vote was inevitable; and that the Government's defeat in a no confidence vote was detrimental to its subsequent electoral performance. The chapter will also particularly consider the effect of a minority government on both major parties, in terms of learning from their experience over the previous five years, in relation to the situation that they were facing in March 1979 itself and their concerns regarding the prospect of future minority/coalition administrations.

When considering the end of the 1970s governments, the focus has often been on the major extra-parliamentary events faced by Heath, Wilson and Callaghan, from the 'Three-Day Week' and European referendum, to the IMF crisis and the 'Winter of Discontent', rather than on the parliamentary strategies and struggles of minority government.[51] Even works challenging some of the myths surrounding the 'Winter of Discontent' understandably focus less on the parliamentary and minority government optic.[52]

The first part of this chapter considers the Government's approach to the failure of the referenda on devolution, often regarded as the trigger for the no confidence vote. Cabinet discussions and internal correspondence show that there was a more strategic dimension. This discussion will also include analysis of Callaghan's meeting with all the Government whips in March 1979, prior to the SNP issuing a no confidence vote. The meeting included a particularly extensive discussion, giving greater insight not only into Callaghan's mindset regarding efforts to avoid a prospective confidence vote, but also the different possible strategies that were being considered by the whips and the assumptions or justifications underpinning their reasoning.

The second part of the chapter, which considers the inevitability of government defeat in the confidence vote after it was issued, re-examines some of the notable efforts to make deals with smaller parties. While studies have concentrated on the Government, this analysis will look at how both main parties approached the no confidence vote, the internal strategic dialogues revealing some assumptions and views that we might find surprising. One example may be seen in the Cabinet's concern to avoid a quick repeal of the Wales Act on devolution 'as this would drive Plaid Cymru into supporting the Conservative Party'.[53]

Planning for interparty deals, even where these were not implemented, such as building a Northern Ireland gas pipeline to ensure Ulster Unionist support, also provides new perspectives on strategic approaches to the no confidence vote. While both Labour and the Conservatives publicly refuted the gas pipeline plan, the Conservatives did examine the political and financial implications of this measure, as well as their possible responses if the Government ended up supporting it.

The third part of the chapter will look at the effects of the no confidence defeat, arguing that, contrary to the experience of some minority governments elsewhere, while the defeat may have been discouraging for Labour MPs, in practice, its effect on the Government's poll rating and the party's electoral campaign was not significant.

The final chapter will consider how these different myths of 1970s Britain, which we have deconstructed in the preceding chapters, continue to resonate with contemporary politics, including, in particular, the June 2017 Conservative Minority Government. Longer-term implications of this study for future political decision-making regarding minority governments and coalition will be assessed, as well as the potential impact on future scholarship.

There have been few works over the last thirty years which have specifically addressed the context and comparative history of British minority governments on a national level. One of the most notable and often overlooked, David Butler's 1983 book on *Governing without a Majority*, does not deal with the historical experiences of any one minority government in significant detail.[54]

Our examination of the legacy of the 1970s will include a brief re-evaluation of the impact of this era on the short periods of Major's Minority Governments in 1993–94 and 1996–97, a development often ignored in both scholarly and popular commentary. The impact on the 2010–15 Westminster coalition will similarly be considered, as will the fears of a minority government in the run-up to the 2010 and 2015 general elections, with a particular focus on the use of history by commentators and political participants.

The chapter will analyse the aftermath of the June 2017 election, comparing the formation of and potential challenges for the Conservative Minority Government and Labour Opposition to those faced by their 1970s counterparts, and exploring how the work of the previous chapters may provide insights into understanding current and future developments. For all these comparisons, the documentation used will include additional material for the later periods, derived from a combination of files released after 2008, and from publicly available sources, including Hansard, newspapers, interviews and television news coverage.

The final part of the chapter will consider how the June 2017 minority government at Westminster may affect planning for future indecisive election results at a UK and devolved level, taking into account as far as possible the significant ongoing political changes. The section will, in addition, consider the subsequent application of the method established in this book to future studies which might further our understanding of the 'British tradition of minority government', gain new insights into minority governments domestically and internationally, and challenge historical myths in other areas.

Notes

1 The National Archives (TNA): PREM 16/1621, Note for the Record: The Outcome of the Next General Election, 7 February 1978.

2 *BBC News* (10 June 2017).

3 A. Seldon, M. Finn and I. Thomas (eds), *The Coalition Effect, 2010–2015* (Cambridge: Cambridge University Press, 2015), pp. 31–58, 87.

4 See Chapter 2.

5 H. J. Perkin, *The Third Revolution: Professional Elites in the Modern World* (London: Routledge, 1996), pp. 65–6; G. Dietze, *America's Political Dilemma: From Limited to Unlimited Democracy* (London: University Press of America, 1985), p. 191.

6 R. Elgie, *Semi-Presidentialism: Sub Types and Democratic Performance* (Oxford: Oxford University Press, 2011), pp. 179–82; J. A. Cheibub, *Presidentialism, Parliamentarism, and Democracy* (Cambridge: Cambridge University Press, 2007), pp. 5, 11–12, 60–2; K. Strøm, W. C. Muller and T. Bergman (eds), *Delegation and Accountability in Parliamentary Democracies* (Oxford: Oxford University Press, 2006), p. 328.

7 'Balanced Parliament: No Need to Rush', *Guardian* (5 May 2010); A. Blick and S. Wilks-Heeg, 'Governing without Majorities: Coming to Terms with Balanced Parliaments in UK Politics', *Democratic Audit General Election Briefing*, 1 (2010), 1–2; A. Brazier and S. Kalitowski (eds), *No Overall Control* (London: Hansard Society, 2008), pp. 1–4.

8   W. Bagehot, *The English Constitution* (Brighton: Sussex Academic Press, 1997), p. ix.

9   D. Butler and D. Kavanagh, *The British General Election of October 1974* (London: Macmillan, 1975).

10 P. Hennessy, *Distilling the Frenzy: Writing the History of One's Own Times* (London: Biteback Publishing, 2013); D. Butler, *Governing without a Majority: Dilemmas for Hung Parliaments in Britain* (London: Collins, 1983).

11 A. Seldon and K. Hickson (eds), *New Labour, Old Labour: The Wilson and Callaghan Governments* (London: Routledge, 2004), pp. 1–5, 190–206.

12 A. Thorpe, *A History of the British Labour Party* (London: Palgrave Macmillan, 4th edn, 2015), pp. 195–208.

13 D. Sandbrook, *Seasons in the Sun: The Battle for Britain, 1974–1979* (London: Penguin, 2012).

14 K. Strøm, *Minority Government and Majority Rule* (Cambridge: Cambridge University Press, 1990), pp. 1–4, 42, 90–1, 126.

15 T. Bergman, 'Formation Rules and Minority Governments', *European Journal of Political Research*, 23:1 (1993), 60.

16 R. Blackburn, R. Fox, O. Gay and L. Maer, 'Who Governs? Forming a Coalition or a Minority Government in the Event of a Hung Parliament', Hansard Society: Study of Parliament Group (2010); A. Paun and R. Hazell, 'Hung Parliaments and the Challenges for Westminster and Whitehall: How to Make Minority and Multiparty Governance Work', *The Political Quarterly*, 81:2 (2010), 213–27; Blick and Wilks-Heeg, 'Governing without Majorities', 6–9.

17 R. Hazell and A. Paun (eds), *Making Minority Government Work: Hung Parliaments and the Challenges for Westminster and Whitehall* (London: UCL Constitution Unit, 2009); Brazier and Kalitowski (eds), *No Overall Control?*

18 B. N. Field, *Why Minority Governments Work: Multilevel Territorial Politics in Spain* (Houndmills: Palgrave Macmillan, 2016); B. Prosser and R. Denniss, *Minority Policy: Rethinking Governance when Parliament Matters* (Melbourne: Melbourne University Publishing, 2015).

19 See, for example, J. Kaarbo, *Coalition Politics and Cabinet Decision Making: A Comparative Analysis of Foreign Policy Choices* (Ann Arbor, MI: University of Michigan Press, 2012); R. B. Andeweg, L. De Winter and P. Dumont (eds), *Puzzles of Government Formation: Coalition Theory and Deviant Cases* (London: Routledge, 2011), pp. 9, 88–90, 112; G. Tsebelis, *Veto Players: How Political Institutions Work* (Princeton, NJ: Princeton University Press, 2011), pp. 93–9, 214–20; D. Arter, *Democracy in Scandinavia: Consensual, Majoritarian or Mixed?* (Manchester: Manchester University Press, 2006), pp. 8–11, 59, 98–9, 238–57; Strøm, Muller and Bergman (eds), *Delegation and Accountability in Parliamentary Democracies*, pp. 282, 291–3, 297–8, 430, 629; M. Laver and N. Schofield, *Multiparty Government: The Politics of Coalition in Europe* (Oxford: Oxford University Press, 1998), pp. 6, 53, 72–81.

20 W. Riker, *The Theory of Political Coalitions* (New Haven, CT: Yale University Press, 1962), pp. 1–6, 47.

21 Strøm, *Minority Government and Majority Rule*, pp. 17, 23–4, 93–131; K. Strøm, 'Minority Governments in Parliamentary Democracies: The Rationality of Nonwinning Cabinet Solutions', *Comparative Political Studies*, 17:2 (1984), 199–227.

22 L. W. Martin and R. T. Stevenson, 'The Conditional Impact of Incumbency on Government Formation', *American Political Science Review*, 104:3 (2010), 503–18.

23 Hazell and Paun (eds), *Making Minority Government Work*, pp. 1–18, 45; Arter, *Democracy in Scandinavia*, pp. 8, 16–18, 99–105; C. Green-Pedersen, 'Minority Governments and Party Politics: The Political and Institutional Background to the "Danish Miracle"', *Journal of Public Policy*, 21:1 (2001), 53–70; Strøm, *Minority Government and Majority Rule*, pp. 60–3; V. Herman and J. Pope, 'Minority Government in Western Democracies', *British Journal of Political Science*, 3:2 (1973), 195, 198–201; M. Taylor and M. Laver, 'Government Coalitions in Western Europe', *European Journal of Political Research*, 1:3 (1973), 229–33.

24 T. Bergman, *Constitutional Rules and Party Goals in Coalition Formation: An Analysis of Winning Minority Governments in Sweden* (Umeå: Umeå University, 1995), pp. 1–10, 167, 181.

25 Y. Dufresne and N. Nevitte, 'Why do Publics Support Minority Governments? Three Tests', *Parliamentary Affairs*, 67:4 (2014), 825–40; T. C. Lundberg, 'Politics is Still an Adversarial Business: Minority Government and Mixed-Member Proportional Representation in Scotland and in New Zealand', *British Journal of Politics and International Relations*, 15:4 (2013), 609–25.

26 Green-Pedersen, 'Minority Governments and Party Politics', 53–70; Strøm, *Minority Government and Majority Rule*, pp. 4–5, 18–19.

27 M. Pugh, *Speak for Britain! A New History of the Labour Party* (London: Vintage, 2011), pp. 354, 389; G. Rosen, *Old Labour to New: The Dreams that Inspired, the Battles that Divided* (London: Politico's, 2005), p. 383; P. Diamond, *New Labour's Old Roots: Revisionist Thinkers in Labour's History, 1931–97* (Exeter: Imprint Academic, 2004), pp. 4, 168; Seldon and Hickson (eds), *New Labour, Old Labour*, pp. i, 1, 321–2; P. Gould, 'The Land that Labour Forgot', in A. Chadwick, *The New Labour Reader* (Cambridge: Polity Press, 2003), pp. 39–42; P. Whitehead, *The Writing on the Wall: Britain in the Seventies* (London: Joseph, 1985); P. Whiteley, *The Labour Party in Crisis* (London: Methuen & Co., 1983), pp. 1–5, 129, 185, 207.

28 *BBC News* (26 March 2005).

29 For example: BBC Documentary Series, *The 70s* (April–May 2012); *The Iron Lady* (film, 2011).

30 BBC Documentary, *The Night the Government Fell (A Parliamentary Coup)* (31 May 2009).

31 See, for example, A. S. Crines and K. Hickson (eds), *Harold Wilson: The Unprincipled Prime Minister? Reappraising Harold Wilson* (London: Biteback Publishing, 2016); C. Moore, *Margaret Thatcher: The Authorised Biography*, vol. 1: *Not for Turning* (London: Allen Lane, 2013); D. Torrance, *David Steel: Rising Hope to Elder Statesman* (London: Biteback Publishing, 2012); K. O. Morgan, *Michael Foot: A Life* (London: HarperCollins, 2007); R. Jenkins, *A Life at the Centre* (London: Politico's Publishing, 2006); B. Donoughue, *Downing Street Diary: With James Callaghan in No. 10*, vol. 2 (London: Jonathan Cape, 2008); K. O. Morgan, *Callaghan: A Life* (Oxford: Oxford University Press, 1997); T. Benn, *Conflicts of Interest: Diaries, 1977–80* (London: Arrow Books, 1991); M. Thatcher, *The Path to Power* (London: HarperCollins, 1995); D. Healey, *The Time of My Life* (London: Penguin Books, 1990); W. Whitelaw, *The Whitelaw Memoirs* (London: Aurum Press, 1989); J. Callaghan, *Time and Chance* (London: HarperCollins, 1987); J. Barnett, *Inside the Treasury* (London: André Deutsch Limited, 1982).

32 Some studies that have been undertaken concerning underlying strategic processes include: J. T. Callaghan, S. Fielding and S. Ludlam, *Interpreting the Labour Party: Approaches to*

Labour Politics and History (Manchester: Manchester University Press, 2003), pp. 18, 49, 161; A. Warde, *Consensus and Beyond: The Development of Labour Party Strategy since the Second World War* (Manchester: Manchester University Press, 1982); J. Ramsden, *The Making of Conservative Party Policy: The Conservative Research Department since 1929* (London: Longman, 1980).

33 See, for example, Conservative Party Archive (CPA): CCO 20/68/2, 1st Meeting, 20 May 1974.

34 K. Hickson, *The IMF Crisis of 1976 and British Politics* (London: I.B.Tauris & Co., 2005).

35 Thorpe, *A History of the British Labour Party*, pp. 195–6; Seldon and Hickson (eds), *New Labour, Old Labour*, pp. 76–7, 190–2; P. Hennessy, *The Prime Minister: The Office and its Holders since 1945* (London: Penguin Books, 2001), pp. 378, 386–9.

36 Hennessy, *Distilling the Frenzy*, pp. 206–29.

37 Our analysis includes a record of events kept by Heath's Principal Private Secretary, retrieved under Freedom of Information legislation by the Margaret Thatcher Foundation, Thatcher MSS: PREM 16/231, 'Note for the Record – Events Leading to the Resignation of Mr Heath's Administration on 4 March 1974', 1–4 March 1974.

38 TNA: PREM 16/1045, Merlyn Rees to Prime Minister, 26 April 1976.

39 J. Shepherd, 'The Fall of the Callaghan Government, 1979', in T. Heppell and K. Theakston (eds), *How Labour Governments Fall: From Ramsay Macdonald to Gordon Brown* (London: Palgrave Macmillan, 2013), pp. 113–41; P. Norton, 'Parliament', in Seldon and Hickson (eds), *New Labour, Old Labour*, pp. 190–206; Hennessy, *The Prime Minister*, pp. 378, 386–9, 395–6; K. O. Morgan, *Britain since 1945: The People's Peace* (Oxford: Oxford University Press, 2001), pp. 382–4, 399–401, 422; D. Tanner, P. Thane and N. Tiratsoo, *Labour's First Century* (Cambridge: Cambridge University Press, 2000), pp. 142, 233.

40 P. Norton, *Dissension in the House of Commons: 1974–1979* (Oxford: Oxford University Press, 1980).

41 P. Bartram, *David Steel: His Life and Politics* (London: W. H. Allen, 1981), pp. 140–78; D. Steel, *A House Divided: The Lib–Lab Pact and the Future of British Politics* (London: Weidenfeld & Nicolson, 1980); A. Michie and S. Hoggart, *The Pact: The Inside Story of the Lib–Lab Government, 1977–8* (London: Quartet Books, 1978).

42 J. Kirkup, *The Lib–Lab Pact: A Parliamentary Agreement, 1977–78* (Houndmills: Palgrave Macmillan, 2016).

43 M. Oaten, *Coalition: The Politics and Personalities of Coalition Government from 1850* (Petersfield: Harriman House, 2007), pp. 174–96.

44 Seldon and Hickson (eds), *New Labour, Old Labour*, pp. 199–201, 252.

45 Representative examples of these studies include G. Wilson, *SNP: The Turbulent Years 1960–1990* (Stirling: Scots Independent, 2009); G. Walker, *A History of the Ulster Unionist Party: Protest, Pragmatism and Pessimism* (Manchester: Manchester University Press, 2004), p. 223; L. McAllister, *Plaid Cymru: The Emergence of a Political Party* (Bridgend: Seren Books, 2001).

46 A. Smith, *Election Timing* (Cambridge: Cambridge University Press, 2004).

47 The Conservatives had even considered the possibility of an election late in 1975, and, while this was dismissed as unlikely, still intended to make preparations in the event of an unexpected poll. See CPA: SC 14, 35th Meeting, 3 November 1975; LCC 1/3/11, 123rd Meeting, 12 July 1976; Thorpe, *A History of the British Labour Party*, pp. 204–5; Smith, *Election Timing*, pp. 216–17.

48 For an example of the regularly updated attempts to anticipate and plan for defeat of major legislation, see, TNA: PREM 16/1045, 'Factors Affecting the Timing of a General Election, Revision as of 4 May 1978'; 16/1621, 'General Election Contingency Planning', 14 November 1977.

49 K. Coates (ed.), *What Went Wrong: Explaining the Fall of the Labour Government* (Nottingham: Spokesman Books, 2nd edn, 2008), pp. 7–11, 28–32.

50 G. R. Searle, *Country before Party: Coalition and the Idea of 'National Government' in Modern Britain, 1885–1987* (London: Longman, 1995).

51 T. Martin-López, *The Winter of Discontent: Myth, Memory and History* (Liverpool: Liverpool University Press, 2014); C. Hay, 'The Winter of Discontent Thirty Years On', *The Political Quarterly*, 80:4 (2009), 545–52; D. Hayter, *Fightback! Labour's Traditional Right in the 1970s and 1980s* (Manchester: Manchester University Press, 2005).

52 J. Shepherd, *Crisis? What Crisis? The Callaghan Government and the British Winter of Discontent* (Manchester: Manchester University Press, 2013); Shepherd, 'The Fall of the Callaghan Government, 1979', pp. 113–41.

53 TNA: CAB 128/65, 12th Meeting, 15 March 1979.

54 Butler, *Governing without a Majority*.

2

Myths about leaders:
personalities and strategy-making

'Hung Parliaments' have been more common than might be supposed. Minority governments have often been formed, usually at periods when the Party system has been in transition, e.g. when the Peelites were drifting slowly from Conservative to Liberal allegiance, or when the Liberal Unionists were moving rapidly from the Gladstonian to the Conservative camp, or when Labour was taking over from the Liberal Party. Sir Ivor Jennings, in *Cabinet Government*: 3rd Edition, 1961, cited no less than eleven cases of minority governments since the 1832 Reform Act. These were 1839 to 1841 (L [Liberal]); 1846–1852 (L); 1852 (C [Conservative]); 1858 to 1859 (C); 1866 to 1868 (C); 1885 to 1886 (C); 1886 (L); 1886 to 1892 (C); 1910 to 1915 (L); 1924 (Lab. [Labour]); and 1929 to 1931 (Lab.). To these one may add the Labour Administration of March–October 1974 which had no overall majority when elected.[1]

This entry from a Conservative internal strategy paper in 1978 briefly encapsulates the historical context of British minority governments as perceived by strategy-makers during the 1974–79 parliamentary term. However, the entry also reveals some of the challenges we face in understanding the contemporary setting in which such papers were written. This chapter will examine the historical context, will chart the evolution of the strategy-making process within the two main parties during the 1970s, and will identify the protagonists and their methods of operating.

Minority and coalition before 1974

In one sense, political coalitions of different forms have played significant roles in shaping both the historic experience of minority government and modern British politics. Labour and the Conservatives are themselves historic interparty coalitions of the late nineteenth and early twentieth century. Labour was formed from the trade union movement and was (and still is) allied to the Co-operative Party, while the Conservatives combined with different parties over time, including the Liberal Unionists and later the National Liberals. Nevertheless, no new unions had occurred within the main parties after the Second World War up to

1974, other than the final merger between Conservatives and National Liberals in 1947, both parties already having been effectively operating as one entity for over two decades.[2]

However, these combinations of different parties did not often translate into formalised interparty governments in Parliament, bearing out the frequently cited stricture by nineteenth-century Prime Minister Benjamin Disraeli that 'England does not love coalitions'.[3] As already indicated in Chapter 1, it is difficult to compare some of the earlier minority governments in the nineteenth century with their twentieth-century counterparts. Recurrent features of earlier minority governments tended to include reliance upon tacit or temporary agreements with smaller parties, and minority administrations were often brought down before the end of their term by no confidence votes. Twentieth-century minority governments before the 1970s shared some of these traits, as was the case with the short-lived Labour Government of 1924, which relied on Liberal support and was defeated in a no confidence vote. However, the other cases in the early twentieth century were somewhat atypical, and have coloured perceptions of minority and coalition administrations in Britain. The Liberal Minority Administration of 1910–15 relied tacitly on the support of smaller parties, including Irish Nationalists, but became a unity coalition involving other parties on account of the First World War. The Labour Government of 1929–31 began as a minority but, in response to the serious global economic crisis, and the resulting split within the party itself, became a National Government, bringing together MPs from Labour, the Conservatives and the two Liberal parties.[4]

During the 1970s, some political elites and sections of the public, informed by the legacy of these unity governments and by the loss of confidence in traditional single-party majority rule, were increasingly interested in interparty coalition government. However, there was also significant parliamentary opposition to formalised cooperation. In Labour and the Conservatives, this took the form of deep-seated hostility. The 1930s National Governments were still largely perceived by Labour MPs and party members as a betrayal of their fundamental values. The wartime coalitions that had taken place were not usually raised in strategy discussions, but were viewed as having emerged as a necessary reaction to exceptionally adverse circumstances not replicated in peacetime. Hostility to interparty cooperation was also fostered by negative perceptions of coalitions in other European countries, which were, and continue to be, regarded as more consensual than Britain in their political culture, but whose governments were also characterised as weaker, prone to more frequent changes when coalitions collapsed.[5]

Domestic political changes in the early 1970s also presented fresh challenges to the possibility of interparty cooperation. The postwar political consensus in Britain on Keynesian economics had ensured that both main parties supported the institutions underpinning the welfare state, nationalised industries and full employment. There was, however, by the 1970s, increasing political polarisation and antagonism between Labour and the Conservatives, ultimately leading to the breakdown of this consensus and the rise of monetarist economics, begun in part during the period of the Callaghan Government, but which culminated in Friedmanian-influenced Thatcher Governments of the 1980s.

The 1970s also witnessed the rise of new parties and groupings not inclined towards formal interparty cooperation with Labour and the Conservatives. National parties in Scotland and Wales, including the SNP and Plaid Cymru, achieved electoral success against a backdrop of economic difficulties and political dissatisfaction, seeking to challenge the Westminster establishment and to win greater recognition and freedoms for their respective nations. An ongoing political crisis in Northern Ireland had led to the deployment of British soldiers there from 1969 onwards to maintain order, and the implementation of direct rule from Westminster in 1972. The Northern Ireland Unionist parties, in opposition to this latter decision, formed a coalition, albeit primarily a platform to contest the 1974 Westminster elections. This included the Ulster Unionists who had previously voted with the Conservatives in Parliament. Even within the Liberals, the party perhaps most favourably disposed to formalised cooperation, historic experiences of their decline following participation in coalition governments had fostered opposition to interparty deals, expressed, not least, in attacks on a prospective deal with the Conservatives following the 1974 February general election.[6]

Wilson and Callaghan 1974–79

In this historical context, Labour's return to power in 1974 marked the beginning of the minority governments in the 1970s. Heath's Conservative Government of 1970–74 faced significant problems during its final days in office, including the adverse economic effects of the oil crisis which had quadrupled petrol prices in 1973, and the political crisis of the coal miners' strike against government pay restraint policies aimed at curbing inflation. The most noticeable effect of the strike was that of limiting electricity supplies for homes and businesses to what infamously became known as the 'Three-Day Week'. Heath called an early general election for February 1974 in an effort to receive a new mandate that would strengthen his hand in negotiations with the strikers. The result was the first election since 1929 in which no one party had an overall majority. This situation led to abortive coalition talks between the Conservatives and the Liberal Party, and, within four days, to the formation of a Labour Minority Government led by Wilson.[7]

Although Wilson had not expected to return to No. 10 following his election defeat in 1970, he was in some ways as well prepared as anyone to tackle the challenges of minority government, having long-standing institutional experience of government and the civil service. Wilson (born 1916) went to university on a grant, reading Modern History and achieving outstanding results in Politics, Philosophy and Economics at Jesus College, Oxford. Thereafter, he had become one the youngest Oxford dons in history, worked as a Lecturer in Economic History, a Research Fellow, and then as a specialist civil servant in different government departments during the Second World War. By 1974, he had been an MP for nearly thirty years and was one of few figures remaining in Labour to have had ministerial experience from the Attlee Government in the 1940s, as President of the Board of Trade. Having held significant shadow cabinet portfolios including Shadow Chancellor and Shadow Foreign Secretary, he was elected Labour leader in 1963, winning the 1964 and 1966 general elections, becoming Prime Minister of two majority Labour Governments between 1964–70, and continuing to lead the party over the previous three and half years in opposition.[8]

While the new Government was limited in its ability to take action, Wilson's experience and that of those advising him assisted in the devising of strategies for coping with the minority status. They were also able to achieve certain successes: negotiating an end to the strikes; passing some legislation favourable to Labour supporters; and setting out the plans a majority Labour Government would pursue. From the outset, Wilson and his advisers, both in Cabinet and in the No. 10 Policy Unit, had not regarded minority government as a workable long-term solution, and recognised the need for another early election in order to try to obtain a majority. An unprecedented number of parliamentary defeats for the Government before the summer recess, seventeen in the space of two months, further reinforced this imperative. The general election, called by Wilson for October 1974, gave Labour a majority of only three, but this proved sufficient to pass a significant amount of legislation over the course of the next two years, some of which continues to have considerable impact upon current politics, such as the Health and Safety at Work Act 1974 or the Sex Discrimination Act 1975.[9]

This period also marked changes in the leadership and composition of opposition parties. Heath's loss of the previous elections increased grievances against him from within the Conservatives, the pressure culminating in his accepting reforms that would require annual re-election of the leader by Conservative MPs. The contest that followed unexpectedly led to Thatcher being elected as the new Conservative leader on 11 February 1975. The emergence of personal scandals in 1975 forced Liberal leader Jeremy Thorpe to resign during the early days of Callaghan's ministry on 9 May 1976, and to be replaced by Steel on 7 July, following a contest voted on by members of the Liberal Party nationwide. Growing dissatisfaction with the two main parties, the rise of nationalism in Scotland and Wales, and increased political and civil unrest in Northern Ireland, prompted a substantial increase in parliamentary representation for smaller political parties, some of which gained seats for the first time in 1974. These parties held over 42 out of the 650 seats, and influenced the options available to and challenges faced by the subsequent minority governments.[10]

One of the most important events between the two minority administrations was the UK-wide referendum in 1975 on whether Britain should remain in the European Economic Community (EEC), which it had joined in 1973. There will be many comparisons made between this referendum and the European referendum in 2016. From a parliamentary perspective, there would appear to be some significant similarities, both Wilson and Cameron only having small majorities. In both cases, the promise of a referendum posed a threat to the Government's parliamentary position, being an issue which bitterly divided Labour and Conservative MPs respectively. Wilson's approach, which arguably informed later efforts, allowed his MPs to take different sides. The favourable conditions in 1975, including support from members of other parties in campaigning, helped to secure a decisive victory in the referendum on 6 June, approving Britain's remaining in the Community by more than a two thirds majority, while also holding the Government together.[11] This victory strengthened Wilson's position, but ongoing divisions meant that his continued success in Parliament was not always guaranteed. There were several parliamentary defeats through rebellions during this time, perhaps the most significant of which was on 10 March 1976, when a group of left-wing Labour MPs voted with opposition parties to defeat the White Paper detailing the Government's expenditure plans. This defeat was considered as calling into question Labour's ability to govern, and was only settled after Wilson organised and successfully managed to win a subsequent confidence vote. Not long after this, Wilson shocked most colleagues and commentators by announcing his retirement, triggering a contest for a new Labour leader.[12]

Callaghan became Prime Minister on 5 April 1976, after winning a contest voted on by Labour MPs, defeating five other candidates over three ballots. Although new to the job, Callaghan, could, as his predecessor had done, draw on a wealth of experience. Moving from his humble beginnings in Portsmouth (born 1912), Callaghan joined the Inland Revenue as a clerk, aged seventeen, working his way up to tax inspector, helping establish a trade union for tax inspectors, being employed as a full time union official from 1936 and serving in the Second World War in the Royal Navy. His experience within formal politics up until 1976 was also substantial, consisting of thirty years' continuous service as a Labour MP, and a long ministerial career which had ranged across the whole spectrum of government, as the only person to have held all three Great Offices of State (Chancellor, Home Secretary and Foreign Secretary) before becoming Prime Minister. The Government which he headed in 1976 was similarly very experienced, including ministers who had served in the Wilson Governments of the 1960s and 1970s. From 1974–76, Callaghan was also particularly involved with managing government business and the passage of parliamentary legislation, not least through weekly meetings with Wilson and Government Chief Whip Bob Mellish.[13]

Within a day of Callaghan taking office, the Government lost its *de facto* majority in Parliament in what can only be described as one of the most bizarre defections in history. John Stonehouse had originally been elected as the Labour MP for Wednesbury in 1957, retaining the seat in subsequent elections along with its successor constituency of Walsall North in 1974. He faked his own death in November 1974 to escape fraud charges, and was found a month later living under a false identity in Australia. Deported six months thereafter, and temporarily incarcerated in Britain, Stonehouse nevertheless remained a Labour MP and was able to return to his duties from August 1975 onwards, pending a further trial. The day after Callaghan became Prime Minister, Stonehouse defected from Labour, ultimately joining the English National Party, as its only sitting MP. Although there were times thereafter when the Government was more secure than others, whether through political manoeuvring, its use of institutional powers or its agreements with smaller parties, it would never again hold a majority in its own right for the remainder of the Parliament, up until its eventual defeat in the general election of 3 May 1979.[14]

While summaries of the Callaghan Government have rightly discussed major economic or policy events with which leaders had to grapple, it is important always to juxtapose these with the precarious parliamentary situation. From April until December 1976, the UK faced a worsening economic crisis through devaluation of the currency, culminating in Chancellor Denis Healey needing to apply to the IMF for a bailout in September. Negotiation of the precise terms and a fear that the Government could split over the issue led to Callaghan devoting significant time and energy to talking the problem through in a marathon series of Cabinet meetings across two months. Although the emphasis was primarily extra-parliamentary, seeking a viable solution which would prevent the party from splitting, questions over whether an economic package would obtain the requisite parliamentary approval in light of the Government not having a majority did feature in these discussions.[15] In part, these fears were informed by an often-forgotten crisis in Parliament during this period.

In May 1976, whether intentionally or by accident, the Government broke a pairing agreement on a particularly contentious piece of legislation that sought to nationalise the aircraft and shipbuilding industries: a Labour MP who had arranged to be absent at the same time as his Conservative counterpart, was present, voted and thereby allowed the bill to pass its second reading by one vote. Accusations of cheating led to an acrimonious breakdown of relations between the Government and Opposition, the Conservatives withdrawing from day-to-day cooperation, including all pairing agreements. The finely balanced minority situation in Parliament meant that, in the resulting environment of uncertainty, all MPs had constantly to be in attendance to avoid or attempt to ensure government defeats in parliamentary votes. An agreement was eventually reached in July to restore normal relations. In spite of there not being many actual vote losses during this period, government business had been significantly delayed, leading to further conflicts with opposing parties.[16]

Labour's unexpected loss of two by-elections in November heightened the Government's vulnerability to parliamentary defeat. Although significant legislation, including the Government's flagship Devolution Bill, had been passed successfully, the timetable motion for debates on the devolution legislation, considered as essential to ensure it could be passed without using up what was regarded as too much parliamentary time, was defeated on 22 February 1977, effectively leading to the abandonment of the bill.[17]

A further government climbdown over a vote on child benefits led to the Conservatives tabling a no confidence motion for 23 March. Facing the prospect of losing such a vote, and thereby being forced into an early election which would likely result in defeat, the Callaghan Government sought a more formal deal with other smaller parties in Parliament, establishing a Pact with the Liberals that would last until the middle of 1978, as well as a more informal and publicly denied understanding with some MPs from the UUP.[18] The six Ulster Unionist MPs were part of a larger electoral and parliamentary coalition of Northern Ireland parties: the United Ulster Unionist Council (UUUC). An internal row in May 1977 broke up this grouping into its constituent parties, the culmination of a series of internal divisions. For the six UUP MPs, led in the Westminster Parliament by James Molyneaux, the terms Ulster Unionists or UUP will be used.[19]

The Lib–Lab Pact itself initially had a shaky start, not least in a conflict over increasing petrol duty in the Budget, but subsequently held together and allowed the Government to survive, including in a no confidence vote in July. The Pact, initially agreed for only a few months, was renewed in the summer of 1977 for a further year. Increasingly, over time some Liberal Party MPs and members became frustrated with the apparent lack of Liberal successes within the Pact, other than perhaps that of a scheme to encourage profit-sharing. These concerns prompted a Special Liberal Conference on 21 January 1978, which considered ending the agreement with the Government, but ultimately supported Steel's desire to continue, with the caveat of a majority of the Government supporting a proportional representation (PR) system for direct elections to the European Assembly. The PR system was rejected on 26 January 1978, with a large number of Labour MPs voting against, although the Government did fulfil the letter of its commitment to consider the proposal. Partly as a result of this decision, the Liberals did not renew the Pact in May, and it ended in July 1978.[20]

The Pact had not completely protected the Government's legislative programme, which suffered a particularly bad spate of defeats during the early months of 1978 as a result of rebellions by Labour backbenchers, particularly on attempts to renew the flagship devolution legislation as separate bills for Scotland and Wales. The most notable defeat was perhaps the amendment on 25 January, imposing a 40 per cent minimum population turnout of those voting in favour in Scotland and Wales if the results were to be considered valid. Government attempts to overturn such changes were unsuccessful, and would ultimately wreck their plans for devolution. In May, some further damaging Conservative amendments to the Finance Bill were successfully passed, including cuts to income tax and the raising of tax thresholds.[21]

Throughout 1977 and 1978 especially, both main parties sought to anticipate the possible date of an election, taking into account a variety of factors, including the state of the economy, local or national holidays, the implementation of politically desirable legislation, the proximity of other elections, whether local, European or the devolution referenda, and the effect of sporting events such as the Football World Cup in June 1978 (particularly the fear of SNP gains if Scotland were to be successful).[22]

In spite of their previous difficulties, the Callaghan Government was enjoying greater success by early 1978. An improving economic situation, the ending of the Pact without incident and the Labour gains in the opinion polls, raised the prospect of the Prime Minister calling an autumn election. One of the most replayed television clips, which has become synonymous with indecision over this election, was of Callaghan addressing the Trades Union Congress (TUC) in 1978, singing the classic song *Waiting at the Church*, prolonging the uncertainty. The deception of electoral expectations among commentators, and even within the Government itself, was further sustained until two days later, on 7 September, when Callaghan went on television to announce that there would be no autumn election. The Prime Minister's fear was that the best result would not bring Labour a clear government majority, and that it was better to aim for an election in either spring or summer 1979, near the end of the five-year parliamentary term. There has been particularly intense speculative debate over whether or not Callaghan should have called the election at this point, and whether the result in autumn 1978 would have been more favourable to Labour, given the subsequent events of the winter.[23]

What began on 22 September as an unofficial strike by workers at the Ford Motor Company factories turned into an official union-backed strike. This dispute ended only two months later with a 16.5 per cent pay rise, far in excess of the recommended 5 per cent guidelines published as part of the Government's income policy in July and originally stated by Callaghan as early as January. The Government's proposed response on 28 September had been to impose sanctions on Ford and other companies who had broken the limit. However, this initiative was defeated in Parliament on 13 December, resulting in the public abandonment of sanctions as an option. Although such sanctions may have been seen as questionable in their effectiveness, even by contemporaries, the parliamentary defeat and the example set by Ford and other firms opened the way for further industrial action by workers in the public and private sectors, demanding settlements far above the Government's target. A series of strikes or threatened strikes from December 1978 to February 1979, described by contemporaries and encapsulated in popular folklore as the 'Winter of Discontent', had significant impact, compounded by harsh weather of snowdrifts and blizzards across the country in what was the coldest winter for sixteen years. Official and unofficial strikes of professions whose work had particularly tangible impact on people's everyday lives – petrol tanker drivers, lorry drivers, ambulance drivers, gravediggers, refuse collectors, to name but a few – and the Government's apparent inability to respond, served significantly to undermine Labour's political support. Even where these strikes were perhaps more localised, as with the Liverpool and Tameside gravediggers, media coverage gave them nationwide impact – some of the most disturbing and emotive television pictures being of coffins remaining unburied. Although an agreement between the Government and unions was eventually reached by 14 February, it did not significantly help to regain voters' trust over the following months, with some strikes continuing to occur into April, not least, for example, those of gravediggers in Lewisham, which only served to reinforce notions of the Government's powerlessness.[24]

Plans for the flagship devolution legislation, set in motion the previous autumn, now compounded Callaghan's parliamentary problems, triggering a crisis that would ultimately bring down the Government. Passage of the Devolution Bills in 1978 had only been accomplished after placating Labour MPs who opposed the plans, accepting that public referenda would be required in Scotland and Wales in order to approve devolution. Even after these concessions, backbench Labour rebels had been able to defeat the Government on a number of amendments to the bills. Perhaps the most crucial of these newly attached provisions required that any result in favour of devolution would need at least 40 per cent of the votes from the entire electorate in order to be valid. Efforts by the Government to overturn this amendment had been unsuccessful. The referenda themselves had been set for 1 March 1979, the unintentional consequence of which was that the campaigns took place against the bleak backdrop of the winter strikes. As was widely expected, the result was a No vote in Wales, but, perhaps surprisingly given hostility to the Government and Callaghan, whose image had been widely used in the campaign, a small majority Yes vote in Scotland. Nevertheless, the votes in favour were insufficient to reach the 40 per cent turnout, requiring the Government by law to repeal the Act. Attempts by government leaders to talk with other parties and to find some way of continuing to bring in Scottish devolution were not considered satisfactory by the SNP, who subsequently ceased their support for the Government, thereby removing Labour's temporary majority, and called for a vote of no confidence. Emboldened by the SNP's decision, the Conservatives quickly followed in tabling their own no confidence motion, which, being that of the Official Opposition, was to be debated first.[25]

The resulting vote came on 28 March 1979, preceded by frantic efforts of the Opposition to marshal their supporters and by government ministers and whips attempting to make last-minute deals that would stave off defeat. In the end, the Government lost by one vote, 311 to 310, becoming the first administration since the Labour Minority Government of 1924 to lose a vote of no confidence and thereby be forced out of office. After what has been described as a largely uneventful election campaign, the Conservative Opposition won the general election on 3 May 1979 with what was regarded by contemporaries as a substantial majority of forty-three.[26]

Strategy-making process

Labour and the Conservatives

Reconstructing processes of political strategy-making poses a number of interpretative challenges. Nevertheless, we can to some extent discern these processes by examining the particular contributions of individuals and organisations in both Labour and the Conservatives. Exploring both implemented strategy and plans that were never codified or enacted gives us insights into the mindset of the principal actors.

Parliamentary strategies and electoral planning were largely the purview of the Labour and Conservative leadership. While detailing the different decision-making bodies, a few individuals or groups will be singled out. Any omission is not to disparage the strategic contribution of people not named here, but rather to concentrate on the particular minority government focus of this book. Although limited, their contributions did sometimes serve as a counterpoint to the more established strategic discourse, and, in some cases, influenced the plans pursued.

The 1974 Wilson Government, the first minority government in Britain for more than forty-five years, had presented both Labour and the Conservatives with significant gaps in terms of their own recent experience, and a comparatively sparse theoretical scholarship to draw on.

Although in some ways the machinery of legislative strategy was very similar to previous governments, through the involvement of the Prime Minister, Cabinet and whips, the challenges of policy implementation in Wilson's 1960s Administrations prompted a number of reforms in strategy-making in 1974. Special advisers, now a ubiquitous feature of British politics, were formally introduced for the first time by Wilson. However, in spite of having some impact on the design and implementation of policy, their role in minority government was more limited on account of restrictions in their remit. The civil service regarded these new arrivals with suspicion, and the government leadership was particularly hostile to advisers participating in policymaking outside their respective departments.

Another innovation which had a greater impact in this area was the No. 10 Policy Unit, introduced under Wilson in 1974 as a group of government-appointed experts, led by Dr Bernard Donoughue from the LSE. Although its creation had been intended as a more broad-ranging support structure to advise the Prime Minister on matters of policy, a key focus of the Unit became that of the Government lacking a majority and the particulars of legislative strategy.

The Conservative Opposition did not face the same challenges of attempting to get legislation passed, but the state of minority government posed unique challenges for them which also served to affect processes of strategy formation. Conservative leaders typically had fewer formal restrictions placed on them than on their Labour counterparts. Heath directed and took decisions in discussion with his closest advisers or with the full Shadow Cabinet (formally known as the Leader's Consultative Committee while in opposition) on a weekly or more regular basis. In addition, there was a formalised Leader's Steering Committee, something of an inner Shadow Cabinet, that also included other figures from within the Conservative leadership, and met to consider wider questions of strategy, addressing how to respond to government policy decisions, studying internal briefing papers, and deciding on the focus of campaigns and publicity. When first confronted with the new reality of minority government in 1974, the CRD, who provided invaluable detailed briefing for policymaking, had been tasked to search for academic literature on the subject of minority government. Very few useful guides were found, the most relevant identified within a month as being an article published in 1973 on Canadian minority government, which does not appear to have featured thereafter in subsequent planning. Alongside this, the earliest meetings of the new Steering Committee sought to consider strategic questions ranging from whether or not to stress the minority nature of the government, the balancing of backbench Conservative desire for confrontation with a public mood of giving the Government 'a chance to govern' and comparable historical precedents. The resulting approach was one of mainly opposing through speeches and avoiding voting against the Government, building on the withdrawal from confrontation over the Queen's Speech.[27]

Historically, parties had, on a number of occasions, responded to significant political changes by forming bodies to consider their strategy, as was the case of the Conservatives' Tactical Staff Committee created in 1947 following Labour's historic landslide electoral victory two years previously. Throughout the 1970s, neither main party created new strategy groups to address specifically the holistic challenges of minority government. The only new body which was potentially a direct response was that of the Conservative 'Party Strategy Group', created by Heath during 1974. The stated aim of the group was to facilitate consideration

of longer-term political issues, considering, amongst other things, minority government questions and radical ideas of interparty cooperation with the Liberals,
such as through establishing an electoral pact. The group was disbanded for
largely political reasons shortly after Thatcher became leader in 1975.[28]

This latter example of bureaucratic change following Thatcher's election as
leader reflects one of the problems in strategic continuity. Some of the leading
figures on both sides had retired or been replaced in the interim, including
both party leaders, the Government Chief Whip, the Leader of the House of
Commons, both party chairmen and figures from the different internal party
strategy-making bodies. Significant differences in the creation and parliamentary experiences of the Wilson and Callaghan Governments further limited the
possibility for strategic crossover. It is difficult to ascertain how much of the
written material developed during the Wilson era was used thereafter. While
occasional references were made to the experience of 1974 decision-makers,
there are only a few citations of previous papers being directly consulted when
formulating minority government strategy. There is also no evidence to suggest
that either main party established any special unit that was dedicated specifically
to addressing questions of minority government.[29]

On the government side in 1974 and 1976, the overall direction of parliamentary strategy was decided by the Prime Minister in consultation with Cabinet
ministers, either on an individual or small committee basis, or in regular meetings
of the full Cabinet. The Leader of the House of Commons, Edward Short in 1974
and Michael Foot from 1976 onwards, was principally responsible for formulating the details of the Government's legislative programme, which would then be
approved by the Cabinet. The Commons Leader also helped to set and manage
the timetable of legislation in Parliament, along with the Government's Chief
Whip, Mellish in 1974 and Michael Cocks from 1976. The Government whips
were largely responsible for ensuring the implementation of the Government's
legislative programme, through communication with and monitoring of the
activities of MPs and opposition parties.[30]

A number of innovations relating to these traditional strategy-making
arrangements changed the way in which bodies including Cabinet, the Shadow
Cabinet and researchers for both parties operated to accommodate the exigencies of minority government. An increasing amount of time in Cabinet discussions was spent considering parliamentary strategy and how to approach
the problems of minority government, something of which is captured by the
recording of debates in minutes and memoranda, as well as by contemporary
recollections, such as a 1976 entry in Donoughue's diary: '*Thursday, 24 June
1976* Cabinet, mainly on "Parliamentary Business". It is quite striking how, compared to two years ago, this item has expanded in Cabinet business. Discussing
how to manage our Commons minority now sometimes takes over an hour.'[31]
Formulation of the parliamentary legislative programme included the Commons

Leader chairing discussions of the Government's Future Legislation Committee, which assumed an increasingly important role in considering how to tailor the legislative programme to the problems of not having a majority.

Alongside the traditional liaison between government leaders and the Chief Whip, the possibility of periodic meetings involving the Prime Minister and all the Government whips was raised under Wilson in 1975, although the first meeting did not actually take place until Callaghan's ministry. These consultations seem to have been created as part of a more general effort towards better ensuring party communication. However, the context of the initial meeting, taking place in the immediate aftermath of the Lib–Lab Pact being formed in 1977, gave a particular focus to this grouping, discussion concentrating on the maintaining of good relations with Labour MPs and those of other parties during the agreement, and, after the end of the Pact, strategies for maintaining a government majority. Conversations that began on primarily parliamentary business ended up taking in wider related aspects of strategy, including electoral timing.

In stark contrast to 1974, the latter stages of the Callaghan Government saw the establishment of formal meetings between the special advisers and ministers from all departments, chaired by Foot, in order to discuss, amongst other matters, broader questions of government strategy, including aspects relating to minority government. Donoughue thought that his appointment was coming to end when Wilson resigned in 1976, but was asked by the new Prime Minister to stay on as Head of the No. 10 Policy Unit. Callaghan made significant use of the Unit, which continued to produce papers on issues facing the Government, including on questions of policy and legislative strategy. A number of these papers sought to address questions posed by minority government, such as the prospect of greater interparty cooperation and the forecasting of the likely future survival of the Government. An important illustration of the work on minority government done by the Unit is given by one of its members, David Lipsey, who had previously served as a Government Special Adviser until mid-1977. His papers for the Prime Minister included analysing the possible implications of the Lib–Lab Pact, as well as considering potential courses of action following a further indecisive general election.[32]

It is sometimes difficult to differentiate precisely between the traditional civil service role of providing non-political advice to the Government and what effectively amounts to political strategy. This has become an increasingly contentious issue among some commentators, not least when considering the role of civil servants in Britain's 2010 coalition formation. John Hunt was Cabinet Secretary throughout the period of the Wilson and Callaghan Governments, while Robert Armstrong and Kenneth Stowe served as their respective Principal Private Secretaries. For the most part, the advice provided represented the traditionally non-politicised setting out of options. Hunt, Armstrong and Stowe do, however, give a window on the strategy development process through minuting otherwise private conversations and meetings, such as those between Callaghan and Steel during the Lib–Lab Pact, or their own conversations with regard to the minority situation with Wilson and Callaghan.[33] Another body of civil servants which made a particular contribution was the Central Policy Review Staff (CPRS), originally created by Heath in 1971. Callaghan found the CPRS to be particularly useful in terms of producing long-term and detailed considerations of issues and potential policies, not least responses to the economic crisis in 1976. However, while the work of the CPRS was affected by the state of minority government, their input into what was specifically political strategy was limited. In one of the few instances where a CPRS paper discussed future questions that had direct implications for minority government strategy, it was largely passed over by the Cabinet.[34]

The main alternative strategy-making body in Labour outside the party leadership was that of the NEC, elected by the party membership. Their duties included monitoring policymaking and drawing up the manifesto. During this period, the frequent conflicts between the Labour Government's leadership and the NEC over issues of policy and party management led to the emergence of alternative strategies in a number of different areas. For the most part, however, the government leadership pursued its own strategies in terms of parliamentary management and the NEC's emphasis was on policy implementation rather than minority government. In spite of this focus, the NEC and its subcommittees, particularly Labour's International Department, did spend some time considering questions of minority government, although, as discussed further in the section 'International inspiration', they did not tend to apply work done on minority governments in other countries to the UK situation.[35]

There were also bodies within or attached to the Labour Party, which, in addition to serving as alternative sources of power or sometimes conflict with the leadership, acted as focal points for strategy-making. While these groups were primarily concerned more with policymaking and implementation, questions relating to minority government were sometimes raised. These groups featured organisations formally constituted by Labour, including the Backbench Liaison Committee and TUC-Liaison Committee involving trade union leaders, as well as groups of MPs pursuing the implementation of a particular ideological agenda within Labour, from the more long-established left-wing Tribune Group to the more right-wing Manifesto Group (set up in December 1974 following Wilson's Minority Government). The membership of these different groups also sometimes overlapped with that of decision-makers in other bodies more directly involved in minority government strategy, including Cabinet ministers. Weekly meetings of all the Parliamentary Labour Party (PLP) MPs served to provide a forum for groups within the party to air their respective strategic approaches to minority government. A few insights may be gained from these discussions, although often contributions were more expressions of frustration with legislative concessions made to other parties, or philosophical conflicts over government policy, rather than issues arising from minority government.[36]

While the party conference and affiliated trade unions had an important role and provided significant input into government policymaking, their contributions did not normally address minority government questions beyond general endorsement or criticism of the Government's approach, along with the desire for implementation of particular policies. Labour's Research Department similarly concentrated largely on policymaking and did not apparently consider strategic questions of minority government.[37]

After the inauguration of the Lib–Lab Pact in 1977, government strategy-making also had to incorporate the Consultative Committee, bilateral meetings between ministers and Liberal spokespersons, and private meetings between the party leaders, Callaghan and Steel, some of which considered the issues of minority government in much greater depth.[38]

For the Conservatives in 1976 there does not appear to have been the same initial search for a minority government strategy as had been the case in 1974. Thatcher, as with Heath, largely shaped the direction of overall parliamentary strategy in discussion with small numbers of parliamentary colleagues or in the full Shadow Cabinet or Steering Committee. The CRD contributed significant work to the strategy-making process, both in terms of the detail of policymaking and papers on broader strategy. Although it was largely staffed by those loyal to the previous administration and distrusted by the Thatcher leadership, the CRD continued to play an important role during the Conservatives' time in opposition in the late 1970s. Prior to Conservative electoral victory, Thatcher's hold on the party remained tenuous, and her own pragmatic style limited far-reaching organisational changes in the early stages. As a result, CRD input to strategy-making could still prove important in certain areas, not least in providing briefing in terms of parliamentary strategy, and establishing frameworks for Shadow Cabinet discussions. There were, in addition, other committees within the Conservatives whose work came to involve aspects of minority government strategy, including that of the directors' meetings and the party chairman's committee.[39]

As with the Government, a number of additional groups were formed or re-formed by the Conservatives, including the Co-ordinating Committee chaired by Joseph. Although not specifically created to deal with minority government, this committee was tasked to examine, amongst other things, Conservative contingency plans in the event of a future 'hung parliament' and possibilities for minority government or coalition.[40]

Other bodies from outside the Conservatives that were more ideologically aligned with Thatcher, including the Centre for Policy Studies, instrumental in formulating future economic policy, were not involved so much in day-to-day parliamentary management, although some of their contributions had relevance with regard to planning for a future minority government.[41]

Some Labour Party bodies and internal groupings were mirrored within the Conservative Party. These groups did not tend to address questions of minority government directly, but focused more on policies. The regular meetings of the powerful Conservative 1922 Committee, containing all the party's backbenchers, may similarly be regarded as a counterpart to PLP meetings, in terms of expressing views regarding party management, while not necessarily focusing particularly on the minority government question. The committee did, however, have added influence in terms of the contacts maintained with the Conservative leadership by its proactive executive members. The largely undocumented nature of these contacts makes it more difficult to assess their contribution to the strategy-making process.[42]

International inspiration

While both main parties during this period had greater interaction with their international counterparts than their predecessors, and conducted closer observation of minority governments in other countries than is commonly recognised, the records of their discussions concerning how to cope with the minority government situation appear only to have drawn on past British experiences when formulating strategy. There was certainly no shortage of instances of centre-left minority governments occurring in the early 1970s, which may have served as potential exemplars, from that of Trygve Bratteli's minority Labour Governments in Norway between 1971–72 and 1973–76, to that of Pierre Trudeau's Liberal Canadian Administration in 1974.[43]

Both Labour and the Conservatives had well-established International Departments within their party bureaucracies which monitored political developments in other countries and produced reports. Tom McNally, who served as Callaghan's Political Adviser and Head of the Political Office in No. 10, was himself a former Head of Labour's International Department. There were also many instances during this period in which party leaders and those advising them met with their counterparts from other countries. The 1970s witnessed a period of growing cooperation among parties internationally, partly facilitated by the reduced costs of air travel and telecommunications, as well as the growing importance of transnational bodies including the EEC. Both Labour and the Conservatives were important participants in the setting up or maintaining of party organisations in this context, whether within the European Parliament or at an extra-parliamentary level globally. However, while there are some recorded instances of government and opposition leaders raising the question of minority government in their discussion or correspondence with their international counterparts, these show little more than acknowledgement of the situation, rather than indicating any desire to seek or to engage in strategic exchange. In spite of occasional references in government and opposition official papers and diaries which recognised some of the above-cited minority governments in other countries, there is no indication that these translated into any significant impact on their subsequent contributions to strategy-making. There were some instances recorded of parties seeking greater cooperation with their counterparts in terms of strategy-making, whether in the European Parliament or globally, but, again, there is no direct indication of these interactions providing input into the process of strategy-making for domestic minority government. In these cases, almost all examples drawn on are of previous British experiences during the twentieth century.[44]

When Labour and the Conservatives considered facilitating transnational cooperation with ideologically similar parties, discussions were always framed as distinct and separate from the interparty cooperative dimension of domestic politics. A possible reason for this division may have been the fear that drawing comparisons with other political systems where minority or coalition governments were an accepted norm would give greater legitimacy to such alternative governing arrangements in Britain.[45] One such example of this mindset may be seen during the Lib–Lab Pact in April 1977. While debating plans for direct elections to the European Parliament, initial notions of the Government making a positive recommendation of PR for these elections were shelved, not least reflecting the fear of some Cabinet members that 'Substantial Liberal representation in the Assembly would greatly strengthen the pressure for proportional representation in our national elections.'[46] Such fears were further expressed at a subsequent meeting:

> [A] recommendation in favour of proportional representation for European Assembly elections would inevitably be regarded as foreshadowing proportional representation at Westminster. It would accordingly provoke united opposition from opponents of the system and from opponents of our membership of the Community, and it would be seen as gravely damaging to the interests of the Labour Party. It would transform the British Party system paving the way for coalitions and the undermining of the legitimacy of Governments. These consequences were too high a price to pay for Liberal support.[47]

The term 'hung parliament' was first created and used during the 1970s in response to the Wilson and Callaghan Minority Governments, as a derogatory reference to the perceived powerlessness and weakness of these administrations. It is also worth noting that those parties, including the Liberals, who most favoured the idea of 'hung' or, as they described them, 'balanced' parliaments, were also the ones who were unafraid to draw upon and acknowledge international examples in their internal strategy papers and in their public statements on the subject of minority government.[48]

The Wilson Minority Government of 1974 compelled both main parties to confront the challenges of non-majority governance, as well as establishing the only recent British experience available to the Callaghan Administration and Opposition. The events of 1974–76 further set up the overarching political and economic conditions within which both governments were formed and which affected their planning.

While the existence of minority government did not lead to new dedicated strategy-making bodies in the two main parties, it contributed to the methods of operation for other strategy-making groups, whether new or long-established. Despite using the experience of international political counterparts and seeking to facilitate greater transnational cooperation, both Labour and the Conservatives showed a continued reluctance during this period to draw comparisons with, and experience from, other political systems when framing their responses to strategic questions of minority or coalition government, possibly fearing the idea of these then being legitimised as norms in the British system. As such, the Government and Opposition tended to draw on examples exclusively, whether consciously or subconsciously, from the British tradition of minority government when presenting their papers to decision-makers, encapsulating an understanding of the British experience and political system as being exceptional and distinct in its form of operation from that of other countries.

Notes

1 Churchill Archives Centre (CAC): THCR 2/1/6/194: Appendix E, 'The Hung Parliament', 12 April 1978; emphasis in the original.
2 S. Ball and A. Seldon (eds), *Recovering Power: The Conservatives in Opposition since 1867* (Houndmills: Palgrave Macmillan, 2005), pp. 23, 121, 183; Searle, *Country before Party*, pp. 26–9, 221–2; A. Seldon (ed.), *UK Political Parties since 1945* (Hemel Hempstead: Philip Allan, 1990), pp. 22–3; P. Adelman, *The Rise of the Labour Party 1880–1945* (New York: Longman, 2nd edn, 1986), pp. 19–37, 90; R. McKibbin, *The Evolution of the Labour Party 1910–1924* (Oxford: Oxford University Press, 1974), pp. xv–2, 240–8.
3 Searle, *Country before Party*, p. 5.
4 The Liberal Party had divided in 1931 between those opposing the National Governments – the Independent Liberals – and those supporting them, known as the National Liberals. Thorpe, *A History of the British Labour Party*, pp. 1–2; Searle, *Country before Party*, pp. 1–12, 70–1, 150–5.
5 Seldon and Hickson (eds), *New Labour, Old Labour*, pp. 224–9; Searle, *Country before Party*, pp. 245–59.
6 Unsuccessful attempts at formalised interparty cooperation were made during the 1950s, which did lead to some informal electoral pacts operating at a local level. Kirkup, *The Lib-Lab Pact*, pp. 11–14; Walker, *A History of the Ulster Unionist Party*, pp. 219–26; Morgan, *Britain since 1945*, pp. 365–74; Bartram, *David Steel*, pp. 137–9; D. Butler and D. Kavanagh, *The British General Election of 1979* (London: Macmillan, 1980), pp. 2–10, 423–4.

7 Thorpe, *A History of the British Labour Party*, pp. 191–2; A. Beckett, *When the Lights Went Out: What Really Happened to Britain in the Seventies* (London: Faber & Faber Ltd., 2009), pp. 128–34, 152–4; J. Campbell, *Edward Heath: A Biography* (London: Jonathan Cape, 1993), pp. 598–9, 613.

8 Hennessy, *The Prime Minister*, pp. 37, 354–61.

9 Labour History Archive Study Centre (LHASC): Campaign Committee Paper, 15 May 1974, 'Party Strategy'; MS. Wilson, c. 1288, Confidential Meeting, 1 July 1974; Sandbrook, *Seasons in the Sun*, pp. 43–4, 152–3; Beckett, *When the Lights Went Out*, pp. 170–1, 230–1, 297; Seldon and Hickson (eds), *New Labour, Old Labour*, pp. 191–2.

10 This number includes MPs Stonehouse, Robertson and Alex Neil, after their defection from Labour. C. Cook, *A Short History of the Liberal Party, 1900–1976* (London: Macmillan, 1976), pp. 162–3; Morgan, *Britain since 1945*, pp. 359–61.

11 Thorpe, *A History of the British Labour Party*, pp. 193–4; Seldon and Hickson (eds), *New Labour, Old Labour*, pp. 139, 145–7; Hennessy, *The Prime Minister*, pp. 360, 365–9.

12 Seldon and Hickson (eds), *New Labour, Old Labour*, pp. 195–6; Hennessy, *The Prime Minister*, pp. 366–71; Morgan, *Britain since 1945*, pp. 361, 364–8, 381.

13 Hennessy, *The Prime Minister*, pp. 23, 358, 378–9; Morgan, *Callaghan*, pp. 469–83. For short chronological summaries of key events in the Wilson/Callaghan Governments, see Seldon and Hickson (eds), *New Labour, Old Labour*, pp. xii–xvii; Butler and Kavanagh, *The British General Election of 1979*, pp. 19–22.

14 Seldon and Hickson (eds), *New Labour, Old Labour*, pp. 192–7; Hennessy, *The Prime Minister*, pp. 378, 393.

15 Thorpe, *A History of the British Labour Party*, pp. 199–201; Hennessy, *The Prime Minister*, pp. 382–9; Morgan, *Britain since 1945*, pp. 383–6.

16 Sandbrook, *Seasons in the Sun*, pp. 466–7.

17 Thorpe, *A History of the British Labour Party*, p. 203; Seldon and Hickson (eds), *New Labour, Old Labour*, pp. 230–1.

18 Hazell and Paun (eds), *Making Minority Government Work*, pp. 20–1; Cook, *A Short History of the Liberal Party*, p. 163; Seldon and Hickson (eds), *New Labour, Old Labour*, pp. 200, 231; Morgan, *Britain since 1945*, pp. 400–1.

19 Walker, *A History of the Ulster Unionist Party*, p. 226; Mitchie and Hoggart, *The Pact*, pp. 30–1.

20 Hazell and Paun (eds), *Making Minority Government Work*, p. 23; Cook, *A Short History of the Liberal Party*, pp. 164–6; Butler, *Governing without a Majority*, pp. 53–4.

21 Seldon and Hickson (eds), *New Labour, Old Labour*, pp. 193–200, 231.

22 CPA: CRD/D/7/19, The General Election, 3 January 1978; CRD/L/4/46/4, Note of Research Department Meeting, 3 April 1978; LCC 1/3/14, 186th Meeting, 18 January 1978; 1/3/15, 208th Meeting, 7 June 1978; 1/3/16, 216th Meeting, 19 July 1978; 218th Meeting, 31 July 1978; Donoughue, *Downing Street Diary*, vol. 2, pp. 304–5. See Chapter 7.

23 Thorpe, *A History of the British Labour Party*, pp. 204–5; Sandbrook, *Seasons in the Sun*, pp. 706–9, 803–4; Seldon and Hickson (eds), *New Labour, Old Labour*, p. 96; Morgan, *Britain since 1945*, pp. 416–17.

24 Sandbrook, *Seasons in the Sun*, pp. 718–21, 753–9; Seldon and Hickson (eds), *New Labour, Old Labour*, pp. xvi–xvii, 96–7, 286–7; Morgan, *Britain since 1945*, pp. 418–20; Butler and Kavanagh, *The British General Election of 1979*, p. 29.

25 Seldon and Hickson (eds), *New Labour, Old Labour*, pp. 233–4; Morgan, *Britain since 1945*, pp. 410–11.

26 Sandbrook, *Seasons in the Sun*, pp. 769–81; J. Campbell, *Margaret Thatcher: Grocer's Daughter to Iron Lady* (London: Vintage, 2009), pp. 107–112; Morgan, *Britain since 1945*, pp. 421–2.

27 CPA: CCO 20/8/17, Correspondence between Heath and Geoffrey Howe, 11–23 April 1974; LCC 1/3/1, 3rd Meeting, 18 March 1974; SC 12 (2), 2nd Meeting, 25 March 1974.

28 CPA: CCO 20/68/2, 1st Meeting, 20 May 1974.

29 TNA: CAB 128/54, 1st Meeting, 5 March 1974; 2nd Meeting, 7 March 1974; B. Donoughue, *Downing Street Diary: With Harold Wilson in No. 10*, vol. 1 (London: Pimlico, 2006), pp. 68–73; P. Bell, *The Labour Party in Opposition, 1970–1974* (London: Routledge, 2004), p. 237; T. Benn, *Against the Tide: 1973–76* (London: Arrow Books, 1990), p. 116; B. Castle, *The Castle Diaries 1974–1976* (London: Weidenfeld & Nicolson, 1980), pp. 41–5; H. Wilson, *Final Term: The Labour Government 1974–1976* (London: Weidenfeld & Nicolson, 1979), pp. 13, 39. See Chapter 4.

30 Sandbrook, *Seasons in the Sun*, p. 464; Morgan, *Michael Foot*, pp. 332–7; Seldon and Hickson (eds), *New Labour, Old Labour*, pp. 175–186, 207–10; B. Donoughue, *Prime Minister: The Conduct of Policy under Harold Wilson and James Callaghan* (London: Jonathan Cape, 1987), pp. 20–9, 36–7.

31 Donoughue, *Downing Street Diary*, vol. 2, pp. 43–4.

32 Morgan, *Michael Foot*, pp. 332–7; Seldon and Hickson (eds), *New Labour, Old Labour*, pp. 173–84. See Chapters 5 and 8.

33 TNA: PREM 16/1621, Note for the Record: The Outcome of the Next General Election, 7 February 1978.

34 See Chapter 5.

35 Seldon and Hickson (eds), *New Labour, Old Labour*, pp. 73–4, 261–70. See Chapter 6.

36 Seldon and Hickson (eds), *New Labour, Old Labour*, pp. 7–8, 72–3; Searle, *Country before Party*, pp. 247–8. See Chapter 5.

37 Seldon and Hickson (eds), *New Labour, Old Labour*, pp. 70–103, 322–7. See Chapter 7.

38 Torrance, *David Steel*, pp. 90–131; Cook, *A Short History of the Liberal Party*, pp. 163–4; Steel, *A House Divided*, pp. 36–7, 43–8. See Chapter 5.

39 CPA: SC 14, 42nd Meeting, 3 May 1976; 45th Meeting, 13 December 1976; R. Behrens, *The Conservative Party from Heath to Thatcher: Policies and Politics, 1974–1979* (Farnborough: Saxon House, 1980), pp. 48–9, 60, 62–3. See Chapter 8.

40 Behrens, *The Conservative Party*, pp. 52, 62.

41 *Ibid.*

42 Division and conflict between these groups was not on the same scale as within Labour during this period. S. Ball (ed.), *The Conservative Party since 1945* (Manchester: Manchester University Press, 1998), pp. 5, 8, 21, 54–5; Behrens, *The Conservative Party*, pp. 23–4, 28–9.

43 J. Bickerton and A. Gagnon (eds), *Canadian Politics* (Plymouth: University of Toronto Press, 5th edn, 2009), pp. 134–41; P. Russell, *Two Cheers for Minority Government: The Evolution of Canadian Parliamentary Democracy* (Toronto: Emond Montgomery, 2008), pp. 33–5; Strøm, *Minority Government and Majority Rule*, pp. 210, 225; Benn, *Against the Tide*, p. 150; Herman and Pope, 'Minority Government in Western Democracies', 192–8.

44 See, for example, CAC: THCR 2/1/6/194: Appendix E, 'The Hung Parliament', 12 April 1978; CPA: CRD/L/4/46/6, 'The Hung Parliament Contingency', 16 March 1978; darties, republicans, unionists,r chapter no.LCC 1/3/15, 200th Meeting, 19 April 1978; Callaghan Papers, Box 19, 2737: Lab/Elec: 78–9, David Lipsey to the Prime Minister, 2 May 1979; 'In

the Event of Deadlock', 2 May 1979; Brazier and Kalitowski (eds), *No Overall Control?*, pp. 83–93; N. J. Crowson, *The Conservative Party and European Integration since 1945: At the Heart of Europe* (London: Routledge, 2006), pp. 125, 192–4; Seldon and Hickson (eds), *New Labour, Old Labour*, pp. 176–7.

45 TNA: CAB 128/61, 5th Meeting, 10 February 1977; 8th Meeting, 25 February 1977; Searle, *Country before Party*, pp. 251–4, 259.

46 TNA: CAB 128/62, 17th Meeting, 28 April 1977.

47 TNA: CAB 128/62, 23rd Meeting, 23 June 1977.

48 'Balanced Parliament: No Need to Rush', *Guardian* (5 May 2010); Blick and Wilks-Heeg, 'Governing without Majorities', 1–2; Brazier and Kalitowski (eds), *No Overall Control?*, pp. 1–4.

3

The birth of myths:
alternatives to government formation

[F]or the Labour Party to be dependent on the SDLP at Westminster would put us in the Catholic camp in Northern Ireland [...] Our stance in Northern Ireland must be that of a party which is not sectarian but socialist.[1]

In a strange parallel to some of the publicly articulated arguments against Conservative/DUP cooperation in June 2017, Northern Ireland Secretary Merlyn Rees' warning, in a letter to Callaghan after the Government became a minority in Parliament in April 1976, was in response to a proposed plan to bring the SDLP into a coalition with Labour, in order to restore this majority. The fact that this proposal was being considered by the Prime Minister, at a time of significant political volatility in Northern Ireland, shows how seriously the minority government situation was perceived. While not enacted, proposals of this nature demonstrate that the formation of a minority government without formalised interparty cooperation was by no means a foregone conclusion.

A number of pervasive assumptions have served to shape analysis of the Labour Minority Governments during the 1970s, including the ideas that the creation of these were inevitable and that some of the preceding Labour Majority Governments during the 1960s and 1970s were essentially similar to minority administrations because of their small majorities and internal party divisions.[2] However, Wilson's 1974 Minority Government represented an unexpected outcome, while Callaghan's Administration actually does not fit neatly either into orthodox or revisionist theoretical models of minority government. Even works that have given greater recognition to the importance of the minority status of the Wilson and Callaghan Governments do not engage in significant analysis of the government-formation process, nor do they consider potential alternative outcomes which were explored by contemporaries.[3]

1974: transitions to minority

Heath's resignation and the establishment of Wilson's Minority Government after the election in February 1974 have often been accepted as inevitable and unrelated to the actions taken by the leadership of the main parties. While hindsight would tend to reinforce this perception of inevitability, the outcome after the election was by no means certain to contemporaries, who put forward different possibilities in an effort to come to terms with the new political reality.[4]

The particular context of the election as a snap poll made it more difficult to formulate strategies to deal with a hung parliament. Unlike the 2010 election, the contest in February 1974 had only been called by Heath three weeks prior to polling day. The result was also largely unpredicted, with the consequence that the main parties were unprepared. Almost every opinion poll conducted, even on election day itself, had inaccurately predicted Heath's re-election at the head of a majority government, many Conservative-supporting newspapers printing their early editions with stories prematurely indicating a Conservative victory and such headlines as 'A Handsome Win for Heath'. The finely balanced nature of the result of only four seats difference between the two main parties (Labour 301, Conservatives 297), and the fact that the winner in some seats was not known until several days after the election, added to this confusion. As a consequence, the leadership of the main parties were often compelled merely to react to events as they occurred in the days following the election.[5]

Although both parties were aware of, and cited examples from, previous hung parliaments in discussions about strategy, most commentators have not appreciated the main conclusion of the February 1974 election that was reached and recognised by contemporaries. The Conservative Cabinet, meeting the day after the election, perhaps best sums up the fact that the result was 'confusing to interpret' and 'without precedent in recent times'.[6] Both 1920s Minority Labour Governments had won more votes than any other party at the preceding election, demonstrating political momentum by gaining over a hundred seats in each case, often from the incumbent Conservative Government. In both cases, there had also been a clear gap of twenty to seventy seats between the two parties. By contrast, in February 1974, the numbers voting for Labour and their percentage share of the vote declined significantly, their gain of only thirteen seats overall being comparatively small and offset by losses to smaller parties. The Conservatives had 200,000 more votes in total, and the gap between the two main parties meant that both were practically equal in their seat numbers. Other precedents actually served to suggest contradictory possibilities, such as Conservatives remaining in power in spite of not holding as many seats as Labour and of having lost their majority during the election. Labour's 1924 Administration had held sixty-seven fewer seats than the Conservatives, and the Liberals had continued in government after the election of January 1910 in spite of losing their majority and a hundred seats. The Liberal Minority Government in 1910 and both previous Labour Minority Administrations had also taken office only after receiving assurances of support from other parties that would ensure a viable, stable majority. The history of coalitions formed in the 1910s and

1930s apparently provided further precedents for interparty agreements to form governments irrespective of which party had made the most gains in an election.[7] Conceptual models relating to minority governance that are now more widely recognised were, in many cases, developed only after the 1974 experience. One of the most notable frameworks is David Butler's 'mysticism about pluralities', which suggests that even a small lead in the number of seats held by one party over another may often be successfully portrayed as outright 'victory', as was arguably partly the case for the SNP, which gained one seat more than Labour in the 2007 Scottish Parliament election.[8]

Heath's efforts to remain in office have often been characterised as a desperate attempt to cling to power or a genuine but naive initiative to ensure stable government for Britain. There is almost universal agreement that Conservative negotiations to form a coalition could not have succeeded or have ensured a governing majority even if successful.[9] Labour is portrayed as almost entirely passive in this process, the leadership issuing a press release, after which they were said to be 'resting' over the weekend before being inexorably ushered into forming a minority government. One commentator even goes so far as to state that 'Wilson simply did nothing'.[10]

However, the detail in internal papers reveals the greater complexities in how both sides approached and sought to navigate this process. Two declassified files provide some particularly interesting insights, the first being a collection of minutes and memoranda, including conversations between the Prime Minister and Thorpe, while the second, a memorandum by Armstrong, records the efforts to form a government in the days preceding Heath's resignation. Labour's internal dialogue during this period is revealed by records including those of Shadow Cabinet meetings and Donoughue's diaries.

On 1 March 1974, the first day following the election, the main parties set out what their overall approaches would be. Heath's plans on the day of the election and discussion immediately thereafter are recorded in Armstrong's minute, along with the challenges of the unexpected situation:

> The Prime Minister told me in conversation the previous day that, if the situation after the election was that his party had more seats than Labour but no overall majority, his inclination would be to stay in office and meet Parliament, rather than make any approach to the Liberals. But the actual situation was that the Labour Party had more seats than the Conservative Party, albeit by a narrow margin; and there was general agreement that in that situation it would not be honourable for the Government simply to continue in office and face Parliament.[11]

A recurring feature of these discussions was to avoid any notion of 'cheating' that would negatively impact on the Conservatives' future election prospects. Although there was talk of an interparty agreement with the Liberals as an option, it was not necessarily the favoured approach initially.

In spite of the belief that any Conservative negotiations with other parties would be unsuccessful, the Labour leadership attempted to anticipate other outcomes at the Friday morning Shadow Cabinet on 1 March. They decided on what would be the general content of their amendment to the Queen's Speech if Heath chose to meet with Parliament, and discussed what issue could politically compel the Liberals to vote with Labour in order to bring down Heath. Another notable problem which the meeting addressed was the issue of how Labour should immediately respond publicly to Heath's efforts to construct a new administration. The view adopted, that was expressed most notably by Callaghan and supported by figures including Roy Jenkins, Shadow Home Secretary, was to remain relatively silent on the matter, beyond an initial press release, and for senior Labour members not to give any kind of briefings to the press over the weekend.[12]

The subsequent press release emphasised the Conservatives had lost 'the authority' to govern, but the end paragraph set out the fact that Labour was not seeking deals or coalitions: 'In these circumstances, the Labour Party is prepared to form a government and to submit its programme for the endorsement of Parliament.'[13] In some ways, this statement was unsurprising. The possibility of a coalition had been rejected during the campaign in response to journalists' questions, and Joe Haines, Wilson's Press Secretary, had privately suggested to Donoughue that 'in a minority his [Wilson's] policy would be to govern until brought down'. This attitude was largely conditioned by the experience of Ramsay MacDonald, the 1920s Labour leader who had been ostracised by the party when he made a peacetime coalition deal. In the early 1970s, this fear of such a post-electoral coalition continued to form an important part of Labour's psyche, evident not least in the widespread endorsement of a 1973 Labour conference motion against any deals with other parties.[14]

Although the release was merely a restatement of Labour's position, in the new reality of there being no overall majority, it impacted on developments for the Government and other smaller parties. The Shadow Cabinet meeting had emphasised various benefits of this approach, including appearing dignified as the government-in-waiting, and that the attempt and failure of Heath to establish any deal would buttress the position of a Labour Minority Government, demonstrating from the outset that there was no immediately viable alternative administration, and making it more difficult for the Opposition to attempt to defeat the Government in the House of Commons, which would only threaten another election rather than any early return to power as part of a coalition.[15] In subsequent Conservative meetings, one of the main points raised was the fact that Labour had committed itself to attempting to form a 'minority government' without any firm promise of support from smaller parties, as had been the case with previous minority administrations. As far as the Conservatives could determine, this statement meant that there was no prospect of Labour trying and failing to construct an interparty agreement. This gave greater impetus to Conservative efforts to form a government, fearing, as indicated in Armstrong's minute, that, if they resigned, the outcome would be politically very damaging:

> Mr Wilson would be given greater initiative in choosing the ground and the timing of the next election, and greater power to shape events so as to put his party in the most favourable position to win it. He would presumably follow the same sort of tactics as he followed after his narrow victory in 1964. If he took office now, the Labour Party might well be in office until 1980 or later.[16]

At the same time, paradoxically, Labour's statement also reduced other fears which could have galvanised the Conservatives into making a more substantial interparty deal. The main obstacle to agreement with the Liberals was that of electoral reform. Unlike 2010, when the Conservative coalition offer to the Liberal Democrats on electoral reform was increased in response to a prospective Labour offer, the absence of any competing deal in 1974 also removed potential Liberal leverage, Conservatives knowing that reform would not be delivered if they could not get an agreement.

Heath and selected groups of ministers managed the government talks, consisting mainly of bilateral meetings between the Conservative and Liberal leaders, and informal contacts, which were largely entered into as a result of the initiative taken by other parties, including the UUP and the SNP.[17] When Heath first met Thorpe, he did have a typed paper, 'Points for Talk with Mr Thorpe', outlining areas of potential agreement between the two parties, and indicating the scope for either a minority or formal coalition government:

> This could be either an understanding with the Liberal Party to support the Government on measures within a programme to be agreed, but without formal participation in Government; or formal participation of the Liberals in Government, with a seat in the Cabinet for Mr Thorpe and one (? or two) other ministerial appointments for Liberals. [Possibly two Cabinet appointments?] Prepared to contemplate either basis.[18]

However, while in some ways far-reaching, the paper amounted to little more than a restatement of what options for cooperation had been discussed at the Cabinet the previous day and a list of topics that might provide a starting point for a common platform, rather than any detailed basis for discussions. This absence of negotiating strategy further hampered any potential deal. While the initial Conservative options for the Liberals had included 'minority government' or 'coalition', this position had changed by the following day, Cabinet members insisting that only a full coalition would be satisfactory, fearing that the Liberals could not otherwise be guaranteed to support drastic economic measures.[19] By setting out a broader opening bid and then restricting the options for any deal to what many Liberals regarded as a less desirable formal coalition, the Government gave the impression that they were not taking the negotiations seriously. This limitation of possible arrangements also ignored or closed down otherwise viable options which the Liberals could have been more likely to countenance, including limited support for the Government on certain issues, or even abstaining on selected votes. Given Labour's rejection of interparty deals, and the precedents of parties governing without holding the most parliamentary seats, it is not inconceivable that such an arrangement could have been agreed, if combined with support or abstention of other parties on an issue-by-issue basis. Whether this 'alliance' could have survived is another matter, but its very formation would have significantly altered the context of minority government.[20]

The manner in which practical arrangements were organised further increased Liberal hostility. The decision to arrange secretly informal talks between only Heath and Thorpe spread resentment among senior Liberal MPs, who felt that they were being excluded from the negotiations. The calling of Thorpe to Downing Street, rather than both leaders travelling to a neutral venue, also allowed sections of the media to portray Thorpe as someone 'desperate for power', and helped further persuade his colleagues to oppose the idea of coalition.[21] Other informal contacts were established between Conservatives and Liberals, but these were largely ad hoc, and initiated later on over the weekend, amounting to little more than unguided conversations where Liberals confirmed they would personally oppose or advise Thorpe to resist any deal.[22] While there was relative unity within the Cabinet over the approach to the Liberals, the Conservatives failed to engage with and coordinate their own parliamentarians, leading to mixed messages emerging, even from those who ostensibly claimed to support coalition. Newspaper reports talked of unnamed Conservative MPs calling on Heath to be replaced as Prime Minister by William Whitelaw, a Conservative frontbencher widely regarded as a moderate who would have been more acceptable to the Liberals. Certainly, one of the two main conditions which Thorpe initially proposed as the price of his party's support included the removal of Heath as leader. However, while some Liberals regarded this proposal as serious, it was much more likely to have been an opening bid reflecting a conventional negotiating tactic. Thorpe quickly suggested to the Prime Minister that he could 'handle' his party on the issue of Heath's leadership in order to secure his second demand of a commitment on electoral reform.[23] The Conservative attempt to put discussions into writing through drafting a letter to Thorpe on 3 March reinforces our perception of a lack of proper coordination. This letter may have been regarded as a reassurance to other senior Liberals, giving a more concrete form to the leaders' discussions and proposals being made, or to prompt further Liberal action. However, even after redrafting by Heath and the Cabinet, the letter sent out did not reflect the most recent meetings and discussions, a fact highlighted by Thorpe through a hint of irritation in his reply.[24]

It may be argued that the negotiations were not taken seriously by the Conservatives because they viewed them as merely a political tactic. While scholars, including Butler and Kavanagh, have refuted this possibility in the past, there was undoubtedly a tactical dimension to the Conservative negotiation effort, as suggested during the Cabinet meeting on 1 March. By showing willingness to form a coalition, Heath could appeal to more moderate voters ahead of another election, and discredit the Liberals if they refused a coalition offer. Nevertheless, even if these negotiations were conducted primarily as a political tactic for future electioneering, their method of execution did not represent good strategy. There was insufficient effort made by the Conservatives to anticipate or counter the emergence of the damaging perception that they had attempted to 'hang on' to power unfairly; the greatest conscious attempt to shape such a narrative consisted of sporadic newspaper comments by isolated MPs and some slight redrafts of the statements issued by Heath prior to his resignation as Prime Minister. Heath also could not rely on the influential Conservative press to support this narrative, their credibility weakened by the stark contrast between early headlines of Conservative victory and subsequent retraction through headlines including, 'Heath's Election Gamble Fails'.[25]

Communication with other smaller parties concerning potential agreements were pursued in parallel to these negotiations, although in a less high-profile way. These discussions were similarly disorganised, reactive rather than proactive, responsive to initial approaches made by the smaller parties. Some commentators have suggested that if UUP MPs had not broken away from the Government during the previous parliament then their seats would have been counted in the Conservative total, making them the largest party bloc in the Commons. Certain Cabinet members initially advocated working closely together with the UUP, even suggesting that this would enable them to form a minority government that possessed a plurality of the seats in Parliament.[26] The UUP themselves used informal contacts to indicate their disapproval at being counted by commentators as 'separate' from the Conservative seat total. They also expected to receive the Conservative Whip, as had been customary in previous parliaments. Any form of deal with the UUP that involved the end of the Sunningdale Agreement, which had set up the Northern Ireland Assembly, was ruled out automatically, but efforts were made by both sides to set up a meeting between Heath and UUP leader Harry West.[27] However, the majority view within the Conservative leadership was more realistic in appraising the political implications of this approach. Heath's meetings with selected Cabinet colleagues over the weekend tended to conclude, even from as early as Saturday, that any attempt to count the UUP towards the Conservative total after the emergence of the final results would appear as an attempt to 'cheat', and would likely cause significant political damage to the Conservatives in a future election. The fact that the UUP had won their seats on a coalition ticket with other Unionist parties that explicitly opposed the main Conservative policy regarding Northern Ireland reinforced the political difficulty of coming to any formal arrangement. The UUP voting record in the previous parliament was also cited as not being consistently Conservative, even on issues not concerned with Northern Ireland, implying that their support could not be relied upon.[28] To avoid political damage, contact with the UUP was limited to written correspondence and the offer of a phone conversation, as well as the decision not to pursue any face-to-face meetings once West's intentions were known more clearly. One of the concerns had been to avoid West bringing along politicians, such as Rev. Ian Paisley, who were part of the UUUC coalition but were perceived by the Government as likely to undermine any agreement with the Liberals.[29]

Another avenue which was pursued, and which has been mostly overlooked by commentators, involved seeking SNP support for the Conservatives on a limited minority government basis. Informal contacts, encouraged although not initiated by Heath, made between Conservative MP Teddy Taylor and Scottish National MPs, considered the possibility of providing assistance in the event of confidence and supply votes. These contacts even reached the stage of the SNP setting out specific policy conditions under which they would support a Conservative Minority Administration, including a settlement that would get the miners back to work, a Scottish Assembly with substantial powers, and the freezing of prices, rents and rates. The SNP suggested numerous options, depending on how far their conditions were met, whereby their MPs could provide full support or else be committed to backing the Conservatives only on confidence votes.[30] While there were areas of common ground and Conservative support for a Scottish Assembly, the Government's ability to meet even the most limited form of these terms would have been problematic both practically and ideologically, and would have involved substantial changes, not least in terms of significant public subsidies to bring about price freezes. This avenue of approach barely featured in the records of weekend discussions, suggesting that it was swiftly dismissed as unworkable. When the notion of an agreement with the SNP was raised again in the Cabinet meeting on 4 March, it was much more briefly dealt with than discussions concerning other parties, ideological incompatibility being cited as the primary reason this could not be pursued. The fact that it was even raised, however, does show the difference that some forty years makes in politics (given the SNP's explicitly anti-Conservative resolve in 2017), and foreshadowed further consideration of diverse interparty deals in the later 1970s.[31]

The Conservative leadership showed some political awareness in their dealings with the smaller parties, but their lack of preparedness and inability to coordinate and plan sufficiently in the aftermath of the election precipitated failures in their negotiations with the Liberals, which prevented any possibility of a successful attempt at minority government or coalition.

Although Labour's original plan had been to remain quiet while the Government's negotiations were ongoing, there were clearly concerns within the leadership about this strategy. Wilson and his closest advisers from the campaign (including Donoughue, Haines, his Political Secretary, Marcia Williams, and his Personal Assistant, Albert Murray) were involved in discussions over the following days about taking a much more proactive approach against the Conservative efforts to construct a coalition. Ideas that were raised and debated varied from privately putting pressure on Heath and Buckingham Palace through sending a strongly worded letter, or taking a more strident tone in publicly demanding the resignation of the Government in speeches and/or press releases. Callaghan's response to Wilson's telephoned request for such a statement was rejected, urging that they should continue to say nothing. There were some private initiatives, such as Donoughue attempting to convince those he was in contact with from the Liberals to undermine the negotiation efforts, anticipating Labour's initiatives towards the Liberal Democrats in 2010, but these were limited in scope. After the weekend, it would appear that there were moves towards a more assertive stance when members of the Shadow Cabinet were instructed on Monday 4 March to draft a press release for the evening attacking Heath's attempt at interparty negotiations. Ultimately, the draft document was never released, being overtaken by the collapse of Conservative negotiations with the Liberals, and the installation of Wilson as Prime Minister on 4 March.[32]

1976: minority government revisited

As with regard to studies on the Wilson Government, investigations of Callaghan's Administration often do not go beyond considering his election as Labour leader, his character and some of the aspects of his early days as the new Prime Minister. While revisionist works have given some greater recognition to Callaghan's loss of a parliamentary majority, the formation process is still unquestioningly regarded as inevitable.[33]

In part, this scholarly omission understandably reflects the greater focus on the change of government leader immediately preceding the loss of a government majority, the surprise resignation of Wilson and the politics of the fiercely contested Labour leadership election which followed. The omission is also reflective of a perception of there being little real difference between a government with a very slim majority and a government lacking a theoretical or working majority by only a handful of seats. The Labour Governments from October 1964 to March 1966 and from October 1974, up to Callaghan becoming leader in April 1976, would appear to lend credence to this idea. These governments possessed a majority of up to only four seats in the House of Commons, and experienced internal divisions which had, on several occasions, led to defeat or the prospect of defeat on major policies.[34]

Measuring both the Wilson and Callaghan Administrations against the Riker-led orthodox and Strøm-led revisionist scholarship, would, at first glance, appear to confirm the idea that Labour's continuation as a minority government was inevitable. Both governments appeared to fulfil conditions set out in these theoretical approaches that predisposed them towards minority administration rather than any alternative form of government such as a coalition.[35] In many ways, both reflected the orthodox position on minority administrations, not least that of representing an unusual (deviant) case in a country which had normally produced single-party majority governments over the preceding decades. In spite of Heath's efforts to construct a deal with the Liberals, decision-makers in the main parties also did not regard themselves as having any established British tradition of coalition formation outside of wartime. Indeed, the only reference made by an MP in Parliament to a possible British coalition government in April 1976 was in Conservative backbencher Sir Raymond Gower's denial that he was advocating one in the face of economic turmoil.[36] Britain also appeared to fit the criteria of party fractionalisation, smaller parties seeking to challenge the established political settlement, having gained a significant number of seats in Parliament after the 1974 elections. When trying to secure a parliamentary majority for passing legislation, whether on a vote-by-vote basis or in forma-tion of the Lib–Lab Pact, the Callaghan Government mindset appears to have been one of securing a 'minimal winning' position, even on legislation of major constitutional importance.[37]

At the same time, the formation of both governments also clearly shared some characteristics identified by more revisionist theoreticians. In many cases, minority governments formed in other countries can be a significant number of seats short of having a legislative majority, possessing only 40 per cent of parliamentary seats, or, even, in some cases, as little as 15–20 per cent.[38] By con-trast, Labour in 1974 and 1976 was only, at most, a few seats short of an overall majority in a Parliament of 635 members, echoing Taylor and Laver's theory of being 'almost a majority government' in practice.[39]

Other structural aspects of the revisionist models were also present. Opposition in the British parliaments of the 1970s was divided between Conservatives, Liberals and a combination of parties, including nationalists from Scotland and Wales and unionists and republicans from Northern Ireland, making it less likely to be able to form an alternative coalition to the Government. Britain's institutional setups would also appear to have favoured minority rather than coalition government in the case of indecisive electoral results. The negative framing of investiture rules allowed a government to exist if merely tolerated by the opposition, while *de facto* near-absolute government control over time-tabling business in the House of Commons, committee appointments and the absence of independent bodies capable of vetoing policies, as well as significant administrative powers granted to ministers through the Crown prerogative, strengthened the Government's capacity to stay in power in spite of not having a legislative majority.[40]

Callaghan Government: a special case

However, while all these factors had an important influence, they by no means inevitably determined the formation and operation of the Callaghan Government. The 1976 Administration actually differed significantly from these theoretical norms and even from previous British experience of minority governments up to 1974, making it particularly important as a case study, not only for British history, but also for consideration of wider minority government theory and the formation of minority administrations internationally. Unlike most administrations considered in this theoretical corpus, Callaghan's Government formed after losing its majority during a parliamentary term through by-elections and the defection of MPs, rather than as a result of a general election or coalition break-up. The Government's formation actually ran contrary to twentieth-century British precedents, all four instances of minority governments up until 1976 having been formed in the period immediately following general elections, whereas the formation of a new government midway through a parliamentary term had, on five occasions because of special circumstances, resulted in coalitions, in spite of certain sections of the main political parties standing opposed to such an outcome. Much theoretical discussion has concentrated purely on the political leadership, considering parties as united actors, with an assumed high level of homogeneity. Party leaderships acted as the main coordinators of parliamentary strategy during this period, and, as such, are the primary focus of this book. At the same time, however, parties represented in Parliament during the Callaghan Administration, whether in government or opposition, suffered from deep-seated divisions which frequently manifested themselves, and served to influence the power dynamics and political interactions. The approaches pursued thereby did not necessarily represent the rational considerations of a single political actor, but were rather the end product of a complex series of negotiations between actors within the same party pursuing their own particular set of objectives. Different actors also considered alternative strategies which, even if not enacted, formed part of the debate and remained as potential options in the event of the situation changing.[41]

Labour's continuance as a minority government in April 1976 was the most likely course of action, but was not inevitable. A number of alternatives existed, some of which were given greater consideration by the Government while others were rejected. These potential alternatives included that of Callaghan calling an early election, an agreement between opposition parties to bring down the Government in a confidence vote or even to form an alternative government, or the formation of a coalition by the incumbent government to retain their majority. Examining why these courses of action were not pursued will give something of an insight into the formulation of strategy, and establish the context within which subsequent responses to the situation of minority government were developed by both main parties.

Early election

Minority governments in other countries have often pursued the escape route of calling an early election, when their strategists calculate there is an opportunity to win a legislative majority, whether or not this actually turns out to be the case. Alternatively, the loss of a majority may compel a government to seek an early election, if it leaves them unable to continue passing the legislation necessary in order to govern. While it is certainly the case that governments with small majorities in postwar Britain tended to experience difficulties in passing controversial legislation and facing the prospect of early general elections, minority government as experienced in 1976 was recognised as a different entity, reflected in both the perceptions and practices of contemporary political actors. The minority government definition was initially resisted by the Government, who continued largely to adhere to majoritarian principles, as discussed further in Chapter 4. However, government leaders were forced to acknowledge the changed situation. These perceptions of a distinct difference appear not only in the public language of parliamentary debates or press releases from early April 1976 onwards, but also in the subsequent private correspondence between Callaghan and other world leaders – the Prime Minister having to explain the loss of the Government's majority – as well as in Cabinet and Shadow Cabinet discussions, beginning in April 1976, on how to deal with the 'new' minority situation.[42] When faced with difficulties of passing a major piece of legislation in June, the Cabinet emphasised that 'the first need was to restore the Government's majority'. A Cabinet memorandum in May by Foot on the Government's legislative programme recognised that the absence of a majority would make it more difficult to get certain legislation passed, and provided detailed charts that prioritised some bills, while also providing an assessment of some possible compromises that could be made.[43]

Callaghan's message upon entering office did not, contrary to some perceptions, completely reject the possibility of an early election, although, as with Wilson's press release in March 1974, it was framed very much within a traditional British majoritarian view of the parliamentary system, emphasising the Government's relative strength over opposing parties and mandate to govern. Callaghan's public address to Labour MPs on becoming Prime Minister on 6 April 1976 included highlighting that, in spite of their overall majority being small, their position relative to the main opposition party was strong, as they possessed 'a majority over the Tories of 40', and indicated that 'We [Labour] can and we shall continue to govern.'[44] On 8 April, in a debate following the defection which had taken away Labour's majority, Callaghan responded to an interruption in his answer to a question by baiting the Opposition with an ambiguous jibe about their fears of him calling an early election.[45] Answering a further question on 29 April, Callaghan's apparent denial of a possible early election was not emphatic, but rather made conditional on the Government's ability to continue to get its legislation passed. These statements and others were not a categorical rejection of an early poll, certainly not when contrasted with Callaghan's clear message two years later, which ended speculation of an election in the autumn of 1978. Callaghan's public acknowledgement of the conditional state of governance, albeit in a manner aiming for the greatest room for manoeuvre, showed recognition of changes in the political reality and the possible need for contingency planning in light of his precarious parliamentary situation. Although most among the government leadership leaned away from embarking upon an early election, some were considering the possibility in April 1976, weighing up a number of different factors. Foot's remarks to a local election rally on 5 May 1976, seeking an early election 'as speedily as we can get it sensibly, in which we can get a full and proper majority in the House of Commons', prompted calls by the Opposition for an early election and a denial by the Prime Minister two days later.[46] It is difficult to ascertain whether this was a genuine reflection of Foot's view, or a remark taken out of context. Foot was already recognising potential challenges when discussing legislative strategy in April and May Cabinet meetings, and bore great responsibility for dealing with these issues, not least in his role of managing the increasingly difficult passage of legislation without a majority.[47]

When considering electoral timing in more detail, as will be seen in Chapter 7, those formulating strategy in both parties tended to attach particular weight to recent British political history, which, in April 1976, offered something of a mixed set of results for governments calling early elections. Wilson had successfully used early dissolutions to bolster his majority in 1966 and to transform his minority government into a majority one in October 1974, but, equally, had lost after going early in 1970, as had Heath after the early election in February 1974.[48] Although the loss of the government majority was, from the outset, portrayed by opposition parties as a sign of failure, Labour's leadership election and Callaghan's recent takeover as Prime Minister had been greeted as positive changes, and potentially provided both a momentum for a campaign and a legitimate reason for an election. Anthony Eden had sought an immediate election upon becoming Prime Minister in 1955, albeit later on in the parliamentary term and already possessing a sizeable majority. Nevertheless, this precedent was cited by contemporary commentators when considering the possibility, not least in speculation by *The Times* Political Editor about potential outcomes of the Labour leadership contest. A new leader deciding to seek the legitimacy of a fresh mandate in such an instance could have perhaps been regarded as showing both statesmanship and political strength, and, as acknowledged by the Government themselves, a large proportion of legislation promised by the October 1974 manifesto had already been passed into law. There appeared to be a temporary lull in the emerging economic crises of 1975 and 1976. There had been a Conservative poll lead in the preceding months, but this was by no means assured of surviving an electoral campaign, the Opposition particularly suffering continued questions of internal divisions and problems over policy for Thatcher, still relatively new to the position of Conservative leader. In fact, following Callaghan being selected as leader, Labour briefly enjoyed a lead of 6 per cent to 7 per cent, as highlighted in an Ipsos MORI poll of 8–9 April 1976.[49]

However, the change to a minority in April did not lead the Callaghan Government to give any serious consideration to an immediate election in their formal strategy meetings. The brief poll lead was not sustained in subsequent soundings of public opinion, and did not provide a solid enough basis for the Government to risk an election. Callaghan's fear of winning an election without achieving an overall majority was perhaps one of the strongest reasons for not seeking a snap dissolution, a stance which would also dominate his decision-making over future electoral timing.[50] A particularly interesting insight into Callaghan's mindset in the early stages of his Government may be gained from a transcribed extract of a call held with German Chancellor Helmut Schmidt on 28 April 1976. Schmidt had heard about the loss of the Government's majority and asked 'does it mean anything?' Callaghan not only restated his public pronouncements about having a party majority of forty over the Conservatives, but also indicated more clearly his position on not needing an early election, as well as forecasting the potential lifespan of the Government:

> My view is unless we lose by-elections and have obviously lost the confidence of the people we can carry on for a couple of years if we want to. [...] there's no need for me to feel that I've got to rush to the country in order to try and do something. I want a period of steady government if we can get it.[51]

Other reasons for the Government fearing an early election at this stage included concerns over electoral fatigue among both the populace in terms of lack of interest, and the party in terms of exhausted resources, having fought two general elections and a nationwide referendum campaign in the space of the previous two years. Although much legislation had been passed, there were significant manifesto commitments which had not been realised and difficult unresolved political questions including devolution, which, it was calculated, could lead to significant Labour losses in any elections in Scotland and Wales. In spite of making calls for an early election and enjoying greater polling success, the Opposition were similarly not expecting a dissolution at this stage, and were still working on their own manifesto and strategic preparations for such a contest.[52]

Opposition coalition/election

In some cases, the loss of a government majority or attempted formation of a minority government following an election has led opposing parties to respond either by vigorous attempts to defeat a government in the legislature, and thereby force its dismissal through an election, or even to establish an alternative majority or minority coalition of opposition parties and replace the incumbent government without the need for an election. The latter approach occurred in Germany in 1982, following the collapse of a centre-left Social Democrat/Free Democrat coalition and replacement of the resulting Social Democrat Minority Government with a centre-right governing coalition of opposition parties.[53] In contrast to some of the more consensual democracies, the traditional adversarial approach characterising British politics has led to an Official Opposition which generally desires to defeat the incumbent government in parliamentary votes and ultimately to replace it in office. Any prospect of this occurring in Britain had, in 1974, as indicated, been prevented by the Conservative failure to form a coalition, which led to Wilson's Minority Government. Stonehouse, whose defection gave the opposition parties a majority in April 1976, followed his resignation from Labour with calls for an immediate election. The Opposition had, in the preceding month, been particularly vociferous in their calls for the Government's resignation and for a general election. These calls were further encouraged in March 1976 by Labour rebels inflicting a significant defeat on the Government over public expenditure when it still had an overall majority, even although the defeat was subsequently reversed by the Government winning a confidence vote. Thatcher continued to call for an early election, and in particular for the resignation of the Prime Minister. These calls were renewed in May in response to Foot's statement about an election. However, while publicly critical of Labour's loss of a majority in April 1976, and periodically calling for an early election, the Conservatives did not consider preventing the minority government from taking office by forcing their defeat over a confidence vote and subsequent general election at this stage. Although there were the occasional public comments from opposition MPs mentioning the prospect of an early election, the Conservatives' internal strategic discourse in April was focused much more upon immediate parliamentary considerations in terms of their attempts to change party representation on committees.[54] In the first Shadow Cabinet that followed the loss of the government majority on 7 April, the main response to the Stonehouse defection was to press 'for an Opposition majority of one on all Standing Committees which were set up on future Bills' to reflect the new political balance of the House of Commons. While removal of the government majority formed an important consideration, this was only one topic of the meeting, other discussions focusing on local government, how to respond to aspects of the Budget and to the Government publishing its devolution proposals in June. No indication was made during the meeting of any notion of trying to force an early election.[55]

Shadow Cabinet references to a possible early election only occurred in July 1976, and even these were speculative, 'in the event of an election this Autumn'.

The Conservatives were still revising policy throughout 1976, and making preparations for a future campaign, not least through the reporting of policy groups so as to enable the acceleration of electoral preparations if necessary. Correspondence between Chris Patten, Head of the CRD, and other researchers, considered an autumn election as a remote possibility, but not likely enough to warrant any significant acceleration of preparations, such as the rapid production and regular updating of emergency manifestos, as had been the case during 1974.[56] Although votes were tabled against the Government, no single issue at this stage presented itself as likely to unite opposition parties and enable them to force an early election through a no confidence vote.[57]

Additionally, there was no indication that the Conservatives in April 1976 thought that it would be appropriate to form any kind of voting agreement with other parties in Parliament towards defeating and/or replacing the Government without an election. Indeed, it is unlikely that such an alliance would have been possible, as it would have had to rely on a disparate mix of opposition parties, including Liberals, different nationalist parties, republicans, unionists and independent socialists, as well as potential Labour rebels, there being significant lines of division between these groups. There have been cases in the past of so-called 'rainbow coalitions' formed in other countries which incorporated counterintuitive groupings of parties across the political spectrum. However, these instances tend to occur only when there is no alternative, and rely to some degree on the different parties accepting certain pre-existing norms of coalition in their domestic political culture. Britain's experience of such unity governments has, up until September 2017 at least, been limited to cross-party coalitions during the two World Wars, and those of the National Governments during the economic crisis of the 1930s. There have also been two (depending on the definition used) unsuccessful attempts to form particularly broadly based coalition governments since 2007. The first was that of a proposed coalition between Welsh nationalists Plaid Cymru, the Conservatives and the Liberal Democrats in the Welsh Assembly following the 2007 election, while the second was an attempt at a Labour–Liberal Democrat coalition including nationalist and Green MPs, following the 2010 general election.[58] While the confidence vote which eventually brought down the Callaghan Government in 1979 did involve many of the different opposition groups voting on the same side, this situation was a case of parties choosing for different reasons to oppose the Labour Administration, rather than actively cooperating with one another. Although some of the smaller parties appeared more willing to challenge the Government, others were in politically unfavourable positions in April 1976 in terms of their electoral prospects, not least the Liberals, their ongoing poll ratings falling to around half of their previous electoral result, and with the then recent revelation of scandals surrounding their leader Thorpe.[59] There is no evidence to suggest that negotiating an alternative opposition coalition government was even being contemplated by the Conservatives following Callaghan's loss of a majority.[60]

This is not to say that the Opposition was completely averse to discussing potentially radical forms of coalition during this period. The Conservative Steering Committee had briefly considered the coalition question over a couple of meetings almost a year earlier in May 1975, at a time when the Government faced serious financial concerns, as well as the prospect of an internal Labour split over the referendum on the European Community. The conclusion from this important Conservative committee was that 'if the Government were ready to drop damaging measures such as nationalisation, a basis for discussing the possibility of a coalition might exist'. Conservative Chair Lord Thorneycroft had also suggested that, facing any crisis election, the best plan would be to campaign for a 'Doctor's Mandate', along the lines of the National Governments in the 1930s.[61] The CRD was tasked to prepare a paper on the possible 'crisis scenarios' for the Steering Committee meetings, which helped to inform the discussion. It was written by Patten, and raised a number of potential questions to be considered, as well as courses of action for the Opposition in the event that the economic crisis forced the Government to seek Conservative support, including:

(i)   to abstain – this would probably not be politically possible or desirable;

(ii)   to support the Government on their terms – unless we take an initiative ourselves we may be driven into this position;

(iii) to bargain our support in return for dropping the nationalisation programme [...]

(iv) to insist on a General Election – but could we govern if we won? And do we really want to do all the dirty work on our own?

(v)   to seek to bring about a coalition or national government.[62]

The Steering Committee were not ruling out becoming part of a unity government in these circumstances, but considered it as very much something to be avoided if possible.

Discussions in late 1975 also considered a prospective minority government caused by a by-election/defection of a few government MPs, and the uncertainty of whether or not this would prompt a general election. When such a prospect was raised at the Conservative Steering Committee in November 1975, it was viewed as very unlikely to lead to an early poll, as a result of ongoing economic conditions unfavourable to the Government. In response to concern about a possible election, Thorneycroft suggested that the Conservatives could 'move into General Election gear at short notice if necessary'. Other preparations during this time included the production in July of a supplement to the standard campaign guide, which, it was suggested, could rapidly be copied and sent to candidates if required (though even at this stage caution was urged).[63]

The Government's successful navigation through the European referendum in early June 1975 without lasting internal divisions helped to reduce the perceived threat of a Labour split and need for any unity government. Thatcher subsequently sought to deny leaked newspaper reports of these discussions on coalition ever having occurred, fearing that they would do damage to the party's primary goal of electoral victory.[64]

By contrast, in the Steering Committee meeting in May 1976, following the loss of the Callaghan Government's majority, the primary parliamentary concern was the battle over achieving greater opposition representation on committees in Parliament. There was no discussion of coalition, nor a call for any paper similar to that of the 1975 'crisis scenarios', the Conservative emphasis clearly being upon seeking to follow the traditional role of opposing the Government where appropriate, as well as making the policy and campaign preparations necessary to win an outright victory at a subsequent election.[65]

Government coalition/interparty agreement

An alternative strategy which governments have frequently pursued to avoid losing their majority is that of forming a coalition or making agreements with other parties.[66] While ultimately ruling out an early election, and not facing an opposition coalition, the use of interparty cooperation to secure a majority was given some consideration from the outset by the Callaghan Government, although this idea did not ultimately yield any substantive results. The only seriously considered proposal was that of inviting Gerry Fitt MP (Leader of the SDLP) to take the Labour Whip, and, in effect, be counted as part of the Government. Such a move would have addressed the one-seat gap needed for a majority, and theoretically secured the Government's position in confidence votes, as well as the retention of government majorities in the composition of legislative committees. In one sense, this initiative was more a search for psychological legitimacy than an attempt at an interparty voting agreement or coalition; Fitt already either abstained on many votes, or tended to vote with the Government. No mention was made of any negotiations, formal or informal, nor any specific incentives to be offered other than general commitment to continued informal consultation between the SDLP and Labour. This action would appear very much in line with the traditional theoretical position of minority governments seeking a 'minimal winning' position, the smallest number of MPs required to secure a majority, in return for the least amount of political concessions to other parties. However, this plan was never brought before the Cabinet, being ultimately rejected by the government leadership. The idea was opposed, particularly by Rees, who feared that the costs of the move would outweigh the benefits, and, as highlighted in the fears of the chapter's opening quote, that being 'dependent on the SDLP at Westminster' could compromise the Government's position in Northern

Ireland.[67] As indicated, this debate resonates with the post-June 2017 reporting of the Conservatives' reliance on the DUP in Parliament.[68]

It was also feared that alignment with what was regarded by some voters as an ostensibly Catholic party could have undermined efforts to resolve ongoing problems of security and governance in Northern Ireland. The initiative would, in addition, be perceived badly in the country as a whole, as being a deceitful backroom deal on the part of the Government, thereby diminishing rather than reinforcing any sense of legitimacy. Any perceived coalition with the SDLP would probably have led to greater opposition to legislation by the eleven UUUC MPs. Rees was, to some extent, also thinking of long-term potential political gains, positing the possibility 'that one day we will have a strong Labour Party in Northern Ireland', although this appears as much to have been an aspiration, part of a plea to avoid Labour reducing their political funding to the very small associated Northern Ireland Labour Party (NILP), which had no parliamentary seats, rather than specifically a strategic argument that seriously considered seat gains as being likely in the immediate future.[69]

The particular political culture and history within Labour helped to discourage other suggestions of interparty cooperation. This contributed not only to both main political parties' views of minority government as weak and unstable, but also to a distrust of interparty cooperation. Labour's First Minority Government in 1924 was brought down by a no confidence vote, in spite of having survived initially by relying on Liberal support, while the Second Labour Minority Government in 1929–31 ultimately ended in a major disagreement which split the party and was compounded by MacDonald's subsequent decision to form a coalition with Conservatives and with elements of the Liberals. MacDonald's perceived 'treachery' made him one of the most reviled figures within the party when accounts were written of Labour's history during this period. That this view continued to be prevalent throughout the political system in the 1970s is evident not least from the aforementioned Labour Party Conference motion in 1973, alongside the private references made regarding the event in the meetings of party leaders, who feared emulating the coalition approach.[70] In both Labour and Conservative strategy papers that considered questions of minority and coalition government during this period, there are references to MacDonald's experience as providing both an example and a warning to the Labour leadership.[71]

In contrast to previous academic assumptions, the formation of both the Wilson and Callaghan Governments as minority administrations was not inevitable. Contemporary strategy-makers and party leaders contemplated a number of different possibilities. Leaders of the governments and their opposition counterparts, while publicly adhering to majoritarian principles, privately recognised the fundamental difference between majority and minority administrations. Heath's efforts to form an interparty coalition or minority government, while unsuccessful, involved greater complexity in the negotiations and internal strategic dialogue than has been acknowledged. In turn, rather than being passive observers, Wilson and his team considered how to approach the challenges of positioning themselves to take advantage of any breakdown of the Government's interparty negotiations. Two years later, the continuation of the Callaghan Administration as a minority government was the most likely outcome, but was by no means the only option – historical precedents favouring coalition and alternative courses of action being considered from the outset by some within the Government, including the prospect of an interparty agreement with the SDLP to maintain a parliamentary majority. The Conservatives, having considered the option of a coalition in 1975, did not revisit this possibility as a means to topple Callaghan. The Opposition similarly did not view an early election as either desirable or likely to occur at this point, not taking action to attempt to force the Government from office in a no confidence vote. The government-formation processes in March 1974 and April 1976 raised questions and potential governmental alternatives for contemporaries which would influence their thinking from 1976 onwards when facing further challenges imposed by the state of minority government.

The Callaghan Government's formation is an atypical case in international theory, not fitting neatly into existing theoretical models of minority governance, not least in terms of it beginning midway through a parliamentary term and not resulting from any coalition break-up. In its formation, it acted very much as an embodiment of the distinctive British tradition of minority government, seeking to adhere to a majoritarian mindset and practices, while simultaneously contemplating and, where necessary, adopting pragmatic changes to adapt to not having an overall majority.

Notes

1 TNA: PREM 16/1045, Merlyn Rees to Prime Minister, 26 April 1976.
2 Moore, *Margaret Thatcher*, pp. 334–6; Pugh, *Speak for Britain!*, pp. 354–60; P. Whitehead, 'The Labour Governments: 1974–1979', in P. Hennessy and A. Seldon (eds), *Ruling Performance: British Governments from Attlee to Thatcher* (Oxford: Basil Blackwell, 1989), pp. 241–2, 256; Butler and Kavanagh, *The British General Election of 1979*; J. Beavan, 'The Westminster Scene', *The Political Quarterly*, 47:2 (1976), 203–14.
3 Hazell and Paun (eds), *Making Minority Government Work*, pp. 10–19; Seldon and Hickson (eds), *New Labour, Old Labour*, pp. 190–2; Hennessy's work includes insight into previous civil service contingency plans for potential hung parliaments, such as following the 1964 general election, see Hennessy, *The Prime Minister*, pp. 21–35.
4 G. P. Thomas, *Prime Minister and Cabinet Today* (Manchester: Manchester University Press, 1998), p. 30; Campbell, *Edward Heath*, pp. 598–9, 613.
5 *The Times* (28 February 1974), pp. 1, 6; 1 March 1974, p. 1; 2 March 1974, p. 1; *Daily Mail* (28 February 1974), p. 1; CAC: Hailsham MSS (1/1/8), 10 January 1974; Donoughue,

Downing Street Diary, vol. 1, pp. 45–51; Jenkins, *A Life at the Centre*, p. 365; Bell, *The Labour Party in Opposition*, p. ix; P. Warwick, *Government Survival in Parliamentary Democracies* (Cambridge: Cambridge University Press, 1994), pp. 29, 37; A. Morgan, *Harold Wilson* (London: Pluto Press, 1992), pp. 428, 431–2; Benn, *Against the Tide*, p. 106; Butler, *Governing without a Majority*, p. 102.

6 Thatcher MSS: PREM 15/2069, 7.

7 Paun and Hazell, 'Hung Parliaments and the Challenges for Westminster and Whitehall', 214–15; Beckett, *When the Lights Went Out*, p. 161; C. Turpin and A. Tomkins, *British Government and the Constitution: Text and Materials* (Cambridge: Cambridge University Press, 2007), pp. 357–8; R. Brazier, *Constitutional Practice: The Foundations of British Government* (Oxford: Oxford University Press, 1999), pp. 32–6; J. Rasmussen, 'Constitutional Aspects of Government Formation in a Hung Parliament', *Parliamentary Affairs*, 40:2 (1987), 140–1.

8 There were also other factors in the 2007 case, including electoral momentum and division among unionist parties. Oaten, *Coalition*, pp. 215–19, 313; C. Crombez, 'Minority Governments, Minimal Winning Coalitions and Surplus Majorities in Parliamentary Systems', *European Journal of Political Research*, 29:1 (1996), 9–10; Butler, *Governing without a Majority*, p. 102.

9 Oaten, *Coalition*, pp. 168–72, 312; Seldon and Hickson (eds), *New Labour, Old Labour*, pp. 13, 190, 286; R. Blake, *The Conservative Party from Peel to Major* (London: Arrow Books, 1998), pp. 316–17; J. Ramsden, *An Appetite for Power: A History of the Conservative Party since 1830* (London: HarperCollins, 1998), p. 494.

10 Hennessy, *The Prime Minister*, p. 359; B. Pimlott, *Harold Wilson* (London: HarperCollins, 1992), p. 614; Donoughue, *Prime Minister*, p. 45.

11 Thatcher MSS: PREM 16/231, 1 March 1974.

12 LHASC: PC Minutes 1973–74, 1 March 1974.

13 Thatcher MSS: PREM 15/2069, 4.

14 LHASC: NEC Minutes, 23 January–6 March 1974, Various Meetings; MS. Wilson, c. 1336, Loose Papers and Articles on the Liberals in 1973–74; Donoughue, *Downing Street Diary*, vol. 1, pp. 22–4, 32, 36–7, 41.

15 LHASC: PC Minutes 1973–74, 1 March 1974; Jenkins, *A Life at the Centre*, pp. 367–8; Hennessy, *The Prime Minister*, pp. 23, 358–9.

16 Thatcher MSS: PREM 16/231, 1 March 1974.

17 CAC: Hailsham MSS (1/1/8), 1 March 1974; Thatcher MSS: PREM 16/231, 1–4 March 1974.

18 Thatcher MSS: PREM 15/2069, 4; PREM 16/231, 2 March 1974. The square brackets in this quote were added to the original document in pen.

19 *Ibid.*

20 TNA: PREM 15/2069, 7, 13, 15, 19, 21; CAB 128/53, 10th Meeting, 4 March 1974; Thatcher MSS: PREM 16/231, 1–4 March 1974; Warwick, *Government Survival in Parliamentary Democracies*, p. 29; Bergman, 'Formation Rules and Minority Governments', 55–66; Rasmussen, 'Constitutional Aspects of Government Formation', 140–1. For the contrary view that such an arrangement would have been insufficient, see Oaten, *Coalition*, p. 173.

21 D. Dutton, *A History of the Liberal Party in the Twentieth Century* (Houndmills: Palgrave Macmillan, 2004), p. 222; D. Walter, *Strange Rebirth of Liberal England* (London: Politico's, 2003), pp. 49–51; Cook, *A Short History of the Liberal Party*, pp. 157–8; T. F. Lindsay and M. Harrington, *The Conservative Party, 1918–1979* (London: Macmillan, 1979), p. 279.

22 Thatcher MSS: PREM 16/231, 2–4 March 1974; TNA: CAB 128/53, 10th Meeting, 4 March 1974.

23 The only three Cabinet ministers who were opposed to the move were Margaret Thatcher, Keith Joseph and Maurice Macmillan. CAC: Hailsham MSS (1/1/8), 1 March 1974; TNA: PREM 15/2069, 11, 13; *The Times* (2 March 1974), pp. 2–4.

24 TNA: PREM 15/2069, 14, 19, 21; CAB 128/53, 10th Meeting, 4 March 1974.

25 TNA: PREM 15/2069, 23–5; CAB 128/53, 9th Meeting, 1 March 1974; D. Butler and D. Kavanagh, *The British General Election of February 1974* (London: Macmillan, 1974), p. 258. See Chapter 1.

26 TNA: CAB 128/53, 9th Meeting, 1 March 1974; I. McLean, *Rational Choice and British Politics: An Analysis of Rhetoric and Manipulation from Peel to Blair* (Oxford: Oxford University Press, 2001), pp. 145–6.

27 Thatcher MSS: PREM 16/231, 1–2 March 1974.

28 *The Times* (2 March 1974), p. 2; Thatcher MSS: PREM 16/231, 2 March 1974; CAB 128/53, 10th Meeting, 4 March 1974.

29 TNA: PREM 15/2069, 5–6, 9, Telegram from Harry West MP; Note Setting Out Plan for Response and Reply Telegram, 2 March 1974; Thatcher MSS: PREM 16/231, 1–2 March 1974.

30 TNA: PREM 15/2069/10–11, 20, Record of Information Conveyed by Edward Taylor MP to Prime Minister on 2 and 4 March 1974; Thatcher MSS: PREM 16/231, 2 and 4 March 1974.

31 TNA: CAB 128/53, 10th Meeting, 4 March 1974.

32 LHASC: PC Minutes 1973–74, 4 March 1974; Castle, *The Castle Diaries*, p. 32; Donoughue, *Downing Street Diary*, vol. 1, pp. 45–55; Wilson, *Final Term*, pp. 10, 25–6; Butler and Kavanagh, *The British General Election of February 1974*, p. 255.

33 Sandbrook, *Seasons in the Sun*, pp. 459–68; Thorpe, *A History of the British Labour Party*, pp. 195–6; Seldon and Hickson (eds), *New Labour, Old Labour*, pp. 1–2, 173–80; Hennessy, *The Prime Minister*, pp. 376–81; Morgan, *Britain since 1945*, pp. 381–3, 399.

34 Seldon and Hickson (eds), *New Labour, Old Labour*, pp. 190–2; Taylor and Laver, 'Government Coalitions in Western Europe', 229–33. Other commentators have highlighted a clear difference, including Sandbrook, *Seasons in the Sun*, pp. 163, 466.

35 See Chapter 1.

36 HC Hansard, vol. 909, cols 303–4 (6 April 1976).

37 Sandbrook, *Seasons in the Sun*, pp. 459–60; Andeweg, De Vinter, and Dumont (eds), *Puzzles of Government Formation*, pp. 1–10, 98–104, 112–13, 195–6; Seldon and Hickson (eds), *New Labour, Old Labour*, pp. 192–3; Hennessy, *The Prime Minister*, p. 385; Strøm, *Minority Government and Majority Rule*, pp. 7–16, 56–92.

38 One of the smallest minority administrations in terms of seat numbers was the 1973–75 Danish Government of Poul Hartling, which had only 22 seats out of 179 in Parliament (12.3%). Minority governments' capacity to govern effectively, as opposed to merely surviving, is another matter – which continues to be subjected to much scholarly debate. See Chapter 1: International minority government theory.

39 See Chapter 2.

40 R. Rogers and R. Walters, *How Parliament Works* (London: Routledge, 6th edn, 2013), pp. 43, 56–7, 93–4; Seldon and Hickson (eds), *New Labour, Old Labour*, pp. 192–4; Tsebelis, *Veto Players*, pp. 97–8, 184; Bergman, *Constitutional Rules and Party Goals in Coalition*

Formation, pp. 45, 162–3; Strøm, *Minority Government and Majority Rule*, pp. 1–2, 8–14, 65, 90–1.

41 Hazell and Paun (eds), *Making Minority Government Work*, pp. 18–19; C. Nikolenyi, *Minority Governments in India: The Puzzle of Elusive Majorities* (Abingdon: Routledge, 2010), pp. 1–24, 90–6; Seldon and Hickson (eds), *New Labour, Old Labour*, pp. 190–204; Hennessy, *The Prime Minister*, pp. 386–8, 393–4; W. C. Müller and K. Strøm, *Policy, Office, or Votes? How Political Parties in Western Europe Make Hard Decisions* (Cambridge: Cambridge University Press, 1999), pp. 1–35, 55, 63–6; Strøm, *Minority Government and Majority Rule*, pp. 1–16, 89–92. See Chapter 1.

42 Callaghan Papers, 118, Prime Minister's Third Carbons: April 1976, Letter to Henry Kissinger, 28 April 1976; TNA: PREM 16/1045, PM's Talk with Chancellor Schmidt [extract], 28 April 1976.

43 TNA: CAB 128/59, 1st Meeting, 13 April 1976; 2nd Meeting, 29 April 1976; 5th Meeting, 18 May 1976; 6th Meeting, 17 June 1976; 12th Meeting, 1 July 1976; 128/89, Legislative Programme 1976–77, 14 May 1976; PREM 16/2214, 'Note of a Meeting Held at […] No. 10 Downing Street', 16 June 1976; George Clark, Political Correspondent, 'Mr Stonehouse Resigns and Leaves Labour in a Minority of Two', *The Times* (8 April 1976); Donoughue, *Downing Street Diary*, vol. 2, pp. 43–4.

44 George Clark and Michael Hatfield, 'No Need for Early Election, Mr Callaghan Tells Party', *The Times* (6 April 1976).

45 HC Hansard, vol. 909, cols 634–5 (8 April 1976); vol. 910, cols 552–3 (29 April 1976).

46 Our Parliamentary Correspondent, 'Prime Minister Rejects Call by Mrs Thatcher for an Early General Election', *The Times* (7 May 1976).

47 See Chapters 3 and 5.

48 Hazell and Paun (eds), *Making Minority Government Work*, pp. 7, 30–1; Smith, *Election Timing*, pp. 88–90; W. C. Müller and K. Strøm (eds), *Coalition Governments in Western Europe* (Oxford: Oxford University Press, 2000), pp. 258–61.

49 David Wood, Political Editor, '17 Vote Victory for Government in Confidence Challenge', *The Times* (12 March 1976); 'Mr Callaghan Likely Successor after Shock Decision by Mr Wilson', *The Times* (17 March 1976); George Clark, 'New Prime Minister Warns Labour Factions to Get into Line', *The Times* (6 April 1976); George Hutchinson, 'The 90 Days that could Make or Break the Tories', *The Times* (1 May 1976); Ipsos MORI, Voting Intentions in Great Britain 1976–87.

50 See Chapter 7.

51 TNA: PREM 16/1045, PM's Talk with Chancellor Schmidt [extract], 28 April 1976.

52 TNA: CAB 128/59, 1st Meeting, 13 April 1976; 2nd Meeting, 29 April 1976; PREM 16/2214, 'Note of a Meeting Held at […] No. 10 Downing Street', 16 June 1976; 'The Context of the Choice', *The Times* (19 March 1976); 'An Early Election? Probably Not', *The Times* (22 April 1976); Donoughue, *Downing Street Diary*, vol. 2, pp. 13–27.

53 K. H. Cerny, *Germany at the Polls: The Bundestag Elections of the 1980s* (Durham, NC: Duke University Press, 1990), pp. 28–32.

54 HC Hansard, vol. 907, cols 565–75 (10 March 1976); cols 634–758 (11 March 1976); vol. 909, cols 779–81, 798–800 (9 April 1976); Moore, *Margaret Thatcher*, pp. 334–7. See Chapter 4.

55 CPA: LCC 1/3/10, 106th Meeting, 7 April 1976.

56 CPA: CRD/D/7/20, Chris Patten to Angus Maude, 29 October 1976; /21, Charles Bellaire to Chris Patten, 23 July 1976; LCC 1/3/11, 122nd Meeting, 7 July 1976; 1/3/11–12, 123rd

Meeting, 12 July 1976; OG 52: 50th Meeting, 21 March 1974; 51st Meeting, 4 April 1974; OG74/145, 'Preparing for a June Election: Notes towards a New Part I', 19 April 1974; 52nd Meeting, 25 April 1974; MF: Reel 95, 00211–30, Letter from Michael Fraser to Heath, 23 April 1974.

57 CPA LCC 1/3/11, 113th Meeting, 7 June 1976.

58 A. Boulton and J. Jones, *Hung Together: The Cameron–Clegg Coalition* (London: Simon & Schuster, 2012), pp. 168–9, 230–1, 242–3; Andeweg, De Winter and Dumont (eds), *Puzzles of Government Formation*, pp. 131–6, 143–4, 165–6; J. Osmond, *Crossing the Rubicon: Coalition Politics Welsh Style* (Cardiff: Institute of Welsh Affairs, 2007), pp. 27–42; Arter, *Democracy in Scandinavia*, pp. 26–7, 96–7; Searle, *Country before Party*, pp. 242–5; Strøm, *Minority Government and Majority Rule*, p. 91.

59 David Leigh, 'SNP Hopeful of an Early Election', *The Times* (31 May 1976); Torrance, *David Steel*, pp. 77–81, 126–9.

60 CPA: LCC 1/3/10, 7 April 1976; SC 14, 41st Meeting, 29 March 1976; 42nd Meeting, 3 May 1976; Our Parliamentary Correspondent, 'Prime Minister Rejects Call by Mrs Thatcher for an Early General Election', *The Times* (7 May 1976).

61 See Chapter 3: 1974: transitions to minority.

62 CPA: SC 14, 'The Present Crisis: Some Scenarios and Questions': Note by the Research Department, 13 May 1975.

63 CPA: CRD/D/7/16, Letter from Humphrey Atkins to Chris Patten, 13 June 1975; CRD/D/7/20, 'State of Readiness for an Election', 25 April 1975; CRD/D/7/20, Chris Patten to Angus Maude, 26 July 1976; LCC 1/3/15, 199th Meeting, 17 April 1978; SC 14, 35th Meeting, 3 November 1975.

64 CPA: SC 14, 26th Meeting, 12 May 1975; 27th Meeting, 13 May 1975; 28th Meeting, 9 June 1975.

65 CPA: SC 14, 42nd Meeting, 3 May 1976.

66 Hazell and Paun (eds), *Making Minority Government Work*, pp. 13–14. See Chapter 5: Formation of the Pact.

67 TNA: PREM 16/1045, Merlyn Rees to Prime Minister, 26 April 1976.

68 See Chapter 10.

69 TNA: PREM 16/1045, Ken Stowe to Prime Minister, 8 April 1976; Merlyn Rees to Prime Minister, 26 April 1976.

70 LHASC: NEC Minutes, 23 January–6 March 1974, Various Meetings; MS. Wilson, c. 1336, Loose Papers and Articles on the Liberals in 1973–74; Donoughue, *Downing Street Diary*, vol. 1, pp. 22–4, 32, 36–7, 41; Searle, *Country before Party*, pp. 245–6, 251, 259; Morgan, *Harold Wilson*, p. 434.

71 See Chapters 5 and 8.

4

The myth of weakness:
legislative management

[T]he Government had to consider what strategy to adopt while without a parliamentary majority [...] whether to introduce Bills which would be popular with the
Government's own supporters but likely to be defeated in Parliament, or whether
to take special steps to obtain the necessary support for Government legislation.[1]

Callaghan's summary of a Cabinet discussion on 3 March 1977 is representative
of the many deliberations which were engaged in by the 1970s governments, and
some of the radical options which were considered as they sought to find ways in
which to manage their absence of an overall majority in Parliament.

The Wilson and Callaghan Governments have often been characterised as
weak and lacking strategic vision, on account of their suffering a large number
of parliamentary defeats. Although both governments suffered a significantly
greater number of legislative defeats than majority administrations, these have
been magnified in scholarly and popular discourses, and have contributed to a
wider British understanding of minority government as an ineffectual model of
governance. The resulting myth has identified both main parties as being entirely
reactive to legislative defeats and lacking strategy. This dismissal in historical
studies situates the administrations within the pre-1970s orthodox models of
weak minority government. Another interpretation has been to accept these
weaknesses as endemic, but, at the same time, to take a more revisionist view with
regard to the circumstantial or accidental nature of most parliamentary defeats,
which occurred despite divisions within and between opposition parties.[2]

However, this chapter will demonstrate that both Labour and the Conservatives
were far more strategically proactive than has previously been recognised in considering the legislative aspects of minority government and evolving strategies
for passing or opposing bills. Furthermore, while both parties' strategic doctrine
was largely influenced by and framed within the context of previous British
experience, strategies were considered which, however consciously assimilated,
reflected aspects that are features of minority government elsewhere. The focus
here will be on the management of parliamentary defeats by governments and
oppositions, and their use of methods that did not involve direct cooperation

or negotiation with the MPs of other political parties, which is a subject for consideration in Chapters 5–6.

Labour considered and adopted some approaches much deployed by minority governments elsewhere, in terms of accepting certain parliamentary defeats, overturning some and circumventing others. At the same time, some other, more radical tactics were contemplated, including that of actively seeking parliamentary defeats and widespread reform of Parliament. The Opposition and other parties also faced a complex and novel situation of parliamentary management, in which Labour's defeats could raise the possible dangers of appearing obstructionist or even forcing an election on unfavourable terms. Moreover, even the threat of defeat, or else the use of institutional mechanisms to filibuster or delay legislation, had to be selectively applied to achieve greatest impact. Conflicts between the Government and Opposition over traditional institutional arrangements helped to shape, and were shaped by, the strategies and interactions of both main parties.

Daring defeat

One of the simplest ways for a minority government to function is to act as if the situation is no different from that of a majority government, making full use of institutional powers by putting forward controversial legislation without amendment or accommodation of other parties and daring opponents to vote it down. Rather than seeking defeat, the goal is to pass legislation and to continue to survive as a government by calling the bluff of opposition parties. Variations of the approach may incorporate institutional tools discussed in the section 'Avoiding defeat', such as making particular votes matters of confidence in the incumbent government. This approach has historically been widely used by minority governments in other countries, either applied to a particular piece of legislation or as an overall strategy. One less successful example in the 1970s included Canadian Prime Minister Joe Clark's 1979 Minority Government, which operated in a constant state of daring opposition parties to defeat it, and, as a consequence, survived for less than seven months (most of which was a parliamentary recess) before being brought down.[3] The Wilson Minority Government of 1974 was very much inclined towards calling the other parties' bluff, which worked initially because of Conservative fears over appearing unnecessarily obstructionist or of triggering an early election. Later in the year, the Opposition became less reserved about attempting to defeat the Government, but this did not prevent Wilson from being able successfully to gain a majority in the subsequent autumn 1974 election. In the early stages of Callaghan's Government, far-reaching and contentious bills over policies including nationalisation were still brought forward, and an especially heavy programme of legislation tabled, seemingly no different from operations under a majority government. However, Callaghan faced an opposition party which did not have the same reservations about trying to defeat the Government as had been the case for Wilson, a factor that would prove important throughout the life of his administration.[4]

Often the dynamics of how a minority government operates are determined during its formative stages. In Wilson's experience, a successful confrontation with the Opposition over the Queen's Speech in March 1974 set the tone for subsequent interactions. Callaghan, by contrast, faced a confrontation in the early months of his minority government which, although not much discussed by commentators, had a significant impact upon subsequent government and opposition strategy-making.[5]

1974: Confrontation over the Queen's Speech

The first major parliamentary test of Wilson's Minority Government in March 1974 was to pass the Queen's Speech, which set out the Government's legislative programme for the forthcoming session. The typical narrative portrays this contest as a straightforward clash of wills between the two leaders, an example of 'parliamentary brinkmanship', which ultimately ended in the Opposition backing down. The Conservatives followed the normal convention of submitting an amendment and implied that, after the debate, they would vote against the Speech. In response, Wilson publicly threatened an immediate election in the event of the Speech being defeated. Particular praise is given by contemporaries and some commentators to Foot's performance during the debate, suggesting that the force and eloquence of his speech persuaded the Conservatives to withdraw subsequently their amendment. However, the underlying strategic debates that took place in the days prior to the amendment's withdrawal present a far more complex picture.[6]

In spite of assertive public rhetoric suggesting that the Government would retain their legislative programme in its entirety and attempt to call the Opposition's bluff, there is no doubt that privately the absence of a majority had an effect on strategy relating to the Speech. The decision to prepare a Speech with a 'normal' year-length legislative programme was justified internally for tactical reasons, psychologically suggesting an air of 'business as usual' while leaving open the possibility of an early general election. At the same time, however, the government leadership thought that the lack of a secure majority on any committee would probably lead to more bills being debated in the House of Commons as a whole in order to ensure they were enacted, therefore reducing the number which could be passed.[7] Those entrusted with formulating strategy also proposed alternative courses of action as to the timing and tactics to be employed concerning the Queen's Speech. The prospect of a delay was raised, in order to allow for more time to develop sections of the Speech, but ruled out for fear that it would limit already precious parliamentary time for other business and portray Labour as being unable to govern. There were also differences of opinion within the Cabinet over whether it was best to pursue successful passage of the Speech or to try to use it tactically to provoke a defeat and an immediate election, taking advantage of a 'honeymoon period' and a negative public response to Conservative obstruction. The greater weight of opinion, however, was with those who opposed such a move, including Wilson. Their reasoning was that another immediate election would be harmful to Labour: the campaigning resources of the party in terms of activist manpower and money had been significantly drained by the February campaign; the public were likely to respond with hostility or indifference having just endured one election, which would make it difficult to motivate potential supporters to turn out; and it could not be guaranteed that fighting an election on a single issue of government being obstructed in its policies (as Heath had discovered) would produce any decisive outcome.[8]

The resulting government approach was developed to send a clear signal to the Opposition and to allow for various possible outcomes. The officially minuted action appeared reminiscent of Labour's quiet but dignified post-election posture, getting Callaghan to make a speech emphasising 'the need for stable government'. Wilson, however, also sought to buttress this statement with other actions that would give the Government greater room for manoeuvre. His publicly stated threat of dissolving Parliament for a further election represented a clear challenge to the Conservatives, with the credibility of such a threat being enhanced by two senior constitutional lawyers, who were tasked to assure the Conservatives covertly that any such dissolution would be constitutionally viable. Sympathetic Labour and Independent Labour MPs in the debate on the Queen's Speech further reinforced this idea of dissolution following defeat, and of the adverse political consequences which an opposition party would face by bringing about such an event. Any decisions over further substantive action were remitted to a Cabinet that would meet the morning after any vote on the Speech. Wilson's decision to schedule such a meeting in advance was itself a form of contingency planning, providing cover for emergency discussions in the event of a government defeat. Wilson also sought to increase the Government's options in such a situation, not least through his opening remarks in the debate on the Speech. By raising the idea that there were different types of binding and non-binding votes in the Commons, Wilson attempted to allow the Government discretion to interpret a vote against it on a particular issue as a mere tactical move by the Opposition rather than an issue which would compel his resignation. This development would have represented a significant constitutional innovation, and could theoretically have led to the Government continuing in spite of a defeat in a confidence vote. However, the analysis provided by Wilson was less than convincing – efforts from opposition backbenchers to get these remarks clarified two weeks later being summarily rebuffed. Although a defeat became increasingly unlikely, senior Labour figures did consider their response, agreeing that the most likely approach would be for the Government to carry on until it was able to hold a subsequent vote of confidence over an issue, such as the Budget, that could provide greater political ammunition if the Opposition tried to block it.[9]

The Opposition's approach to the Queen's Speech was similarly subject to deliberations and divisions, and was, in fact, much more cautious from the outset than has typically been recognised. Although the Conservatives had tabled an amendment and publicly indicated their intentions, the internal papers suggest that there was little enthusiasm to defeat the Government. The first Shadow Cabinet meeting bemoaned the omission of certain expected Labour policies in the Queen's Speech that had been seen as likely to produce economic uncertainty, but also implied that their removal reduced the political imperative to vote against it. This cautious view was not necessarily shared by all within the party leadership. Maurice Macmillan, son of former Prime Minister Harold Macmillan, and an MP who had himself held a number of offices in Heath's Administration, sent a letter to Heath the day after the meeting. In the letter, Macmillan criticised the planned opposition abstention, stressing the need for the leader to reconsider his position and to seize the opportunity to defeat the Government.[10]

Macmillan's position does not, however, appear to have been given much consideration. Subsequent meetings of the Shadow Cabinet and Steering Committee only served to confirm the usefulness of refraining from confrontation, while examining the possible implications of amendments that it was thought would be proposed by smaller parties. Foot's contribution to the debate did play a role in Conservative deliberations, though one of reassurance rather than intimidation, strategists fixing upon what they perceived as indicators in his speech against any immediate abandonment of counter-inflation policy as a good enough reason to render their proposed amendment no longer necessary, or as a means of justifying their abstention.[11]

In this situation, daring defeat had worked, enabling the Government to pass the Queen's Speech. Although we cannot know the alternative course of action for certain, in some respects, the Conservatives were correct in their decision to back down. If they had defeated the Government, the Opposition would likely have been labelled with the charge of obstructionism, removing a government that had just taken office. The defeat would also have been on the abstract issue of Labour's legislative programme in its entirety, rather than on a distinctive controversial policy, making it less likely for the Conservatives to be successful in any subsequent election campaign. However, while avoiding this outcome, Heath's choice to engage in this battle in the first place turned it into a defeat. By publicly preparing to fight and then backing down, the Opposition had allowed the perspective of their 'losing' this initial confrontation to form. The meetings

conducted had not sufficiently considered how to respond strategically, resulting in the Conservatives being outflanked by Wilson. Heath's reflection on the
entire episode during a subsequent meeting provides perhaps the best recognition that the Conservatives in early March still had to work out how to cope
with opposing a minority government: 'Mr Heath said [...] There were definite
tactical lessons for the Party to learn in the present situation in the House. [...]
[These] would have to be discussed and resolved as they would govern the Party's
pattern of behaviour on Parliamentary business. They were not yet sufficiently
understood.'[12]

Although the Conservatives were later able to inflict defeats on the Government
in June and July, the loss of this first battle established the dynamics which
allowed Wilson to achieve a number of successes in his short-lived administration. The prospect of the same scenario being repeated on other major legislation
had emboldened the Government and increased the cautiousness of opposition
members. Just over two years later, a confrontation occurred in the early days
of the Callaghan Administration which in some ways mirrored Wilson and
Heath's manoeuvres, setting the tone for the rest of the Parliament. However,
this often-forgotten battle in May 1976 was more prolonged and ultimately more
damaging to the Government.

Whipping system: disruption of the 'usual channels'

An essential component of day-to-day legislative management and timetabling of
parliamentary business in Westminster occurs through informal discussion and
contacts between Government and Opposition whips, referred to as the 'usual
channels'. This archaic mechanism enables pairing agreements for parliamentarians to be absent from specific votes, so as to negate the need for a constant
full turnout of MPs from all sides. This is particularly important in that it allows
ministers to be away from Parliament while conducting their official duties.
The institution of pairing helps governments maintain their existing majority
on legislation, or may even, in a state of minority government, help to secure
a day-to-day majority, such as through pairing members not normally voting
because of illness or serving as officers of the House (i.e. Deputy Speaker). Even
contemporary pairing arrangements continue to be a source of both strength
and controversy for minority governments in other countries, one notable
recent example being in Australia between 2010 and 2013.[13] During the Wilson
Government, Labour Party whips also sought to maintain a sufficient number of
MPs within close proximity to the House of Commons in order to counter the
possibility of being caught off guard and defeated in votes called unexpectedly by
opposition MPs. As such, their arrangements had become more rigorous, ending
the previously accepted practice of informal agreements which had been made
between MPs, and creating a rota system to ensure that at least 100 Labour MPs

were in close proximity to Westminster each day during the week.[14] All Labour MPs had been required to attend when it was possible that the Government could be defeated on an important piece of legislation, but the cross-party connections with the Conservatives had nevertheless been maintained, not least the negotiation and agreement between the Government and Opposition on issues such as timing for debates and committee stages for bills.[15]

However, the Callaghan Government's minority status helped provoke an incident during parliamentary votes in May 1976 on the controversial bill to nationalise large parts of the aircraft and shipbuilding industries. On 27 May, the Government won an important parliamentary division on the bill by one vote, on a motion already anticipated as likely to be close. It later transpired that the government victory resulted from the breaking of a pairing arrangement: a Labour MP had voted when it had been previously agreed that both he and his Conservative counterpart would abstain. The Wilson Government had witnessed a comparable incident when Labour MP Harold Lever was counted as being on the premises for voting purposes, when, in fact, he had left the Westminster precincts. In that case, although the Conservatives had cried foul, Heath ultimately backed down, in response to evidence presented by Wilson that had been ignored by the Opposition whips at the time.[16] By contrast, in retaliation to the 1976 infringement, the Conservatives suspended all pairing arrangements. The result of this action was that the Government whips could not be sure of how many opposition MPs would be in attendance at any given vote.[17]

Although arguments have continued in political memoirs, it is difficult to find evidence of either the Government breaking this pairing deliberately or the Opposition's subsequent withdrawal of cooperation as being anything other than reactive and unplanned.[18] Some members of the Opposition did later seek to capitalise on what they considered to be success in delaying government business, raising the matter in strategy meetings. Thatcher was encouraged deliberately to extend the tactic for as long as possible in a way that was manageable for the Opposition, as advocated by Nigel Lawson, then an adviser to the leader, in his letter of 30 May:

> Provided it is accepted that, on all except essential business, our people can – within reason – register as 'absent unpaired', this will inconvenience the Government infinitely more than [...] the Opposition; whereas not to implement the threat would, I suspect, be seen as a sign of weakness.[19]

The success of this opposition tactic is debatable. A vote of censure called by the Conservatives on 9 June 1976 was defeated by a clear majority. Only one government defeat occurred in the House of Commons during the breakdown in cooperation, that of 28 June 1976, when the Government abstained on a motion of adjournment, fearing defeat in any case from a likely rebellion of its own backbenchers. The vote on the controversial Aircraft and Shipbuilding Bill was retaken at the request of the Opposition, along with amendments.[20] There was also a perception expressed in government and opposition strategy meetings that Labour's likely victory in an upcoming by-election would restore a situation in which the Government could effectively operate as if they possessed a majority. The Conservative leadership did not extend the tactic indefinitely, recognising that such a situation was, in the long term, as unsustainable for their MPs as for Labour, and that government attempts to portray them as being unnecessarily obstructionist could cause more damage politically. Withdrawal of cooperation similarly prevented the prospect of traditional opposition influence or input into government legislation through negotiation. The absence of communication with the Government meant the withholding of information normally provided about the schedule for parliamentary business, forcing the Opposition to guess on a daily basis the timetable for upcoming legislation and to manage the attendance of their MPs accordingly.

Although the threat of cooperation being withdrawn remained an option and continued to be discussed at various points by the leadership through the autumn of 1976, it was not acted on during the remainder of the Parliament. There were occasional selective refusals to provide pairs for particularly important votes, but this was very much in line with existing procedures. When it appeared not long after the resumption of cooperation that the Government was seeking to extend the length of time the House of Commons would sit, in order to give more opportunity to pass legislation, the Shadow Cabinet decided that any attempt to prolong the session, or to force through controversial legislation using allocation of time (guillotine) motions to curtail debates, would be met by a fresh withdrawal of all cooperation. However, in spite of the session extending into August and the Government using guillotines to pass certain bills, it does not appear that further withdrawal of cooperation was either implemented by the Opposition or, if implemented, had significant impact. The Government was able to pass their guillotines successfully, and, of the six divisions that occurred in the first week of August, only one, on an opposition motion, had an almost full turnout of MPs, being comfortably won by the Government.[21]

The closest to a further breakdown was the Opposition's cancelling of the pairing of ill members in a series of important votes on the shipbuilding industry on 29 July 1976, leading to the bringing in of a number of seriously ill government MPs for the purposes of ensuring passage of these votes. The particular approach on this occasion backfired somewhat for the Opposition, the presence of the ill members enabling the Government to win the vote and be able to characterise their opponents as disruptive. There is no record of this tactic being discussed in the Shadow Cabinet meetings. In part, the failure of this move may account for hesitation over pressing the Government further in the August sitting.[22]

However, the withdrawal of cooperation also had more of a detrimental impact on the Government than might otherwise have been expected. While such a breakdown in relations could have caused significant difficulties either for majority or minority governments, the absence of a majority made it particularly damaging for Callaghan. Although the number of defeats was small, the ever-present possibility of defeat meant that a sizeable number of Labour MPs had to be permanently in attendance at Parliament, increasing their workload and making it more difficult to undertake either constituency or government-related business away from Westminster. The Government, as had been the case during the 1974 Minority Administration, did adopt a rota for its MPs, to keep the requisite numbers in attendance. Nevertheless, there were other factors which compounded the long-term impact of the opposition approach. Government concern at not being able to reliably get business passed served to delay important legislation, making it more difficult to enact bills in what was already a crowded legislative schedule. The record summer heatwave and drought of 1976, combined with the requisite late-night sittings in Parliament, served to wear out government members. One indication of the physical toll exacted during this period, which included Cabinet ministers struggling to stay awake in meetings as a result of the late-night sittings, is recorded in Donoughue's diary.[23]

The withdrawal of cooperation showed the Government how far the Opposition were willing to go in order to challenge perceived changes or alterations to existing practices. Although the Government was able to pass some guillotine motions and to extend the session, the conflict had set the tone for subsequent parliamentary relations. Difficulties over pairing, and the Government's failure to learn lessons of minority governance at this early stage, made it more problematic for them to carry major legislation in subsequent parliamentary sessions.

While a quasi-majoritarian and directly confrontational approach was adopted in the early and lattermost stages of the Callaghan Administration, the limitation of the administration's success was not dissimilar to that of a number of other minority governments globally. The breakdown of the usual channels in 1976 had caused significant disruption of government business, leading some within the Government to re-evaluate their approach thereafter. For the most part, the Callaghan Government sought henceforth other methods to handle both the serious prospect and the reality of parliamentary defeats.

Avoiding defeat

There are three principal ways, beyond interparty cooperation or daring defeat, in which a minority government can seek to manage legislative defeats. The first, and arguably the most appealing, is that of avoiding defeat – either by not putting forward or withdrawing legislation considered unlikely to succeed, or using institutional mechanisms of control to enable the passage of legislation that would otherwise fail. The second, accepting defeat, involves reacting to legislative losses or opposition amendments by endeavouring to accommodate the changes in policy, and possibly planning or publicly indicating that these would be reversed by the Government if it won a majority at a subsequent general election. The third, as contemplated by the Wilson Administration during the confrontation over the Queen's Speech, is that of a government actively seeking its own defeat, putting forward legislation known to have no chance of success and maybe even deliberately encouraging the Opposition to block it as part of a broader political strategy.

Avoiding/preventing defeat

Many minority and majority governments around the world, including those in Britain, have not submitted or else have withdrawn prospective legislation which is known to be particularly contentious, or unable to command a majority.[24]

Both the Wilson and Callaghan Governments showed private recognition from the outset that the passage of some bills could not be assured, and contemplated adapting their programme accordingly. Some of Labour's more controversial and significant proposals in 1974 were not put forward, including a prospective referendum on membership of the EEC. However, these omissions were also conditioned by the brevity of the 1974 Government's parliamentary session before a likely autumn election. As such, not all proposed legislative commitments could have been accomplished in the time available.

The Callaghan Administration, by contrast, already more than eighteen months into a new Parliament, largely continued to press ahead with some controversial legislation in its early stages. In spite of Foot's Cabinet report in May 1976 prioritising some bills and indicating possible compromises, it was only later on in the Parliament that the Government began seriously to scale back its legislative programme. The abandoning of prospective legislation caused significant internal strategic debates within the Government. One of the greatest fears expressed was that the absence of politically important legislation would depress Labour supporters and undermine subsequent electoral campaigns. The absence of controversial legislation was, paradoxically, not merely a hindrance to the Government, but also to the Opposition. In a notable Shadow Cabinet discussion, concern was expressed that the legislation being put through Parliament did not allow for major points of disagreement between the two main parties, thereby depriving the Opposition of 'ammunition' for subsequent political campaigns.[25]

Where the decision was made to pursue legislation which could prove to be controversial, the Government relied in the first instance on its considerable institutional powers in order to attempt to get bills through Parliament. The UK government leadership has historically enjoyed very substantial control over setting the agenda for parliamentary business. It has been argued by Tsebelis that minority governments generally seek to make greater use of the institutional mechanisms available to control the agenda and force Parliament to comply with their will.[26] Such experiences are consistent with minority governments internationally, notably in Canada. The UK Government of the period, perhaps even more so in the early twenty-first century, possessed considerable institutional control over Parliament when compared to both European and American counterparts. Governments over the last few decades, whether in a majority or minority, have increasingly resorted to more frequent use of institutional devices to strengthen their control over Parliament. However, the Callaghan Government's use of powers over Parliament to manage the legislative process was significantly affected in unique ways by the minority government situation.

Some of these institutions affected included the composition of parliamentary committees that considered and amended legislation, and devices affecting the timing and amount of legislation that could be passed, including guillotine votes or timetable motions, as well as the length of parliamentary recesses. The state of minority government also presented the Callaghan Administration with additional challenges, and indeed opportunities, through the device of confidence votes. Opposition from the House of Lords also raised the prospect of the Parliament Act being used.

Voting arrangements

The institution of a strong party Whip system to manage MPs served as the Callaghan Government's first main method of controlling Parliament. Changes to established voting arrangements for MPs were considered by the Government as one means of securing their majority. One change considered in the light of confrontations with the Opposition was that of altering pairing agreements. In September 1976, the Government Chief Whip, Michael Cocks, raised the possibility with his counterpart of pairing ill members of Parliament who were unable to attend, of which Labour had at that time a greater number, with opposition members even if they were in good health. Such a procedure would have changed the existing practice of only pairing ill MPs with others who were ill. Opposition Chief Whip Humphrey Atkins' preliminary memorandum was very much against this suggestion, arguing that it was unreasonable for an MP in good health to have to 'justify [their] actions to [their] constituents' for choosing not to vote on an important issue when their counterpart's health restricted them from voting, and that it would be difficult for a party leader 'to enforce it'. Consequently, this potential alteration was not pursued further. The question of proxy voting also arose, specifically that of allowing either ill members or ministers who were absent on government business to cast a vote. This would have marked a significant departure from established practice, and was likewise rejected.[27] The only form of proxy already allowed at the time was the 'nodding through' of ill members who were within the Palace of Westminster but physically unable to walk through the division lobby. This concession led to the infamous scenes of several ambulances being parked outside Parliament, so that the MPs within them could have their votes counted. The Government's continued reliance on the votes of these members, even in its latter stages after the end of the Lib–Lab Pact, shows something of a continued majoritarian mindset and desire to avoid interparty cooperation where possible.[28]

Committee composition

Some parliamentary systems afford greater influence to opposition parties through the composition and powers of parliamentary committees. These committees' roles can include the oversight of government departments, approval of appointments and, particularly, the examining, amending and even delaying of legislation. Their composition is, in many cases, determined by party strength in a Parliament, and thereby they may come to play an increasingly important role during periods when a government is in the minority.[29]

Legislative committee composition was one of the first issues confronting Callaghan following Stonehouse's defection on 7 April 1976. The system of parliamentary committees served as an integral part of the legislative process, all bills having to pass through individual standing committees of MPs, assembled on an ad hoc basis, which examined legislation and could amend it.[30] Since committee composition normally reflected the political strength of parties in the House of Commons, names being supplied by the whips, the absence of a government majority led to calls by both Conservative and Liberal Press releases for committees, then dominated by Labour, to have additional members assigned to reflect the new 'majority' of opposition MPs.[31]

The Government's first instincts were to resist any changes to committee composition, in the knowledge that it would make it more difficult in the future to avoid amendments or delays to legislation at the committee stage, which could prevent the passage of important bills. In the Cabinet meeting of 29 April, there was even the suggestion by Foot that the Government was not, in fact, in a minority, attempting to count 'Mr Robertson and Mr Sillars' (who had defected from Labour to form a separate party) and 'the two Northern Ireland members who regularly voted with the Government' as not part of the Opposition, and even perhaps constituting part of the Government's own total.[32] This seeming unwillingness to acknowledge minority status is a further reflection of the continued majoritarian mindset of members of the Callaghan Cabinet in its early stages. The Committee of Selection, a body of MPs whose role it was formally to put forward any appointments to committees, and itself with a Labour majority of five members to four, initially ruled that there should be no changes to new standing committees. Nevertheless, the Government, recognising the constraints of not having a majority and seeking to avoid providing political ammunition to their opponents, subsequently recognised opposition demands by conceding that the composition of any newly formed standing committees for future legislation would reflect the change. This approach was in line with that of Wilson's Minority Government of 1974, which had similarly conceded the question of standing committee composition. It was suggested that the addition of extra committee members from among the smaller parties might be strategically used by the Government whips, presumably through allocating members more likely to be sympathetic to Labour to committees regarded as particularly important. Maintaining the status quo on existing committees was also thought likely to help limit the number of adverse effects on government policy. The Cabinet considered possible alternative ways to circumvent the changes, such as through the suggestion, first raised on 29 April and discussed at greater length on 6 May, that the composition of standing committees 'reflect the majority for that Bill on Second Reading, rather than the composition of the House'. This method was rejected, however, in terms of strategy: it was feared that opposition MPs would be encouraged either into more vigorous resistance and 'to vote against the Second Readings of Bills', or even to vote for a bill and then claim extra places on a committee, representing themselves as constituting part of the bill's majority, but then 'not necessarily support the Government when voting on amendments' in the committee. Cabinet discussions concluded that, in the light of the 'present parliamentary circumstances', it would not be practical to implement any change and that such a measure would be fiercely resisted by all opposition parties.[33]

As with the withdrawal of pairing arrangements, the Opposition's first approach to demanding the change in committee appointments was purely reactive. However, although less high profile, there were some instances in which the Opposition consciously judged that it would be better to allow bills to proceed rather than oppose them in the Commons, but then possibly to attempt to amend the legislation at the committee stage. Although defeats for the Government at the committee stage were not given the same high profile as parliamentary losses, and, in some ways, the Opposition were merely following established practices, the lack of a Commons majority prevented the usual response of a government overturning some of the more damaging amendments in a meeting of the full House of Commons.[34] Often the Government expressed fears that while legislation was expected to pass through Parliament, it could suffer significant amendment at the committee stage. A possible means of countering this threat was putting legislation to a committee of the entire House (a standard practice on constitutional legislation), where it was potentially easier for the Government to achieve majorities through such tactics as dividing the larger numbers of opposing MPs. Time pressures and the dangers of further delays or more damaging backbench amendments being brought forward limited the extent to which such an approach could be implemented successfully.[35]

Timing

The process of getting a bill through Parliament typically occupies a significant amount of time, going through three readings and a committee stage in both Houses. Technically, the Government controls the timetabling of the House of Commons, and does not, as of September 2017, have to answer to any all-party committee, as is the case with many of their European counterparts. In spite of this, in practice, the institutional set-up of Parliament provides some accommodation to opposition parties in terms of time for debates. Both majority and minority governments have had to face time constraints when introducing legislation, significant proportions of parliamentary time already being allocated for various essential items including the annual Budget and Queen's Speech, Prime Minister's Questions, general debates, and days given to opposition parties and individual MPs. In other countries, minority governments are able to have a significant influence on legislative timing, compelling longer periods for the consideration of bills, reducing the amount of legislation put forward by a government or even changing the allocation of parliamentary time further to accommodate opposition parties.[36]

During the Callaghan Government, neither side considered pushing for a fundamental alteration of existing arrangements regarding government control over legislative timetabling. Any question of removing parliamentary time allocated to opposition parties and individual MPs was similarly not entertained as a viable option, the Government fearing that the Opposition would break off all cooperation and voters would see the move as being inherently unfair. As in the case of whipping arrangements, government attempts to use institutional mechanisms to overcome timing problems were very much shaped by the minority government situation.

One method which had already been in place during periods of majority government was that of combining pieces of legislation that would otherwise have been considered as separate bills. Although bills were also combined for administrative or legislative clarity, strategic reasons did play an important part in discussions within the Callaghan Government, particularly on politically sensitive measures. There were, of course, limits as to how far such a tactic could be employed. The approach could make it more difficult to ensure passage of the legislation, whether through uniting opposition parties and government rebels who objected to different parts of the bill, as in the case of the Scotland and Wales Bill in 1976–77, or legislation being more susceptible to failing because of a technicality, as in the Aircraft and Shipbuilding Bill. The prospect of further combining of bills to save time was considered by the Government occasionally, particularly in late 1976, such as in the case of those concerning conspiracy and criminal justice (which were combined), or two Post Office Bills on industrial democracy and borrowing powers (which were not). The practice does not, however, appear to have been widely used.[37]

Another institutional device increasingly used by postwar governments to pack more legislation into a crowded schedule has been that of votes designed to shorten the amount of time spent debating legislation, establishing a timetable, or guillotine votes, to set limits on the amount of parliamentary time to be allocated to a debate or piece of legislation, or to end an ongoing debate on a particular issue and compel a vote. The Callaghan Government had sought to use these devices in order to continue with a heavy legislative programme through late 1976 and into 1977 (in part making up for delays during the breakdown in cooperation with the Opposition). However, the exigencies of minority government restricted the occasions on which such votes could be successfully employed, their use often being fiercely resisted not only by opposition parties, but also by some backbench government MPs who resented the practice. While the Scotland and Wales Bill of 1976–77 was never defeated in the Commons, the loss of a timetable motion setting out the limits for debate was effectively regarded as having prevented its passage. Although the Government could have allocated more time to what was essentially an important piece of constitutional legislation, this would have required the dropping of other legislation regarded as politically important. The principal aim of this devolution legislation was to address increased support for the nationalist parties in both Scotland and Wales, which posed a threat to Labour at a subsequent general election. Labour MPs were bitterly divided over the issue, some of those from Scotland and Wales being particularly vociferous opponents of the legislation. Whereas there had initially been reluctance by the Government to drop legislation in order to find the necessary time to complete passage of the rest of the legislative programme, some prospective bills were dropped from 1977–78 onwards.[38] This change reflected, in part, the increased difficulty of ensuring the passing of guillotines or timetable motions after the failure of the Scotland and Wales Bill. In spite of this setback, the Government still, paradoxically, made use of some timetable motions and guillotines in order to curtail debate and enact parts of the legislative programme – although their use remained controversial – primarily on matters where the major parties suffered internal divisions, such as over the European Elections Bill in early 1978. Alternatively, guillotines were used after negotiation, with the backing of the Opposition. Guillotines also continued to be used on major legislation such as devolution, helping contribute to legislative defeats through increasing the intransigent resistance of opposing MPs both within and outside the Government.[39]

Recesses

The question of minority government dictated the Callaghan Administration's approach to their control of the length of parliamentary recesses, raising significant questions and prompting internal disagreements. An important difference of opinion was over the issue of whether to shorten recesses and thereby provide more time for Parliament to pass legislation, or to increase the number of days and thereby reduce the time available to deal with prospective parliamentary defeats. Other concerns raised regarding shorter recesses included the greater physical pressure on Labour MPs, and that the parliamentary party had been under a particular strain over the previous three years in government. An alternative suggestion of holding more late-night sessions, requiring that over 100 Labour MPs be kept at Westminster to ensure a sufficient majority for closure motions, was met with similar disquiet. These debates built on the experience of the Wilson Minority Government in 1974, where a long summer recess had served as relief from parliamentary defeats in June, and had provided a successful launch platform for the Government's October election campaign without having to recall Parliament. Discussions both in Callaghan's Cabinet, and in the Cabinet Future Legislation Committee, particularly on 10 March 1977, highlight the Government's changing approach over time. Initially, the preference in 1976 until early 1977 was to reduce the length of recesses in order to accommodate more bills. By March 1977, however, the Government was clearly moving in favour of maintaining and even lengthening the amount of time when Parliament was not in session, partly as a response to the increasing instances of legislative defeats.[40]

Referenda

In some parliamentary systems, constitutional arrangements provide for the possibility of appealing directly to the population to settle a particularly contentious political issue or seek support for a major policy through a referendum. This mechanism has not historically been much used in Britain. However, majority and coalition governments within the UK since 1998 have held referenda on a number of significant issues, including devolution, reform of the voting system, Scottish independence and the exiting of the European Union (EU). A referendum can also potentially be used by a minority government that desires to get an important policy through a deadlocked legislature but is unwilling to call an election, as was the case with the successful Danish referendum in 1986 over ratification of the Single European Act. This prospective use of referenda is, of course, conditioned by particular institutional and political constraints, such as where there is a requirement for a referendum proposal to be approved by a parliamentary majority.[41]

The need for parliamentary approval would appear to make such a device inappropriate for British minority governments, although there are situations in which opposition parties may sometimes be less inclined to oppose referenda for fear of the adverse political consequences of denying the population a vote on a particular issue. Britain had also had recent experience of a nationwide referendum through the EEC vote in 1975. After parliamentary defeats on the devolution timetable motion in early 1977, Callaghan's Government briefly considered holding pre-legislative national referenda, in order to secure an additional mandate and pressure MPs not to block devolution legislation. In not pursuing this approach, a number of justifications were brought forward in Cabinet which reflected strategic assessments that continued to be weighed against established majoritarian principles. One concern was that the legislation for any such move would be unlikely to pass without a secure government majority. Even if referenda legislation were passed, it was further argued that there was no guarantee of a positive referendum result when voters did not know what a finalised bill would contain. Furthermore, it was concluded that even a positive result could not guarantee majority support in Parliament for government devolution proposals. Labour's concession of referenda over devolution in Scotland and Wales, held in 1979, rather than being pre-legislative, were principally seen as a means of defusing opposition to the legislation in Parliament.[42]

The thought of using referenda to reinforce particular policies was not restricted to the Government. During the early stages of the Parliament, and even latterly, the Conservative leadership contemplated the acceptance of referenda proposed by others, albeit reluctantly, or even the initiation of referenda themselves, both in terms of devolution and in order to buttress support for the passage of potentially controversial legislation concerning the restriction of trade union power. Although this device was ultimately unused, discussion surrounding it illustrates something of the opposition mindset. Some concerns were raised when an opposition committee was formed to consider the matter. Shadow Cabinet discussions in relation to a prospective referendum manifesto pledge prompted a number of objections, including the danger of creating a 'two-tier' system of legislation, where laws backed by referenda could acquire greater legitimacy than those that had only been passed by Parliament, and that the use of referenda to entrench legislation could challenge the established notion of one British Parliament not binding its successor. It would appear that the Shadow Cabinet feared that their acceptance of referenda would also enable Labour Governments 'to secure popular endorsement for certain superficially appealing socialist measures'. It was agreed at this stage to include a passage on the usefulness of referenda in the manifesto, and there were further references made by the Opposition to the prospect of referenda being used in order to pass popular legislation 'resisted by a minority', although this was conceived of more as a response to widespread industrial action, rather than as a remedy to a minority government situation.[43]

House of Lords

Another institutional challenge which both the Wilson and Callaghan Governments faced was that of the legislative defeats inflicted by the House of Lords, which were more numerous during this period than those in the House of Commons. This trend has continued in the twenty-first century, the House of Lords inflicting a number of significant defeats on both Labour and Conservative Governments with majorities in the Commons. In part, the Callaghan Government's situation was also exacerbated by the practical difficulties imposed by the heavy legislative timetable and associated pressure to get bills passed, which led to late nights and increased opposition from the Lords.[44] While the Lords had previously been more inclined to vote against certain measures, and Labour Governments permanently lacked any majority in the Upper House, traditionally the second chamber had accepted the will of the incumbent government in the Commons, especially over manifesto commitments. However, the absence of a Commons majority made it much more difficult to overturn reasoned amendments made by the Lords as would normally have been the case. Theoretically, there were several institutional approaches which might have helped the 1970s governments to overcome their difficulties with the second chamber, including some particularly radical options. One such sanction was the creation or threatened creation of enough new peers to achieve a government majority or reform of the second chamber to reduce its powers. The former threat had been used historically to enable the passage of the first Parliament Act in 1911 that limited the power of the Lords, and reform had been seriously considered by governments into the 1960s and 1970s.[45] While reform proposals were being worked on by Labour during this period, implementation of such policies as arbitrary creation of new peers or rapid changes to established procedures were not pursued as solutions to the immediate day-to-day problems of parliamentary majorities. It was recognised by both governments that any such approach would appear unconstitutional, would likely lead to intransigent opposition in Parliament and would not solve the lack of a Commons majority. Abolition of the second chamber was supported by the wider Labour Party, but not given any significant consideration by either government, knowing that it would be impossible without an electoral mandate and Commons majority. Although abolition of the Lords was put forward by the NEC, and years later was adopted as a Labour manifesto commitment, this proposal arose more from an adherence to socialist philosophy, rather than specifically as a response to minority government.[46]

The only institutional option seriously countenanced by the Callaghan Government was that of using the Parliament Act, which would allow a

Commons vote to override the House of Lords' opposition to legislation. The prospect of its use was raised selectively in Cabinet, particularly in the case of the Health Services Bill in late July 1976, and the Aircraft and Shipbuilding Bill in November 1976 and February 1977. Consideration of whether or not to try to override the Lords' veto on this latter bill produced debates in Cabinet, and a difference of opinion between the principal government strategy-makers.

In the November 1976 Cabinet, the Government was more inclined towards the approach of daring defeat. Foot advocated the use of the Parliament Act to compel passage of the Aircraft and Shipbuilding Bill, potentially leading to the loss of one or more other pieces of less important prospective legislation from the timetable. In discussion, concerns were raised about losing the Aircraft and Shipbuilding Bill completely, although there would also appear to have been considerable frustration with the Lords' actions on rejecting a major government policy as being 'intolerable and unconstitutional'. Callaghan, in summarising the debate, recognised the need for further consideration of options, but emphasised the continued pursuit of the legislation, and stated that the fault of losing any bills would rest with the Lords:

> The Government could not allow their programme for next Session to be affected by the behaviour of the Lords, and the legislative proposals in The Queen's Speech should all be maintained. If, because of the need to invoke the Parliament Act next Session, it was not possible to complete some other measures it would be clear where the blame lay.[47]

A shorter discussion of an Education Bill was also couched in terms of compelling passage through the Parliament Act in the event of Lords' opposition.

By contrast, the Cabinet meeting of 24 February 1977 shows something of a different approach. The Government once again considered invoking the Parliament Act to ensure passage of the Aircraft and Shipbuilding Bill. However, rather than losing the legislation, the alternative proposed was seeking a deal with the Opposition. Foot's personal preference once again was to use the Parliament Act, citing some of the political dangers involved in any deal:

> The reaction of Government supporters would be hostile, and they were likely to vote against these amendments while Ministers had to vote in the same lobby as the Conservatives [...] parliamentary difficulties of a deal with the Opposition would also be very great, and the Cabinet should consider very carefully before deciding to seek such a deal.[48]

Various points were raised in the subsequent discussion, including the possibility that it was better as a minority government to fight and lose. However, it was emphasised that there was not much time for the Government to make a decision to challenge the Lords, and the argument was ultimately settled by Callaghan, coming down against the use of the Parliament Act: 'THE PRIME MINISTER, summing up the discussion, said that the majority of the Cabinet took the view that the better course was to decide now to seek a deal with the Opposition.' Foot had also earlier acknowledged that his was a minority opinion, and that a majority of the group which had been tasked to consider the options for the bill: 'had reluctantly reached the conclusion that the industrial consequences of delay and the political risks of proceeding under the Parliament Acts made it necessary to adopt the second option'.[49]

Once again, the minority government situation proved a crucial determining factor, discussions being set in the context of the Government having recently lost two Commons votes attempting to overturn Lords' amendments. The Government's fear was that any Parliament Act vote would be perceived by the smaller parties as an attempt to force through controversial legislation without due consideration, and would almost certainly be blocked, damaging the prospects for future legislation. The Parliament Act was not invoked by the Callaghan Government during its time in office, and not even raised as a serious option in Cabinet after February 1977. As discussed later in this chapter, the blaming of the Lords on wholesale obstruction of bills was also not carried through, Cabinet preferring the quiet withdrawal of legislation rather than its defeat. In the case of the Aircraft and Shipbuilding Bill, the Government went for cooperation with the Opposition, excluding the ship-repairing industry in return for passing the bill in early 1977.[50]

The Conservatives recognised the advantages of the Lords as a block on legislation, and sometimes chose to allow government bills to pass in the Commons, planning stronger resistance to them in the Lords, where there was less danger of the Opposition being characterised as obstructionist. In Shadow Cabinet meetings, the preservation of Lords' amendments to legislation was given high priority on several occasions when deciding where Conservative MPs should try to achieve a maximum turnout in their numbers.[51]

Confidence motions

Votes of confidence or of no confidence, the Queen's Speech and the Budget are crucial tests for a UK government's survival. The loss of any such vote would normally lead to the Prime Minister's resignation, and, probably, a general election or change of party in government. This practice has largely been upheld since the first precedent for resigning on a confidence vote, often cited as Lord North's Government leaving office in 1782, although the precise origins of the convention have divided scholars. Past British administrations, whether in a minority or majority in Parliament, have used the confidence motion as a tool to bolster political support, normally after the defeat of a major piece of legislation or perceived failure of a particular policy.[52]

As of September 2017, the Callaghan Government is the only British administration in over ninety years to have been brought down in a motion of no confidence. This no confidence defeat will be considered at greater length in Chapter 9 since it marks the end point of the 1970s minority governments. The vote in March 1979 has already received some attention from scholars. However, the previous confidence votes won by Callaghan's Administration have, surprisingly, been comparatively neglected. These include five confidence votes called by the Government, several no confidence votes called by opposition parties, three Queen's Speeches and three Budgets.[53]

Theoretical perspectives on minority governments have mainly concentrated on confidence votes at the time of investiture, as an obstacle to the initial formation of a minority government. In some countries, governments have to win a vote in the legislature when taking up office, as, for example, in Scotland and Wales, where one of the first orders of business is to appoint a First Minister. Countries where this rule does not apply, as is the case in England, have been perceived as more likely to form minority governments rather than coalitions. There is also a general acceptance in the literature that minority governments are more susceptible to being defeated on confidence motions, a trend borne out in twentieth-century British history, where the administrations that have fallen as a result of no confidence votes have all been minority governments (twice in 1924 and once in 1979). In some countries, such as Canada, the confidence motion has been used by minority governments either to compel opposition compliance with particularly controversial legislation for fear of otherwise leading to an election, or designed to enable the Government's own defeat and to trigger a general election which can then be fought on the grounds of opposition obstructionism.[54]

Although in a minority, the Callaghan Government's use of confidence motions was very much in line with the traditional British conception of strengthening a government, rather than some of the potential uses of reversing legislative defeats or holding charges of obstructionism against opposition parties. While the Government did suffer from increased backbench rebellions, Labour MPs were, in fact, far more disciplined when it came to explicit confidence votes. The success of those confidence motions put down by the Government partly relied on circumstances but also upon careful selection and strategic calculations. Callaghan and the Labour whips recognised that, on certain divisive issues, even the strictures of a confidence motion could not be guaranteed to gain the support of all government MPs, or that making something an issue of confidence would unite the other parties in voting against the Government.

Several backbench amendments to Scottish devolution legislation in early 1978, as a result of government defeats in the Commons, created significant political difficulties. One of the most difficult problems was the imposed requirement of a 40 per cent minimum turnout threshold voting in favour of devolution to carry the proposal. Even the prospect of finally passing both bills into law was considered to be in serious doubt. The Government considered whether votes to overturn these amendments, or, indeed, the passage of the entire bills, should be made matters of confidence. Nevertheless, it was concluded that invoking a confidence vote would actually lessen the chances of success, shifting the emphasis from the particular issue, which was, at this stage, supported by the crucial votes of some pro-devolution Conservatives and SNP/Plaid Cymru MPs, to that of a more general endorsement of confidence in the Government, more likely sharply to divide MPs along party lines and push opposition parties into uniting against Labour. While the bills were successfully passed and the Scottish referendum campaign in 1979 delivered a Yes vote, the failure to overturn the amendments prevented the implementation of devolution.[55]

Conversely, the Government chose to make other less-well-publicised issues into confidence motions. The attempted opposition vote to reduce the salary of the Chancellor of the Exchequer in June 1978 was taken to represent a direct challenge to the Government's economic policy, which, after careful deliberation, made the issue into a confidence vote which Labour won. While there was an increase in actual and threatened rebellions by government MPs during this period, Labour remained remarkably disciplined on motions of confidence, reflecting the Government's strategic judgement and judicious selection.[56]

Wilson's Minority Government of 1974 had attempted to set precedents with regard to confidence votes, such as creating different categories of confidence vote, to build in some flexibility as to a government's response. The apparent aim was to allow the opportunity to call another formally titled confidence vote even if defeated on the Queen's Speech or Budget, which would previously have been regarded as necessitating the resignation of the Government. While this attempted reconceptualisation of confidence motions does not appear to have gained wider acceptance among MPs or been subsequently taken up by the Callaghan Government, the latter administration did face internal debates over whether some major pieces of legislation should really be regarded in their traditional role as being implicit 'confidence' issues. When there was concern about losing the Devolution Bills in February 1978, some in the Cabinet regarded these pieces of legislation as implicit 'confidence' issues, and that the loss of such major items in the Government's legislative programme would necessitate resignation. Others in the Cabinet suggested that this was not necessarily the case unless the bills were made explicit confidence votes.[57] There have been instances in other countries of minority governments seeking to reconceptualise the notion of confidence votes, not least, for example, that of the Canadian Liberal Minority Government in May 2005, which dismissed a defeat over a committee report as not being a confidence vote, and subsequently put forward and won a Budget Bill.[58]

While the prospect of confidence votes created problems for the Government, the Opposition could also suffer political damage when they decided to hold no confidence votes and were then unsuccessful in winning them. Indeed, it led to questions being asked about the judgement of the opposition leadership on more than one occasion. Conservative preparations for such votes may be regarded in part as reflecting normal debate preparation, but also considered other factors. Increasingly, these preparations included greater discussion on framing confidence motions in a way that would appeal to the smaller parties. There were also debates over timing, with the tendency being to avoid confidence votes unless there was a relative assurance that other parties would support them.[59]

One of the most informative cases during the Callaghan Government is that of the defeat in the vote on sanctions in December 1978. The vote, on an opposition motion criticising the Government's use of sanctions on companies awarding workers a higher pay rises than the 5 per cent target limit, helped to open the floodgates to a subsequent wave of strikes.[60] Even if such sanctions would have been ineffective in the case of Ford, the contemporary view of the Cabinet was very much that the threat of sanctions in other cases had proved to have a significant impact, and that the parliamentary difficulties 'stemmed from the absence of a Government majority'.[61] This vote also remains particularly instructive in terms of how Labour and the Conservatives handled minority government in Parliament; from the government perspective, the decision not to make implementation of the sanctions a confidence vote, and, from the opposition perspective, the ability to vote against sanctions but avoid being blamed for the subsequent industrial turmoil. It may appear strange that the Government lost the vote on sanctions but then called and won a general vote of confidence the next day, without attempting to overturn the earlier decision. Why did they not make the sanctions issue itself a confidence motion, given the perceived importance of the 5 per cent figure? In an indication of the seriousness of the issue, Callaghan himself, along with Foot, met with members of the Tribune Group who had threatened to vote against the sanctions. A minute of their conversation suggests that even the threat of a confidence motion would not necessarily have prevented defections. As had been the case with devolution legislation, it would appear that the Government believed their initiation of a confidence motion would compel all opposition parties into voting against. Such a prospective defeat, leading to a January 1979 election in bad weather and against the background of striking trade unions, conjured images of the Conservatives' defeat in February 1974, counselling the Labour leadership against linking the two issues. This vote also represents something of a paradox in terms of the Opposition's approach. In part, their victory resulted from their downplaying the vote as not being a major confrontation between the Government and Opposition. The use of a technical motion, rather than an explicit confidence vote, enabled some Labour backbenchers who disagreed with the Government's policy on pay sanctions to feel that they could vote with opposition parties without endangering the existence of the Government. The Conservatives were able subsequently to criticise the

Government's lack of effective action concerning the industrial disputes, while having simultaneously disempowered ministers by voting down sanctions. The Opposition's approach relied on an emphasis that the Government's policy had been flawed, the Conservative shift to a tougher stance regarding the regulation of trade unions and on the subsequent offer made by Thatcher during January 1979 to cooperate with the Government over passing measures to mitigate strike action.[62] The defeat over sanctions also continued to limit the Government's legislative response to the industrial situation in the early months of 1979, not least, for example, when attempting to pass an order limiting the prices charged by the road haulage industry. Callaghan expressed his fears to Cabinet, suggesting that: 'The Government might well be defeated by a combination of its own backbenchers with the Opposition.'[63]

Accepting defeat

An alternative to minority governments avoiding parliamentary defeat, either through use of institutional resources or not putting contentious legislation forward, is to accept defeat as a consequence of not having a majority. A government may either publicly accept this, or publicly reject defeat but tacitly accept it by not seeking to overturn a decision. Minority (and indeed majority) governments around the world have often accepted losing votes on certain pieces of legislation, without the need for a change of government or an election. The 1974 Wilson Minority Government tacitly accepted certain defeats, such as over six-monthly pension upratings, while maintaining a robust public rhetoric, in anticipation that these measures could be reintroduced if Labour gained a majority at a subsequent general election.[64]

The Callaghan Government similarly maintained a defiant public stance, retaining very much a majoritarian mindset and stressing in strategy meetings that the Government could not formally and publicly 'accept' defeats over its major policies. Nevertheless, it is clear that, on some issues at least, the leadership accepted legislative defeats, prioritising their efforts in terms of only trying to reverse particular decisions by Parliament.

Scholars have often emphasised the large number of defeats suffered by the Wilson and Callaghan Minority Governments, eighteen and thirty-four respectively. However, although much greater than those of majority governments before and after these administrations, not all the defeats were of equal importance. Contemporary political actors recognised that there was a hierarchy of parliamentary defeats. Some losses of parliamentary votes barely feature in official records of Cabinet discussions, meetings of strategy-makers or political memoirs, such as that over an adjournment motion on teacher training colleges in Scotland in April 1977 or the Firearms (Variation of Fees) Order in March 1979.[65] By contrast, other defeats, including over devolution, income tax reductions and, of course, the defeat over a vote of no confidence in 1979, were of much greater importance, and had significant space dedicated to discussions concerning the response to them.[66]

One government tactic, used in the early stages of the Callaghan Administration, was to accept defeat by abstaining on a vote which they knew could not be won because of rebellion among their own MPs and/or unity of opposition parties. The aim of this approach, when first applied to an adjournment debate on child benefit on 28 June 1976, was to lessen the humiliation of defeat or even refute that a defeat had occurred at all so as to deny political ammunition to the Opposition. The approach does not appear to have been especially successful, however, only being used on one other occasion, over an adjournment debate on a public expenditure White Paper on 11 March 1977. The abandonment of the tactic may reflect this latter experience, providing little more than a breathing space and serving as an encouragement to the Opposition's motion of no confidence that was subsequently tabled and seriously threatened the survival of the Government.[67]

In other cases, defeat was swiftly followed by the modification of government policy. When defeated on an adjournment motion concerning the set-up of a contentious government inquiry on 5 December 1977, the Government's reaction was immediately 'to accept the will of the House' and change the format of the inquiry. Indeed, Callaghan's statement to the Commons on the matter was amended more clearly to express that the Government 'accepted' the decision, rather than the original and more obscure formulation: 'did not intend to stand in the way of'. After suffering an unexpected defeat on a clause of the devolution legislation for Wales, the Government planned to try to reinstate the clause at a later stage, but also showed willingness to concede the loss of the clause if it would facilitate easier passage of the bill.[68]

Accepting defeat was not restricted to procedural questions but also featured in some more major aspects of government policy. Conservative amendments to the 1978 Finance Bill, reducing income tax from 34 per cent to 33 per cent and increasing the personal allowance, were initially regarded as intolerable by the Government when successfully passed through the Commons by a combination of opposition MPs. Ultimately, however, the amendments became accepted when the Cabinet concluded that the risks of defeat in trying to reverse the decisions were too great, that further defeats over these issues would lead to the collapse of the Government and that, even if successful, restoration of the previous rates would be unpopular among the wider electorate.[69]

Some theoreticians have even gone so far as to suggest that regular defeats of a minority government that change policy need not challenge the viability of the incumbent administration. In Denmark, for example, there were frequent cases in the 1980s of minority governments being overruled by an 'alternative majority' of the legislature on certain aspects of policy and of the Government's leadership accepting these changes.[70]

Although, as indicated, the Callaghan Administration accepted certain opposition victories while regarding some others as intolerable, there are significant
differences between the attitudes of Danish and British political elites, as well as
in the scope of this approach. The Callaghan Government's acceptance of legislative defeats was a begrudging recognition of their inability to reverse particular
votes on single issues, rather than on whole policy areas. Defeats were also still
regarded very much within the British political establishment as a sign of outright government weakness and a deviation from the expected 'norm' of strong
majority government. While Labour sought to lessen the impact of particular
defeats, there is no indication of any sustained effort to normalise such setbacks
as an acceptable expression of minority government.

Seeking defeat

A third and rather unusual possibility for governments dealing with parliamentary defeat is to actually want it or even actively work towards this outcome.
This paradoxical practice is actually far more common than might otherwise be
expected. Theoretical discussions of minority government highlight two 'unusual' situations in which such defeat may be sought. Either a government may
wish to provide an excuse for calling an early election because of 'obstructionist'
opposition politicians (as was the case in Canada in 1974), or, in preparing issues
for a future campaign, may wish to establish a policy objective it seriously wants
to accomplish as being blocked by the efforts of opposition parties.[71]

Wilson's Government in 1974 certainly appears to have made some use of
unwinnable bills as signposts for a future administration. Concerns had been
raised among Wilson's advisers in May and early June, when the Government
had not suffered any defeats. Partly as a result of these worries, Labour put
forward legislation that would refund £10 million in tax to trade unions. The
opposition parties voted down the measure on 19 June 1974, marking the first
parliamentary defeat for the Wilson Minority Government. Typically inter-
preted as a loss, this particular defeat was actually welcomed by Labour MPs,
who hoped that it would provide them with good political ammunition for a
subsequent election campaign. Rhetoric used by both sides in Parliament itself
and in media communications prior to the actual vote was particularly heated,
from Heath's declaration in an interview regarding the end of the 'Phoney War'
to Denis Healey's use of language designed to goad Conservative MPs into
action.[72]

Callaghan's Government built on this kind of experience a couple of years
later, suggesting that certain bills should be put forward which ministers knew
would be defeated, but highlighted potential future campaign policies. These
bills were also perceived by Labour as seeking to satisfy supporters, both within
Parliament and the wider country, who demanded action on such issues as

occupational pensions schemes legislation, Post Office reforms or the Dock Labour Scheme. Various strategy meetings had highlighted concerns by leading figures that the Government could not win an election if it could not pass controversial legislation. For example, the Cabinet meeting of 3 March 1977 considered the question of what future legislation the Government should put forward given the ongoing state of minority government and recent defeats. Callaghan summarised the discussion, as indicated in this chapter's opening quote, highlighting the different proposed approaches over seeking parliamentary defeat, and whether the Government would 'introduce Bills which would be popular with the Government's own supporters but likely to be defeated in Parliament' as opposed to finding the 'necessary support for Government legislation'.[73]

The Cabinet Legislation Committee was tasked to respond to this discussion, looking to address these concerns in their meeting of 10 March 1977 by, amongst other things, recommending a series of bills which were unlikely to pass but were judged to have use as political 'signposts' and electoral campaign ammunition. However, although sentiments were expressed on several occasions favouring this approach, there is little evidence to suggest that these signpost bills were actually pursued unless support could be secured for them. In fact, Callaghan and the Cabinet increasingly perceived any Commons legislative defeat as undesirable and damaging to the Government. A reflection of this approach is the fact that only two government defeats involved the loss of entire bills, both occurring earlier on during Callaghan's Administration, on low turnouts of fewer than 200 MPs in the Commons, seemingly as much a result of miscalculation rather than planned confrontation between the Government and Opposition. After July 1977, all the Callaghan Government's parliamentary defeats were of amendments to bills or motions, rather than entire pieces of legislation. Where government legislation was partway through the parliamentary process but unlikely to be completed successfully, the preference was quietly to abandon work on the bills, rather than risk their being defeated in Parliament.[74]

One such example of the Government's fear of defeat may be seen in the case of the Aircraft and Shipbuilding Bill, discussed earlier in this chapter. While the November 1976 Cabinet was more confrontational in terms of it being 'preferable to lose the Bill this session rather than give way to the Lords', the meeting of February 1977 made a deal with the Opposition.[75] Another particularly interesting example may be seen in the Occupational Pension Schemes Bill. In meetings in 1976 and 1977, the TUC had stressed that they particularly wanted the Government to proceed with passage of the bill, even if controversial provisions were 'amended or deleted'.[76] However, having ascertained the likely defeat of these proposals, subsequent Cabinet discussions in May 1977 highlighted that, even if the bill could be passed in a significantly amended form, the amendments constituted an unacceptable political price, as indicated in the minute:

[S]trong doubts were expressed whether it would be advisable to introduce a Bill containing these provisions, which would be to court a humiliating defeat at the hands of the Opposition and the minority Parties. Defeats in Parliament on issues of importance damaged the Government and its electoral prospects.[77]

Callaghan very much shared this view, summarising that 'the standing of the Government was only weakened by defeats on issues of this kind'.[78] The legislation was quietly shelved, as referred to in a rather more perfunctory note in the Cabinet discussion of 20 October 1977, 'because it would not secure sufficient support in the present Parliament'.[79]

Conversely, the prospect of the Government seeking its own defeat led the Opposition to contemplate how to avoid the dangers of being lured into a trap. The Conservative Opposition to Wilson's Minority Government had attempted to grapple with this problem in 1974, either through choosing not to vote against the Government, or deliberately to withdraw certain backbenchers from a vote to ensure government victory. However, the Conservative strategy not to oppose was applied on an almost indiscriminate basis to begin with and did not include sufficient consideration of how to address either the problems of party morale or the counterstrategies of the Government. From the outset, Heath was aware that trying to avoid defeating a government that could be more easily defeated would not be popular with their supporters. Efforts to counter this problem by the Conservative leadership, communicating strategic reasoning through speeches, media interviews and visits to local Conservative associations, remained ineffective, with frustration being expressed in subsequent internal meetings that the message on strategy was not getting through. There was also little development of tactics that could counter Labour's efforts to goad the Opposition through legislation on such issues as rates and changes to VAT. The result was to enhance the perception and reality of the Conservatives as a divided party, some backbenchers disobeying the leadership's instruction to abstain by voting against the Government.[80] One mechanism developed to allow more active challenging of the Government was that of deliberately keeping a number of Conservative backbenchers away from the vote, removing the danger of engineering a defeat at a strategically inopportune moment. It is unclear, however, how far this was a codified facet of Conservative strategy as opposed to an informal arrangement. The labelling of this phenomenon as a 'strategy' was, in fact, made by their opponents, in particular the Liberals, who repeatedly expressed their frustration, both in Parliament and in their own strategy meetings, at being unable to defeat legislation because of the Conservatives' approach.[81]

While there was no repeat of these tactics during the Callaghan Administration, the Opposition did modify their approach at times to address this strategic dilemma. In some instances, the Conservatives supported the Government over legislation or in particular votes which would otherwise have led to defeat by the actions of rebel Labour MPs. While sometimes this was very much in line with pre-existing practices, there were other cases where the Conservatives clearly envisaged the move as a tactical response to minority government, and an attempt increasingly to divide the government leadership against its rebel members.[82]

In addition to the disunity between different opposition parties, there were other factors limiting the ability or desire of the respective oppositions to defeat these governments. Some of the most major pieces of legislation were those over which the Conservatives themselves were divided, such as devolution, or else had a particular interest in seeing implemented, such as direct elections to the European Parliament. As a result, there were a number of instances when the Opposition actively supported the Government in the passage of legislation, or, at least, did not hinder its progress.[83]

Contrary to what has previously been acknowledged, both Labour and the Conservatives were more proactive in their strategic approaches to managing legislation and defeats during a minority government. Wilson's confrontation over the Queen's Speech in 1974, and the initial conflict over pairing agreements during the Callaghan Government, set the tone for subsequent government–opposition relations in both cases, and conditioned the strategy-making process for the main parties in ways that have often been overlooked in studies of this period.

Both the Wilson and Callaghan Governments at times operated in accordance with what has subsequently been deemed as 'almost a majority government', making increased use of institutional powers to ensure passage of a full legislative programme. At the same time, however, both governments recognised the limitations of their minority position. The Wilson Government used parliamentary timetabling to their advantage, but also avoided putting forward some major legislation until after regaining their majority. In Callaghan's case, wholesale institutional changes in the legislative process that could have increased the Government's ability to pass bills were not pursued, such as over reform of the House of Lords or use of referenda.

Over time, the Callaghan Government's position increasingly evolved to one more accepting of added limitations in terms of what bills could be passed, ready to drop entire pieces of legislation rather than risk their defeat. A largely majoritarian approach was maintained, with no effort being made to normalise the process of legislative defeats, while the practice of actively seeking defeats for tactical purposes was considered too radical an option to be pursued, beyond the potentially limited use by Wilson in 1974. The selective use of confidence votes played a much more important role than has hitherto been accepted. While mistakes were made, adoption of these strategies helped to enable the Callaghan Government to survive for a prolonged period of time without a majority, even in instances where interparty cooperation was not guaranteed.

The Conservatives' ability to thwart government legislative efforts remained very much dependent on factors beyond their control. Confrontation over the Queen's Speech in 1974 was not well handled, and their subsequent early caution against opposing legislation or selectively withdrawing backbenchers to avoid engineering a defeat, had mainly served to frustrate their supporters. Nevertheless, over time, both the Heath and later Thatcher Oppositions learned to modify their approach, consciously recognising some of the potential minority government traps. The Conservatives placed increased reliance on committees and the House of Lords to avoid charges of obstructionism, while also sometimes offering cooperation to the Government against its own rebelling backbenchers. These initiatives, combined with selective opposition to legislation, reflected conscious efforts by the Conservatives to think strategically about how to engineer government defeat.

However, as the state of minority government continued in the later 1970s, both sides would increasingly need to consider cooperation with other parties in Parliament. Conservative success in forcing the Callaghan Government to the brink of a confidence vote defeat in early 1977 led to the most notable instance of interparty cooperation during the period, in the form of the Lib–Lab Pact.

Notes

1 TNA: CAB 128/61, 9th Meeting, 3 March 1977.
2 Thorpe, *A History of the British Labour Party*, pp. 207–8; Seldon and Hickson (eds), *New Labour, Old Labour*, pp. 190–4; Hennessy and Seldon (eds), *Ruling Performance*, pp. 241–2, 256.
3 Canada's Harper Government of 2008–11 also acted more along the lines of daring defeat, converting a minority into a majority government at the subsequent election. Hazell and Paun (eds), *Making Minority Government Work*, pp. 31–2; Russell, *Two Cheers for Minority Government*, pp. 35–8; Paun and Hazell, 'Hung Parliaments and the Challenges for Westminster and Whitehall', 216–17, 223.
4 Seldon and Hickson (eds), *New Labour, Old Labour*, pp. 190–3, 198; V. Bogdanor, *Coalition Government in Western Europe* (London: Heinemann, 1983), pp. 5–7; I. Burton and G. Drewry, 'Public Legislation: A Survey of the Session 1974', *Parliamentary Affairs*, 29:2 (1976), 155; Butler and Kavanagh, *The British General Election of October 1974*, pp. 18–19.
5 CPA: SC (located in LCC 1/3/1), 1st Meeting, 18 March 1974; MS. Wilson, c. 1322; c. 1436, loose papers; TNA: CAB 128/54, 3rd Meeting, 14 March 1974; Castle, *The Castle Diaries*, pp. 41–3; Wilson, *Final Term*, pp. 15–16.
6 Paun and Hazell, 'Hung Parliaments and the Challenges for Westminster and Whitehall', 219–20; P. Ziegler, *Edward Heath: The Authorised Biography* (London: HarperCollins, 2010), pp. 452–3; Benn, *Against the Tide*, p. 122.
7 TNA: CAB 128/54, 1st Meeting, 5 March 1974; 2nd Meeting, 7 March 1974; MS. Wilson, c. 1597, Prime Minister's Personal Minutes 1974, M11W/74; Benn, *Against the Tide*, p. 116; Wilson, *Final Term*, p. 13.

8 TNA: CAB 128/54, 1st Meeting, 5 March 1974; Castle, *The Castle Diaries*, pp. 41–5; Donoughue, *Downing Street Diary*, vol. 1, pp. 68–73; Wilson, *Final Term*, p. 39; Bell, *The Labour Party in Opposition*, p. 237.

9 HC Hansard, vol. 870, cols 70–2 (12 March 1974); cols 734–5, 751–2, 760–2 (18 March 1974); vol. 871, col. 177w (28 March 1974); TNA: CAB 128/54, 3rd Meeting, 14 March 1974; Castle, *The Castle Diaries*, pp. 41–3; Wilson, *Final Term*, pp. 15–16; Paun and Hazell, 'Hung Parliaments and the Challenges for Westminster and Whitehall', 218. There remains substantial debate as to whether such a dissolution would have been granted. Turpin and Tomkins, *British Government and the Constitution*, p. 363; Rasmussen, 'Constitutional Aspects of Government Formation', 144–8; Butler and Kavanagh, *The British General Election of October 1974*, p. 20.

10 CPA: LCC 1/3/1, 1st Meeting, 11 March 1974; Letter from Maurice Macmillan to Heath, 12 March 1974.

11 CPA: LCC 1/3/1, 1st Meeting, 11 March 1974; 2nd Meeting, 13 March 1974; 3rd Meeting, 18 March 1974; SC (located in LCC 1/3/1), 1st Meeting, 18 March 1974; HC Hansard, vol. 870, cols 679–80, 793–4 (18 March 1974).

12 CPA: LCC 1/3/1, 3rd Meeting, 18 March 1974.

13 Rogers and Walters, *How Parliament Works*, pp. 73–4, 95–101; M. Simms and J. Wanna, *Julia 2010: The Caretaker Election* (Canberra: ANU E Press, 2012), pp. 365–6.

14 LHASC: Parliamentary Committee, 10 April 1974; TNA: CAB 128/54, 5th Meeting, 21 March 1974.

15 LHASC: Parliamentary Committee, 8 May 1974; 17 July 1974.

16 TNA: PREM 16/233, Correspondence between Harold Wilson and Edward Heath, Bob Mellish and Humphrey Atkins, 11–22 July 1974.

17 TNA: CAB 128/59, 7th Meeting, 25 May 1976. Although highlighted, the incident has not often been discussed in great detail by commentaries, which concentrate on events after the debate, when Conservative spokesman Michael Heseltine picked up the ceremonial mace in response to the taunts and singing of Labour backbenchers. While this incident may serve as an amusing anecdote, it also illustrated the seriousness of tensions between the Government and Opposition. See J. Aitken, *Margaret Thatcher: Power and Personality* (A&C Black, 2013); Moore, *Margaret Thatcher*, p. 336; Campbell, *Margaret Thatcher*, pp. 320–1; Morgan, *Michael Foot*, p. 340; Seldon and Hickson (eds), *New Labour, Old Labour*, p. 193.

18 Thatcher, *The Path to Power*, pp. 313–14. See Chapter 4: Daring defeat.

19 CAC: THCR/2/1/1/42A, Nigel Lawson to Margaret Thatcher, 30 May 1976; CPA: LCC 1/3/11, 114th Meeting, 9 June 1976; 117th Meeting, 21 June 1976.

20 HC Hansard, vol. 916, cols 977–8, 1037, 1047, 1051, 1057 (29 July 1976); Donoughue, *Downing Street Diary*, vol. 2, pp. 37, 60–1. Further technical and political complications when the bill reached the House of Lords did give the Opposition a partial victory.

21 CPA: LCC 1/3/11, 119th Meeting, 30 June 1976; 122nd Meeting, 7 July 1976; 1/3/12, 124th Meeting, 14 July 1976; 1/3/14, 168th Meeting, 6 July 1977; 187th Meeting, 25 January 1978; SC 14, 42nd Meeting, 3 May 1976; HC Hansard, vol. 915, cols 1661–71 (20 July 1976); vol. 916, cols 1217–20, 1344–51 (2 August 1976); TNA: CAB 128/59, 8th Meeting, 10 June 1976; 16th Meeting, 19 July 1976.

22 CPA: LCC 1/3/13, 129th Meeting, 28 July 1976; 131st Meeting, 4 August 1976; HC Hansard, vol. 916, cols 1252–3 (2 August 1976); Donoughue, *Downing Street Diary*, vol. 2, pp. 54, 58–62.

23 CPA LCC 1/3/12, 124th Meeting, 14 July 1976; TNA: CAB 128/59, 22nd Meeting, 3 August 1976; Donoughue, *Downing Street Diary*, vol. 2, pp. 43–4, 48–9, 51.

24 Hazell and Paun (eds), *Making Minority Government Work*, p. 60.

25 TNA: CAB 129/189, 'Legislative Programme 1976–77 – Memorandum by the Lord President of the Council', 14 May 1976. See Chapter 4: Daring defeat.

26 Tsebelis, *Veto Players*, p. 98.

27 CAC: THCR/2/6/1/191, Humphrey Atkins to Thatcher, 4 October 1976; Humphrey Atkins to Michael Cocks, and Attached Memorandum: 'The Recording of Votes by Members who are Ill – Some Thoughts for Discussion', 2 September 1976.

28 Rogers and Walters, *How Parliament Works*, pp. 53, 172–6.

29 Rogers and Walters, *How Parliament Works*, p. 132; Hazell and Paun (eds), *Making Minority Government Work*, pp. 33, 50–1; Strøm, *Minority Government and Majority Rule*, pp. 42–4, 152–3.

30 Rogers and Walters, *How Parliament Works*, pp. 100, 354–5, 360.

31 CAC: THCR/2/1/1/54, 'Statement by the Rt. Hon. Humphrey Atkins, M.P., Opposition Chief Whip', 7 April 1976; 'Statement from Alan Beith, MP, the Liberal Chief Whip', 7 April 1976; *House of Commons Information Office: General Committees*, Factsheet L6 Legislative Series, pp. 2–3.

32 TNA: CAB 128/59, 2nd Meeting, 29 April 1976.

33 TNA: CAB 128/59, 3rd Meeting, 6 May 1976; PREM 16/1045, Ken Stowe to Prime Minister, 8 April 1976; Meeting Held in the Prime Minister's Office, 26 April 1976.

34 CPA: LCC 1/3/15, 198th Meeting, 12 April 1978; SC 14, 42nd Meeting, 3 May 1976.

35 J. Brand, *British Parliamentary Parties: Policy and Power* (Oxford: Oxford University Press, 1992), pp. 101, 292–3, 343.

36 Twenty-five per cent more time was allocated to opposition parties under the SNP Minority Government of 2007–11. Rogers and Walters, *How Parliament Works*, pp. 189–229; Hazell and Paun (eds), *Making Minority Government Work*, pp. 58–9.

37 TNA: CAB 128/59, 5th Meeting, 18 May 1976; 128/61, 9th Meeting, 3 March 1977; 128/62, 27th Meeting, 21 July 1977; Seldon and Hickson (eds), *New Labour, Old Labour*, pp. 198, 227.

38 TNA: CAB 128/62, 27th Meeting, 21 July 1977; 128/64, 21st Meeting, 8 June 1978.

39 TNA: CAB 128/61, 2nd Meeting, 20 January 1977; 4th Meeting, 3 February 1977; 6th Meeting, 17 February 1977; 7th Meeting, 24 February 1977; 11th Meeting, 17 March 1977; 128/63, 1st Meeting, 19 January 1978; 2nd Meeting, 26 January 1978; 10th Meeting, 16 March 1978.

40 A closure motion may be called by any MP to end a debate and to put the question to a vote, requiring a majority voting in favour that consists of at least 100 MPs. Callaghan Papers, 2741: PP/Lib-Lab: 77, Report to the Prime Minister – 'Government Business during the Rest of the 1976/77 Session', 14 March 1977; TNA: CAB 128/60, 28th Meeting, 26 October 1976; 128/61, 9th Meeting, 3 March 1977; 11th Meeting, 17 March 1977; 128/63, 10th Meeting, 16 March 1978; K. Jefferys, *The Labour Party since 1945* (London: Macmillan, 2002), p. 89; Butler, *Governing without a Majority*, pp. 30–2; M. Holmes, *The Labour Government, 1974–79: Political Aims and Economic Reality* (London: Macmillan, 1985), pp. 15–18; Butler and Kavanagh, *The British General Election of October 1974*, pp. 97–100.

41 It is also worth noting that referenda on constitutional changes are a codified part of the Danish political system. S. Tierney, *Constitutional Referendums: The Theory*

and Practice of Republican Deliberation (Oxford: Oxford University Press, 2012), pp. 117, 126, 146, 156–7; M. Setälä and T. Schiller (eds), *Referendums and Representative Democracy: Responsiveness, Accountability and Deliberation* (London: Routledge, 2009), pp. 6, 87–91, 111, 218; R. Hazell, K. Donnelly and N. Smith, *Report of the Commission on the Conduct of Referendums* (London: UCL Constitution Unit, 1996), pp. 30, 37–40, 43, 73. Pre-legislative referenda were subsequently used in 1998 by Tony Blair's Labour Government to strengthen the case for subsequent devolution legislation. A. McDonald (ed.), *Reinventing Britain: Constitutional Change under New Labour* (London: University of California Press, 2007), pp. 6, 38, 49.

42 TNA: CAB 128/61, 7th Meeting, 24 February 1977.

43 CPA: LCC 1/3/13, 132nd Meeting, 28 September 1976; 1/3/14, 177th Meeting, 2 November 1977; 1/3/16, 230th Meeting, 29 January 1979.

44 See, for example, TNA: CAB 128/60, 27th Meeting, 21 October 1976.

45 Rogers and Walters, *How Parliament Works*, pp. 139–42, 187, 240–2, 266; M. Minogue (ed.), *Documents on Contemporary British Government*, vol. 1: *British Government and Constitutional Change* (Cambridge: Cambridge University Press, 1977), pp. 71–9. The provisions of the revised Parliament Act in 1949 were only first invoked in 1991, the original 1911 Act having only been used three times.

46 LHASC: HART 12/31, Reform of the House of Commons, April 1978; NEC Minutes, Machinery of Government Study Group, 29 June 1976; Seldon and Hickson (eds), *New Labour, Old Labour*, pp. 32, 191–8.

47 TNA: CAB 128/60, 32nd Meeting, 18 November 1976.

48 TNA: CAB 128/61, 7th Meeting, 24 February 1977.

49 *Ibid.*

50 Callaghan Papers, 2744 Lab/Cab 76, Callaghan to Lord Peart, 19 April 1977; TNA: CAB 128/59, 16th Meeting, 19 July 1976; 128/61, 7th Meeting, 24 February 1.

51 See Chapter 4: Daring defeat.

52 Rogers and Walters, *How Parliament Works*, pp. 139–40, 284, 288; Hazell and Paun (eds), *Making Minority Government Work*; J. Cannon, *The Fox–North Coalition: Crisis of the Constitution 1782–4* (Cambridge: Cambridge University Press, 1969), pp. 1–4.

53 Sandbrook, *Seasons in the Sun*, pp. 769–81; Seldon and Hickson (eds), *New Labour, Old Labour*, pp. 198–203.

54 Brazier and Kalitowski (eds), *No Overall Control*, pp. 83–93; Laver and Schofield, *Multiparty Government*, pp. 74–5.

55 TNA: CAB 128/63, 5th Meeting, 16 February 1978.

56 Seldon and Hickson (eds), *New Labour, Old Labour*, pp. 190–204; Norton, *Dissension in the House of Commons*.

57 TNA: CAB 128/63, 5th Meeting, 16 February 1978.

58 Hazell and Paun (eds), *Making Minority Government Work*, p. 35.

59 Donoughue, *Downing Street Diary*, vol. 2, p. 37; Thatcher, *The Path to Power*, pp. 314–15, 327–9, 431–2.

60 Thorpe, *A History of the British Labour Party*, p. 205.

61 TNA: CAB 128/64, 42nd Meeting, 7 December 1978.

62 CPA: CRD/D/7/24, Memorandum from Peter Utley to Lord Thorneycroft, 12 January 1979; TNA: CAB 128/64, 41st Meeting, 30 November 1978; 43rd Meeting, 14 December 1978; Donoughue, *Downing Street Diary*, vol. 2, pp. 398–402; Thatcher, *The Path to Power*, pp. 419, 423–30.

63 TNA: CAB 128/65, 8th Meeting, 18 January 1979.

64 LHASC: CC, Paper, 15 May 1974, 'Party Strategy'; TNA: CAB 128/54, 7th Meeting, 28 March 1974; 8th Meeting, 4 April 1974; 9th Meeting, 9 April 1974; 21st Meeting, 27 June 1974.

65 TNA: CAB 128/61, 15th Meeting, 21 April 1977; 128/62, 25th Meeting, 14 July 1977; Donoughue, *Downing Street Diary*, vol. 2, pp. 176–8, 464–7.

66 Seldon and Hickson (eds), *New Labour, Old Labour*, p. 193; Minogue (ed.), *Documents on Contemporary British Government*, p. 85.

67 TNA: CAB 128/59, 11th Meeting, 24 June 1976.

68 TNA: CAB 128/62, 35th Meeting, 10 November 1977; 39th Meeting, 8 December 1977; 128/63, 15th Meeting, 20 April 1978.

69 TNA: CAB 128/63, 18th Meeting, 11 May 1978; 128/64, 21st Meeting, 8 June 1978. The Government had itself advocated and carried out reductions in income tax over preceding budgets. While accepting defeat, the Government did attempt to recover the lost revenue through other means. See Chapter 6: Government cooperation.

70 Green-Pedersen, 'Minority Governments and Party Politics', 15–16, 20.

71 B. E. Rasch and G. Tsebelis (eds), *The Role of Governments in Legislative Agenda Setting* (London: Routledge, 2013), pp. 89–90; Hazell and Paun (eds), *Making Minority Government Work*, p. 31; Russell, *Two Cheers for Minority Government*, pp. 34–8; P. Cowley, *The Rebels: How Blair Mislaid His Majority* (London: Politico's, 2005), p. 286.

72 Castle, *The Castle Diaries*, p. 118; Hazell and Paun (eds), *Making Minority Government Work*, p. 65; Campbell, *Edward Heath*, pp. 635–6; Burton and Drewry, 'Public Legislation', 158–60; F. Stacey, *British Government 1966–1975: Years of Reform* (Oxford: Oxford University Press, 1975), p. 52.

73 TNA: CAB 128/61, 9th Meeting, 3 March 1977.

74 Callaghan Papers, 2741: PP/Lib-Lab: 77, Report to the Prime Minister – 'Government Business during the Rest of the 1976/77 Session', 14 March 1977; TNA: 128/61, 5th Meeting, 10 February 1977; 9th Meeting, 3 March 1977; 11th Meeting, 17 March 1977; CAB 128/62, 35th Meeting, 10 November 1977; 40th Meeting, 15 December 1977; CAB 128/63, 18th Meeting, 11 May 1978; 128/64, 27th Meeting, 20 July 1978.

75 See Chapter 4.

76 TNA: CAB 128/60, 29th Meeting, 28 October 1976; 31st Meeting, 11 November 1976.

77 TNA: CAB 128/61, 20th Meeting, 19 May 1977.

78 *Ibid.*

79 TNA: CAB 128/62, 32nd Meeting, 20 October 1977.

80 CPA: CCO 20/61/5, PCM, 1 May 1974; LCC 1/3/1, 5th Meeting, 27 March 1974; 7th Meeting, 10 April 1974; 8th Meeting, 29 April 1974; 12th Meeting, 8 May 1974; NHCA 1/10, 26 April 1974; SC 12 (2), 2nd Meeting, 25 March 1974; HC Hansard, vol. 878, cols 478–9 (30 July 1974).

81 CPA: LCC 1/3/1, 9th Meeting, 1 May 1974; 12th Meeting, 8 May 1974; Liberal Party Archive, LSE: CA17/LIBERAL PARTY/1/8, Meetings 4 March–25 July 1974; HC Hansard, vol. 874, cols 578–80 (23 May 1974); cols 1377–8 (10 June 1974); vol. 875, cols 356–8 (18 June 1974); cols 1803–4 (27 June 1974); Burton and Drewry, 'Public Legislation', 157–8.

82 CPA: LCC 1/3/1, 6th Meeting, 4 April 1974; 9th Meeting, 1 May 1974; 12th Meeting, 8 May 1974; 1/3/13, 160th Meeting, 27 April 1977; SC 12 (2), 2nd Meeting, 25 March 1974; LSE: CA17/LIBERAL PARTY/1/8, Meetings 4 March–25 July 1974.

83 CPA: LCC 1/3/13, 160th Meeting, 27 April 1977.

5

The myth of coalition:
the Lib–Lab Pact

[Callaghan said that the Cabinet] could now consider at more leisure whether to continue with the Liberals on agreed terms or to go on at greater risk by themselves. [...] whether the deal should be for an ordinary 12-month session or for an 18-month one to the spring of 1979 as a public announcement of the latter might dishearten the Conservatives. [...] [He] hoped that those of his colleagues whose style it was would 'set the Thames on fire' at least in moderation. [...] Some Ulster Unionists were well disposed towards the Government and they and other small groups should not be overlooked [...] otherwise the election campaign would begin almost immediately.[1]

The Prime Minister's country retreat, Chequers, 26 June 1977. At a secret strategy meeting, three months after the beginning of the Lib–Lab Pact, Callaghan's Cabinet discussed whether or not to renew their cooperation with the Liberals through extension of the Pact, to seek an early election or to create an entirely different agreement with another political party.

This interparty cooperation built on the abortive attempt at coalition between the Conservatives and the Liberals in 1974, but also moved beyond the experiences of that earlier period. Wilson had eschewed any formal collaboration with the Liberals in 1974 for reasons identified in Chapters 2 and 3, including the majoritarian stance of Labour, the shortness of the term and the different political climate. By contrast, the Callaghan Government was only able to survive until nearly the end of its parliamentary term because of the formal cooperation with the Liberals in the Pact.

Studies and reflections by participants on interparty cooperation during the Callaghan Administration have been dominated by the subject of the Pact between the Liberals and Labour during the period of March 1977 to September 1978. The Pact presents something of a conundrum for any study on minority government, appearing to be nearer to a coalition.[2] Both main parties have typically been perceived as subscribing to the previously cited 'minimal winning' formula, demonstrated not least in a general preference for ad hoc deals to ensure a government majority in particular votes and the general hostility towards any notion of coalition. Subscription to the Lib–Lab Pact could well be regarded through this optic of applying only minimal conditions on both the Government and the Liberals.[3]

In addition, the agreement has generally been viewed as representing a lack of strategy-making, authored primarily as a political expediency, solely as a reactive measure, entered into reluctantly by Labour and largely leaving neither party's goals satisfied beyond the sustaining of the Government in office. The alternative was defeat and a snap general election, at a time when the Conservatives held a significant opinion poll lead of up to 15 per cent.[4] Even government advisers including Lipsey, who considered the most optimistic polling scenario at only a 7 per cent opposition lead, advised against an early election. While this option received some consideration by the Government, as will be discussed in Chapter 7, it was still rejected as unlikely to deliver a victory.[5]

However, while the Government's participation in a formal interparty agreement may have been compelled by circumstances when facing defeat in 1977, the shape of this agreement was by no means certain, being conditioned particularly by the contemporary experiences of minority government. The Government's handling of the negotiation, renegotiation and operation of the agreement did, in fact, involve strategic consideration and discussion about how to deal with interparty cooperation in a minority government setting. Selected examples of this strategic deliberation include Donoughue's paper for the June 1977 Strategy Cabinet, or the paper by Lipsey in his role as a Special Adviser, indicating possible responses to the March 1977 confidence vote. In fact, in some ways, Labour's use of the Pact may have been as much a psychological tool, with the Government even willing to consider only monthly renewal as better than having no agreement. Other possibilities for cooperation that presented themselves to both main parties, before, during and after the Pact, as well as extra-parliamentary agreements and the prospect of post-electoral deals, will be discussed at length in Chapters 6 and 8.

To understand fully the strategic dynamics involved in the Callaghan Government's approach to the Pact, this chapter will begin by examining the distinctive nature of the agreement and the formation process in light of aspects of the negotiations which shaped and were shaped by the state of minority government. Thereafter, we will consider aspects that have been overlooked, including the confrontation over raising petrol tax which shaped the renegotiation, the strategic discourse during the renewal of the Pact, the Government's changing strategic approach during the course of the Pact and the development of an exit strategy. Some aspects which play an important part in negotiations or the scholarship applying to them will be highlighted insofar as they relate to questions of minority government, but will not be re-examined at greater length.

Formation of the Pact

Distinctive

The Lib–Lab Pact, as with the Callaghan Government as a whole, provides an important case study in minority government because of its distinctive characteristics compared to formal interparty legislative agreements elsewhere. In part, these features can be explained as having arisen from inexperience of formalised interparty cooperation or the particular political circumstances in 1977. However, this format also reflected the distinct British tradition of minority government, which helped to enable the survival of the Pact. Given the historic hostility to interparty agreements, the Government did not countenance the formation of a coalition, party leaders repeatedly seeking to reassure MPs and the wider party that their deal with the Liberals did not amount to one.

As indicated, the formation of the Pact lacked mechanisms characteristic of other interparty agreements abroad, such as, for example, obtaining a mandate from MPs or party members before entering negotiations.[6] There were no formally constituted teams, nor apparent briefing notes and pre-arranged strategy for talks.[7] The negotiations were also supplemented by a number of undirected individual initiatives in response to the prospect of imminent government defeat. These included Liberal MP Cyril Smith's attempted approach to Callaghan, and Foot's approaches to Ulster Unionist (former Conservative) MP Enoch Powell. Even narratives highlighting the overall strategic visions being pursued by individuals, particularly that of Steel, recognise this initial formation process as largely unstructured on both sides.[8]

Devices for interparty cooperation that were employed, such as a formal written agreement, took on a different shape from experiences of interparty cooperation and coalition elsewhere.[9] The Government's preferred written agreement was of an exchange of letters between party leaders, rather than a more formal 'contract'. These letters were subject to extensive redrafting by the Government, not least to prevent the agreement from being perceived as a coalition. One amendment, for example, included that the commitment to consultation on paper was to be between the two party leaders, rather than the wider parties, designed to frame the agreement as being limited to within Parliament. Another change was the removal of references to what government plans were being dropped in terms of further nationalisation and the Direct Labour Bill. Even though, as highlighted in Lipsey's paper, it would have been difficult in any case to proceed with these measures, the Government wanted to avoid the perception of the Liberals blocking policy or forcing concessions. Steel accepted the deletion of this paragraph in return for the change itself being 'conveyed in briefing'. Changes also sought to prevent the Government from being tied to specific timetabled legislative commitments.[10]

Furthermore, there were few attempts to create any long-term commissions to solve intractable policy differences, as has happened in coalitions both in Britain and overseas. The Labour–Liberal Consultative Committee, comprising several representatives from both parties, was more of a system for resolving day-to-day legislative disputes, and justified by the Government merely as an extension of pre-existing consultative mechanisms between itself and bodies such as the TUC, and as not attaining a higher priority than internal Labour mechanisms when formulating government plans.[11]

During this period, a Speaker's Conference would sometimes be proposed as part of interparty negotiations. These conferences, chaired by the House of Commons Speaker, were formal inquiries that had historically been used for dealing with important constitutional questions concerning electoral arrangements, but were limited in their usefulness. Terms of reference and composition of the conferences were set by the Government and dominated by the two main parties. Their primary purpose was to confer legitimacy on a policy agreed between the Government and Opposition, rather than as a genuine tool for interparty negotiation. During negotiations in 1977, Callaghan did offer a conference on increased Northern Ireland parliamentary representation to the UUP, but there was no similar offer to the Liberals concerning PR in direct elections.[12] In the failed 1974 negotiations, by contrast, Heath had gone so far as to offer Thorpe a conference on PR for House of Commons elections. Steel, however, desired a more solid commitment to legislation in 1977, mindful of the previous coalition attempt.[13]

The Callaghan Government ended up using a promised free vote on PR for direct elections to deal with the issue. Dialogue between government leaders would suggest that this method was accepted more because it would deal with problems Labour would have, in any case, faced through its own divisions over the issue of direct elections, rather than as a specific concession to the Liberals or device for facilitating interparty cooperation.[14]

Conditions set down in the Pact would, at first glance, suggest a limited 'Confidence and Supply' agreement, in which an MP, party or group of parties agrees either to vote with a minority government or to abstain on votes of confidence or some/all monetary-spending bills ('Supply'). In such an agreement, usually, but not always, participants remain separate from the Government itself and do not take up ministerial posts. The agreement is normally established to operate over a set period of months or years, with the Government supplying some added legislative benefits to those providing support, such as greater influence in the formation of legislation, or support for particular bills or policies advocated by the smaller parties.[15] These arrangements may secure a government majority on certain issues, but their incomplete coverage and potential vulnerability of the Government on other legislation, may, in practice, mean that the Government is still formally in a 'minority'.

However, this misconception is rightly challenged by Kirkup. The Pact was not a typical 'Confidence and Supply' agreement, the Liberals only committing themselves to backing the Government in formally declared votes of confidence, rather than necessarily the 'Supply' of monetary spending bills.[16] In fact, going beyond this argument, in practice the Pact did not even qualify as a 'Confidence' agreement. Liberal MPs considered opposing and, in some cases, ultimately voted against government Budget items with which they disagreed, in spite of such measures traditionally being matters of confidence. These ambiguities served to lay the foundations for the first major conflict of the Pact over the raising of petrol tax, as well as setting up further significant government defeats over Budget items in both 1977 and 1978. Furthermore, typical 'Confidence and Supply' arrangements would tend to last a minimum of twelve to eighteen months and could even extend up to the full length of a four- to five-year Parliament. By contrast, the initial Pact only committed both sides until the end of the parliamentary session in the summer of 1977, a time period of around three months. The continued insecurity arising from such a short-term agreement seems at odds with the Government having sought mainly to justify its efforts to secure a formal deal on the basis of ending uncertainty and reducing the need for vote-by-vote negotiations. Furthermore, the Pact was negotiated in less than five days, a much shorter time frame than most interparty negotiations elsewhere, albeit the same time taken to form the UK coalition government in 2010. The immovable deadline of a no confidence vote played an important role in pressuring parties into an agreement.[17]

While this short-term outcome would seem, at first glance, paradoxical, not satisfying the objectives of either party and indicative of the Pact's reactive formation process, it was not totally counterintuitive. In other countries, minority coalition governments have been formed and have governed successfully for a full term without a parliamentary majority.[18] There are, however, other advantages of an agreement in these instances, not least in terms of raising governments to the 'almost' majority threshold. Other psychological advantages include the perception of greater governing legitimacy among commentators and the wider public, and the dissuading of opposing parties from attempting repeatedly to bring down a government, by the implied failure of any prospective no confidence vote. The distinct form of the Lib–Lab Pact as a short-term 'experiment', as it was dubbed by participants, actually helped to enable its successful enactment and renewal, as represented in internal dialogues between Callaghan and other decision-makers. While, as stated, the Government entered into the Pact without being as well prepared as their overseas counterparts, the final shape of the Pact was significantly affected by strategic considerations in the negotiating process. By looking at the employment of potential negotiating tactics and their wider implications, it is possible to trace the forces shaping the agreement and, further, to highlight the main parties' adherence to a particular British tradition of minority government.

Other issues raised by the negotiations provide even more direct insight into the Government's strategy when forming the Pact and during its subsequent renewal: use of rhetoric to pre-signal negotiating preferences, planning in advance for interparty cooperation and addressing a prospective bidding war between parties.

Rhetoric and pre-signalling preferences

The exchange of statements of intent prior to negotiations, whether through party leaders' correspondence or through press releases and television/radio interviews, tends to allow parties to reassure their supporters, citing continued commitment to particular electoral promises and criticising political opponents. In political systems where majoritarian government has historically been preferred, such as in Britain, the Government's mandate to govern will also be rhetorically presented. In March 1977, the Callaghan Government's public rhetoric was one of daring opposition parties to trigger an early election.[19] There appear to have been some attempts by Labour to use communications to put pressure on the Liberals, and vice versa, whether through strongly worded press releases, newspaper comments, TV interviews, telephone conversations or letters warning of the impending election that would follow defeat. In the Liberals' case, for example, these indications were echoed in Steel's statement on 19 March, threatening that 'either' the Government could seek interparty cooperation over its wider legislative programme 'or else we have a General Election'. From the Government side, references made were primarily brief factual statements, without specifying details of ongoing discussions, and generally refuting the use of such words as 'deal' when asked if the Government was pursuing formal interparty cooperation. Similarly, Labour spokesmen took a belligerent line against the prospect of the Liberals bringing down the Government, not least, for example, in Rees' implied threat of 'so be it' on 21 March.[20]

These exchanges may also set out parties' negotiating positions and flag up a small number of crucial 'red lines' that are non-negotiable, while indicating particular aspirations that are then revised in subsequent discussions. In the 2010 general election, for example, the Liberal Democrat manifesto included four top priorities considered critical to any post-electoral interparty agreement, while Conservative leader David Cameron's speech following the result set out 'red lines' on foreign and economic policy.[21]

However, while the Callaghan Government was endeavouring to communicate their position and criticise their opponents through the media, this approach was grounded in pre-existing majoritarian practices in an effort to discourage opposition parties from voting against the Government, rather than being consciously engineered as part of signalling policy preferences for a negotiating strategy. The Government did seek to keep informed of statements by the smaller parties in the run-up to the vote, including through written reports to Callaghan, which helped to inform their efforts at interparty cooperation.[22]

The Government preferred communicating negotiating points through private channels, particularly through letters and meetings between individuals in the party leadership and those of other parties. Limiting the agreement's scope to a parliamentary arrangement with MPs of other parties, rather than wider party memberships, was also considered likely to help justify the deal to the Labour Party. Unlike Heath's failed coalition of 1974, the secrecy of the Pact's initial formation process, the absence of leaking concrete information about the discussions and the perception that any successful outcome was considered less likely by participants in both Labour and the Liberals, helped to lessen the possibility of greater attacks in advance.[23]

Planning for cooperation

As indicated, the reactive nature of the Pact negotiations and ad hoc approach meant that there does not appear to have been as much planning by the Government on how to tackle such a situation. Callaghan did ask his civil service advisers for additional information in order to help facilitate the negotiations, including a summary of the present and future proposed legislation which detailed the Liberals' parliamentary actions regarding recent bills.[24] At the same time, however, members of the Government were also engaging in some strategic consideration as to the implications for prospective pacts, not least in Lipsey's strategy paper, which suggested that an agreement with the Liberals was the preferred option in the circumstances. Having examined and ruled out the alternatives of a UUP deal and early election, Lipsey detailed some of the different potential obstacles to a Lib–Lab agreement and how these would be dealt with. Thereafter, the paper went on to explore the various conditions which, it was expected, would be attached by the Liberals to any such deal, concluding that enough could be offered by the Government to ensure an agreement without making any significant compromises from the perspective of the Government's leadership. Conditions in terms of dropping legislation, such as the Direct Labour Organisation Bill, were viewed either as merely fulfilling the Government's existing intentions or even as a positive excuse to avoid politically difficult issues: 'We were going to have to anyway', 'There is no such Bill' and, on the Bullock report on industrial democracy, 'an excuse to escape from the TUC/Jack Jones axis on this issue is much to be desired'.[25] Where it appeared that the Government would struggle to gain support for legislative demands, such as a stronger Devolution Bill and PR for European direct elections, Lipsey suggested that these could still be discussed with the Liberals or even offered 'on the understanding that the decision [...] is ultimately one for the House of Commons'. Lipsey's paper represents one of the few instances of an example outside the British experience being employed in the illustrations of strategy-makers during this period. In this case, the example was of the then Italian Government maintaining its unity while entering into a pact with a party of a different ideological persuasion: 'The Andreotti example of keeping the Communists with the Government, without splitting his Party, shows what can be done.' The use of this particular example does not appear to have been widely taken up in subsequent planning, reflecting the general preference for drawing on British parliamentary precedents. That Lipsey himself advocated the arrangement with the Liberals is perhaps more surprising given his own strong dislike of the party, which he admitted in the closing paragraph. However, dismissing other options as 'hideously unattractive', he ended by challenging the Ramsay MacDonald example which had helped to influence Labour's hostility to interparty cooperation, hoping that such an aversion would 'not entice us into an act of electoral suicide'. While it is difficult to ascertain the full impact of Lipsey's paper, the sentiments expressed and suggestions made appear to have been very much in line with the eventual outcome of forming and justifying the Pact to Labour as a temporary measure borne out of necessity and not imposing significant burdens upon the Government.

Prospective bidding war

Another side of simultaneous negotiations, although more unusual, is that of trying to compel potential political partners to outbid each other, or to pressure one to sign a barely acceptable deal for fear of losing out to another party, as occurred following the 1996 New Zealand election. Following the 2010 UK election, disclosure of Liberal Democrat negotiations occurring both with the Conservatives and Labour has been characterised as 'bidding' for coalition part-ners.[26] However, although the Callaghan Government could approach different smaller parties in 1977 it could not necessarily promise delivery of what they wanted, whether PR for the Liberals or Northern Ireland devolution along lines favoured by the UUP. Negotiations were conducted secretly, and there was no attempt by the Government to get smaller parties into a bidding competition with one another. Some prospective combinations with other small parties were also ruled out for strategic and/or political reasons, as we shall see in Chapter 6.

Correspondence and Cabinet discussions suggested that talks between the Government and UUP in March 1977 were initially regarded as more likely to lead to a successful agreement.[27] However, the Cabinet, special advisers and the Policy Unit opposed reliance on a UUP deal. Members of these groups believed such a deal would be unworkable based on the previous UUP voting record and policy differences. Concerns were raised that any formal agreement between Labour and the UUP would lose electoral support of Catholics in important UK constituencies.[28] Both sides questioned how far the Government could deliver policies to sustain any long-term deal, fearing the need for endless bargaining, a sentiment expressed not least in the paper by Lipsey, that the UUP were:

> mostly Conservative by temperament and it is difficult to believe that we should permanently win any auction for their votes (e.g. by promising tougher security measures). We might just buy their abstention for Wednesday, but the alliance would be unstable, especially since Enoch Powell's support would probably disappear if we introduced a Direct Elections Bill.[29]

Callaghan and Foot referred to parallel talks or offers to both parties during their meetings with the Liberals and the UUP, but there is no evidence that this was a conscious tactic, or that it had any effect on pressuring a deal. While any formal agreement with the Liberals could, and necessarily would, be made public, formalised cooperation with the UUP remained secret. Although both sets of discussions were subsequently acknowledged in the confidence debate, government and UUP leaders strenuously sought to deny any formal deal.[30]

Any possibility of a bidding war was further diminished when, from the outset, the Government gave the assurance that increased Northern Ireland representation would be granted regardless of the conclusion of a parliamentary deal. This move appears to have been designed as a gesture of goodwill, aiming to secure the support of a handful of UUP MPs over a longer timescale than the immediate confidence vote, even without a formal deal. While this opening offer may have limited the prospect of extracting greater concessions, it is questionable as to whether a conditional offer would have yielded better results.[31] A limited deal with the UUP was done through an exchange of letters between party leaders, but, being kept secret, could not provide the public psychological reassurance of giving the Government the appearance of a majority. The continued support of the Government by certain UUP members during the course of the Lib–Lab Pact would suggest that this tactic had some success. Lacking the same immediate electoral challengers which were faced by the parties in constituencies in Scotland, England and Wales, the UUP were not under the same pressures to do any deal with the Government as was the case with their Liberal counterparts.[32] At the same time, the arrangement also created challenges for Labour's future parliamentary strategy. In spite of attempted secrecy, news reporting of the ongoing discussions taking place and the subsequent actions of the UUP sustaining the Government (which lessened the believability of denials), prompted increased opposition from the SDLP and independents, including Frank Maguire.[33]

Petrol tax

Although the agreement's formation and the confidence vote on 23 March 1977 have rightly been regarded as important, a particularly crucial experience conditioning the long-term operation of the Pact was, in fact, the dispute which flared up in the following weeks over the government plans to raise petrol tax by 5.5p. In the same way that the disruption of the usual channels in the summer of 1976 had influenced party approaches to minority government, the petrol tax conflict significantly shaped the Government's approach to Liberal–Labour interactions and the workings of an interparty agreement. Liberal MPs judged this increase to be of particular concern to their supporters in rural constituencies and decided to vote against. While Kirkup rightly suggests that the episode reflected a lack of 'experience of coalition politics' for all sides, it is important to recognise that the Callaghan Government had as much to learn from the episode as the Liberals.[34] The initial public reaction of the Government was more majoritarian, seeking to compel Liberal support through raising the spectre of a defeat over the issue as leading to the resignation of the Government and an immediate election. At the PLP meeting on 21 April 1977, Callaghan, as recorded by Chief Secretary to the Treasury Joel Barnett, stressed the importance of avoiding the appearance of 'solely reacting to the Liberals'.[35] Nevertheless, from the outset, the Government sought privately to balance these threats with potential compromises, albeit limited and disguised so as to avoid the appearance of concessions. Meetings were held, not least Callaghan's secret meeting with Steel on 31 March 1977 in an attempt, early on in the row, to persuade Liberal abstention in return for agreeing later changes to the Budget. Other discussions between government members and their Liberal counterparts also took place in an effort to resolve the issue, including a meeting between Barnett and John Pardoe, as Liberal Treasury Spokesman, to consider the matter at length on 20 April. An immediate motivating factor for the Liberals was highlighted during this meeting, Pardoe suggesting that the reduction in petrol tax would be an important tangible gain for Liberals facing upcoming local elections in May. Barnett proposed delaying the date of the increase to 5 August on the grounds of it being easier from an administrative point of view, which Pardoe approved. However, no agreement was reached at this stage on the possible figure of the reduction, with Barnett ostensibly claiming that he could not offer any concession while floating the possibility of a 2p reduction before the local elections, while Pardoe said that his colleagues would not settle for less than 3p, and threatened the possibility of their voting against other parts of the Budget.[36]

At the same time as these discussions were taking place, the Government was also formulating contingency plans in the event of a defeat, including how to raise lost revenue from elsewhere. Discussions between the Chief Whip and Barnett had concluded that the Liberal amendment was likely to succeed. Following on from this, and his meeting with Pardoe, Barnett prepared a short paper for the Chancellor and Prime Minister on potential tactics for handling the issue. The two options considered were either outright opposition to an amendment, accepting defeat but seeking a way to recoup the lost revenue, or seeking to make the more limited reduction of 2p, rather than cancelling the 5.5p rise as demanded by the Liberals. This latter option was also framed in terms of attempting to justify the measure as dealing with concerns about the rising petrol price 'which has come not only from the Liberals, but from [our] own backbenchers and the unions'.[37] This offer thereby sought to disguise a concession to the Liberals under the veil of the Government addressing concerns of its primary participants. Although Callaghan was, in his own annotations of the paper, 'in favour of [the] Government standing by the increase', he also recognised the need for consultation and the fact that 'if we are going to lose we had better consider how it is reflected'.

The subsequent compromise that emerged introduced the increase, but included a private promise by the Government to reverse the policy in full by amendment at a later stage, as previously indicated in the Barnett/Pardoe discussions, in return for Liberal support on the other aspects of the Budget. The compromise allowed the Government to avoid the appearance at that stage of having given any concession to the Liberals which could have reduced its credibility in the eyes of Labour backbenchers. At the same time, the offer arose from the recognition that the position of daring defeat without any notion of an alternative approach would also not appear credible in the eyes of many Labour supporters or the Liberals, the Government having only just avoided an early election through their recent negotiation of the Pact. Labour was in no better position than before the 23 March confidence vote, indeed, it would have been far worse, cutting a deal a week earlier only to then have to fight an unpopular campaign on the basis of petrol tax increases. The Government's conclusion, as expressed in Cabinet, was that even if the petrol tax vote could be won without Liberal support, it would make further cooperation over subsequent votes more difficult and effectively nullify any advantage that had been gained through the Pact. Even if the vote were not treated as a matter of confidence, such a rift between the Pact members at this early stage would also have likely encouraged further confidence vote challenges by the Opposition, with no guarantee of the Government's survival.[38]

Renegotiating the Pact

Renewal of the Pact in July 1977 has often been seen as inevitable or unimportant, the terms largely remaining unaltered and the Liberals continuing not to gain any significant concessions in terms of policy. Indeed, even some more scholarly considerations of Callaghan's Government tend to omit any reference to renewal of the Pact, treating the agreement as a single, uninterrupted period. An exception to this is Kirkup, whose does devote a chapter to examining renewal.[39] This process of renewal was of far greater importance to the minority government situation, the conflict over increased petrol tax providing a context within which the Government sought alternatives to the established agreement, as well as reconsidering its longer-term implications. In key strategy meetings considering renewal, the Government contemplated alternative options, which would lead either to an early election or to a different interparty agreement.

In contrast to the relative passivity of the Cabinet in agreeing the Pact, the renegotiation was preceded by Callaghan calling a Strategy Cabinet at Chequers for 26 June 1977. The meeting's purpose was to discuss the deal with the Liberals, alongside the Government's economic strategy.[40] Uncirculated records were taken by the Prime Minister's staff during the meeting, which were supposed not to have been retained, but, in fact, were deposited in the archives.[41] These provide a particularly interesting insight into the Government's approach to the renegotiation and some of the alternative approaches or formulations of the Pact that were proposed.

When Callaghan opened the Chequers Strategy Cabinet he 'said that the first question was whether to go on or to have a general election forthwith [...] whether to go on or not was a valid question for a minority government'.[42] That Callaghan chose to frame the meeting in this manner, had chosen to have it at Chequers with no officials present and had emphasised the importance of free discussion by ministers, shows the significance of all options being on the table regarding the Pact. Although some sentiments were expressed in favour of an early election, there was 'unanimous agreement' to accept the 'price' of Pact renewal, the Cabinet believing that an election at that time would not yield any positive result for the Government.

Callaghan's original preference towards renegotiation appears to have been one of simply continuing the agreement on the basis already established. The government leadership feared that a fresh round of negotiations would not only undermine the Pact, by eliciting further demands from the Liberals, but would also invite criticism and even wholesale rejection of the strategy by Labour MPs. Some Liberal MPs also appear to have preferred an extension of the Pact on this basis. However, the experience of the petrol tax dispute, along with backbench rebels defeating the Government over Finance Bill Committee votes, led others to question the Pact's basis. Liberal MPs, seeking reasons to justify to their wider party membership continuation of the agreement, pressed for further policy concessions as prerequisite to any renewal. These demands, alongside Steel's insistence that continuation of the Pact necessitated PLP approval, sought to bind the Government to their commitments.[43] This development necessitated both closer government consultation among decision-makers, and sensitive management of relations with the PLP.

In some cases, parties cooperating with each other have split, some members of a party choosing to continue to support a government or even becoming a full or associated part of the governing party, while others break away to return to being an independent political entity in opposition. A repeat of the historic 1931 Labour split upon entering coalition was much feared by Callaghan and other members of the Government during negotiations over the IMF loan in 1976.[44] Fears of a similar division arising from the Pact were given some serious consideration. While there had been initial disagreements, the Government perceived the relatively loose nature of the arrangement and lack of overt concessions as mitigating the potential for any irreparable grievances regarding the Pact on the part of Labour MPs. The greater risk of an intra-party split was perhaps that of the Liberals themselves, although the Government does not appear to have considered this contingency as distinct from the more general dissolution of the Pact.[45] A rather cryptic comment by Callaghan in a meeting with Steel on 14 December 1977 suggested that if, as seemed a distinct possibility at the time, the Liberals rejected the Pact, and, by extension, compelled their leader to stand down, the Prime Minister would try to find another position for him.[46] In the event, the Pact survived this particular hurdle and there are no other references to such a possibility in future meetings. It is more likely that such a statement possibly referred to a public appointment of some kind, rather than an invitation to join the Government. Nevertheless, that the offer was made shows something of the positive spirit of the working relationship between the two leaders.

While the short-term nature of the first stage of the Pact perpetuated a degree of uncertainty and necessitated renegotiation, this factor may also have, paradoxically, contributed to the agreement's successful continuation. The initial period acted as something of a trial run, demonstrating the working of the Pact to some of the Labour MPs who would otherwise have been likely to oppose it – showing that the Liberals could provide useful support to the Government in votes. Callaghan was also able to use the argument of a limited trial period in both private and public communication in order to counter criticisms that the NEC and other Labour decision-making bodies had been bypassed. The breathing space allowed the Government time to consider and talk out some of the issues of interparty cooperation, as well as to consult and gain the, albeit reluctant, approval of the PLP.[47]

As with the initial stage of Pact negotiation, there appears to have been some codified consideration of strategic implications, but not that of detailed negotiation briefings. The Policy Unit did prepare a memo for the Chequers Strategy Cabinet, at Callaghan's request, which considered questions of strategy. The paper was much commended by members of the Cabinet, and appears to have been particularly valued by Callaghan, as indicated not least through the annotations on his copy. While the bulk of the document was focused on electoral considerations, it does contain useful insights into how government strategy-makers conceived of their overarching approach to minority government and to formalised interparty cooperation. The paper stressed the significant opposition poll lead and the unrealistic chances of winning any early election. Further to this, and underlined by Callaghan, the paper set out that the 'first objective must be to stay in office beyond the present discontents'.[48] To meet this objective, maintaining the Pact was perceived as crucial to the Government, and was the only formalised interparty cooperation envisaged. At the same time, this arrangement was not viewed as being totally exclusive. Some emphasis was also briefly placed on obtaining informal support from other parties, including the SNP, to buttress the Government's position: 'It obviously follows from this that maintaining the Liberal "alliance" is of prime importance (and that detaching the Scottish Nationalists from committed Opposition by a Devolution Bill would also help).'

Following on from this, the paper sought to forecast how long the Government could hold its current majority, based on the state of the parties in Parliament and historic by-election trends and results since the Second World War. The conclusion reached was that the Government could potentially *'survive for roughly two years – virtually to the end of this Parliament if we want*, unless we had a bad run of deaths against us [of Labour MPs] or if swings against us [in by-elections] were all of Ashfield proportions' (Ashfield being a formerly safe Labour seat that was lost on 28 April 1977 with a very large swing of over 20 per cent to the Conservatives).[49] Ironically, this last forecast of the Government's ability to retain its majority was in some ways actually remarkably prescient. Although Labour had to defend a further nine seats in by-elections up to the fall of the Government on 28 March 1979 (eight through death and one resignation), they only lost one of these seats to the Conservatives.[50]

One of the other main papers at the meeting, 'A Strategy for the 1980s', compiled by the CPRS, identified the Liberal Pact among its headings, but did not go into much detail in terms of maintaining interparty cooperation.[51] The paper was, in any case, widely criticised by government members for its tone.

Although not explicitly stated, the prospect of not renewing the Liberal agreement was briefly raised at the Strategy Cabinet, alongside the fact that the UUP did not want an election and might offer potential for a more complete Pact. Such a view followed on from perceptions of the UUP as more reliable than the Liberals in providing parliamentary support for the Government through abstentions. The break-up of the wider UUUC coalition in May 1977 enabled a potential deal with the UUP alone that would not raise some of the previous political difficulties of involving the DUP or Vanguard Party. However, the pre-existing issues were once again re-articulated: the Liberal deal was still seen as more likely to deliver the support of its MPs which the UUP could not guarantee, along with the potential backlash from Catholic voters and MPs if there were a more formalised UUP deal.[52]

It was preferred that renewal of the Pact would be for a further parliamentary session lasting twelve months. However, other possible timescales for the agreement were contemplated by both the Government and the Liberals.[53] Foot had raised the possibility of the Pact being renewed on a monthly basis, an idea rejected by other government decision-makers as too short term and uncertain. However, Foot raised this option only as a possible compromise to gain Liberal acceptance in the event that the Liberals would not commit to another full session, monthly renewal being favoured by some Liberal MPs, but not by Steel himself. From Foot's perspective, even a more short-term agreement that yielded greater uncertainty was better than no agreement and the prospect of an immediate election. Foot's actual preference, as expressed in the Strategy Cabinet, was for an even longer arrangement than twelve months, lasting until 'Autumn 1979'. The meeting initially endorsed this sentiment of making a deal with the Liberals 'for the next year and longer if necessary'.[54] Members from both parties had sought to explore lengthening the proposed Pact. In a conversation on 21 June, five days before the Strategy Cabinet, Pardoe approached Donoughue wanting to explore the possibility of an eighteen-month Pact, lasting until 1979. However, a meeting of Government Special Advisers the following day, as well as the aforementioned Strategy Cabinet, both ultimately endorsed renewal for a twelve-month session as the preferred option.[55] One fear, expressed in later discussion at the Strategy Cabinet, was that an extended deal would effectively commit the Government to a single eighteen-month parliamentary session, as opposed to the normal twelve months. Another concern was that this change in procedure would appear as 'cheating' to both MPs and the public. Further objections included the argument that the resulting difficulties in parliamentary management of MPs – whether curtailing Labour backbenchers' expectations for more controversial legislation, or preventing a repeat of the Opposition suspending cooperation with the Government as had happened over the Aircraft and Shipbuilding Bill – would outweigh any potential benefits. By talking through these alternative courses of action, managing potential opposition and making limited concessions, the Government was, in large part, able to maintain the substantive initial tenets of the Pact.[56] Like the initial setup, renewal of the Pact was concluded on 27 July by an exchange of letters between Callaghan and Steel.

As with the formation of the Pact, any changes in the proposed arrangements appear to have been aimed at giving the Government greater room for manoeuvre, avoiding firm legislative commitments or timetables which might have proved difficult to implement, justified as such in meetings between Callaghan and Steel. The most visible change in Steel's first draft, highlighted in annotations, was the watering down of any commitment on profit-sharing, from 'the Government intends to legislate in next year's Finance Bill for tax incentives' to the somewhat vaguer 'would consider what help could be given'. The final wording, while being slightly more positive, nevertheless did not reflect a firm timetabled commitment with defined policies, the Government's involvement in the area being 'to consider ways [...] with a view to legislation'.[57] The second draft, which was more heavily annotated, similarly removed references committing the Government to particular bills. For example, 'legislation to assist the agricultural industry' and a 'land bank' were changed to 'assistance to meet the special financial problems of farmers'.[58] In the same way, the definitive statement on 'a reduction of the burdens of taxation on income' was changed to a 'shift' in taxation 'so far as is permitted'. Where firm commitments to legislation were given, these redrafts also sought to stress primacy of the Government's input, as indicated in the case of 'legislation to provide help for first-time home buyers' through the addition of 'on the lines suggested in the Government's Green Paper on Housing Policy'.

Operation of the Pact

The successful operation of any formalised interparty agreement within a legislature typically (but not always) requires the creation and maintenance of certain structures and good relations between decision-makers. In addition to providing the basis for continuing an agreement, these structures may also be used strategically by parties to advance their own particular interests. Although the limitations of the Pact for both parties are often stressed, its operation demonstrated that the Government was attempting to engage in greater strategic consideration of how to handle formalised interparty cooperation with the Liberals, albeit with mixed success.[59]

The Government rejected commentators' and MPs' claims that the Pact was a formal coalition. Privately, however, some of the Government's strategy-makers, including Donoughue, did refer to the grouping of parties supporting the Government as a 'coalition', or as the 'alliance', and began to adapt their strategies over time to try to take advantage of some of the different mechanisms involved in formalised interparty cooperation, to strengthen the Government's legislative position.[60]

Following on from the formation process, a written agreement was able to be used by one or more parties to legitimise the rejection of further demands by other deal participants and help to lessen threats of such demands leading to the breakdown of the agreement.[61] After a December 1977 vote on the European Elections Bill, in which the Liberal preference for PR was defeated, the Liberals accused the Government of not fulfilling the deal and Steel sought privately to negotiate with Callaghan for further action on both this and other policy areas. Callaghan, supplied with briefing notes to counter these accusations, was able to quote the relevant part of their original written agreement from March 1977, along with lists of those supporting the bill supplied by the Government whips, in order to prove that he was upholding the deal, a contention which Steel subsequently accepted.[62]

Consultation mechanisms for managing any agreement may also be used strategically by a minority government in order to achieve their aims in terms of parliamentary legislation. Although the Consultative Committee is much cited as the public face of the Pact, much discussion and negotiation occurred between Callaghan and Steel in their regular meetings, along with other important figures, Foot and Pardoe in particular, who had significant input. Undoubtedly the lack of previous governmental experience, the inability at times to agree a common line and the absence of significant administrative support, were all factors that helped to undermine the Liberals in their negotiating with the Government. At the same time, the Government also sought to use ongoing negotiations as a means to realise their preferences.[63] As Kirkup has rightly emphasised, bilateral discussions between the two leaders were, to some extent, used by Callaghan to ensure government preferences in the face of potential Liberal opposition, from sharing information with Steel on Privy Counsellor terms which he could not then circulate to his colleagues but which also encouraged him to tone down his demands, to negating Liberal Defence Spokesman Emlyn Hooson's call for a reversal to defence cuts.[64]

The failure to resolve disputes has, in the past, frequently led to the breakdown of coalitions or interparty agreements, and, often as a direct consequence of this, the collapse of governments. A strategic approach to this problem may include formal or informal mechanisms of conflict resolution, or more belligerent courses of action. For example, in some cases, parties may actually deliberately seek a dispute with partners in order to: threaten the stability of an agreement as a means to enforce their will over a particular policy; obtain a stronger negotiating position for a potential compromise; gain credit with potential voters for having stood up for a particular position, even if unsuccessful; or, provide an excuse to terminate the agreement prematurely. Where the breaking of an agreement is concerned, different factions within the parties may seek to pursue this approach, contrary to the wishes of their leadership.[65]

The Government's response to disagreements with the Liberals, and the resultant possibility of being defeated on particular issues, were themselves the subjects of internal debates. Some Labour MPs consistently advocated a policy of no compromise, believing that, if a government bill were defeated by the Liberals voting against, then the public would blame Steel and Liberal MPs.[66] One example of this approach was that of Labour MP Dennis Skinner arguing for pursuit of the Electricity Bill in the face of Liberal opposition in February 1978. While not necessarily informed by historical analogy, Skinner's approach was reminiscent of Wilson's attitude during the Short Parliament of 1974, and the more general tactic of daring opposition parties to vote down government proposals. However, while this approach had proved relatively successful in the past, this was in the context of a recently defeated Conservative Opposition, itself unwilling to trigger another election in early 1974. In 1977, the Government recognised that there were many equally significant issues where the Opposition would not abstain. Foot, reflecting the government position that had arisen after the petrol tax dispute, and desiring good relations with the Liberals to ensure the passage of future legislation, diplomatically refused to countenance Skinner's approach, publicly stressing the greater danger of losing the Electricity Bill, while rejecting the notion that the Government was making concessions to the Liberals.[67] In general, the Government endeavoured to get Liberal and other party support for such legislation where they feared the prospect of defeat.

By their own admission, the Liberals 'stumbled' into the dispute over petrol tax, and, as Kirkup suggests, continued to be divided and institutionally inhibited in terms of their approach to negotiations with the Government.[68] However, the record of meetings between Liberal MPs suggests that they did grasp the strategic importance of dispute as a means to ensure their continued independent identity. As a consequence of this, the Government sought to avoid being drawn into public quarrels with the Liberals by not raising issues or not putting forward legislation judged likely to spark disagreement. To avoid acknowledging Liberal influence on the prevention of this government legislation, various pretexts were used, including that of there being insufficient time given the crowded parliamentary schedule. While these reasons may not have always convinced those among the Government's critics, they allowed the defusing of potential conflicts that would have challenged the Pact. The Government also sometimes conceded points in discussions about legislation, some of which Liberals had either expected or even wanted to use to compel a dispute, or even modified or dropped legislation entirely, including over occupational pensions, restructuring of the electricity industry and reform of the Official Secrets Act.[69]

In addition to ensuring dispute resolution between governing parties, agreements also rely upon the resolution of disputes that can arise within a governing party. While unable to resolve Labour's divisions, the Government was able to avoid an internal party split. Greater consultation of Labour backbenchers had been raised even before the Government lost its majority in April 1976, formal reports looking into ways of improving coordination between ministers and backbench groupings. Callaghan had also stressed the importance of good liaison with backbenchers following April 1976. One of the first questions Callaghan was asked in Parliament following his announcement of the Pact was an intervention from Skinner, seeking reassurances over continued consultation of Labour MPs. Callaghan subsequently sent a minute to Cabinet ministers on interparty cooperation, emphasising the need to avoid any perception that the Liberals were being given preferential treatment or consultation in advance of existing internal Labour Party and TUC consultations.[70] There was also an open letter to the Prime Minister in May 1977, signed by sixty-seven left-wing backbenchers, who, by virtue of their numbers, demanded the same facilities of consultation as had been extended to the thirteen Liberal MPs.[71] This initiative does not appear to have been acted on by Callaghan, nor further pursued by the MPs in question. While Kirkup may be right to suggest that Callaghan's citing of the existing methods of cooperation negated the impact of the letter, the Prime Minister was clearly concerned about the problem.[72] In meetings with all the Government whips in later May and June 1977, Callaghan cited this letter, stressing the need to ensure PLP cooperation was working.[73] In spite of continued vocal opposition to the

Pact by some members of the PLP, and backbench rebellions in Parliament, there was no further sustained attempt by a large group of Labour MPs to challenge formally the Pact, suggesting that the Government's management of perceived Liberal influence was, to some extent, effective.

Smaller parties will usually seek to publicise their particular contribution to a government by relying on interparty cooperation. In some agreements or coalitions there are even specific mechanisms designed to ensure that individual parties have their input highlighted. It is, of course, equally possible that parties, large or small, will seek to circumvent such mechanisms and claim all credit for policies.[74] Although some members of the Callaghan Government were sympathetic to the Liberals, there was a general desire to avoid giving them credit in terms of policy-making, in spite of this being a clearly articulated Liberal goal. Callaghan himself stipulated to Steel from the outset that he saw the agreement as providing Liberal input into the general process of policymaking, but not having policies that would be identified or labelled as 'Liberal' contributions to the government programme. This view reflected existing majoritarian attitudes, but also concerns that such publicity would encourage greater Labour backbench opposition to the Pact and to those particular policies. In response to Liberal demands, some additions to speeches were made, but these did not explicitly acknowledge Liberal input into the policymaking process beyond thanking them for sharing and supporting the intentions of the Labour Government on a particular subject.[75]

Exit strategy

Arguably one of the most important elements of any interparty deal is how the end of the agreement is handled. If conducted well, the different parties determine the timing, have control over the process and, while returning to a state of greater interparty competition, remain on good terms and able to continue cooperating in the future, either informally or through another agreement. If the exit is handled badly, then an often unexpected, acrimonious and unilateral breakdown of relations ensues, which can lead to an immediate election and adverse political consequences for some or all of the participants. Regardless of the circumstances, the Pact would still have had to be ended at some point, renewed indefinitely or transformed into some other kind of interparty agreement, possibly a full coalition. The former option presented the only realistic outcome. The Pact was only ever conceived of by most within the Government as a temporary expedient, had faced much criticism from MPs and members of both parties, and could not deliver policies on PR or other substantive measures that were crucial to continued Liberal participation.[76]

However, in spite of this apparent lack of benefits for the Liberals and increased hostility between some members of the two parties, the ending of the Pact was actually relatively well handled by both sides. An end date was formally agreed in advance, the Liberals maintained their commitment to ensure the passage of the Devolution Bills after the end of the agreement and Steel's public statement signalling the end of the Pact was cleared by the Prime Minister's staff with only minimal amendments – seeking a more positive portrayal by removing references to the 'no confidence debate' that had led to the agreement, and maintaining government flexibility on timing by removing a suggestion that the session would finish at the 'end of July'.[77] While the end of the Pact followed the failure to deliver PR and proved to be a disappointment for the Liberals, the fact that the Pact was ended by mutual agreement was, in itself, a successful accomplishment for both sides, and did not seriously imperil the position of the Labour Minority Government. Although the Government was largely dependent on the Liberals' deciding whether or not to renew the Pact, there was greater awareness and consideration of the strategic implications of exiting the agreement than is normally appreciated.[78]

From the outset of the Pact, the Government recognised that the agreement would end at some point, and that this process would need to be managed, although there does not appear to have been any initial attempt to explore or to codify an exit strategy. Discussions over the issue in the early months particularly manifested themselves in terms of fears of a sudden collapse. Even when renewing the Pact, concerns were raised in Cabinet on 28 July 1977 that the Liberals might have drafted parts of the agreement, including over pay policy, as a deliberate means to allow themselves the prospect of breaking the deal early if it were judged to be politically advantageous. It does not appear that this was viewed as a significant threat by the Government, although contingencies were put in place for having to fight an autumn 1977 election, as discussed in Chapter 7. While this 'escape clause' does indeed appear to have been intended by some Liberal MPs and peers, the prospect of using it as a means to break the Pact was never seriously considered as an option.[79] Just as the Government feared that calling an election over a legislative defeat would not prove popular in the country, the Liberals recognised the danger of breaking the agreement and forcing an election over an issue which would be perceived as 'obscure' by the public, such as over PR in European elections, or which would be directly unpopular, such as that of preventing high pay rises for low-paid workers. Steel's personal investment in the Pact succeeding as part of his wider political strategy gave added incentive for him to ensure it was maintained.[80] At the same time, there was some recognition in the early stages of future agreement, not least in the cited Policy Unit Strategy paper in June 1977, which briefly pondered the question of the Pact ending in the future as part of an attempt to forecast its likely lifespan, linking longevity to political and economic success as an effect upon the decision-making of participants: 'Whether, in fact, the Government would wish to go on to the bitter end, and whether the Liberals would wish to go along with the Government, will of course depend upon whether our prospects improve and demoralisation does not set in.'[81]

There has been some suggestion from Donoughue that Steel's acceptance of the ending of the Pact had been based on the assumption of an autumn 1978 election, and that both he and Pardoe, who in any case favoured a longer deal, would have sought to keep the agreement going if they had known that there would be no election until 1979.[82] Callaghan had expressed his preference for continuing the agreement into 1979 during a meeting with Foot, Steel and Pardoe in May 1978, although without contradicting their perception of the inevitability of an early autumn election in the event of the Pact ending. Even if it were the case that the Liberals had misinterpreted Callaghan's intentions, it is unlikely that renewal of the Pact could have worked given the defeat of PR for direct elections and the Liberals' disagreement over the 1978 Finance Bill – the Government did not seriously attempt to pursue ways of further renewing the Pact. Both Steel and Callaghan agreed in one of their meetings that the Liberals no longer had 'anything they could reasonably ask for', and that there was nothing that the Government could muster its MPs to support, which would justify continuation of the agreement. Substantive proposals of getting an amendment for PR in the Devolution Bills or a nationwide referendum on PR were suggested by Steel in a subsequent meeting as possible bases for renewal.[83] However, these policies appear to have been recognised by all participants as being undeliverable by the Government, there being a sizeable number of Labour MPs who would likely oppose most vigorously any deal that sought to deliver PR. In a special meeting of the Cabinet on 25 May 1978, held to discuss the end of the Pact (albeit without any officials being present), Callaghan, based on his prior consultation with Cabinet colleagues, began by dismissing the PR amendment plan as unworkable.[84]

At the same time, the Government did engage in attempting strategically to manage the end of the Pact and its aftermath as far as possible. Even when the non-renewal of the Pact became a certainty in a meeting with Steel in April 1978, Callaghan suggested that the best outcome was a 'clean break', rather than an acrimonious breakdown over a row about the Budget. In terms of presentation, Callaghan preferred a unilateral statement, with the Liberals resuming their independence, rather than both parties ending the agreement, an alteration to the proposed mutual ending announcement, which was accepted by Steel. Such a change enabled both parties to regain their full independence for fighting the subsequent election, while seeking to lessen the notion that the agreement had been broken by the Government. The Prime Minister also sought to delay the timing of the announcement of the end of the Pact. He stressed the potential harm to the markets that would be caused by an early announcement, and played for time by asking to take the Liberal proposals on devolution PR to a meeting of the full Cabinet, allowing for a further two-week delay. However, while there were disagreements between the two sides, the managed ending of the Pact enabled continued interparty cooperation between Labour and the Liberals, including in such areas as: continued work on the Devolution Bills; the discussions in the following months between government members and their Liberal counterparts; and the contacts between Callaghan and Steel.[85] Indications from internal Liberal planning in early 1979 for possible future coalition preferences were more positive about another agreement with Labour, in spite of the difficult experiences of the Pact, and showed that the disengagement from the agreement had left open the possibility for future dialogue and potential cooperation between the two parties.[86]

The Lib–Lab Pact began largely as a reactive and ad hoc measure to prevent an imminent election, but its shape and method of operating were by no means foregone conclusions. Greater strategic consideration by the Government than has previously been recognised included the preparation of briefings by the Policy Unit that examined some of the implications of interparty cooperation with the Liberals and other parties prior to and during the lifetime of the Pact. The less-publicised agreement with the UUP, while never representing a true alternative to the Liberals as had been originally envisaged by some within the Government, nevertheless helped serve to complement the Pact in ensuring parliamentary majorities for legislation. This agreement did, however, also store up problems for the Government in terms of cooperation with the SDLP and other supporting parties.

The confrontation over petrol tax and the renegotiation process involved further strategic deliberation and led to the modification of government tactics. Alternative formulations of the Pact were considered, including monthly renewal or an even longer agreement into 1979, but were rejected for strategic reasons. Different mechanisms established by the Pact were utilised to varying degrees of success by the Government as means of pursuing its own objectives, whether in terms of curtailing some Liberal demands for additional policies by reference to the original written terms of the Pact, or engaging in negotiations with individual Liberal spokesmen while having access to greater briefing resources and channels for communication. The Government managed increasingly to use the facets of interparty cooperation in order to tie the Liberals into accepting Labour policy preferences on various issues, and withdrew legislation or conceded points to avoid disputes desired by the Liberals for tactical reasons.

Even though the Liberals ultimately voted to bring down the Government in 1979, disengagement from the Pact itself was managed remarkably well given tensions over the issue of PR for direct elections. The mediated conclusion of the Pact allowed for future cooperation between Labour and the Liberals, not least in terms of continued dialogue and mutual support on issues including passage of the devolution legislation.

While much attention has been focused on the Pact during this period, there were other arrangements of more informal interparty cooperation that were given serious consideration, both within the Government and Opposition.

Notes

1 TNA: PREM 16/1227, Conclusions of a Meeting of Ministers Held at Chequers, 26 June 1977.
2 For a discussion of some of the weaknesses of existing studies, see Kirkup, *The Lib–Lab Pact*, pp. 1–3, 50–1.
3 Andeweg, De Vinter and Dumont (eds), *Puzzles of Government Formation*, pp. 7–10, 48–9, 174, 191–3; Thorpe, *A History of the British Labour Party*, pp. 202–3; C. Mershon, *The Costs of Coalition* (Stanford, CA: Stanford University Press, 2002), pp. 9–10; Strøm, *Minority Government and Majority Rule*, pp. 13, 31–40, 68–70; R. Axelrod, *Conflict of Interest: A Theory of Divergent Goals with Applications to Politics* (Chicago: Markham, 1970), p. 16; Riker, *The Theory of Political Coalitions*, pp. 47, 255–7.
4 Oaten, *Coalition*, pp. 174–96; Seldon and Hickson (eds), *New Labour, Old Labour*, pp. 198–201; Morgan, *Britain since 1945*, pp. 400–1; Searle, *Country before Party*, pp. 256–7; I. Marsh, 'Liberal Priorities, the Lib–Lab Pact and the Requirements for Policy Influence', *Parliamentary Affairs*, 43:3 (1990), 292–321; Bartram, *David Steel*, pp. 140–78; Butler and Kavanagh, *The British General Election of 1979*, pp. 8, 34–7, 42–3, 93–7.
5 CAC: DNGH 1/1/16, David Lipsey – Personal and Confidential/The Political Situation, 21 March 1977. See Chapters 5 and 7.
6 D. Giannetti and K. Ineoit (eds), *Intra-Party Politics and Coalition Governments* (London: Routledge, 2008), pp. 174–5.
7 Teams are typically around four to five individuals, although can be far more substantial. Negotiations following the 2005 German federal election included 16 people in each of the two main teams, and a total of 190 negotiators in attached working groups. C. Clemens and T. Saalfeld (eds), *The German General Election of 2005: Voters, Parties and Grand Coalition Politics* (London: Routledge, 2013), pp. 176–8; Andeweg, De Vinter and Dumont (eds), *Puzzles of Government Formation*, pp. 39–40; Hazell and Paun (eds), *Making Minority Government Work*, pp. 43–4, 86.
8 Callaghan Papers, Box 19, 2741, Michael Foot and Roy Mason Report – Ken Stowe to Prime Minister, 18 March 1977; Kirkup, *The Lib–Lab Pact*, pp. 40–2, 50–1; Morgan, *Britain since 1945*, pp. 400–1; Mitchie and Hoggart, *The Pact*, pp. 10–11, 30–64; Bartram, *David Steel*, pp. 143–52.
9 C. Moury, *Coalition Government and Party Mandate: How Coalition Agreements Constrain Ministerial Action* (London: Routledge, 2013), pp. 1–8, 34–6, 74–5; Hazell and Paun (eds), *Making Minority Government Work*, pp. 69, 71–3; Butler, *Governing without a Majority*, pp. 56–71, 110–21.
10 Callaghan Papers, Box 19, 2741, Various Annotated Papers and Handwritten Notes on the Wording of the Lib–Lab Agreement, 20–23 March 1977; TNA: CAB 128/61, 12th Meeting, 23 March 1977; 128/62, 28th Meeting, 28 July 1977; PREM 16/1399, Stowe to Callaghan, 23 March 1977; Donoughue, *Downing Street Diary*, vol. 2, pp. 168–9.
11 TNA: PREM 16/1399, Cabinet: Liberal Party Agreement, 23 March 1977; Lord President and Mr Steel Meeting, 28 March 1977; Kirkup, *The Lib–Lab Pact*, pp. 86, 102–6; Bartram, *David Steel*, pp. 148–50; Steel, *A House Divided*, pp. 36–7.
12 *House of Commons*, Parliamentary Briefing Paper (2009), SN/PC/04426, 'Speaker's Conferences', pp. 1–10; TNA: PREM 16/842, Note of a Meeting to Discuss Representation at Westminster in the Context of Devolution, 12 October 1976; Donoughue, *Downing Street Diary*, vol. 2, p. 167.

13 TNA: 16/2069, Cabinet Meeting, 4 March 1974.

14 Callaghan Papers, Box 19, 2741, Assorted Papers, Written and with Annotations, 21–23 March 1977; TNA: CAB 128/61, 12th Meeting, 23 March 1977.

15 Callaghan Papers, Box 19, Prime Minister's Third Carbons, March 1977, Prime Minister to Leslie Spriggs, 30 March 1977; Callaghan, *Time and Chance*, pp. 458–9; Hazell and Paun (eds), *Making Minority Government Work*, pp. 6–7, 15, 42–3, 47, 86–7; Brazier and Kalitowski (eds), *No Overall Control*, pp. 10–18, 79, 84–111; Strøm, *Minority Government and Majority Rule*, pp. 19–20, 93–108; Butler, *Governing without a Majority*, pp. 53–5; L. Geller-Schwartz, 'Minority Government Reconsidered', *Journal of Canadian Studies*, 14:2 (1979), 1, 67–9.

16 Kirkup, *The Lib–Lab Pact*, pp. 1, 122, 157.

17 A short-term agreement of this nature was also at odds with Steel's public and private discourse. TNA: CAB 128/61, 12th Meeting, 23 March 1977; Donoughue, *Downing Street Diary*, vol. 2, pp. 168–71; Seldon and Hickson (eds), *New Labour, Old Labour*, pp. 193, 200; L. W. Martin and G. Vanberg, 'Wasting Time? The Impact of Ideology and Size on Delay in Coalition Formation', *British Journal of Political Science*, 33:2 (2003), 323–32; Bartram, *David Steel*, pp. 143–51.

18 The second Reinfeldt (2010–14) and first Löfven (2014–ongoing) Governments in Sweden, for example, both constitute minority coalitions.

19 Torrance, *David Steel*, pp. 92–9; Hazell and Paun (eds), *Making Minority Government Work*, pp. 34, 42–3; Brazier and Kalitowski (eds), *No Overall Control*, pp. 56–62, 99; Bartram, *David Steel*, pp. 145–51; Mitchie and Hoggart, *The Pact*, pp. 35–40.

20 George Clark, Political Correspondent, 'Tories Table Motion of No Confidence in the Government', *The Times* (19 March 1977); Our Political Staff, 'Alter Course or Face Election, Liberals Say', *The Times* (19 March 1977); Our Political Staff, 'Government Considers Deal with Liberals and Unionists as Means to Avoid Election', *The Times* (21 March 1977).

21 T. Quinn, J. Bara and J. Bartle, 'The UK Coalition Agreement of 2010: Who Won?', *Journal of Elections, Public Opinion and Parties*, 21:2 (2011), 304–9; Boulton and Jones, *Hung Together*, pp. 140–1.

22 Callaghan Papers, Box 19, 2741, Duty Clerk to Prime Minister, 19 March 1977; Cledwyn Hughes to Prime Minister, 17 March 1977; Christopher Walker, 'Ulster Unionists Want Devolved Assembly as Condition of Support in Confidence Vote', *The Times* (21 March 1977).

23 CAC: Hailsham MSS (1/1/8), 1 March 1974; Callaghan Papers, Box 19, 2741, Assorted Papers, Written and with Annotations, 20–23 March 1977; POLL 9/1/9, Telegram to Enoch Powell, 18 March 1977; TNA: PREM 15/2069; Donoughue, *Downing Street Diary*, vol. 2, pp. 167–70.

24 Callaghan Papers, Box 19, 2741, The 1976–77 Legislative Programme, 21 March 1977.

25 CAC: DNGH 1/1/16, David Lipsey – Personal and Confidential/The Political Situation, 21 March 1977.

26 Alternative reasons have been suggested for simultaneous negotiations in the UK 2010 case, including Clegg's desire to satisfy those within the Liberal Democrats who favoured a deal with Labour. The existence of a theoretical alternative partnership may have compelled Conservative acceptance of the alternative vote referendum, as signified in William Hague's statement on 10 May 2010, but the perception of bad faith may also have, in fact, reduced Liberal Democrat bargaining power in subsequent Conservative negotiations. Quinn, Bara

and Bartle, 'The UK Coalition Agreement of 2010', 301, 309; BBC Documentary, *Five Days that Changed Britain* (10 January 2011); 'Hung Parliament: Tories' "Final Offer" on Vote Reform', *BBC News* (10 May 2010); P. Webster, T. Baldwin and R. Watson, 'Brown's Parting Shot Starts Coalition Bidding War', *The Times* (11 May 2010); Boulton and Jones, *Hung Together*, pp. 166–70, 183–99, 227–31; J. Boston, S. Levine, E. McLeay and N. S. Roberts (eds), *From Campaign to Coalition: New Zealand's First Election under Proportional Representation* (Wellington: Dunmore Press, 1997), pp. 207–46.

27 TNA: CAB 128/61, 12th Meeting, 23 March 1977; Donoughue, *Downing Street Diary*, vol. 2, pp. 165–9; Seldon and Hickson (eds), *New Labour, Old Labour*, pp. 254–5.

28 Callaghan Papers, Box 19, 2741, Roy Mason to Prime Minister, 23 March 1977; Michael Foot and Roy Mason Report – Ken Stowe to Prime Minister, 18 March 1977; MF + LJC and Powell drafts, [n. d.].

29 CAC: DNGH 1/1/16, David Lipsey – Personal and Confidential/The Political Situation, 21 March 1977.

30 CAC: POLL 9/1/9, Harry West to James Molyneaux, 21 July 1977; HC Hansard, vol. 928, cols 1303–6, 1360–2, 1367–8, 1404–6 (23 March 1977).

31 Callaghan, *Time and Chance*, pp. 454–5; Kirkup, *The Lib–Lab Pact*, pp. 42–5, 84.

32 CAC: POLL 9/1/9, Correspondence between Enoch Powell and Michael Foot, 14–29 November 1977; James Molyneaux to Harry West, 27 July 1977; Letter to Ian O'Loan, 24 March 1977.

33 Callaghan Papers, Box 19, 2741, Foot and Powell Annotated Draft Letters of Matters Discussed, [n. d.]; Roy Mason to Prime Minister, 23 March 1977.

34 Kirkup, *The Lib–Lab Pact*, pp. 122–5, 157.

35 TNA: PREM 16/1225, 'Petrol Duty and the Liberals', 22 April 1977.

36 TNA: PREM 16/1225, 'Note for the Record', 20 April 1977.

37 TNA: PREM 16/1225, 'Petrol Duty and the Liberals', 22 April 1977.

38 TNA: CAB 128/61, 15th Meeting, 31 March 1977; 18th Meeting, 5 May 1977; PREM 16/1225, Meeting between the Prime Minister and David Steel, 31 March 1977; 3 May 1977; 'Petrol Duty and the Liberals', 25 April 1977; Donoughue, *Downing Street Diary*, vol. 2, pp. 174, 176.

39 Kirkup, *The Lib–Lab Pact*, pp. 165–82; Hazell and Paun (eds), *Making Minority Government Work*, pp. 20–3; Seldon and Hickson (eds), *New Labour, Old Labour*, p. 193; Morgan, *Britain since 1945*, pp. 400–1; Bartram, *David Steel*, pp. 157–60.

40 Donoughue, *Downing Street Diary*, vol. 2, p. 196–7, 204–6, 213, 221; Kirkup, *The Lib–Lab Pact*, pp. 135, 155, 173; Callaghan, *Time and Chance*, pp. 462–6; Seldon and Hickson (eds), *New Labour, Old Labour*, p. 200.

41 TNA: PREM 16/1227, Conclusions of a Meeting of Ministers Held at Chequers, 26 June 1977; Manuscript Notes [and typed-up version] taken by R. J. Meadway at the Chequers Cabinet, 26 June 1977; John Hunt to Prime Minister, 21 June 1977.

42 TNA: PREM 16/1227, Conclusions of a Meeting of Ministers Held at Chequers, 26 June 1977.

43 TNA: PREM 16/1400, Follow Up to the Prime Minister's Meeting with Mr Steel (Annotated), 30 June 1977; Donoughue, *Downing Street Diaries*, vol. 2, pp. 176, 197, 203.

44 Thorpe, *A History of the British Labour Party*, p. 199; Oaten, *Coalition*, pp. 18–19, 84, 93–6; D. Powell, *British Politics, 1910–1935: The Crisis of the Party System* (Abingdon: Routledge, 2004), pp. 4–5, 111–20; Hennessy, *The Prime Minister*, pp. 385–6; Laver and Schofield, *Multiparty Government*, pp. 16–18, 25–7, 221–42.

45 Donoughue, *Downing Street Diary*, vol. 2, p. 178.

46 TNA: PREM 16/1794, Meeting in the Prime Minister's Room at 4.05 p.m., 14 December 1977; Meeting in the Prime Minister's Room at 19:30, 14 December 1977.

47 Callaghan Papers, Prime Minister's Third Carbons, April 1977: Prime Minister to S. McCluskie, 7 April 1977; TNA: CAB 128/61, 17th Meeting, 28 April 1977; PREM 16/2201, Prime Minister's Statement in Labour Weekly, [n. d.].

48 TNA: PREM 16/1227, 'Chequer's Cabinet: Thoughts on the Government's Future Strategy', 2 June 1977.

49 *Ibid.* Emphasis in the original document.

50 P. Rose, 'The Wilson–Callaghan Government of 1974–79: By-opartys to the llowing the indecisive result in June 2017'elections (Eventually) Bring Down a Government', in C. Cook and J. Ramsden (eds), *By-elections in British Politics* (London: Routledge, 1997), pp. 215–27.

51 TNA: PREM 16/1227, CPRS – A Strategy for the 1980s.

52 CAC: DNGH 1/1/12, PU/346, 'Pre-Election Strategy – Prospects, Policies and Options for 1978/9', 22 December 1977; POLL 9/1/9, Correspondence between James Molyneaux and the Managing Director, Press Association, 22–28 November 1978.

53 Hazell and Paun (eds), *Making Minority Government Work*, p. 23.

54 TNA: CAB 128/62, 28th Meeting, 28 July 1977.

55 CAC: DNGH 1/1/17, Meeting of Special Advisers, 22 June 1977; Liberal Party Archive, LSE: STEEL A/3/1, Correspondence between Callaghan and Steel, 27 July 1977; Donoughue, *Downing Street Diary*, vol. 2, pp. 197, 203–5.

56 PREM 16/1401, 'Renewing the Agreement with the Liberals', 21 July 1977.

57 TNA: PREM 16/1401, 'DS's First Draft of Joint Statement', 25 July 1977; Meeting between Prime Minister and David Steel, 26 July 1977; David Steel to Prime Minister, 27 July 1977.

58 TNA: PREM 16/1401, 'Draft of Letter to the Prime Minister', 27 July 1977.

59 G. Loomes, *Party Strategies in Western Europe: Party Competition and Electoral Outcomes* (London: Routledge, 2013), pp. 35–41, 92; Hazell and Paun (eds), *Making Minority Government Work*, pp. 5–6, 15, 41–51.

60 CAC: DNGH 1/1/12, PU/346, 'Pre-Election Strategy – Prospects, Policies and Options for 1978/9', 22 December 1977; Donoughue, *Downing Street Diary*, vol. 2, pp. 170, 175.

61 Moury, *Coalition Government and Party Mandate*, pp. 74–5; C. Moury and A. Timmermans, 'Inter-Party Conflict Management in Coalition Governments: Analyzing the Role of Coalition Agreements in Belgium, Germany, Italy and the Netherlands', *Politics and Governance*, 1:2 (2013), 117–31.

62 TNA: PREM 16/1794, Meeting between Prime Minister and David Steel, 8 December 1977; 14 December 1977; Philip Wood to Prime Minister – Attached Notes, 14 December 1977.

63 Hazell and Paun (eds), *Making Minority Government Work*, pp. 6, 19–23; Butler, *Governing without A Majority*, pp. 52–4; Bogdanor, *Coalition Government in Western Europe*, pp. 32–58, 70, 132–3, 140–52, 269–70.

64 Kirkup, *The Lib–Lab Pact*, pp. 107–8, 120–1, 177.

65 A. Paun, *United We Stand? Coalition Government in the UK* (London: Constitution Unit, 2010), pp. 17–20, 26–7; Butler, *Governing without a Majority*, pp. 114–15.

66 Paun and Hazell, 'Hung Parliaments and the Challenges for Westminster and Whitehall', 216–17, 223; Bogdanor, *Coalition Government in Western Europe*, pp. 5–7; Burton and

Drewry, 'Public Legislation', p. 155; Butler and Kavanagh, *The British General Election of October 1974*, pp. 18–19.

67 LHASC: PLP Minutes, 23 February 1978.

68 Kirkup, *The Lib–Lab Pact*, pp. 122–4, 212.

69 LSE: STEEL A/3/1, Meetings of the Shadow Administration, 30 March 1977–29 June 1977; TNA: CAB 128/61, 17th Meeting, 28 April 1977; 20th Meeting, 19 May 1977; 128/62, 32nd Meeting, 20 October 1977; PREM 16/1795, Extract of a Meeting between the Prime Minister and David Steel, 7 February 1978; John Stevens to Ken Stowe, 9 February 1978; Ken Stowe to John Stevens, 13 February 1978; Legislative Programme 1977–78, 15 March 1978.

70 TNA: PREM 16/1355, Ministerial Consultation with the Labour Party, 29 March 1977; Prime Minister Personal Minute M21/77, 29 March 1977.

71 TNA: PREM 16/1399, Letter (Signed by Sixty-Seven Labour MPs) to Callaghan, 3 May 1977.

72 Kirkup, *The Lib–Lab Pact*, pp. 201–4.

73 TNA: PREM 16/1794, K. R. Stowe to Private Secretary, 2 February 1978; PREM 16/2214, Prime Minister and Whips Meeting, 16 June 1977.

74 Hazell and Paun (eds), *Making Minority Government Work*, pp. 45–51; Paun, *United We Stand?*, pp. 8–9, 36–7.

75 Callaghan Papers, Box 19, 2741, Cledwyn Hughes to Prime Minister, 17 March 1977; TNA: PREM 16/1399, Prime Minister and David Steel Meetings 21–2 March 1977.

76 Paun, *United We Stand?*, pp. 17–20, 36–7; Hazell and Paun (eds), *Making Minority Government Work*, p. 41; Butler, *Governing without a Majority*, pp. 122–34; Seldon and Hickson (eds), *New Labour, Old Labour*, p. 200; Searle, *Country before Party*, pp. 256–7.

77 TNA: PREM 16/2201, 'Draft Statement by the Leader of the Liberal Party' (with Annotations), 25 May 1978.

78 Kirkup, *The Lib–Lab Pact*, pp. 219–23; Steel, *A House Divided*, pp. 138–9.

79 LSE: STEEL A/3/1, Meeting of the Shadow Administration, 18 July 1977; Lord Byers to David Steel, 21 July 1977; TNA: CAB 128/62, 28th Meeting, 28 July 1977; PREM 16/1794, Meeting in the Prime Minister's Room at 4.05p.m., 14 December 1977; Meeting in the Prime Minister's Room at 19:30, 14 December 1977.

80 Kirkup, *The Lib–Lab Pact*, pp. 75, 184. See Chapter 4: Seeking defeat.

81 TNA: PREM 16/1227, 'Chequer's Cabinet: Thoughts on the Government's Future Strategy', 2 June 1977.

82 Donoughue, *Downing Street Diary*, vol. 2, p. 455; BBC Radio 4, *Today Programme* (26 February 2015).

83 TNA: PREM 16/1794, Prime Minister's Meeting with David Steel, 10 April 1978; 26 April 1978; 9 May 1978; Meeting between the Prime Minister and the Liberals, 10 May 1978.

84 TNA: PREM 16/2201, 'Note for the Record', 25 May 1978.

85 TNA: CAB 128/64, 24th Meeting, 29 June 1978; PREM 16/2201, Prime Minister and David Steel Meeting, 6 March 1979; Note for the Record, 27 September 1978; Prime Minister and David Steel Meeting, 19 July 1978; Donoughue, *Downing Street Diary*, vol. 2, pp. 331, 341, 347.

86 See Chapter 8.

6

The myth of exclusivity: informal interparty cooperation

The Prime Minister [Jim Callaghan] referred to other minority groups in the House and said that, as was plain, they were all, in their various ways, up for auction.[1]

This statement from Callaghan in a Strategy Cabinet on 25 May 1978, recorded separately from the official Cabinet meeting, highlights something of the complexity of interparty cooperation during the 1970s. The Wilson Government, while benefiting from the support of smaller parties for particular legislation, had largely eschewed making deals, preferring to dare opponents to defeat them, and being able to recover their majority, albeit slender, by October 1974. The prolonged life of the Callaghan Government, and the inability to drop or delay major legislation entirely, made this approach more difficult and necessitated greater engagement with other parties. While the Lib–Lab Agreement had a significant impact on the Callaghan Government, the particular emphasis on the Pact with the Liberals has served to obscure consideration of other forms of interparty cooperation. Here we will further challenge the myth that the Government's agreement with the Liberals was exclusive. We will also challenge the false assumption that the Opposition adopted an unsophisticated and hostile attitude to the Pact while simultaneously rejecting the possibility of working with other parties.

Half of the Callaghan Government's time in office as a minority administration occurred outside the Pact, ad hoc cooperation or proposed cooperation with other parties continuing throughout the life of the Government. This chapter will consider how these ad hoc deals were implemented by the Government concurrently with the operation of the Pact, as well as after its dissolution up to March 1979. We will then examine the Opposition's reaction to the Pact, their relations with the Liberals during the Parliament as a whole and Conservative initiatives regarding cooperation with other parties.

It should be noted that some communication between parties was routine during this period, rather than a specific response to the minority government situation. Along with the usual channels between Party whips, other circumstances compelled official interparty dialogue, such as, for example, on security policy in Northern Ireland.

Government cooperation

In spite of the Callaghan Government's general reluctance with regard to inter-party deals, the exigencies of minority government increasingly compelled them to confront questions of interparty cooperation. Although they do not appear to have drawn on international exemplars, some approaches adopted by minority governments elsewhere were considered by the Government. In large part, these decisions reinforced their adherence to the British tradition of minority government as instinctively majoritarian but also pragmatic in terms of seeking ad hoc cooperation. A number of devices were considered, including: building informal understandings with other parties; co-authoring legislation across party divides; constructing different majorities for related bills or even within the same legislation; and supplementing formally agreed or implicit understandings of support with case-by-case assistance from other parties.

Sometimes a government lacking a majority may seek to build on relations with other parties, without any negotiations or formal understanding, maybe even enacting policies specifically designed to predispose them towards future legislative support. As already highlighted in Chapters 3–4, Callaghan's early approach to minority government, from April 1976, was, to some extent, mirroring that of Wilson in 1974. Both governments acted as if possessing a majority, daring defeat while, at the same time, attempting to use institutional tools to ensure legislation was passed. Although devolution legislation had the added benefit of attracting the support of nationalist MPs, it was viewed primarily as a means of limiting electoral damage in Scotland and Wales, rather than as securing parliamentary majorities. The first major effort of the Callaghan Government towards seeking deals with the smaller parties followed the defeat of the timetable motion on devolution and the threat posed by the no confidence vote in March 1977 that led directly to the Lib–Lab Pact.

There was, however, at least some earlier consideration by the Government of different forms of interparty cooperation, even during its first months as a minority in mid-1976. As already indicated in Chapter 3, formation of the Government had been accompanied by considerations of greater formalised cooperation with the SDLP to retain a majority in Parliament.[2] Although this initiative was never acted on, Fitt, as the SDLP's single MP, already tended to vote with the Government. The Labour Party, independent of the government leadership, also continued to pursue discussions with the SDLP, not least through meetings between the two parties. In one such meeting with Labour's NEC in June 1976, the SDLP Chairman, Denis Haughey, did raise the issue of greater interparty cooperation in general, suggesting that 'it would be valuable if there were regular contacts between the respective Executive committees to establish friendly relations'.[3] While this sentiment was positively received, the NEC representatives did distinguish between the Government and the wider Labour

Party in their response. In spite of seeking better contacts, such discussions were primarily devoted to extra-parliamentary and longer-term issues, such as SDLP membership of Socialist International, and initiatives to secure greater state funding for the SDLP. These meetings were not considered by the NEC as part of any strategy to secure more parliamentary votes for the Government. Indeed, as set out in Chapter 8, the general sentiment in these meetings was against some of the electoral system reforms in terms of PR that had been proposed by the SDLP, not least because these would have necessitated 'coalitions'.

There have also been many instances in which minority governments have constructed majorities on a case-by-case basis. Formal pacts or agreements may also be supplemented through negotiations with other parties on individual bills, either when a formally supporting party will not back a certain bill or to garner greater legitimacy in the case of particularly important legislation.[4]

Although the Callaghan Government accepted some of the necessities of ad hoc interparty cooperation, their approach did not conform to some of these expectations arising from minority government experiences elsewhere. For example, it has been suggested by Bräuninger and Debus that during periods of weakened minority government (those without formal support from other parties) there is a significant increase in the amount of legislation co-authored by both government and opposition MPs.[5] In spite of greater efforts at infor-mal cross-party cooperation on specific bills, there is no indication during the Callaghan Administration that either of the main party leaderships sought more legislation being co-authored by MPs of different parties. Where such cross-party initiatives occurred, these often conformed to pre-existing arrangements, particularly those of individual backbench MPs introducing Private Members Bills that were, in any case, co-sponsored by fellow backbenchers from other parties. Party leaders would sometimes tacitly support such bills by allowing them more time to be debated or encouraging their MPs to vote in favour, but this was seen by the Government and Opposition primarily as advancing poli-cies favoured by their respective supporters rather than as a means of building further cross-party cooperation. One of the few instances concerning Private Members Bills where the Government considered facilitating such cooperation was on a bill regarding abortion. This initiative was, however, viewed as part of an effort to defuse controversy surrounding the issue and possibly to prevent the reintroduction of the bill, rather than as a result of minority government. The initiative was, in any event, not acted upon.[6] The absence of co-authoring perhaps reflected continuation of the British tradition of legislation largely being initiated by the Government rather than individual MPs, in contrast with the experience of minority governments in more consensus-based systems.

Another widely used option for minority governments is to construct dif-ferent majorities for different parts of a legislative programme. In this way, the support of one party may be used to pass a particular bill and another party to pass a different bill. In some cases, even more confusingly, different parts of the same bill may require almost completely different combinations of other parties in order to be passed.[7]

After the Callaghan Government's defeat on the timetable motion on the Scotland and Wales Bill in February 1977, questions regarding strategy towards future legislation were raised – the suggested approach, presented to the Cabinet by Foot, was that majorities would thereafter have to be constructed on a bill-by-bill basis using the smaller parties. There were, however, limits as to how far the Government would go in terms of using different party combinations. For legislation on the electricity industry, one suggestion brought to the Cabinet was the use of Conservative support to help aid passage of one bill on reconstruction of the industry, the measures being opposed by the Liberals. Conversely, it was suggested that Liberal support be used, at the same time, to pass another separate bill on the Drax B power station and nuclear safety, in a form which would have been opposed by the Conservatives. While the Government had reluctantly made deals with the Conservatives before, not least over the aircraft and shipbuilding industries, these alternate combinations were rejected, the Cabinet fearing that reliance on opposition votes would encourage further rebellions amongst Labour MPs and would also damage future cooperation with the Liberals.[8]

Although government adoption of the different majorities approach was limited, this did not preclude seeking informal cooperation to supplement, or even act as a temporary replacement for, the formal Pact with the Liberals. In the aforementioned Cabinet discussion of 3 March 1977, when the minority government situation was being considered, Callaghan summarised the utility of ad hoc interparty cooperation in terms of future legislation: 'Ministers would have to construct the necessary Parliamentary majorities for their legislative proposals, by putting these proposals to the PLP and obtaining support for them, and by seeking support from the minority Parties, at the planning stage.'[9]

Even after the formation of the Pact, efforts of the Cabinet and whips were directed to build on existing contacts, through ascertaining whether smaller parties would support particular legislation, including, for example, that for-mulated by Stanley Orme, Government Minister for Social Security, reporting to Cabinet in May 1977 on ascertaining the views of the SNP and other par-ties on the Occupational Pension Schemes Bill.[10] The Government was also, in some cases, more actively seeking to encourage the support of these parties in individual votes by making changes to legislation or proposing amendments to accommodate their particular concerns.[11]

While formal approaches were made to both the UUP and the Liberals, there does not appear to have been any attempt during negotiation of the Pact to gain formalised support from the SNP or Plaid Cymru. Nevertheless, as highlighted by Kirkup, this did not prevent the Government from considering other ad hoc forms of cooperation to win the 23 March confidence vote in 1977.[12] By contrast, during the coalition negotiations in February 1974, informal contacts had been established between Heath's Conservative Government and the SNP, including the outlining of potential conditions for nationalists to provide support to a Conservative or Conservative–Liberal Minority Government. Such a course of action may not have been open to the Callaghan Government, given the SNP's desire for an election at this point, which, following the failure of the Government's devolution legislation, offered the potential of electoral gains at the expense of the established parties. Even if an agreement with these parties had been technically feasible, the Cabinet had rejected the possibility, considering the political price of doing a deal with the SNP to be too high – likely to push Scottish Labour MPs into opposing the Government and further endangering the party's seats in Scotland at the subsequent general election. The two ex-government MPs of the breakaway Scottish Labour Party, Robertson and Sillars, had, in the early days of the minority government, still been effectively taken for granted as part of the Government's seat count, as indicated in Chapter 4. The failure of the devolution legislation had removed this support. Both MPs were in correspondence with Foot on 21 March 1977, offering to vote with the Government on the confidence motion in return for reintroducing the guillotine vote on the Devolution Bill and making it a vote of confidence. This offer similarly does not appear to have been followed up, not least, as with the SNP, because of the unacceptable political price and likely opposition from other Labour backbenchers.[13] The prospective two votes were, in these circumstances, in any case insufficient in themselves to stave off defeat.

Only the day after the Pact was formally announced, the Cabinet considered contentious legislation concerning industrial democracy in the Post Office. While favouring Liberal cooperation, the meeting considered that the bill could potentially be secured using SNP and UUP support, even in the face of Liberal opposition. Although the Government's attempt to maintain the general support of Scottish and Welsh nationalist MPs through devolution legislation is more widely recognised, there were also attempts of varying success to encourage their support for other government measures, including the Occupational Pensions Bill and aspects of the 1978 Finance Bill. It does not generally appear, however, that reliance on the SNP and Plaid Cymru was widely countenanced by the Government, fearing the potential negative impact to their own electoral position in Scotland and Wales. It is notable that, during the 1978 passage of the devolution legislation, there was a particular effort by the Government to ensure that the bills were passed by a sufficient margin rather than by a bare parliamentary majority. This was in an effort to counter the potentially politically damaging notion of the Government having to rely on nationalist votes to deliver on devolved assemblies.[14] At times during the Pact when Liberal support was uncertain, particularly concerning conflicts over the 1977–78 Budgets and direct elections, government strategy-makers speculated about a potential future need to rely on alternative party combinations. Donoughue, for example, came to reflect in subsequent months on the possibility that UUP support could theoretically allow the Government to survive even if the Lib–Lab Pact broke down and the SNP voted against the Government.[15]

While dismissing the possibility of a Pact extension, the Strategy Cabinet meeting at Chequers on 25 May 1978 did discuss some alternative ways forward. Suggestions did not include other formal agreements, but rather a recognition that the different groups in Parliament were, in the minuted quote from Callaghan at the beginning of the chapter, 'in their various ways, up for auction'.[16] The absence of further pacts at this stage reflected the widespread perception within the Government that an election would most likely be only a few months away, in the autumn of 1978. In spite of this perception, members of the Cabinet stressed the need to avoid attacking the Liberals directly, and justified this course of action either as a means of preventing Liberal MPs from breaking the Pact early, or in order to encourage the Liberals as a party to focus on attacking the Conservatives.

Following the end of the Pact, the Government did maintain ad hoc cooperation with the Liberals, including on the passing of the devolution legislation, continued support for which had been promised by Steel. When legislation was raised in Cabinet as lacking a stable majority, such as in terms of a proposed National Insurance surcharge in June 1978 to answer a successful Budget amendment by the Opposition, the Government had to concede a lower increase than had been planned in order to obtain Liberal support.[17] Although the Liberals were voting more against the Government, partly to re-establish their independent identity following the Pact, informal contacts did remain between the two parties, with Callaghan being able to meet Steel privately for discussion in July and September 1978. Steel made it clear in the latter meeting that the Liberals would vote with the Opposition against the autumn Queen's Speech. However, Steel also explained that the Liberals were taking this course of action while assuming that the Government would win the vote. Indeed, it is recorded by Stowe in the minute that 'Mr Steel seemed to hope they [the Government] would! [win].' Steel further indicated that the Liberals 'would thereafter deal with each issue on its merits'.[18]

At the same time, this did not mean that the default position became one of the Government making deals to ensure a majority. In some cases, the Government decided not to bargain for potential legislation that was otherwise unlikely to succeed. Instead, as was explicitly stated in private, they would not put forward such measures until they had regained a parliamentary majority, such as over the gilt market or reform of the Official Secrets Act.[19] In other cases, the Government did sometimes decide that daring their opponents to defeat them was a preferable option, rather than negotiating with other parties or shelving legislation. When a prospective Dividend Control Bill became necessary to extend existing controls in July 1978, the Liberals were again considered as the party to be approached. In this case, however, there was division within the Government as to whether they were willing to accept a deal at the Liberal price of setting an earlier date when the temporary legislation would cease operating, a few months as opposed to a full year. Callaghan's summary of the discussion reflected the Government's earlier and instinctively majoritarian approach of daring defeat: 'it would be premature to accept a compromise with the Liberals at this stage'.[20] The Government's preferred aim in this case was very much one of risking defeat and, if it occurred, blaming the Opposition and Liberals. In the event, the Liberal amendments to the Dividends Bill in terms of timing were not passed. The Opposition, not viewing the measure as carrying the same importance or likelihood of success as amendments to the Finance Bill, did not commit their full voting strength to the divisions, allowing the Government to win by margins of over 200. The bill was passed into law by the end of July.[21]

While the Government talked about daring defeat on some other issues, this was not something that they were willing to apply particularly widely and, when applied, was not always successful. The aforementioned Dock Labour Scheme, which was going through Parliament at around the same time as the Dividend Bill, similarly faced the explicit opposition of both Conservatives and Liberals, lacking support from other parties. The Cabinet expressed the concern that 'The overall political situation required that the Government should not unnecessarily risk defeat at this time.'[22] Despite disagreement, the Cabinet decided that the political imperatives, including pressure from the TUC, required them to adopt the approach of daring defeat. However, the Government's leadership did not consider defeat to be a reasonable outcome in this instance, Callaghan stressing that the bill 'should be proceeded with despite the risk of defeat. But it was important that every effort should be made to secure a majority for it.'

The Dock Labour Scheme was subsequently defeated on 24 July 1978 by 301 votes to 291. Although there were calls for it to be reintroduced in the subsequent Queen's Speech in autumn 1978, the lack of support from smaller parties meant that it was instead given as one of the aspirations that Callaghan would address in his speech on the possible measures in a future majority government.[23]

In some instances, concessions may be designed as much to facilitate future cooperation with other parties as to further a particular deal. There were some cases where the Government consciously decided to let the Liberals 'win' in terms of making concessions designed both to ensure the passage of legislation and also to ensure their support – allowing the Liberals to claim that they had influenced government policy, not least, for example, in lowering the aforementioned National Insurance surcharge.[24] Paradoxically, such an acknowledgement of Liberal success would have been previously unacceptable to Labour under the Pact. While the Government's initiative here may well have reflected as much an attempt to limit the taking of Liberal votes by Conservatives at the upcoming general election, it also served as a mechanism to retain Liberal support in parliamentary votes or the prospect of negotiation with them over other legislation.

However, there were limits to the effectiveness of this approach, in terms of what Callaghan could offer and how far the Liberals would feel indebted to the Government for these 'victories'. In addition, the Liberals feared that overt support for Labour would damage them further, given the hostility they were already facing from their membership, and the negative publicity over the then recent legacy of the Pact. Following on from this, it was not possible to retain Liberal support in the final stages of the Government, as witnessed in the no confidence debate of March 1979.

As will be discussed further in Chapter 7, Callaghan's decision not to call an autumn 1978 election was primarily conditioned by the knowledge that he could be relatively certain of a parliamentary majority for another Queen's Speech, through private assurances from the UUP. Callaghan also reported to Cabinet in October 1978 the conclusion from his September meeting with Steel that 'after the Queen's Speech the Liberals would consider each measure on its merits: they would not wish to vote regularly with the Conservatives'. Nevertheless, as with earlier measures, Callaghan also cautioned that implicit support given could not necessarily be relied on, and echoed the sentiments of the March 1977 Cabinet meeting before the Pact was even considered, that, in coordination by Foot and the Chief Whip: 'It would however be necessary to construct a majority for each Bill, and Ministers sponsoring Bills would need to consult individually with the minority Parties.'[25]

Even with the assurances received from some of the smaller parties, the Government did not wish to risk the Queen's Speech in the way that risks had been taken with the Dividends or Dock Bills. When Foot reported on the drafting of the Speech, he began by outlining that the committee: 'had sought to avoid provocation for the minority Parties to vote against the Motion on the Address, and for this reason they had omitted some material which would be attractive to the Government's own supporters and on which the Government's position would need to be reaffirmed'.[26]

Such subjects were instead to be saved for the speech by Callaghan or other ministers in the subsequent debate, highlighting the Government's intended goals for when it gained an overall majority. These speeches, occurring within the normal robust context of parliamentary debate, were viewed as less likely to put pressure on the smaller parties to oppose, while still allowing the Government to communicate its plans.[27] This signposting of future aspirations was very much in line with the experience of other minority governments, and of the Wilson Minority Government, which had used speeches and the publication of White Papers on future policy in 1974.[28] While, to some extent, such a move allowed the Government to survive, there were limits as to how far it ensured a majority on any given issue. When attempting to overturn defeat over the pay sanctions vote in November 1978, the Government did not pursue the matter, believing that the move would not be successful. Callaghan summed up the Government's view of the situation, and stated that, in this instance, 'the minority parties could not be relied upon for support'.[29]

While different forms of informal interparty cooperation were considered, adopted or attempted with varying degrees of success over the course of Callaghan's Administration, the Conservatives also had to deal with the various questions raised when endeavouring to construct majorities and defeat the Government.

Conservative reaction

The Opposition and the Pact

Although the Lib–Lab Pact is usually discussed in terms of Government/Liberal relations, it also had a significant effect on the Opposition, compelling them to confront significant challenges regarding their own approach to interparty cooperation. Questions arising included the potential for an opposition coalition, coordinated efforts to disrupt the Labour–Liberal partnership, and the scope and extent of Conservative relations with the Liberals and other parties.

As during the initial formation of the Callaghan Government, there was no suggestion in March 1977 of any opposition coalition being formed. There was no need for the Conservatives to consider one, the conditions being ripe for the traditional replacement of a government through an election. Opinion polls had given the Opposition a significant lead of up to 15 per cent, the economic situation in the country remained problematic, and important defeats over devolution and economic policy had made it more likely that the smaller parties would vote to bring down the Government and trigger an election which the Conservatives would probably win. While the Shadow Cabinet sought to be supportive of the UUP and to reiterate their calls for a Speaker's Conference on 'Northern Ireland Representation', it was agreed on 16 March that no formal offer should be made to them at that stage.[30] Thatcher did meet with UUP leader James Molyneaux immediately prior to the no confidence vote, but there is no indication that either side was seeking any kind of formal negotiations in terms of voting support. Sometimes a party either directly involved in or excluded from coalition negotiations may aim to gain political advantage by actively seeking to disrupt the formation of any potential agreement, particularly one which allows other parties either to enter or to remain in government. Following the 2010 UK election, Labour figures, including MPs, peers and special advisers, privately contacted Liberal Democrat counterparts, seeking to discourage participation in negotiations with the Conservatives.[31] In March 1977, the Conservatives' favourable electoral position in the opinion polls meant that they certainly would have had an incentive to prevent any deal that would keep the Government in power.

However, there is no indication in the Conservatives' strategic dialogue during March 1977 that they planned to attempt to disrupt negotiations between the Government and the Liberals, or to establish their own dialogue with Steel. Non-consideration of this approach may well have reflected the Opposition being caught unaware by the secrecy in which the Pact was established. Nevertheless, even if the Conservatives had previously known, it seems less than likely that they would have considered active disruption of the Pact in this way. As already outlined, their primary interest was in fighting and winning an election, rather than forming any alternative coalition. Rather, the preferred long-term Conservative approach to dealing with the Pact appears to have been extra-parliamentary. The Opposition wanted to focus on increasing Conservative support in the subsequent general election, as articulated in Shadow Cabinet meetings, by trying to appeal to Liberal supporters who were dissatisfied with the Pact, rather than endeavouring to gain support from Liberal MPs.[32]

Opposition relations with the Liberals

On the surface, it would appear that inauguration of the Pact led to an implacably hostile relationship between Conservatives and Liberals throughout the rest of the Parliament. This view was initially articulated publicly through the adverse reaction of opposition backbenchers and statements by members of the Shadow Cabinet after the Pact was signed. In electoral campaigns, whether local, by-elections or the general election of 1979, Conservatives criticised the Liberals and the Pact for 'propping up' the Labour Government and allowing the perpetuation of harmful socialist policies in the country.[33]

However, the Opposition's approach to the Liberals was, in fact, more complex than this initial impression would suggest. The Conservatives' strategic deliberations show the alternative courses of action under consideration, which sought to retain the possibility of future interparty cooperation with the Liberals during the course of the Parliament. After the Pact began, there were some initial changes in the way in which the Conservatives dealt with the Liberals in Parliament in terms of procedure. A Liberal request in June 1978 to be given one of the parliamentary supply days, allocated for opposition use to conduct a debate, was denied on the grounds that the Liberals formed 'part of the Government' through the Pact. By contrast, after the end of the Pact, a similar request in November 1978 was granted, explicitly justified as a resumption of 'the former practice' and normal parliamentary relations.[34]

The line agreed in the first Shadow Cabinet meeting following the inauguration of the Pact seems surprisingly conciliatory, emphasising 'sorrow rather than anger', targeting the Government rather than attacking the Liberals. In the early stages of the Pact, the CRD also challenged the idea of any condemnatory approach towards the Liberals. A CRD research paper, discussed in the Shadow Cabinet, suggested that this tactic would only work in the short term, that there was significant danger of the Liberals gaining greater electoral credibility if they were seen to be moderating a Labour Government and that there was a need for Conservatives to reach out to rather than blame Liberal MPs.[35] In practice, however, the Opposition's approach appears to have been more condemnatory than accommodating. The harsh language that tended to be employed against the Liberals in debates and electoral campaigns would suggest that the electoral conversion of dissatisfied Liberal supporters was given a higher priority by the party leadership than any attempts to gain the support of Liberal MPs. Nevertheless, there are no indications of contacts being broken off between Liberals and Conservatives in the same way that the Opposition's cooperation with the Government was withdrawn over the disruption to the usual channels in the summer of 1976. In fact, there were some continued instances of discussions between the Opposition and Liberals, and, indeed, of the Conservatives supporting Liberal amendments to parliamentary legislation. Some of the Conservatives' greatest successes in defeating the Government on votes during the lifetime of the Pact were only made possible by cooperation with the Liberals, including the politically important devaluation of the green pound and cutting income tax by 1p in the 1978 Budget.[36]

In this respect, while the Conservatives expressed public and private outrage at the Pact and sought long-term electoral gains at the expense of the Liberals, they continued to pursue some degree of interparty cooperation with them at times to achieve defeats on government legislation.

Opposition relations with other parties

While pursuing different legislative goals, the Conservatives also had to respond to government initiatives and pursue their own relations with other parties. Situated firmly within a majoritarian optic, the Opposition's strategic dialogues nevertheless show recognition of some of the implications of minority government and a desire to coopt other parties to achieve the defeat of government legislation. As highlighted in Chapter 2, the Conservatives had long-established historic experiences of interparty cooperation. In the years immediately preceding the Callaghan Government, the Conservatives had also pursued different forms of interparty cooperation, including through an attempted coalition with the Liberals in March 1974, and a campaign for a government of national unity in October 1974. While Thatcher was undoubtedly more hostile to notions of coalition than her predecessor Heath, she was also a pragmatic leader – a point emphasised in considerations of the Conservative experience in opposition before 1979, and her recognition of the importance of securing the support of other parties to defeat the Government in Parliament.[37] Even in mid-1975, the Shadow Cabinet had not ruled out the possibility of entering a unity coalition government in the event of Wilson's Government collapsing, while a 1922 Executive Committee meeting in late 1976 once again seriously considered the prospect, albeit that these instances were very much responses to looming economic and political crises at the time. Other Conservatives were also very much involved in interparty cooperation during this period, whether in terms of the cross-party campaign on Britain's EEC membership referendum, or the pursuit of formalised cooperation with other centre-right parties in Europe. While a general predisposition towards majority government remained, there was recognition among those formulating Conservative strategy of the need to consider the implications of how to respond to the minority government situation, not least in terms of the Lib–Lab Pact, and the potential for interparty cooperation in Parliament.[38]

By contrast with the overt condemnation of the Pact and limited ad hoc cooperation with the Liberals, the Conservatives adopted a somewhat different line towards the other parties in Parliament. There are clear indications that the Conservatives, while criticising the outcomes of government agreements with other parties, were actively seeking to avoid rebuking some of the smaller parties themselves, recognising the importance of protecting the possibility of future cooperation.

In July 1977, the Shadow Cabinet decided not publicly to criticise a statement by the UUP leader suggesting that there were some instances in which he would support the Labour Government. Similarly, in the aftermath of a deal between Labour and the SNP over a vote, there were calls in the Shadow Cabinet for condemnation, but there was also, however, a recognition by some at the meeting that the Conservatives would need to work with the SNP in the future to achieve anything against the Government's legislative programme. Some within the Opposition even went so far as to link this idea of maintaining working relations to the thought that if the SNP held the balance of power at a future election it might end up being necessary to cooperate with them in order to form a government. Although this line of argument does not appear to have been supported or pursued by the party leadership, the fact that it was even raised in the Shadow Cabinet showed a willingness to contemplate contemporary relations within the context of future interparty cooperation and minority government (discussed further in Chapter 8). This suggestion also reflected something of the effect which the initial success of the Pact had on the opposition mindset, as exemplified in the above-cited correspondence among Conservative strategy-makers, including researchers in the CRD who feared the potential success of the Lib–Lab Pact.[39] The Conservatives would also vote for amendments or no confidence motions put forward by these smaller parties, although this appears as much to have been a reaction to upcoming votes where they tied into pre-existing Conservative policy commitments or strategy for attacking the Government, rather than any deliberate attempt to court smaller party support.

Even prior to the no confidence debate in March 1977, and the subsequent events that led to the Pact, the Conservatives were considering improved cooperation with the UUP, albeit on an informal basis. This, nevertheless, was likely to prove difficult, given the split between the Conservatives and the UUP over the Heath Government's policies in Northern Ireland. An example of how this sentiment affected the UUP approach to the Conservatives during the Callaghan Government may be seen in Molyneaux's comments in a UUUC Executive Committee meeting in June 1976: 'Until such times as they [the Conservatives] came up with policies which were an improvement and which would undo the damage which they did – then they [the Conservatives and the UUUC] could not come to terms.'[40]

Indications of the Conservative approach to the UUP included an early March 1977 Shadow Cabinet paper dedicated to the question of finding ways to achieve better cooperation through continued informal contacts with individual MPs, along with public support for particular policies, including a Speaker's Conference on 'Northern Ireland Representation at Westminster'.[41] Following the inauguration of the Lib–Lab Agreement, the break-up of the UUUC and the Government's promise of a Speaker's Conference on Northern Ireland representation, Conservative efforts regarding cooperation with the UUP continued largely along the same lines, although gathering increased importance in the eyes of the Opposition's leadership. Conservatives voted for particular UUP amendments to legislation, including the desired retention of first-past-the-post in European elections, and pressed the Government on the issue of pursuing greater representation for Northern Ireland in the House of Commons. Towards achieving this end, some potentially more radical suggestions were put forward by the Opposition, one idea being that of promising to push through the increased representation as quickly as possible, and then immediately to hold a special general election in Northern Ireland on the new boundary lines, as a means to separate the UUP from supporting the Government. There were limits, however, as to how far the Conservatives pursued these efforts at improved cooperation, not supporting other amendments and supporting some but not whipping all their MPs to vote. The notion of a special general election was not pursued, nor does it appear that any formal Conservative/UUP voting deal was attempted during the Parliament.[42]

There are few indications of such formalised cooperation being considered. One of the most visible appeared beyond the primary strategy groups, in a 1978 report by the Young Conservatives.[43] The report examined the possibility of establishing formal links with the UUP, Official Unionist Party or even parties traditionally less aligned with the Conservatives, such as the Alliance in Northern Ireland. In part, this approach reflected the already-cited Conservative desire to hold and win a general election outright and UUP reluctance to form deals with the main parties. While emphasising the need to take a tougher line on security, there was also no suggestion among Conservatives of breaking the overall consensus with the Government over the security situation in Northern Ireland by offering the restoration of devolution on majoritarian lines as a means to secure UUP support. This attitude reflected a continuation of the Heath Government's position in 1974 when engaging in post-electoral coalition negotiations, recognising that a formalised UUP deal at that stage would likely drive some of the other smaller parties away from voting with the Conservatives.[44] The possibility of future formal cooperation between the Conservatives and the UUP after the end of the 1974–79 Parliament was, however, promoted by some within the Opposition, as we shall see in Chapter 8.

The forms of interparty cooperation that occurred during the 1970s minority administrations were more complex and involved greater strategic considerations by both the Government and Opposition than has often been appreciated.

Ad hoc cooperation between the Callaghan Government and other parties continued throughout the Pact and afterwards, helping to ensure the Government's majority for particular legislation. The Callaghan Administration did not engage in some forms of cooperation used by other minority governments, such as seeking to build greater ties with other parties in Parliament, co-authoring legislation or constructing alternate electoral alliances for different clauses within the same bill.

The Conservatives did not attempt to foster formal agreements with other parties, and were, to some extent, forced to react to the will of smaller parties and government backbenchers in any given vote. However, while condemning the Liberals' participation in the Pact, the Conservatives recognised the importance of continued cooperation with them to inflict defeats upon the Government. The Opposition's leadership also sought greater informal interparty cooperation with other groupings in Parliament, and did try to avoid taking actions that would dissuade other parties from supporting their attempts to defeat certain government proposals. Over the course of the Parliament, the Conservatives were able to inflict a number of reversals to government policies, culminating in their defeating the Government in a vote of no confidence on 28 March 1979.

The loss of the confidence motion in 1979 was a catastrophic failure for the Callaghan Government. The defeat represented a more majoritarian attitude to cooperation towards the end of the administration, and a miscalculation of how some MPs would vote, including the SNP representatives. Although some deals had been done prior to the vote, the limitations placed on what Callaghan considered to be an acceptable political price, or what ministers considered could be practically delivered in the face of government backbench opposition to forcing through the devolution proposals, served severely to restrict any potential room for manoeuvre.

These different experiments in interparty cooperation as a means to deal with minority government situations would provide an important foundation for the formulation of strategies for coping with the possibility of another indecisive general election. Both main parties, in considering these strategies and making plans, confronted the prospect of their participating in a further minority government, a pact or even a formal governing coalition.

Notes

1 TNA: PREM 16/2201, 'Note for the Record', 25 May 1978.
2 See Chapter 3: 1976: minority government revisited.
3 LHASC: NEC Minutes, 'Report of Meeting with SDLP Representatives', 24 June 1976.
4 Hazell and Paun (eds), *Making Minority Government Work*, pp. 42–8; Strøm, *Minority Government and Majority Rule*, pp. 99–108.
5 T. Bräuninger and M. Debus, 'Legislative Agenda Setting in Parliamentary Democracies', *European Journal of Political Research*, 48:6 (2009), 821–8.
6 The Government did back a Liberal MP's Private Members Bill on Homelessness as part of the Pact. TNA: CAB 128/61, 21st Meeting, 26 May 1977; 128/62, 24th Meeting, 7 July 1977; 25th Meeting, 14 July 1977; PREM 16/1395, Jeremy Bray to Michael Foot, 5 May 1977; Michael Foot to Jeremy Bray, 10 May 1977.
7 Shifting alliances have been much used in Scottish, Irish, Danish and Canadian minority governments. P. Cairney, 'Coalition and Minority Government in Scotland: Lessons for the United Kingdom?', *The Political Quarterly*, 82:2 (2011), 265–6; Hazell and Paun (eds), *Making Minority Government Work*, pp. 14–15, 31, 64; Brazier and Kalitowski (eds), *No Overall Control*, pp. 78–82; Strøm, *Minority Government and Majority Rule*, pp. 103–7.
8 TNA: CAB 128/61, 7th Meeting, 24 February 1977; 9th Meeting, 3 March 1977; 11th Meeting, 17 March 1977; 128/63, 8th Meeting, 2 March 1978; 10th Meeting, 16 March 1978.
9 TNA: CAB 128/61, 9th Meeting, 3 March 1977.
10 TNA: CAB 128/61, 20th Meeting, 19 May 1977.
11 Donoughue, *Downing Street Diary*, vol. 2, pp. 177, 237; Hennessy, *The Prime Minister*, pp. 392–3.
12 Kirkup, *The Lib–Lab Pact*, pp. 49–82.
13 In the actual confidence debate, Robertson and Sillars opposed the Government. Callaghan Papers, Box 19, 2741, Jim Sillars and John Robertson to Michael Foot, 21 March 1977; HC Hansard, vol. 928, cols 1413–17 (23 March 1977); TNA: CAB 128/61, 12th Meeting, 23 March 1977; PREM 15/2069, 10–11, 20, Record of Information Conveyed by Edward Taylor MP to Prime Minister on 2 and 4 March 1974; Thatcher MSS: PREM 16/231, 2 and 4 March 1974; Morgan, *Michael Foot*, pp. 348–52.
14 TNA: CAB 128/61, 13th Meeting, 24 March 1977; 17th Meeting, 28 April 1977; 128/62, 35th Meeting, 10 November 1977; 128/63, 18th Meeting, 11 May 1978.
15 Donoughue, *Downing Street Diary*, vol. 2, pp. 196–7, 204–6, 213, 221.
16 TNA: PREM 16/2201, 'Note for the Record', 25 May 1978.
17 TNA: CAB 128/64, 21st Meeting, 8 June 1978; 24th Meeting, 29 June 1978.

18 TNA: PREM 16/2201, Note for the Record, 27 September 1978.

19 TNA: CAB 128/64, 21st Meeting, 8 June 1978; 33rd Meeting, 28 September 1978.

20 TNA: CAB 128/64, 26th Meeting, 13 July 1978; 27th Meeting, 20 July 1978; 28th Meeting, 27 July 1978.

21 HC Hansard, vol. 954, cols 1939–40, 1984–93 (27 July 1978); HL Hansard, vol. 395, col. 1187 (31 July 1978).

22 TNA: CAB 128/64, 27th Meeting, 20 July 1978.

23 HC Hansard, vol. 954, cols 1320–5 (24 July 1978); TNA: CAB 128/64, 33rd Meeting, 28 September 1978.

24 TNA: CAB 128/64, 21st Meeting, 8 June 1978; 24th Meeting, 29 June 1978.

25 TNA: CAB 128/64, 35th Meeting, 17 October 1978.

26 *Ibid.*

27 TNA: CAB 128/64, 33rd Meeting, 28 September 1978.

28 Holmes, *The Labour Government, 1974–79*, pp. 15–18; Butler and Kavanagh, *The British General Election of October 1974*, pp. 97–100.

29 TNA: CAB 128/64, 41st Meeting, 30 November 1978.

30 CPA: LCC 1/3/13, 155th Meeting, 16 March 1977; 156th Meeting, 23 March 1977.

31 Hazell and Paun (eds), *Making Minority Government Work*, pp. 13, 62; BBC Documentary, *Five Days that Changed Britain* (10 January 2011); Boulton and Jones, *Hung Together*, p. 134; Butler and Kavanagh, *The British General Election of 1979*, p. 36.

32 CAC: Hailsham MSS 1/1/11, Diary Entries, 22–23 March 1977; CPA: LCC 1/3/13, 155th Meeting, 16 March 1977; 156th Meeting, 23 March 1977.

33 For example, see HC Hansard, vol. 928, cols 1317–18, 1334–5, 1353–5, 1360–3, 1372–6, 1393–8, 1403–4 (23 March 1977); Sandbrook, *Seasons in the Sun*, pp. 649, 801; Campbell, *Margaret Thatcher*, p. 90; Donoughue, *Downing Street Diary*, vol. 2, pp. 171, 175–6; Searle, *Country before Party*, pp. 249–50.

34 CPA: LCC 1/3/14, 165th Meeting, 15 June 1977; 1/3/15, 210th Meeting, 21 June 1978; 1/3/16/1, 225th Meeting, 29 November 1978.

35 CPA: LCC 1/3/13, 156th Meeting, 23 March 1977.

36 CPA: LCC 1/3/14, 104th Meeting, 11 January 1978; Seldon and Hickson (eds), *New Labour, Old Labour*, pp. 192–3.

37 Ball and Seldon (eds), *Recovering Power*, pp. 219–42; Searle, *Country before Party*, pp. 220–35, 244–5; Campbell, *Edward Heath*, pp. 630–8; Behrens, *The Conservative Party*, pp. 1–6, 22–9, 126–8.

38 CPA: CCO 20/7/21, Meetings, 17 September–9 October 1974; LCC 1/3/13, Liaison Group, 1st Meeting, 5 November 1975; OG 56/74/158; MF: Reel 95, 00082–7, Letter from Michael Fraser to Heath, 5 October 1974; Thatcher MSS: 1922 Committee Executive Meeting, 20 December 1976; PREM 15/2069.

39 CPA: LCC 1/3/14, 166th Meeting, 22 June 1977; 167th Meeting, 29 June 1977, 168th Meeting, 6 July 1977.

40 CAC: POLL 9/1/8, UUUC, Executive Committee Meeting, 18 June 1976.

41 CPA: LCC 1/3/13 154th Meeting, 9 March 1977.

42 CAC: POLL 9/1/8, UUUC, Executive Committee Meeting, 4 September 1976; 5 November 1976; 2/6/1/102, Memorandum from Philip Goodhart, 6 July 1977; CPA: LCC 1/3/7, 27th Meeting, 13 May 1975; 1/3/13, 130th Meeting, 2 August 1976; 164th Meeting, 25 May 1977; 1/3/14, 183rd Meeting, 14 December 1977; 184th Meeting, 11 January 1978; 9/1/9, Col. E. H. Brush to E. Powell, 24 July 1976.

43 THCR 2/1/3/14, Northern Ireland Report (Attached Covering Letter: Airey Neave to Margaret Thatcher), 11 December 1978.

44 TNA: CAB 128/53, 10th Meeting, 4 March 1974; PREM 15/2069, Telegram from Harry West; Note Setting Out Plan for Response and Reply Telegram, 2 March 1974; Thatcher MSS: PREM 16/231, 1–2 March 1974; 16/1035, Meeting Thatcher–Callaghan, 3 May 1976; Seldon and Hickson (eds), *New Labour, Old Labour*, pp. 254–7.

7

The myth of binary choice: electoral timing

All our considerations over the date of the election assume that Callaghan wants Labour to win with a majority [...] why should he? [...] would it not suit him to risk a hung parliament or even a slender Conservative majority?[1]

The date was 10 January 1979. The Conservative leadership were engaged in much speculation about the possible date of an election. CRD researcher David Nicholson's paper, from which the extract beginning this chapter is taken, questioned whether Callaghan was acting in the rational manner expected of a prime minister, or whether in fact he might not choose to hold an election even at a time which was disadvantageous to Labour. The date was 18 April 2017. Prime Minister Theresa May's sudden announcement of a snap general election caught most commentators by surprise, the Government having spent the previous ten months repeatedly playing down any talk of an early poll. In spite of the differences in contexts, both events highlight the critical importance of election timing, and the challenges faced by parties in government and opposition, seeking to anticipate when elections are to be called.

While many factors contributed to the April 2017 decision, May and her advisers would have been well aware of the historic examples of Callaghan in 1978 and Gordon Brown in 2007.[2] Both Labour leaders, taking over midway through a Parliament and regarded as cautious prime ministers, had allowed election speculation to build when the polls appeared favourable for them, only then not to call an early election for fear that the result was not guaranteed. Their hesitation led to Labour subsequently being swept out of power in 1979 and 2010. The indecisive June 2017 result will likely become a significant historical precedent of its own in years to come, about the contrary dangers of acting decisively by calling an early election.

Frequent media and scholarly reference to the ruling out of an election in 1978 has given rise to the persistent myth on electoral timing – that Callaghan faced a simplistic binary choice between an election in autumn 1978 or May 1979. The absence of commentary on the minority government in 1974 has given rise to a similar, albeit unstated, myth of electoral timing, that Wilson's decision to hold an autumn poll was likewise inevitable. In both cases, the choice is seen as having been made by the Prime Minister, following limited consultation.[3] However, both Wilson and Callaghan considered a broader range of potential dates, consulted a wider group of strategy-makers and engaged in more strategic thinking than has previously been recognised, all conditioned by the state of minority government and depending on factors including government defeats.

Other questions of timing, including the length of an election campaign, will not be considered in detail here, as this was primarily driven more by immediate political factors other than minority government. While, for example, some suggestions of a short campaign were raised during the Callaghan Administration, the Government tended towards holding a long election campaign, with senior figures, including Donoughue, calculating that this would provide more opportunities for the Opposition to make mistakes.[4] When the actual dissolution came in 1979, an added reason for a long campaign was that it would move the country further away from the recent unpopular events of the 'Winter of Discontent'.

Wilson: 1974

Commentators have downplayed the importance of any internal debates in 1974, regarding the choice of an autumn election as effectively pre-determined: it gave sufficient opportunity for publication of a series of official government 'White Papers' that showcased detailed plans for government if given a legislative majority; it occurred during a period when Parliament was in recess, making it easier for Wilson to retain the initiative in terms of presentation; and it came at a time of relative calm in domestic affairs, tangible benefits of Labour's newly enacted spending policies still very much in the public consciousness.[5] However, contrary to the conventional narrative, the choice of date was by no means a certainty; there was a serious prospect of an election occurring in June, or even earlier.

Prior to campaigning events, manifesto policies and media presentation, the timing of an election may have a critical impact on the result. The added parliamentary uncertainty of minority government has typically served to increase debate over electoral timing in countries where election dates are not pre-determined in advance by a constitutional requirement. In addition, there is a greater probability of an unexpected and early poll being called in situations of minority government, either as a result of a conscious government decision or an inability to pass crucial legislation in the face of concerted opposition. The timing of elections in relation to minority government has also not been much considered, possibly reflecting the preponderance of minority governments being formed in political systems where election dates are fixed, including the Scandinavian countries.[6] As a result of their more consensual approach to governance, many such minority governments have survived for a substantial period, or even their full term in office, without a legislative majority.

Both the Canadian and UK government systems have, in the past, operated in a similar way in terms of dissolving Parliament, allowing prime ministers the sole power over when to call elections within a given period. Both countries also show some similarities over dissolutions during periods of minority government, with prime ministers tending to favour, or being forced, to dissolve Parliament early, sometimes as little as a few months to two years after forming a minority government. In a favourable scenario for the incumbent, such a poll has been aimed to occur at a time when there is a likely prospect of the minority government gaining a majority. Following his minority in the February 1974 election, Wilson requested an election in October 1974 in which he gained a small majority.[7]

However, there are also alternatives to this practice which have not, at the time of writing, been adopted in the UK. One such variation on the timing of parliamentary dissolution includes instances of prime ministers who have chosen to fight an early election with the knowledge that the best possible outcome was likely to be a continuation of minority government, such as in New Zealand in 2002 and in Canada in 2008.[8] An election has therefore sometimes been used as a device to buttress the authority of a prospective minority or coalition government by confirming the relative strengths of parties' parliamentary seats, or even, possibly, strengthening the government's bargaining position in negotiations with other parties by gaining seats or votes.

Another variation, as already discussed, is that of prime ministers who either respond to, or deliberately set up, major legislative defeats or confidence votes by calling an immediate election, seeking to increase government electoral support by portraying opposition parties as being deliberately obstructionist or blocking popular legislation. In May 1974, Canadian Prime Minister Pierre Trudeau successfully baited opposition parties into defeating him in a vote on the Budget, calling an election in July which turned his minority into a majority government.[9] Wilson's Minority Government was facing significant parliamentary defeats at around the same time, and they were certainly much aware of this example. Although Wilson's subsequent decision for an autumn election was conditioned by the parliamentary losses, it was a response to them, not framed in the context of international experience, but rather that of British political history and necessity.[10] At the same time, however, Wilson's decision was subject to greater internal discussion.

Wilson sanctioned such debates on electoral timing, drawing on advisory papers, including one prepared for him by the No. 10 Policy Unit, and bringing the matter to a full Cabinet discussion (minus officials) on 2 May 1974. Such a decision may be reflective of Wilson's previous experience, reminiscent of a discussion that he had convened in 1970 concerning proposed election dates. This earlier conversation, however, was very much more restricted to an inner

Cabinet, rather than the full formal body. The discussion revealed clear divisions, with some, including Foot and Mellish, preferring an earlier date, while others, including Wilson, opted for the later date of October. The views put forward by the different sides are reflected to some extent in Labour's strategy papers. One proposition from the meeting advocated the use of government defeats against the Opposition as ammunition in a particularly early electoral campaign. Another argument suggested that more time was needed before any election to ensure that there were enough government successes to justify seeking a further mandate from the public.[11] Diary entries of these discussions, and of those between ministers and their advisers, would seem to indicate that the balance of those for and against a June election in the Cabinet were much more even than has often been appreciated. Wilson himself showed signs of wanting to keep the option for an earlier poll open, asking Donoughue on 22 April to plan 'strategically for an October election and tactically for a June election'. Ultimately Wilson appears to have been dissuaded from pursuing this approach by further discussions in early May, adverse news coverage and his own continued fear of electoral apathy, which he described as 'the big yawn'. There were even one or two more 'radical' voices within the Government who were willing to raise alternatives to a further election in 1974, floating the idea that minority government could be continued over a much longer period. While theoretically possible, this course of action was practically very difficult, and appears to have been largely ignored by contemporaries, although the subsequent experience of the Callaghan Government suggests that such a notion may have become more acceptable, or politically necessary, as the decade progressed. Wilson's control over election timing meant that Labour's internal campaign coordinators felt safe in assuming that there would be an autumn election. This was, in turn, reflected in preparations, the earliest draft manifesto being produced in early June and considered in detail during July.

Wilson's control over the timing of the election left the Opposition very much in the position of having to react, with the bulk of discussions on timing concerned with attempts to anticipate the most likely date of the election, mainly in the form of papers and monitoring conducted by the CRD. They were by no means totally reactive, however, with efforts from the outset also being directed to prepare for a variety of outcomes. Shortly after the February election, the Conservatives created an 'emergency' manifesto, which included multiple different opening sections that could be used depending on how any sudden dissolution had been brought about, including such outcomes as a surprise announcement by Wilson or a government defeat. Efforts were also undertaken to prepare guidelines for the leadership in the event of an early election and to map out a preliminary campaign approach.[12] While it was acknowledged that these documents needed more work, the decision to produce them recognised the need to respond quickly to any sudden dissolution.

Callaghan: 1976 to 1979

In Callaghan's case several years later, the binary choice involving autumn 1978 or May 1979 is a false representation of the internal debate. A contest earlier in 1978, or 1977 or even 1976 was viewed as a possibility, albeit less likely.[13] This added uncertainty over electoral timing affected the subsequent actions and planning of both major political parties, and resulted in a sustained though often obscured conflict, researchers trying to predict when the election would occur and plan their response in a way designed to outmanoeuvre the other side.

Efforts by the Government and Opposition to anticipate possible election dates from 1976 onwards may in one sense be regarded merely as an academic exercise until the actual dissolution of Parliament. It is clear, however, that the strategy of both was influenced by these forecasts. Assessing how seriously parties took the prospect of an early election, or tried to bring one about, requires consideration of potential dates alongside other general election preparations, particularly whether there were changes in the timescale in which the manifesto was assembled or organisational preparations set in motion.

At times when the Callaghan Government stressed the prospect of defeat on an important issue and the triggering of an election, this was primarily seen as a means of attempting to curtail rebellions by backbench Labour MPs, or as a form of brinkmanship to intimidate opposition parties, rather than actually wanting to fight an election over a particular policy defeat. The Government's efforts to avoid defeat through this method had varying degrees of success. Although some major votes in terms of the Budget or devolution were partly secured through this, it did not appear to have helped when Callaghan sought to head off a rebellion over industrial sanctions policy in the winter of 1978–79, a vote which the Government subsequently lost, significantly undermining their economic policy and becoming a key factor in triggering the disastrous strikes in the 'Winter of Discontent'. While the Government did not seek to set up defeats for itself on important matters or confidence votes, it did consider that the response to defeat on certain issues would be to choose to call an election, whether over the Budget or devolution. These were, similarly, threats that were not acted upon, either because the Government was successful in averting defeat, or accepted defeat in votes which would previously have constituted the basis for an election. Timing did play an important factor in some of these decisions, Callaghan wanting to avoid elections when the Opposition enjoyed significant poll leads, when particularly difficult news was scheduled to come out in terms of such issues as the economy and at times of the year that were disadvantageous in terms of holidays or poor winter weather.[14]

Fixed-term parliaments, or requiring a supermajority of votes to achieve an early election, are overseas practices that have only been adopted in Britain since 1999, in the creation of the devolved assemblies, and as a Liberal Democrat initiative in the 2010 coalition at Westminster. While these innovations theoretically provide a greater impetus for minority or coalition governments to be formed that could be viable for the duration of a Parliament, the calling of the early general election in June 2017 would suggest a continued adherence to a majoritarian vision by the main parties. Fixed-term requirements are no guarantee against early elections in other countries either, as witnessed, for example, in the German federal elections of 1983 and 2005.

The Liberals were also supporting the concept of fixed-term parliaments in the late 1970s. However, as far as can be determined, neither main party leadership was willing at this stage to think about giving up the advantages of controlling the timing of an election. In this regard, both Labour and the Conservatives continued to adhere to a primarily majoritarian mindset, desiring to win an election outright, or to adapt to situations of minority governance on a pragmatic case-by-case basis.

Evolving process of planning

There were many aspects of Labour's electoral planning which followed or built on existing procedures, from organisational questions of hiring staff and putting candidates in place to the preparation of the manifesto by the NEC in conjunction with (or often in opposition to) Cabinet ministers and the Prime Minister. Being in government, Labour's main concerns over electoral timing were those of considering when best to call an election or how to respond to an election compelled by parliamentary defeats. Minority government conditioned these preparations, the possibility of an imminent parliamentary dissolution leading to significant work on electoral timing by the Government. When Labour lost its majority in April 1976, the prospect of an immediate election was raised, but the first real consideration of a possible election was in March 1977. This was a purely reactive measure, amounting primarily to a paper supplied to the Prime Minister about the mechanics of election dates when it was feared that a defeat on a vote of confidence was imminent. Even in this paper, it was not suggested that such a defeat made dissolution inevitable, raising the possibility of consultations with the other parties.[15] When considering the response to the March 1977 confidence vote, Lipsey's paper on strategy suggested that the more reliable polling showed a 7 per cent Conservative lead rather than other projected leads of up to 15 per cent. He judged this smaller poll lead against historical precedents and contemporary conditions as being: 'not insuperable [...] about the same as our gains vis-à-vis the Tories in February 1974'.[16] However, even taking the most optimistic projections, Lipsey still counselled against an early election, believing that the prospective indecisive outcome would be undesirable: 'the best we could realistically hope for is a Parliament made up much as the present one is [in March 1977]', while the 'most probable result' was still a Conservative victory.

Wilson's unrealised fears of potential defeat over the Queen's Speech in 1974 had similarly been considered not as necessitating an election, as would have traditionally been expected, but as calling a separate confidence vote to reaffirm support. The subsequent majority secured by Callaghan through the inauguration of the Lib–Lab Pact in 1977 ended any threat of an immediate election.[17]

Most likely as a result of the potential defeat in March 1977, the Government became more proactive in the field of electoral timing as related to the exigencies of minority government. Callaghan requested that special contingency planning be done by the Policy Unit to deal with an election arising from a major legislative defeat. Planning included trying to anticipate when such defeats might occur and producing reports which recommended potential courses of action, papers being updated on a regular basis. Papers were also produced prior to particularly important votes whose passage could not be assured, such as the second reading of Devolution Bills in November 1977, which outlined potential measures to be taken in order to prepare for an election in the event of the legislation being defeated.[18]

Measures were adopted which would suggest that while 1978 was the preferred option, preparations were being made for a more immediate dissolution should the need arise. The joint NEC–Cabinet discussions of February 1977 began by highlighting the absence of a government majority as a crucial determining factor in the timing of an election and emphasising that this presented an urgent need to make preparations, in terms of resolving internal party conflict over a potential manifesto and the development of electoral strategy.[19] After a campaign committee was established in February 1977, the Government sought to calm fears about a sudden poll, placing particular emphasis on such a committee being formed typically eighteen months to two years in advance of an election. Nevertheless, the records of the newly formed Election Committee from March 1977, and reports arising thereafter on proposed organisational planning, reinforce the perceived impact of minority government on election timing. Plans for a summer publicity and membership campaign were framed explicitly in terms of preparing for an election from October 1977 onwards. The model recommended for these campaigns was that used during the minority government of 1974, when summer publicity work had served as preparation for an October general election.[20] As discussed in Chapter 5, Callaghan's framing the June 1977 Strategy Cabinet's renewal of the Pact with the opening question of whether to continue in office 'or to have a general election forthwith', shows the seriousness with which early dissolution was considered by the government leadership.[21] In putting forward the question, Callaghan cited the example of the Labour Government in 1951, which had been viewed as hanging on to the office prior to its defeat in an election later that year, while losing its authority as perceived by civil servants. Callaghan asked his ministers 'whether this was happening in Departments or in the country' in 1977. The meeting concluded that this was not the case, and that the best course of action was to continue in office.

Callaghan also sought to acquire information relating to the holidays in different constituencies from 1977 onwards, a factor long considered of political importance in terms of potential voter turnout. Correspondence entitled 'Election Contingency Planning' in September 1977 was directed at obtaining information about holiday dates while, at the same time, seeking to prevent the fuelling of speculation over a possible early election date. Alternative reasons for enquiring about the information were devised to disguise the true nature of the planning involved, including such devices as the 'provision of information for the planning of [the] Prime Minister's regional industrial visits', which was viewed as 'the best cover'.[22]

It would generally appear, however, that while accepting the possible need for an early dissolution, government strategy-makers did not prefer 1977 as an option for an election. Such sentiments may be seen in the previously cited Policy Unit paper for the Chequers Strategy Cabinet, which emphasised the need to 'stay in office', and advocated a later election in 1978–79.

Following on from such considerations, a potential 1977 election was ultimately ruled out. However, from 1978 onwards, an election seems to have been contemplated as a more realistic option by the Government, either by choice or enforced by a parliamentary defeat. When the possibility of a serious defeat was raised in strategy meetings concerning the Budget in April 1978, there was a much more definitive response from Callaghan, that an election would be held immediately in that instance. This approach is very much in line with minority government experience in other countries and British parliamentary practice – such votes being viewed as confidence motions, which were essential for governments to win. The early months of 1978 show the greatest evidence of immediate pre-election preparations by Labour in terms of organisation, including the hiring of campaign staff, the clearing of outstanding legislation in Parliament and the changing of planned autumn events in consultation with the TUC, such as public rallies. Even up until the point when Callaghan announced there would be no election, many within the Government had come to view dissolution in October as inevitable.[23]

In spite of earlier manifesto preparations being called for, the timing of such work would seem to argue against the influence of minority government and a possible early election. The NEC Home Policy Committee did not produce a draft of their basis for the manifesto until December 1978, and the final acceptance of the manifesto did not occur until the beginning of the election campaign itself in April 1979. However, this prolonged process is as much demonstrative of the level of conflict between the NEC and parliamentary leadership, rather than of any lack of impetus in response to minority government. The decision not to produce the manifesto basis until such a late stage also reflected a desire not to publish a finalised draft too far in advance, for fear of certain policies being undermined by opponents within the party. If an election had been called in the summer or autumn of 1978, the NEC was in a position to publish such a draft at a much earlier stage. When the need arose to finalise election arrangements after the loss of a confidence vote in March 1979, the NEC's ultimate begrudging acceptance of many of the Prime Minister's preferences shows how the impetus of an immediate election could (at least temporarily) resolve such disagreements and enable completion of the manifesto.[24]

Minority government: influence on timing

Much of the analysis of government planning with regard to election timing focuses around Callaghan's fateful decision to delay until 1979 rather than hold an autumn election in 1978 when conditions appeared more favourable for Labour. Academic and media commentators have often suggested that if an election had been held at that earlier stage, it might have led to government victory rather than defeat. The impact of the delay on contemporaries is seen as having been counterproductive for Labour, allowing the portrayal of the Government as clinging on to office, angering potential supporters including trade union leaders, and placing greater reliance upon support from the smaller parties in order to survive without a parliamentary majority. It has also frequently been suggested that Callaghan wished to retain freedom of manoeuvre over the choice of election date, or genuinely had not made up his mind.[25]

However, whatever the consequences of delaying the election, the decision-making process was more complex than has been thought. There were many strategic considerations involved, all of which were primarily conditioned by Callaghan's experiences and situation of minority government: securing a temporary majority for key votes; uncertainty about the potential result; fear over appearing opportunistic; greater consultation over timing; and attempting to negate the Opposition's strength by catching them off guard.

Previous accounts have typically characterised Callaghan as being driven on the choice of the date of the election by only a small handful of Cabinet colleagues, and, partly in response to their advice, making the fateful decision to delay until 1979. Callaghan's own retrospective account also alludes to various letters of advice from other sources, but appears to dismiss them as not having had any significant impact. However, as shown in the declassified files, Callaghan was more proactive in consulting a wide range of people on timing. It is also clear from these papers and from Callaghan's own annotations of strategy documents that his decision over electoral timing was significantly influenced by factors and advice relating to the minority government situation. These consultations included discussions between all the Labour whips, as well as meetings they had with Callaghan, reports from the No. 10 Policy Unit, advice from the full

Cabinet and extensive discussion in a meeting with trade union leaders. The papers from the whips' discussion, forwarded to the Prime Minister on 1 August 1978, showed that seven were against an autumn election, with only two unequivocally in favour. Callaghan's annotation of the paper also suggests some of the issues which had particular impact, including the section of the plan (which he had highlighted) to 'go as far as possible into 1979' before calling an election. There was also, paradoxically, a strong collective sentiment expressed against doing further deals with other political parties to remain in office during such a period. Even in his regular meetings with Steel during the Pact, Callaghan had raised the question of electoral timing, promising not to reach a decision before July or August 1978.[26]

The likelihood that an election would produce another minority government served as a strong deterrent to an early dissolution, as already indicated in Lipsey's March 1977 paper on strategy, and also highlighted through different discussions on election timing within the government leadership over subsequent months. In one such discussion between Callaghan and Stowe in September 1978, an early dissolution was viewed as probably leading to 'a parliamentary stalemate as at present' which would 'help no one'.[27]

Private Labour polling, suggesting that an indecisive result was potentially the best possible outcome of an autumn 1978 election, has been identified by different decision-makers within the Government, including Callaghan himself retrospectively, as one of the major factors which led to the delay in calling an election. Much as with polling in 2010, 2015 and 2017, the experiences of inaccurate forecasting of elections in the 1970s complicated any decision. The examples from history were very much at the forefront of Callaghan's mind. The three preceding general elections, 1970, February 1974 and October 1974, had all been called early, and had delivered poorer results for the incumbent government than predicted by opinion polls.[28] Handwritten notes of Callaghan planning his autumn ministerial broadcast highlighted the minority government political situation of 1974, as well as that of 1931, and indicated the Prime Minister's continued fears over indecisive results and interparty cooperation potentially leading to the breakup of Labour as a party.[29]

The Government also compared the potential limited electoral losses or gains in the light of recent experiences of minority. It was suggested that the 1974 minority government and subsequent Callaghan Administration in 1976 had both been strengthened by the particular nature of their composition; the former had replaced an unpopular Conservative Administration, while the latter had been originally been elected with a majority in October 1974. By contrast, a renewed Minority Labour Government after another election in 1978–79 was viewed as likely to find it very difficult to claim a mandate to carry out its policies, even if it won an increase in votes or seats. The trade-offs required in deals with other parties in a new post-electoral administration were considered to be significantly greater than had been the case for either Wilson or Callaghan. Contrary to other countries whose traditions included a greater acceptance of electing and sustaining governments through interparty deals, there was no desire among most senior Labour figures in autumn 1978 to enter an election whose outcome could, at best, be another minority administration.[30]

One of the factors which gave Callaghan the most reassurance in terms of delaying the election was, as previously discussed, the apparent guarantee of smaller party support to get the next Queen's Speech voted through Parliament. Tacit support from the SNP and at least some members of the UUP theoretically secured Callaghan against being forced to go to the country in late 1978. Even in December 1977, a paper on electoral timing, produced at Callaghan's request by the No. 10 Policy Unit, began by emphasising the importance of the minority government situation, but also argued that a 1978 election was not inevitable, given the parliamentary arithmetic.[31] Certainly, in his meetings with Steel, the Prime Minister had frequently referred to the end of the Pact, and resultant end of a stable government majority, as triggering or likely to lead to an early election. While, as suggested, the Government planned for a possible election being forced by a major legislative defeat, Callaghan wanted to avoid this if possible. There were also differences in terms of what would be considered an 'acceptable' defeat in a parliamentary vote. For example, Callaghan could at least entertain the possible risk of defeat over the Budget, but not over the autumn Queen's Speech. Rather than differences in the legislative issue at stake, this concern was as much a reflection of practical reality. A defeat during the autumn opening of Parliament would necessarily lead to an election in November or December, times deemed particularly bad politically, poor weather likely to affect negatively the turnout of Labour voters.

Callaghan's meeting with Steel in March 1978 is one of the most definitive statements of his reasoning, stipulating that if there were no guarantee of support, an autumn election would be necessary, while simultaneously endeavouring to secure Liberal support for the Queen's Speech, even in absence of the Lib–Lab Pact.[32] The Prime Minister's reactions to internal correspondence with strategy-makers also reinforce the importance of the secured majority for the Queen's Speech as a factor in determining electoral timing. In addition, he sought to lay the groundwork for an autumn session, requesting a paper that outlined what actions would have to be taken to ensure that the Government could carry on if there were no autumn election, in terms of critical votes that could not be delayed and handling other events including the devolution referenda.

One of May's significant justifications for the June 2017 election was that of opposition parties obstructing the Government over Brexit, although even from the outset the decision was criticised by opposing political leaders and some commentators as being opportunistic.[33] There are surprising parallels between this dialogue and Callaghan's mindset in 1978, one of his major concerns being that an autumn election risked appearing opportunistic, given that there was 'no great issue requiring settlement by [a] General Election' and no major piece of legislation whose passage had been prevented by the Opposition. Although the Government had continued to suffer parliamentary defeats, these were on isolated or more technical points, which were not important enough to warrant dissolution. Such issues, as assessed by Callaghan and others, would not serve to move public opinion towards the Government in an election campaign. Although previous preparations had been made in the event of a major parliamentary defeat, the possibility of seeking a dissolution on the basis of an 'obstructionist' opposition was rejected during autumn 1978. The potential charge of opportunism clearly appears to have weighed heavily on the Prime Minister, Callaghan privately fearing that timing any election to accord with the implementation of particular benefits, such as tax concessions, would be likely to produce significant negative publicity. There was also no effort to set up deliberately a major legislative defeat that would trigger an election, as has been practised in other instances of minority governments, and which had been contemplated during 1974 under Wilson. Both Callaghan and his advisers feared that any such loss would be perceived as an unacceptable weakness that would similarly undermine any electoral campaign. When faced with defeat in the March 1979 confidence vote, these attitudes had shifted somewhat, Callaghan increasingly opposing the use of deals with smaller parties to stay in power, even if this led to defeat.[34] Indeed, several whips were even willing to suggest at this stage that such a defeat would give a possible basis for a successful appeal to the country in an election, although presentation of this line of thought appears more to have been an attempt to make light of a desperate situation, rather than an indication of a shift in strategy, as we shall see in Chapter 9.

Another consideration Callaghan faced was that of counterbalancing the uncertainty of having no parliamentary majority by creating electoral uncertainty for the Opposition. By building up to an election without committing to a date and then either calling one if conditions favoured the Government, or delaying, Callaghan could seek to catch his opponents off guard. The experience of minority governments in other countries has shown instances of this approach, such as occurred in the build-up to the New Zealand election in 2002. Prime ministers have also sometimes used a potential election as a threat to compel the Opposition (or their own supporters) not to vote down a particular piece of government legislation, as had been the case for Wilson with the confrontation over the Queen's Speech in 1974. As suggested by some scholars, the calling of elections in relatively quick succession may also be used as a tactic to wear down the material and financial resources of opposition parties, particularly those of smaller parties, or as an attempt to compel those parties to reveal their plans prematurely, in anticipation of elections which are not then called.[35]

While electoral delay after a false build-up has typically been portrayed as an inherently detrimental approach for a government to adopt, popular perceptions during late 1978 were, in reality, more nuanced. Although political elites and groups including trade unions were annoyed by Callaghan's decision not to hold an election, the electorate's response was more mixed. As highlighted during internal Conservative correspondence between Patten and other CRD members, opinion-polling immediately after Callaghan's September announcement of no election showed a relatively even split between those for and those against the election being delayed (42% to 43%).[36] These polls also showed that the delay had not in itself significantly influenced which party people intended to vote for.

Some of those involved in shaping government strategy, including Walter Harrison, Labour's Deputy Chief Whip, viewed unsettling the Opposition as being of particular significance when they gave advice to Callaghan on election timing. By building up the expectation of an election and then delaying, it was thought possible the Conservatives might reveal some of their policy plans or use up funds early on campaigns which, through the changing political climate, would not necessarily be relevant months later during an actual election. The Conservatives' relative financial strength over Labour was even greater during 1977–78 than had previously been the case, and there were certainly calls by some advising Callaghan, including McNally, that it was important to seek a way to offset these material advantages. To some extent, this uncertainty over election timing did have the effect of unsettling the Conservatives, who went to the verge of printing their manifesto in large quantities in September 1978 before the no-election announcement. Conservative groundwork for an autumn campaign had also been laid through various publications and the buying up of costly advertising space which could not be recouped.[37] Spending in anticipation of an autumn election had certainly affected the limited finances of the smaller parties, including the SNP, who used up the then significant sum of £12,000 on poster advertising.[38]

After autumn 1978, the choice over an election date was to some extent restricted by political events, including widespread industrial action during the 'Winter of Discontent', but nevertheless remained an important issue which was given some consideration by the Government.[39] In a meeting with Steel on 6 March 1979, Callaghan discussed the response to the failed devolution referenda and the question of electoral timing. Once again, the absence of a majority conditioned his response. When Steel suggested that October 1979 be announced well in advance as the election date, citing the practice of Sir Alec Douglas-Home in 1964, Callaghan 'pointed out that he was not in the same position as Sir Alec, who had a majority'.[40]

The Opposition was, to some extent, wrong-footed by uncertainties over electoral timing and used up some of their party funds. In spite of this, however, Conservative resources and planning over the timing of the election were also being employed towards endeavouring to cope with alternative outcomes and capitalising on the opportunities presented by subsequent events.

Opposition planning

Conservative planning had begun early on in the Parliament to anticipate the timing of a potential election, as indicated in Chapter 3. The absence of a government majority made an early 'snap' election much more of a possibility, reminiscent of 1974. Efforts to forecast when such an election would be called and how to prepare for it ranged from CRD calendars charting important upcoming events to papers that analysed the multiplicity of factors which could influence Callaghan's decision. There was also significant debate as to how uncertainties caused by minority government should affect electoral preparations.

While the Government principally determined election timing, the Opposition also dedicated significant efforts towards anticipating any future election date. After 1976, the first serious Shadow Cabinet discussions on preparations for a general election were held in April 1977. These meetings concluded that production of the campaign guide in May would enable an election to be fought whenever it was called, and suggested that more policy documents should be produced to supplement existing plans.[41] Although an autumn election in 1977 was briefly considered, it was viewed as very unlikely.

Opposition efforts directed towards anticipating the potential election date largely built on the methods used in 1974, and were increasingly framed against the backdrop of the minority government situation.[42]

Attempts to predict Callaghan's decision considered a multiplicity of factors, including the economy, recent political history, opinion polls, by-elections, the Prime Minister's 'cautious' temperament and even sporting events (particularly major football matches involving Scotland or Wales, victories in which were thought potentially to benefit the SNP and Plaid Cymru). The overall conclusion derived from all these factors was the almost certain belief that the election would occur in 1978 rather than in 1979. Timing of actual preparations for an electoral campaign would suggest that the Opposition expected the dissolution of Parliament to come in the autumn of 1978, including requests for Shadow Cabinet manifesto contributions from January 1978 onwards to the circulation of the first draft manifesto in July.[43] Discussions of organisational arrangements were also very much based on this timetable.

Nevertheless, even in spring 1978, the prospect of an earlier election had not been ruled out. When examining the question of whether a 1978 election would be held in late June, one of the most important factors identified was that of the minority government situation, and the prospect that the Government would face difficulties in securing a majority for getting the Finance Bill through Parliament, without which there would have to be a summer election. Discussion and papers on the drafting process questioned whether it would be necessary to accelerate the pace of manifesto composition in the light of these developments.[44]

The removal of any threat of a June election presented Conservative planners with the challenge of the summer parliamentary recess and prospective autumn election. Prior to the October 1974 election, Wilson had capitalised on a long summer parliamentary recess to lay the groundwork for his successful campaign, and had been able to announce major future policies without being subject to legislative defeats or the same intensity of scrutiny from MPs. The Conservatives sought to thwart any government attempt to recapture political initiative during the 1978 recess, through such measures as a special summer campaign to foster greater awareness of issues that were a core part of the Conservative political programme, to provide a platform in anticipation of an autumn election. In the autumn, some within the Government privately acknowledged the effectiveness of this campaign in allowing the Opposition to maintain political momentum.[45] It is difficult, however, to tell how far these campaigns were inspired by the minority situation, rather than by ongoing general concerns regarding publicity and a desire to build up party membership.

The purpose of some contingency planning, was, by contrast, spelt out more clearly, a Shadow Cabinet in the spring of 1978 recognising the possibility that Callaghan could attempt to wrong-foot the Opposition by delaying the election. Measures were adopted to avoid being caught out by changes in the 'expected' date, not least, for example, in preparing an alternative series of publications on policy for autumn 1978 to be used in place of election literature, and in building up the autumn party conference to act as a substitute 'high point'.[46]

The subsequent delay in September 1978 led to serious reconsideration of Labour's planning by the Conservatives, although it was assumed that no election would be called during the winter period. Callaghan's definitive September announcement reinforced this assumption. Attempts to anticipate timing resumed in the beginning of 1979, although these appear to have presented even more of a challenge in spite of there being fewer than eight months of the Parliament remaining. The CRD January predictions, sent by Nicholson to Patten, of an election in March, June or October, did not carry any firm conclusion as to which was the most likely.[47] In fact, as highlighted in the introductory quote to this chapter, Nicholson went so far as to question whether it was incorrect to assume that Callaghan's sole motivation was that of gaining a parliamentary majority, and that he might, in fact, have more interest in securing longer-term goals rather than immediate political concerns: 'would it not suit him [Callaghan] to risk a hung parliament or even a slender Conservative majority?'

By March 1979, other considerations were being factored in by the Conservatives, such as the possibility of the election being held at the same time as European elections scheduled for June, a development which was seen as creating potential difficulties in campaign finances. This possibility was not, however, viewed as practicable, requiring legislation establishing the UK framework for European elections, which could not be passed by a minority government without opposition support. Similarly, any extension of the Parliament to the final October deadline was viewed as unrealistic, primarily because of the absence of the Government's majority and likely difficulties with important legislation. As such, the most likely election date considered was 10 May, not far from the actual date of 3 May.[48]

Other than attempting to obstruct government business, which itself carried risks of appearing irresponsible, one of the few ways for the Opposition to exercise control over the choice of timing would have been to compel an election by winning a vote of no confidence. A sizeable number of minority governments have been removed from office by being defeated in such votes, both in Britain and abroad. However, while the Conservatives continued to seek to defeat the Callaghan Government, and ultimately succeeded in a no confidence vote on 28 March 1979, there is no indication that opposition leaders perceived a forced dissolution as an integral part of their overall strategy. There is also no indication that the Conservatives wished to try to impose a specifically preferred election date upon the Government, prior to the loss of the confidence vote itself. Delaying an autumn election in 1978, when the Government appeared to be enjoying a period of greater political successes, ultimately benefited the Opposition, but was not necessarily viewed beforehand as a goal. Throughout the period, the main focus for the Conservatives remained that of trying to predict the date and to win the election whenever it was called.

Following the March 1979 confidence vote, the need for an immediate election was established and the question of electoral timing effectively diminished the room for manoeuvre for both of the main parties. However, even at this stage, the Government and Opposition were making final calculations of strategy over the preferred election date. Callaghan wanted to avoid being pressured into an 26 April election, to allow for a full rather than temporary Budget to be passed, albeit with the agreement of the Opposition. The Government's preference remained that of fighting a longer electoral campaign, which it was believed would be to the Conservatives' disadvantage. The Shadow Cabinet, fearing that the Government would seek a postponement to 10 May, decided to 'press strongly for April 26th' following the confidence vote. In the event, 3 May was settled upon as the election date and a largely uncontroversial Budget was agreed by both parties.[49]

The 1979 general election and preceding campaign have, in some ways, been regarded as an anti-climax, when compared to the dramatic events of the 'Winter of Discontent', and of the Government's defeat in the March confidence vote. In spite of some encouraging signs for the Government in individual opinion polls that showed Labour gaining ground during the campaign, a significant

Conservative victory was consistently predicted by commentators and pollsters. In line with previous minority governments in British history and administrations elsewhere, after the no confidence vote the Callaghan Administration was effectively operating as a caretaker government. Such an approach was, in fact, consistent with that of any British government in an immediate pre-election period, avoiding major policy announcements and either putting off substantial political decisions for whatever government was formed after the election, or else taking such decisions with the agreement of the Opposition.[50] However, in the same way that the timing of the election had been subject to the influence of the Government's minority status, the election itself also presented a significant challenge to both main parties, that of potentially leading to another indecisive result, which would necessitate a further immediate election, minority government or even a coalition.

Both main parties sought an exit from minority government through an election, had to confront the particularly important question of electoral timing and had to adapt their strategies accordingly. The considerations faced by Labour and the Conservatives were distinct from those of minority administrations operating in fixed-term parliaments, but were shared by contemporary minority governments in other countries, including Canada. The formulation of strategies conducted by both parties shows the clear and central influence of the state of minority government upon their planning. The Wilson Government's internal debates considered alternatives to an autumn election in 1974, while the Conservatives sought to develop methods to anticipate electoral timing and to have preparations in place, including their 'emergency' manifesto.

In the Callaghan Government's case, the question of deciding when to hold an election and the impact of not having a legislative majority were given much consideration. Labour's planning over election timing, which began even in 1977, drew to some extent on experience from 1974, and sought to anticipate the possibility of an early dissolution or an election being forced by a legislative defeat in Parliament. Callaghan's often discussed 'mistake' of delaying an election in autumn 1978 was based on a wide-ranging consultation within Labour. It showed an understanding of the dynamics of the 'hung parliament', and recognised the inappropriateness of the 'obstructionist opposition' argument often used by minority governments, while simultaneously making construction of a stable majority a central objective. Anticipating the uncertain timing of an election forced the Opposition to consider alternative electoral strategies and compelled researchers to question their assumptions about the mindset of their political opponents. Conservative planning started early on in the Parliament, developing from their existing fears of a snap or crisis election, and sought to anticipate possible election dates and to prepare for contingencies when the expected autumn election in 1978 did not materialise. Even in the final days of the

Government, following the no confidence defeat, both sides continued making strategic calculations over the more limited choice of date for the election, but were also able to continue cooperating where necessary to settle practical issues before the dissolution of Parliament.

Confronting the challenges of electoral timing in a minority government situation helped to develop the strategic understanding of both main parties, and affected their wider approaches to campaigning in the October 1974 and May 1979 general elections. Although political leaders and their advisers sought clear results from these elections, further indecisive outcomes were privately thought to be a significant possibility, particularly in 1977 and 1978. The prospect of another Parliament without a majority government further affected the main parties' planning, both sides seeking to a greater or lesser extent to adapt and develop strategies in order to deal with a future minority or coalition government.

Notes

1 CPA: CRD L/4/46/9: Letter from David Nicholson to Chris Patten, 10 January 1979; Memorandum on Election Timing, 23 February 1979; 'General Election Timetable' [Memorandum to Mrs Thatcher], 8 March 1979.

2 *BBC News* (18 April 2017); M. White, 'Theresa May Won't Call a Snap Election: Voters Don't Want One', *Guardian* (11 August 2016).

3 K. Jefferys (ed.), *Labour Forces: From Ernest Bevin to Gordon Brown* (London: I.B.Tauris, 2002), p. 89; Butler, *Governing without a Majority*, pp. 30–2; Holmes, *The Labour Government, 1974–79*, pp. 15–18.

4 Donoughue, *Downing Street Diary*, vol. 2, pp. 186–7.

5 Butler, *Governing without a Majority*, pp. 30–2; Butler and Kavanagh, *The British General Election of October 1974*, pp. 97–100.

6 Arter, *Democracy in Scandinavia*, pp. 98–100.

7 Russell, *Two Cheers for Minority Government*, pp. 83–4, 134–42; D. Childs, *Britain since 1939: Progress and Decline* (Houndmills: Palgrave Macmillan, 1995), pp. 183–4; Butler, *Governing without a Majority*, pp. 31–2; Strøm, *Minority Government and Majority Rule*, pp. 14, 103.

8 J. Vowles, P. Aimer, J. Karp, S. Banducci and R. Miller (eds), *Voters' Veto: The 2002 Election in New Zealand and the Consolidation of Minority Government* (Auckland: Auckland University Press, 2004), pp. 14–15, 184–5; *BBC News* (7 September 2008).

9 Russell, *Two Cheers for Minority Government*, p. 34.

10 Hazell and Paun (eds), *Making Minority Government Work*, p. 31; M. Laver and K. A. Shepsle, *Making and Breaking Governments: Cabinets and Legislatures in Parliamentary Democracies* (Cambridge: Cambridge University Press, 1996), pp. 210–11, 216.

11 LHASC: Campaign Committee Paper, 15 May 1974, 'Party Strategy'; MS. Wilson, c. 1288, Confidential Meeting, 1 July 1974; Donoughue, *Downing Street Diary*, vol. 1, pp. 68, 76, 99, 103–14; Castle, *The Castle Diaries*, pp. 82–4, 96–7; Seldon and Hickson, *New Labour, Old Labour*, p. 182; Butler and Kavanagh, *The British General Election of October 1974*, p. 4.

12 CPA: OG 52: 50th Meeting, 21 March 1974; 51st Meeting, 4 April 1974; OG 74/145, 'Preparing for a June Election: Notes towards a New Part I', 19 April 1974; 52nd Meeting, 25 April 1974; MF: Reel 95, 00211–30, Letter from Michael Fraser to Heath, 23 April 1974.

13 SC 14, 35th Meeting, 3 November 1975; CPA: LCC 1/3/11, 123rd Meeting, 12 July 1976. Even in March 1976, when the Government still had a majority, defeat over an Expenditure White Paper led to some concerns about an early election. Thorpe, *A History of the British Labour Party*, pp. 204–5; Wilson, *SNP: The Turbulent Years*, p. 130; Smith, *Election Timing*, pp. 216–17; H. Young, *One of Us: A Biography of Margaret Thatcher* (London: Macmillan, 1989), p. 127; Hennessy and Seldon (eds), *Ruling Performance*, pp. 262–3.

14 See Chapter 4: Seeking defeat.

15 Callaghan Papers, Box 19, 2741: PP/Lib–Lab: 77, 'Choice of Date for an Election' (and Covering Letter), 18 March 1977; LHASC: TUC–Labour Party Liaison Committee, 45th Meeting, 21 March 1977; TNA: CAB 128/54, 3rd Meeting, 14 March 1974; TNA: PREM 16/1045, 'Prime Minister's Talk with Chancellor Schmidt' (Extract), 28 April 1976.

16 CAC: DNGH 1/1/16, David Lipsey – Personal and Confidential/The Political Situation, 21 March 1977.

17 Strøm, *Minority Government and Majority Rule*, pp. 4–5, 102, 228; Castle, *The Castle Diaries*, pp. 41–3; Wilson, *Final Term*, pp. 15–16.

18 For an example of the regularly updated attempts to anticipate and plan for defeat of major legislation, see TNA: PREM 16/1045, 'Factors Affecting the Timing of a General Election, Revision as of 4 May 1978'; 16/1621, 'General Election Contingency Planning', 14 November 1977.

19 CAC: DNGH 1/1/18, 'Organisational Arrangements for the Next General Election', 7 July 1977; Callaghan Papers, 2755: NEC–Cabinet Working Groups 1977: 'Paper for Joint NEC/Cabinet Meeting', 14 February 1977; LHASC: NEC Minutes, 16 February 1977, Home Policy Committee: NEC–Cabinet Meeting: 'An Agenda for Agreement'; Donoughue, *Downing Street Diary*, vol. 2, pp. 304–5.

20 LHASC: NEC Minutes, 16 February 1977, Campaign Committee, 1st Meeting, 28 March 1977; 'Organisational Preparation', 1 April 1977; 25 May 1977, Home Policy Committee: 'A Further Note on the Programme of Work'; TNA: PREM 16/1240, Correspondence and Papers Including, for Example, 'Wakes Weeks and Other Traditional Holiday Periods', 1 December 1977; R. J. Meadway to Mr. Brazier, 10 October 1977.

21 TNA: PREM 16/1227, Conclusions of a Meeting of Ministers Held at Chequers, 26 June 1977. See Chapter 5.

22 TNA: PREM 16/1240, Note for the Record: Election Contingency Planning: Wakes Weeks, 29 September 1977.

23 Callaghan Papers, Box 19, 2743: 'Abortive General Election 1978', Annotated by Prime Minister – 'Timing of Elections and Age of Electoral Register' (and Covering Letter, Reg Underhill), 21 December 1977; LHASC: HART 12/10, TUC–Labour Party Liaison Committee, 58th Meeting, 24 July 1978; TNA: PREM 16/2214: 'Note of a Meeting Held in the Cabinet Room', 18 May 1977; Donoughue, *Downing Street Diary*, vol. 2, pp. 353–5.

24 Paradoxically, the fact that it was not introduced until after losing the no confidence vote in March 1979 probably strengthened Callaghan's ability to impose the terms of the secretly pre-prepared document on the NEC. LHASC: RICH 3/1/12, Tribune Group Minutes, 6 July 1978; Seldon and Hickson (eds), *New Labour, Old Labour*, pp. 268–70.

25 Thorpe, *A History of the British Labour Party*, pp. 204–5; Ball and Seldon, *Recovering Power*, p. 229; J. E. Cronin, *New Labour's Pasts: The Labour Party and its Discontents*

(Harlow: Pearson Education, 2004), pp. 189–90; Seldon and Hickson (eds), *New Labour, Old Labour*, p. 96; Morgan, *Britain since 1945*, pp. 216–17; Hennessy, *The Prime Minister*, pp. 393–5; Tanner, Thane and Tiratsoo, *Labour's First Century*, p. 233; E. J. Evans, *Thatcher and Thatcherism* (London: Routledge, 1997), pp. 14–18; Blake, *The Conservative Party*, p. 329; B. Särlvik and I. Crewe, *Decade of Dealignment: The Conservative Victory of 1979 and Electoral Trends in the 1970s* (Cambridge: Cambridge University Press, 1983), pp. 15, 18–19.

26 Callaghan Papers, Box 19, 2743: 'Abortive General Election 1978', Minute of Whips' Discussion concerning Election Timing, Sent to the Prime Minister with Chief Whip's Covering Note, 1 August 1978; TNA: PREM 16/1621; PREM 16/1794, 'Meeting between the Prime Minister and Mr David Steel', 7 February [1978]; PREM 16/2214, 'Minute of a Meeting Held in the Cabinet Room', 8 March 1978; Morgan, *Michael Foot*, pp. 360–1; Callaghan, *Time and Chance*, pp. 514–15.

27 TNA: PREM 16/1621, Note for the Record, 8 September 1978.

28 Thorpe, *A History of the British Labour Party*, pp. 204–5; Seldon and Hickson (eds), *New Labour, Old Labour*, pp. 96–7, 293; N. Moon, *Opinion Polls: History, Theory and Practice* (Manchester: Manchester University Press, 1999), pp. 94–7; Hennessy, *The Prime Minister*, p. 393; Callaghan, *Time and Chance*, p. 516; Penniman, *Britain at the Polls: 1979*, p. 99; Särlvik and Crewe, *Decade of Dealignment*; Butler and Kavanagh, *The British General Election of 1979*, p. 45.

29 Callaghan Papers, Box 19, 2743: PP/Elec/Lab: 78, Handwritten Notes, Various Dates September 1978.

30 Callaghan Papers, Box 19, 2737: Lab/Elec: 78–9, 'Personal and Secret – Prime Minister', 2 May 1979; Callaghan, *Time and Chance*, p. 516.

31 TNA: PREM 16/1621, Bernard Donoughue to Prime Minister, 'Pre-Election Strategy – Prospects, Policies and Options for 1978/9', 22 December 1977.

32 TNA: PREM 16/1794, 'Prime Minister's Meeting with Mr David Steel', 7 March 1978; Callaghan, *Time and Chance*, p. 513.

33 *BBC News* (18 April 2017).

34 Callaghan Papers, Box 19, 2743, 'Abortive General Election 1978', Strategy Paper Annotated by the Prime Minister as 'Very Helpful', Examining Implications of March 1979 Election; TNA: CAB 128/54, 1st Meeting, 5 March 1974; PREM 16/1621, Policy Unit 346, 22 December 1977; 'Note for the Record', 6 September 1978; PREM 16/2214, 'Note of a Meeting Held in the Cabinet Room', 21 March 1979; Castle, *The Castle Diaries*, pp. 41–5; Donoughue, *Downing Street Diary*, vol. 1, pp. 68–73; Wilson, *Final Term*, p. 39; Bell, *The Labour Party in Opposition*, p. 237.

35 Hazell and Paun (eds), *Making Minority Government Work*, pp. 5–8, 18–22; Vowles *et al.*, *Voters' Veto*, pp. 12–15; J. Boston, S. Church, S. Levine, E. McLeay and N. Roberts, *New Zealand Votes: The General Election of 2002* (Wellington: Victoria University Press, 2003), pp. 38–44.

36 CPA: CRD/L/4/46/9, 'The New Political Situation', 12 September 1978; Seldon and Hickson (eds), *New Labour, Old Labour*, p. 96; Boston *et al.*, *New Zealand Votes*, p. 28; Smith, *Election Timing*, pp. 48–9.

37 Callaghan Papers, Box 19, 2742: PP/Elec/Lab: 77, Tom McNally to Prime Minister, 24 June 1977; 2743: Abortive General Election 1978, Minute of Whips Discussion concerning Election Timing, Sent to the Prime Minister with Chief Whip's Covering Note, 1 August 1978; Transcript of Mr William Deedes Interviewed on World at One, 8 September 1978;

TNA: PREM 16/1621, 'Note for the Record', 6 September 1978; Callaghan, *Time and Chance*, p. 517.

38 P. Lynch, *SNP: The History of the Scottish National Party* (Welsh Academic Publishing, 2nd edn, 2013), p. 151; Wilson, *SNP: The Turbulent Years*, p. 156.

39 Donoughue, *Downing Street Diary*, vol. 2, pp. 412–16, 420, 427–8, 434–5, 439–42, 448–9, 452, 455, 458–62.

40 TNA: PREM 16/2201, Prime Minister's Meeting with Mr David Steel, 6 March 1979.

41 CPA: CRD/D/7/20: 'Staff in Confidence' (from Chris Patten), 20 September 1977; LCC 1/3/13, 160th Meeting, 27 April 1977; 1/3/14, 176th Meeting, 26 October 1977.

42 CPA: CRD/D/7/20, Angus Maude to Chris Patten, 29 October 1976; OG 52: 50th Meeting, 21 March 1974; 51st Meeting, 4 April 1974; OG 74/145, 'Preparing for a June Election: Notes towards a New Part I', 19 April 1974; 52nd Meeting, 25 April 1974.

43 CPA: CRD/D/7/19, The General Election, 3 January 1978; CRD/L/4/46/4, Note of Research Department Meeting, 3 April 1978; LCC 1/3/14, 186th Meeting, 18 January 1978; 1/3/15, 208th Meeting, 7th June 1978; 1/3/16, 216th Meeting, 19 July 1978; 218th Meeting, 31 July 1978.

44 CAC: THCR 2/11/9/6, 'Some Thoughts on the Date of the Next General Election', [date unknown – early 1978?]; CPA: CRD/D/7/19: 'A Paper by Lord Thorneycroft', 26 June 1978; CRD/D/7/23: Directors Meeting, 10 January 1978; 'General Election Arrangements', 5 January 1978; LCC 1/3/15, 199th Meeting, 17 April 1978 (and Attached Chairman's Note).

45 CPA: CRD/D/7/23: Directors Meetings, 14 March 1978; 21 March 1978; 23 May 1978; 6 June 1978; LSE: ABEL-SMITH/7/6, Folder 1 of 2, Meeting of Special Advisers, 21 September 1978.

46 CPA: LCC 1/3/15, 'Chairman's Note' – Meeting, 17 April 1978.

47 CPA: CRD L/4/46/9: Letter from David Nicholson to Chris Patten, 10 January 1979.

48 CPA: CRD L/4/46/9: Memorandum on Election Timing, 23 February 1979; 'General Election Timetable' [Memorandum to Mrs Thatcher], 8 March 1979.

49 CPA: LCC 1/3/16 (239th) Meeting, 28 March 1979; TNA: CAB 128/65, 14th Meeting, 29 March 1979.

50 See Chapter 9: Confidence defeat and election result.

8

Myths and secret plans: future minority governments/coalitions

Before and during a general election campaign there can be no public admission that the [Conservative] Party expects anything less than victory with an overall majority: to give any hint that we had planned for any other contingency would tend to increase the minority parties' vote. We have thought it prudent, nevertheless, to set down, in case they are ever needed in the aftermath of an election, some considerations first on the constitutional and historical aspects of a hung parliament, secondly on the contingency itself and thirdly on the psephological background.[1]

This extract from an internal Conservative strategy paper in April 1978 reveals a previously unrecognised dimension to opposition preparations, prior to the 1979 general election, for a post-electoral minority or coalition government. This general election, one of the most crucial events in the development of modern British politics, is well known as having ended the postwar economic consensus and laid the foundations for the transformation of Britain's major political parties. Accounts of the election have tended to follow an established pattern, either exposing the seeming inevitability of Conservative victory and the inexorable decline of Labour, or cautioning that there was considerable uncertainty among contemporaries regarding the result, but without examining the strategic reaction to these attitudes in any great detail.[2]

However, the myth that the parties only considered outright victory in this general election, and indeed, in the often overlooked election of October 1974, has discouraged investigation of their secret plans for a further hung parliament. Both the Government and Opposition were considering contingency scenarios that were publicly unmentionable, and making plans, particularly prior to 1979, for what would happen if there were another indecisive result. This chapter will examine the instances of secret planning by the Government and Opposition, looking at some of the more formal preparations for a future minority government or even a coalition that were explored through internal dialogues between policymakers.

In Labour's case, this was very much a sporadic effort, tied into day-to-day survival as a minority government. Consideration of a future minority administration was evident only from occasional references in meetings, and from papers produced immediately in advance of the 1979 election itself, to consider whether or not Callaghan would stay on as Prime Minister, along with some possible ideas about how to seek formal interparty agreements with the SNP, Liberals or parties from Northern Ireland, including the UUP or SDLP. For the Conservatives, a lot more planning for this eventuality is apparent, from the embryonic plans for a national unity government in 1974 to detailed and documented consideration of alternative options between 1977 and 1978. A short-lived minority government followed by another election appears to have become the preference of the opposition planners when confronted with an indecisive result, although different options for a potential coalition were also formulated, again considering parties including the UUP, Liberals or SNP. Even a grand coalition with Labour was discussed, which, however unlikely, shows something of the detail in the plans, and the intellectual context of radical thinking that these involved.

This chapter will also study some of the approaches used by parties elsewhere to adapt to future minority and/or coalition government, which were either partially implemented or not considered or pursued in 1970s Britain. The form of planning conducted during this period further demonstrates the British tradition of minority government, indicating the extent to which Labour and the Conservatives were prepared to innovate in strategies for dealing with indecisive elections. The approaches considered here will include those aimed at pre-electoral agreements or innovations that would make any minority/coalition easier, and those prior to an election which were directed at dealing with the aftermath of an indecisive result. Discussion of pre-electoral approaches will consider: institutional reforms such as PR; parliamentary committees and devolution; and political alliances, such as electoral pacts. Examination of the post-electoral dimension primarily focuses on the preparation of the groundwork for interparty negotiations, particularly through manifesto commitments.

In a situation very much akin to the inaccurate polling forecasts during the 2015 and 2017 general elections, 1970s policymakers were very much influenced by previous inaccurate forecasting of the general election results in 1970, as well as those of February and October 1974. On two out of three occasions, the polls predicted the wrong winner (Labour in 1970 and the Conservatives in February 1974) and, in the case of the third (October 1974), seriously overestimated the Government's majority. The continuation of significant dichotomies in opinion polls between Conservative strength as a party and Thatcher's perceived unpopularity compared to Callaghan, further reinforced this uncertainty about the prospective electoral result, even during the actual election of 1979.[3]

In the post-mortems of both parties following the 1979 election, there were concerns expressed about the possibility that the result could have been indecisive. The Conservatives' internal 'Inquest on the Election' a week later, opened by asking whether the party had really come close to 'defeat or deadlock' during the campaign.[4]

Scholars considering the breakdown of a minority government and possible subsequent elections have tended to concentrate on explaining the reasons for these elections occurring, or on forecasting what type of government will be formed based on the resulting composition of a legislature. There has also been discussion of countries where the greater frequency of indecisive results has led to their acceptance by political elites, such that planning and strategies are, by default, based on not achieving outright electoral victory.[5] However, these accounts and theoretical models do not provide insights into what is being examined here: how do parties plan for the possibility of future minority or coalition governments, and what the effect of minority government is on any such planning?

When these accounts do discuss Britain, it is frequently identified as a country where electoral majority governments are the norm, and where the political leaders of the main parties would not feel the need to accommodate minority or coalition governments when conducting their electoral planning.[6]

Secret plans for minority or coalition

Government plans

Wilson's approach to questions of coalition in 1974 largely continued existing government policy, which officially rejected any prospect of negotiation with smaller parties. Unofficially, there were discussions of possible coalitions or agreements hinted at by leading figures within Labour, but no indication that these received any systematic development or were seriously considered as potential strategies. Minority government did significantly shape Labour's electoral strategy, but more in how it presented its successes and attacked the coalition plans of its opponents.[7] Wilson took the Conservative proposal of a 'National Unity' administration to be a serious threat, and had been working with his staff on devising a counterstrategy from the early part of July. The subsequent Labour approach attacked Heath's particular conception of coalition through speeches (through such images as Wilson comparing it to a 'con-trick'), while simultaneously adopting Heath's language of 'National Unity' as representative of Labour's goal.[8]

Although many members of the Callaghan Government shared these misgivings with regard to coalition, more serious consideration was given to the prospect of future minority or coalition government. Some government internal papers, such as the Policy Unit's June 1977 work on government strategy, viewed another indecisive general election result as a potentially more favourable outcome than defeat, even though anything other than an outright victory was still regarded as undesirable. However, there is no immediately apparent development of this position, or indeed of any strategic measures being drawn up to handle such an electoral result. Although unwilling publicly to state what he would do in the event of an indecisive result, Callaghan's thoughts on the matter are made clearer in a February 1978 Note for the Record, in which he discussed the matter with his Principal Private Secretary after a meeting with Steel. Callaghan considered the likelihood of an indecisive result to be 'quite conceivable' and that, if the Government had called the election and lost seats, even if it were possible for Labour to get minor parties' support, he would, in the first instance, resign as Prime Minister. If Thatcher failed to construct a majority through agreements with the smaller parties, Callaghan would then attempt to do so, considering that it would not be feasible for the Conservatives to ask for another parliamentary dissolution so soon after an election.[9] In some respects, this approach would seem to build on that recommended by Callaghan following the indecisive election in February 1974, when Labour waited for the Conservative Government to try to form a coalition and then resign after failing to do so, rather than trying to bring pressure on Heath to resign immediately. The consideration was that waiting and allowing the Conservatives to try, for four days in 1974, would then strengthen Labour's position as the incoming minority government, removing any suggestion of an alternative viable opposition majority that could be invited to replace them. It is difficult to tell whether such an approach would have, in fact, been workable in 1978–79. Callaghan's resignation would likely have been viewed as an admission of failure by MPs from the different parties, and by the country at large. Even if the Conservatives had no majority, the removal of Callaghan would still have placed Thatcher as Prime Minister over a *de facto* Conservative Minority Government, with control over the prospect of an early dissolution, as Wilson had had with Labour in 1974.[10]

It would certainly appear that such thoughts were not lost upon those in Labour who were considering the question of a future indecisive result. Up until the end of the election campaign itself in 1979, there is little indication of Callaghan's approach being significantly developed, or of much further work being done on the prospect of another minority government. There were, however, two brief letters in May 1979 from members of the Policy Unit that presented summaries of options for the Prime Minister in the event of another 'hung parliament' – one written by Lipsey, the other by Roger Carroll. These reflections mark a significant departure from earlier sentiments expressed by Callaghan himself. Lipsey's two-page letter argued that the Prime Minister ought to attempt to stay on if the result produced no majority, 'Even if we [Labour] were not the largest party.'[11] The letter also included a phoned-in message from McNally, stating in no uncertain terms '1. At all costs avoid letting her [Thatcher] get a toe-nail in the door' and '2. You have every right to announce that you intend to face Parliament (1923 precedent).' Both of those advising in this instance favoured

Callaghan's staying on and attempting to form a government. The 1923 precedent referred to Conservative Prime Minister Stanley Baldwin meeting Parliament and attempting unsuccessfully to rule as a minority administration after losing his majority in an election. Invoking this precedent, would, in the first instance, suggest a preference for continuing Labour's Minority Government, and maybe even adopting the approach of daring other parties to defeat them, as discussed in Chapter 4. At the same time, these advisers would have been more likely to push for either another interparty agreement in the style of the Lib–Lab Pact, or maybe even a more comprehensive arrangement. Lipsey suggested that the Government's recent practice of ad hoc arrangements with other parties would not be sustainable following another indecisive election: 'Because of the difficulties ahead, if we do stay on, it could not be on the basis that we have operated on since the end of the Lib/Lab pact, seeking to construct a majority from day to day. Something solider would be needed.'

Carroll's letter, 'In the Event of Deadlock', briefly summarised some options for Labour to construct agreements with other parties while considering some potential scenarios.[12] Carroll appears to have favoured Lipsey and McNally's position of Callaghan staying on as Prime Minister, whether Labour or the Conservatives were the largest party, and 'to try and have first crack in any event' of forming a government. The paper also considered, in the event of Labour being a few seats behind the Conservatives, the possibility of reinforcing the legitimacy of Callaghan staying on by presenting it as a 'caretaker government', so as 'not to lose the advantage of being the incumbents'. Carroll's reasoning was that of positioning Labour in the event of Conservative interparty coalition talks failing, stipulating that 'Then, if their talks got nowhere, surely we [Labour] would be entitled to see if we could construct a majority.' The parties considered as potential partners to an agreement in the letter were the Liberals, the SNP and (by inference) the UUP and SDLP. The clearest statement of potential conditions that other parties might set concerned the Liberals, the two policies identified being 'A House of Lords elected by PR', an attempt to present something of a preferred Liberal objective that still had some chance of being delivered by the Government, and 'Allowing the Liberals to Make Some Running on Pay Policy', thereby enjoying some significant economic influence. The letter's potential conditions for the other parties are less clear, referring to a possible review of 'revenue raising power for a Scottish Assembly', and, even more vaguely, to having 'detailed material ready on a possible Northern Ireland initiative' that sought to engage parties from both sides.

While these documents demonstrate the potential willingness of some within the Government to engage with the possibility of further agreements or coalitions, and were considered by Callaghan, they, in of themselves, were also very much reactive, only being authored the day before the election. The options and ideas which they considered do not appear to have been translated into any substantial preparation in such areas as the framing of the manifesto, or the setting up of teams or writing of briefing papers for negotiations which would have helped to realise such plans in the event that these were to be enacted.

Opposition plans

Ironically, given Labour's past experiences of minority government and involvement with the Pact, more significant strategic consideration of a potential minority or coalition government is in evidence from the Conservatives. A number of factors have tended to discourage examination of the possibility that the Conservatives planned for an indecisive result after the 1979 election. As distinct from October 1974, there was no Conservative call for a coalition and Thatcher herself made no secret of her hostility to formal interparty deals during the course of the Parliament and the election campaign itself. While some individuals may have favoured being open to a more consensual approach, the Conservative leadership was firm in putting down any such proposals, as seen, for example, in Central Office's strongly worded denials of reports in *The Times* that the Shadow Cabinet had discussed the possibility of a coalition. Oft-cited internal strategy papers on the election would engage in analysing the strengths and weaknesses of both parties, but tended to refer to a 'hung parliament' as particularly unlikely, and emphasised the objective as being outright Conservative victory. The subsequent electoral successes for the Conservatives during the 1980s and 1990s, and the image of Thatcher as the strong, uncompromising party leader, may also have served to influence scholarly investigation in this area. The seemingly self-assured message and image projected by the Conservatives during the 1979 campaign would suggest that any thought of planning for a future minority government or making deals with other parties would have been flatly rejected by the leadership as unnecessary and defeatist.[13]

However, while the main Conservative emphasis focused on winning, senior party members were, in private, seriously considering the prospect of minority government or even a possible full coalition. The general preference expressed from 1977 onwards by those conducting planning for this eventuality would appear to have been for running a minority government with UUP support before seeking a majority at another early general election after a few weeks or months. A particularly important body in formulating these hypothetical plans was the CRD. Even where the importance of this body may have been diminished or bypassed by the leadership during the late 1970s, particularly in economic matters, it continued to exercise influence over day-to-day parliamentary affairs, as has been highlighted in previous chapters, from considering questions of electoral timing to supplying briefings on confidence debates. Thatcher did not yet have the authority over her Shadow Cabinet that she would later possess, and it is also likely that an indecisive result would have further increased her reliance on the Shadow Cabinet and official strategy-making bodies.

The apparently increasing polarisation of British politics during the 1970s, and the widely perceived loss of the Conservatives' traditional position as the 'natural' party of government, had also served to change opinions within the Opposition. A growing number of influential Conservative voices from 1974 onwards were willing to contemplate radical notions of entering into a coalition or reforming the electoral system if it meant preventing another Labour Government from being formed. Even before the Callaghan Government had lost its majority in 1976, the Conservatives had been confronting the coalition question. During mid-1975 when, as mentioned, an economic crisis or government split appeared imminent, there was serious discussion among political commentators that the only viable alternative to a 'crisis' election would be a national unity government. Conservative Steering Group meetings on the subject in May 1975 suggested that nothing should be said publicly about the prospects of a national unity government, but also went so far as to say that in the event that Labour dropped further nationalisation proposals, there could possibly be a basis for coalition discussions (although there is no evidence of any concrete preparations being made in regard to this eventuality).[14]

While no such government was formed, these discussions provided the back-drop for planning after Labour became a minority government under Callaghan. This planning reflected ongoing uncertainty regarding a Conservative victory, and the belief that factors might conspire to produce another indecisive result: the vote swing required to win was greater than that achieved by an opposition party at any other election since 1945; national opinion polls (NOPs) had already proved themselves unreliable when predicting the result of the three previous general elections; and, in any case, during the Callaghan Government, different polls had been showing periods of very small Conservative leads, or even Labour leads. There were also persistent fears among some senior Conservatives that Callaghan would form a coalition to stay in power in the event of an indecisive poll. One such instance of these concerns being raised came in an October 1978 letter from Conservative Researcher Charles Bellaire to Patten and other senior strategy-makers including Adam Ridley (one of Thatcher's inner circle and future CRD Director), entitled 'The Future Scene'. This letter considered likely political developments following the delay of the prospective autumn election. While the letter was primarily concerned with the Government's economic strategy, Bellaire warned that waiting for Labour's failing on industrial policy could usher in a unity government:

> [I]n such circumstances, Mr Callaghan might take a leaf out of Ramsay MacDonald's book, and urge the formation of a coalition of all the moderates [...] I would hope that the possibility of such action by Mr Callaghan is not dismissed as completely

beyond the realms of possibility. He would certainly be making such an approach from a stronger negotiating position than was the case with Ramsay MacDonald in 1931.[15]

It is this context of continued concerns about the outcome of an election and unity governments that prompted some Conservatives seriously to consider future 'hung parliaments'. In the first instance, it was suggested that the party's public discourse needed to accommodate, even in a subtle way, the possibility of future minority government. In a paper written in November 1977, 'Some Thoughts on Strategy and Tactics: A Note by the Research Department', Patten stressed that while a 'hung parliament' after the next election was unlikely, there was a need for contingency planning ('The subject deserves discussion'), and for the tailoring of publicity to allow for any eventuality by designing 'a form of words which, while making clear our determination to win a majority, does not rule out negotiation with other parties if we fall slightly short of that'. Patten further suggested that 'there may be a case for more positive, if discreet, wooing of other parties in the coming months'.[16] Unsurprisingly perhaps, given the hostility within the party to this concept, such references appear to have been removed from subsequent redrafts of the paper. However, this statement was not only indicative of other discussions on the subject between those planning Conservative strategy that were not minuted, but foreshadowed further officially sanctioned planning within the party.[17]

Such papers were requested and considered by a special Co-ordinating Committee that had been set up in late 1977 to study important issues relating to party strategy and planning. It was chaired by Keith Joseph, with Thatcher kept informed of the planning being conducted.[18] While such strategy-making may not have been on the scale of that conducted by their European counterparts, Conservative preparations appear to have been more extensive than those preceding the October 1974 election. Faced with Wilson's Minority Government and the prospect of further indecisive elections, the Conservative Opposition of 1974 had produced several strategy papers on forming potential coalitions or electoral pacts with other parties, particularly with the Liberals, in order to help ensure victory in a subsequent poll. The purpose of these documents, however, appears to have been as much to justify or condemn their authors' advocacy or rejection of interparty cooperative policies as to provide practical plans for their implementation. It would also appear that the internal argument against electoral pacts was decisively carried, perhaps explaining, as cited, why these political devices did not form a significant part of the Conservatives' 1976–79 planning.[19]

In contrast to Conservative planners' efforts in both 1974 and 1975, interparty agreements for supporting a future Conservative Minority Government and potential coalitions with other parties were considered during the later 1970s. Even from mid-1977 onwards, CRD documents were outlining not only a series of hypothetical post-electoral scenarios involving 'hung parliaments', but were also going into greater detail over the conduct of negotiations, the possibility of reaching agreements with particular parties, and some of the tactics that might be used or required in order successfully to achieve a workable agreement. This planning was very much framed within the British tradition of minority government, asserting a firmly majoritarian vision of the need to keep the planning secret, but also acknowledging the purpose of such planning for alternative outcomes as being a pragmatic preparation. Such sentiments are perhaps best captured in the opening of the April 1978 'Hung Parliament' paper, as quoted at the beginning of this chapter, that there should be 'no public admission that the Party expects anything less than victory' while also putting forward 'some considerations first on the constitutional and historical aspects of a hung parliament, secondly on the contingency itself and thirdly on the psephological background'.[20] While these papers stressed their authors' desire for an outright Conservative victory, they drew different conclusions as to potential minority government or coalition outcomes.

The three documents that will be considered here include that of James Douglas's paper on 27 May 1977, to which subsequent papers make reference, followed by Nicholson's paper of 16 March 1978, 'The Hung Parliament Contingency', and a paper of April 1978, written by Alexander 'Sandy' Walker, 'Appendix E', which appears to have been, in part, derived from Nicholson's paper.

In Douglas's May 1977 paper, it is suggested that, in the event of an indecisive election: 'the most likely outcome […] would be either an exceptionally short Parliament [with a minority government]' or a 'grand coalition' involving at least part of Labour and the Conservatives.[21] Although the idea of a coalition between Labour and the Conservatives was publicly dismissed out of hand as impossible by many contemporary political commentators, the fact that this was even being considered shows something of the mindset of opposition planners at the time, and the influence that the notion of a unity government continued to exercise. Both Labour and the Conservatives had been in coalition around thirty-two years previously, albeit in terms of a wartime government. This paper was also framed within the context of a potential Labour split, discussed in Chapter 3: 1976: minority government revisited, which had dominated previous Conservative consideration of the subject in 1975 and 1976. While the economic turmoil of the IMF bailout had been successfully navigated by Callaghan, the early months of the Lib–Lab Pact and the tensions raised between government leaders and Labour MPs, discussed in Chapters 5–6, once again raised the possibility of a party split in the minds of observers.

By early 1978, the situation had changed significantly, as acknowledged in subsequent CRD papers. The Pact had not only survived, but had demonstrated the value of interparty cooperation, which led opposition researchers considering 'hung parliaments' to fear 'the recent narrowing of the gap between the two major parties in the opinion polls' or that it had become 'more likely that Callaghan would seek to stay in power through a continued arrangement with the Liberals'.[22]

A later development of Conservative planning that addressed these issues may be seen in Nicholson's 'The "Hung Parliament" Contingency', a twenty-nine-page paper considering likely government behaviour, more detailed analysis of possible deals/coalitions between the Conservatives and other political parties, the likely political price of such deals and an assessment of their viability. The twelve-page 'Appendix E: The Hung Parliament', prepared in April 1978, conducted an extended study of plans for a potential minority or coalition government. Both papers share some of their material, not least when setting out the different possible courses of action in a 'hung parliament', where the wording between the two is practically identical:

> If Mr. Callaghan resigned, the main options facing the Conservatives would be:
> (a) to form a minority government with an understanding with some or all of the minor parties;
> (b) to form a minority government without any formal understanding with the minor parties;
> (c) to ask for an immediate dissolution and have another general election within a few weeks;
> (d) to form a coalition with a combination of minor parties or a 'grand coalition' with the Right of the Labour Party and the Liberals.[23]

Both papers also shared the idea of the initiative remaining with Callaghan after the election as the incumbent, seeking to stay on, and citing precedents including Heath's experience in 1974. They both presented the notion of a prime minister losing seats at an election as having 'forfeited' the right to govern, and that this represented a 'powerful' argument for Callaghan's resignation, a notion of electoral momentum that, as discussed in Chapter 3: 1974: transitions to minority, has been applied in other cases of minority government overseas. At the same time, both papers believed that Callaghan could dismiss the argument without facing significant public opposition, but that the Conservatives attempting a similar move would be met by significant trade union opposition that would make governing difficult. This position would appear partly rooted in the Conservatives' experience of the February election of 1974, following industrial action. Walker's 'Appendix E' also highlighted the aforementioned 1923 precedent, showing that both Labour and the Conservatives were drawing on the same exemplars: 'The possibility of the existing Prime Minister (presumably James Callaghan) attempting to soldier on is of importance since there are recent precedents for this.'[24]

After much discussion, the alternatives that Nicholson's paper came up with notably featured the SNP in combinations with either main party, along with a

Conservative–UUP option, while at the same time questioning the strength of such combinations: 'The most likely outcomes of a "hung" parliament would be Labour–SNP, Conservative–SNP, or Conservative–Ulster Unionist arrangements and all of these would exist unstably and possibly involve undesirable policies.'[25]

In part, this focus on the SNP derives originally from Douglas's paper, which forecast the possibility of a significant SNP presence at Westminster, as being the third placed party with around twenty to thirty seats. A remarkable prescience, if lacking realisation until 2015! Although the SNP poll rating had diminished nearly a year later, the subsequent papers still considered an enlarged SNP to be a distinct possibility. Nicholson's paper also examined the three above-cited arrangements in more detail, even going so far as to suggest that there were some conditions that the Conservatives could accept in order to reach an agreement with the SNP, including that of offering a further devolution referendum in the event that the 40 per cent threshold was not passed. Such a proposal was considered to be justified if it gained the parliamentary support of the SNP and could be 'represented as avoiding the need to move into the murkier waters of federalism'. Even more radically, the paper considered the possibility of the Conservatives being prepared to implement devolution even without a further referendum, in order to gain SNP support. Evidence of multiple edits in this section of the paper, and the blotting out of entire paragraphs, shows something of the difficulty of considering these options and reveals that this was very much an area being repeatedly revised in Nicholson's line of thought. Walker's paper similarly considered conditions for an SNP agreement, such as 'the power to raise revenue' for a future Scottish Assembly, but spent less space discussing it, and couched the measures very much as temporary expedients, designed to satisfy moderate devolutionists. Both papers also acknowledged the additional difficulties of such a deal, including the absence of any previous 'tradition' of cooperation with the Scottish Nationalists, and viewed an enlarged SNP as being 'further to the Left and [...] all the harder to make a deal with'.[26]

While Nicholson's paper was very much grounded in the experiences under the Callaghan Administration, Walker's paper initially set out more of a history of minority governments in Britain. Subsequent discussion of options included drawing on nineteenth-century precedents (possibly reflecting the paucity of twentieth-century British precedents for successful minority governments, none of which were Conservative). That the paper was prepared to cite the Derby and Disraeli Minority Governments of the 1850s, rather than contemporary minority governments from elsewhere, once again provides a good example of the British tradition of minority government as self-referential.[27]

In spite of differences, there is, nevertheless, a consistent preference expressed across these different papers, opting for the Conservatives running their own minority government on a temporary basis in the event of an indecisive result, and then seeking another election and majority shortly thereafter. This is very much in line with the aforementioned approach adopted by other minority governments, including those of the Canadian Government under Trudeau in 1974. While the CRD was aware of these international experiences, there is no indication in this planning that the exemplars were drawn from overseas, potential actions being justified either through reference to precedents from British political history and contemporary experience from the Callaghan Minority Government, or through an appeal to pragmatic adaptation that would enable the Conservatives to return to power. Ultimately, the only formal interparty agreement seriously entertained in these proposals was that of a coalition between the Conservatives and the UUP, in a post-election Parliament where it was assumed the Conservatives would be the largest party. In Nicholson's case, 'The Ulster Unionists, of course, present the best basis for a permanent arrangement. Some additional support might be obtained when needed from the Liberals though the strength and reliability of this are both doubtful.'[28]

Even where Walker's paper had criticised some of the views previously expressed in Douglas's 1977 discussion of a prospective unity government, it explicitly cites the earlier work, supporting the conclusion that 'The only feasible course would seem to be the one James Douglas suggested in July 1977: to rule as a minority Government with Ulster Unionist support until another general election.'[29]

In terms of policies that could have been offered to the UUP, the preference appears to have been largely the same as cited in Chapter 6, when the Conservatives were seeking UUP support during the Callaghan Government: increased representation at Westminster and the reconstruction of local government in Northern Ireland along majoritarian lines, while continuing to reject any notion of home rule that did not involve power-sharing. In this regard, Conservative planners recognised that the UUP were divided over the power-sharing issue, majority rule 'not supported by Powell, Molyneaux and other Unionists', and that rejection of power-sharing would lead to wider political damage and loss of Conservative supporters in Britain, negating any short-term benefit. Other policies included modest changes or preservation of existing arrangements in areas from the structure of secondary education to improving security. This is not to say that radical proposals were not being considered. Nicholson's paper ended the section discussing the Ulster Unionists with a scenario reminiscent of the 1974 Wilson Government's Doomsday plan, suggesting that, if events spiralled out of control, a future Conservative Government could be compelled 'with or without the agreement of the Irish Republic or the SDLP to re-draw the border and arrange appropriate exchanges of population'.[30]

Nicholson's closing sentence indicated that he had thoughts on the arrangements for this possibility but that it would not be appropriate 'to specify them in a paper of this nature'. This would suggest that such a proposal was very much a speculative contingency scenario, rather than an attempt to address the paper's focus on preparations for minority or coalition government.

The only other option which came up repeatedly in these Conservative plans was that of the 'grand coalition', cited originally in Douglas's paper. Nicholson considered that the only situation in which a grand coalition would emerge as an issue would be if Callaghan made 'an offer to the Conservatives and possibly the Liberals', but thought that even such an attempt would be 'highly improbable unless the constitutional impasse were to be accompanied by an economic blizzard worse than any previously experienced'. The option of a coalition with Labour was detailed in 'Appendix E' so that it could be dismissed as unworkable. However, the fact that both papers felt it necessary to outline such an option indicates the continued intellectual impact of the 'National Unity idea' among political elites, and the already-cited Conservative fears about Callaghan's propensity for encouraging interparty cooperation.

These fears were not limited to internal discussions, but also involved those outside institutions which were particularly influential in formulating economic strategy for Thatcher. CPS Director Alfred Sherman's extensive memorandum to Conservative strategist John Hoskyns in May 1978 is one example of this, arguing passionately for the need to counter the threat of a prospective government of national unity.[31]

These papers are also indicative of the Conservatives' mindset when presenting their plans for minority or coalition government, as they are framed very much within the continuation of experiences learned in the British political system, rather than looking towards innovation based on contemporary practices abroad. Even where those making plans demonstrated their awareness of the experiences of minority governments in other countries, their papers on potential 'hung parliaments' drew exclusively from British examples. For instance, the April 1978 paper on 'Hung Parliament', as quoted at the beginning of Chapter 2, listed a number of these examples, emphasising that there had been: 'no less than eleven cases of [British] minority governments since the 1832 Reform Act'.[32]

While the Conservatives had largely ruled out the Liberals as potential post-electoral coalition partners, the papers exploring the possibility justified this more on the grounds of projections that the Liberals would not have a significant number of seats in Parliament following any election, rather than from a principled stand against such cooperation. As highlighted in Chapter 6, the Conservatives were more interested in converting Liberal voters, but did not fully cut off cooperation with their Liberal parliamentary counterparts. It is interesting to note that the Liberals' own planning also did not completely rule out future cooperation with the Conservatives. The natural instincts of the Liberals in the country would appear, even in the 1970s, to have been more oriented towards Labour, as is evident from their rejection of coalition with Heath in 1974 and the formation of the Lib–Lab Pact in 1977. However, internal planning by the Liberal leadership in the late 1970s did consider the possibility of working with the Conservatives after an indecisive election. The party's NEC accepted in a June 1978 meeting with Steel that an agreement between the two parties might become necessary depending on the outcome of any election:

> [I]n the event of a hung parliament after the General Election, the Liberal Party would be willing to co-operate with another party in government, whatever its political complexion, in order to achieve certain Liberal objectives, foremost amongst these being positive progress towards the implementation of proportional representation, and therefore the possibility of an agreement with the Conservatives should not be dismissed, but agreed with Mr. Steel who had said that the Tories would have radically to modify their present dogmatic and intransigent attitudes, before such an agreement could be considered.[33]

Precisely what these modifications would have entailed is uncertain. It is very likely, however, that the most significant would have been the removal of Thatcher as leader in favour of someone more palatable to the Liberals, such as the Deputy Conservative Leader, William Whitelaw. This device of leadership change as a price for coalition is very much in line with contemporary and more recent practices of smaller parties seeking to form coalitions, such as the Liberal Democrat demands for Prime Minister Gordon Brown's resignation as a condition for coalition in 2010 and Liberal demands for Heath's removal in 1974.[34] Such a device would have served to remove perhaps the greatest obstacle to a Conservative–Liberal agreement in 1979, that of Thatcher's opposition to such a form of cooperation. At the same time, there was still considerable sensitivity within the Liberals and opposition to agreements with the Conservatives, Steel feeling compelled to respond to a *Guardian* article, suggesting that the Liberal leader had outlined conditions for future Conservative–Liberal cooperation, by apologising and providing reassurance in a letter to Liberal parliamentary candidates: 'I am sorry that "The Guardian" misinterpreted my recent speech intended to illustrate Tory divisions as my "terms for a Lib–Con pact" and even sorrier that it was lifted as such straight into Liberal News.'[35]

While this speculative scenario of a coalition may have appeared unlikely, it is possible that, in the event of the Conservatives failing to gain a majority, Thatcher's position would not have been secure against challengers in 1978–79. Even if a formal coalition could not have been put together, some more informal arrangement between the two parties would not have been totally inconceivable, given their cooperation on important votes during the Callaghan Administration.[36]

In January 1979, Thatcher was persuaded by those advising her to make use of the spirit of 'National Unity' – doing a party political broadcast on 14–15 January in which she offered the Callaghan Government the support of Conservative MPs to pass specific measures in Parliament: seeking to alleviate the industrial crisis through bans on secondary picketing; providing funding of strike ballots; and proposing a no-strike agreement in essential services. Although the offer was made on the premise that it was bound to be rejected, Thatcher voiced her concerns when discussing the approach with those advising her, fearing that a pragmatic Callaghan could accept, and, as a consequence, out-manoeuvre the Conservatives.[37] The offer was, as had been forecast, rejected by the Government. Although this broadcast was couched in terms of a 'National Unity' appeal, it was conceived of primarily as a political device for gaining the support of moderate voters, rather than as a genuine move towards opening up greater interparty cooperation between the two main parties.

Unrealised adaptations

While the main parties engaged in formal planning for minority or coalition government in the late 1970s to a greater or lesser extent, there were other potential innovations adopted elsewhere which were also given some consideration. Where these measures were adopted, their implementation was only partial, and confined within the pragmatic majoritarian optic of the British tradition of minority government, hostile to any notion of making future minority or coalition administrations a more likely occurrence.

Minority governments have had to accommodate pre-existing constitutional conventions, such as, in the British case, of a prime minister remaining the incumbent until resignation (theoretically) irrespective of the majority in Parliament. Some particularly notable methods of dealing with this have been those preparations focusing on pre-electoral arrangements (including institutional reforms, establishing lines of interparty contact prior to the loss of a government's majority, creating pacts or alliances) and/or those which, while conducted in advance of a poll, are primarily post-electoral (including signalling potential negotiating positions through a manifesto or other communications).[38]

While neither of the two main parties harboured any desire for further minority governments and post-electoral political alliances, both sides came to suspect that their principal opponents might, in fact, be attempting to aim for such a situation, as has already been indicated in Chapters 3 and 7. Such fears manifested themselves in different ways, from Labour worries about a Tory-led unity government in the face of economic turmoil, to Conservatives' questioning whether Callaghan was actively seeking a future coalition, during attempts to forecast the timing of the general election.

Institutional reform in advance of elections

In some countries, institutional arrangements have been modified in order to assist the process of forming and operating a minority or coalition government after a subsequent election, whether in terms of extended time before the first meeting of a new Parliament to allow for interparty talks, the provision of official civil service support for such discussions and/or the formal appointment of a person to examine coalition possibilities (i.e. a *formateur*). Some of these arrangements were put in place prior to the UK general elections of 2010 and 2015. A legislature primed for government by minority or coalitions may, additionally, include such arrangements as the timetable for business being worked out through an all-party committee, greater involvement of different parties in the legislative process and a stronger committee system, as seen, for example, in the Nordic countries. Initial acceptance of some of these constitutional reforms has, in many cases, also served as a requirement for larger parties to secure cooperation with potential coalition partners.

The Callaghan Government and Conservative Opposition spent a lot of time considering constitutional reform in terms of legislation on subjects including devolution and direct elections to the European Parliament. However, while devolution was used by the Government in an attempt to retain support of SNP MPs, such reforms were primarily designed to safeguard the political advantage of the main parties against new challengers. There was no serious consideration by either main party of changing constitutional arrangements in order better to facilitate the formation and operation of future minority or coalition governments, nor any suggestion of a move towards a formalised *formateur*. As already highlighted in Chapter 4, Foot's resistance to committee reform was, in fact, specifically motivated in part by a desire not to weaken the power of a future minority government. This was very much in line with Labour policy, not least as expressed in an NEC report of 1978 which, while pressing for reforms to create more powerful committees that responded to the concerns of backbenchers, wanted these to reflect the parliamentary party balance along largely majoritarian lines, seeing 'no future in consensus government'.[39] Conservative efforts to strengthen committees in Parliament during 1974–79, and to ensure more opposition members on them, were conditioned by the minority governments at the time. However, as already discussed in Chapter 4, this initiative was also principally focused on their own parliamentary position and on weakening the Wilson and Callaghan Governments, rather than enabling better cooperation with the other opposition parties.

The only area during this period in which plans for constitutional reform had a direct link to a possible future minority government situation was that of changing the electoral system to PR. Even here, such considerations were limited in scope, and inspired more as an immediate response to circumstances.

Many countries with experience of minority and coalition governments have PR electoral systems, while the two main parties in Britain have traditionally been opposed to PR. The most visible example of PR being contemplated was for the direct elections to the European Parliament. A majority of the Cabinet did consider a proportional list voting system to be their preferred choice for European elections when the matter was discussed. This preference was, however, out of a desire to prevent the Conservatives gaining large numbers of seats at European elections, predicted to be the case under a first-past-the-post system, rather than as a means to facilitate future interparty cooperation in a minority or coalition situation at Westminster. That barely half of Labour MPs backed the PR system in the subsequent vote on European elections meant that it would have been very difficult, if not politically impossible, for the Government to get PR approved as the electoral system for the House of Commons. As highlighted in Chapter 3, the hostility of some Cabinet members to PR in direct elections reflected wider Labour fears that PR reform at Westminster would be 'paving the way for coalitions and the undermining of the legitimacy of Governments'.[40]

Another instance in which PR was raised was in relation to Northern Ireland. While the Cabinet had shown some understanding of the unique political situation there, this was not ultimately acted upon. When meetings had occurred between Labour NEC representatives and the SDLP in the early months of the Callaghan Government, the SDLP wanted the alternative vote system to be considered for use in elections in Northern Ireland. The response from the NEC representatives confirmed the wider Labour hostility to notions of reform that necessitated formal interparty cooperation, considering that such a move would pressure reform at Westminster and that 'there was not a wish for a system which would force coalitions on Britain'.[41]

The main Conservative considerations of PR, as part of internal discussions involving the Shadow Cabinet in 1975, were, as indicated in Chapter 3, primarily a response to a crisis situation when a Labour split still appeared likely and the Liberals continued to enjoy a high poll rating.

Pre-electoral pacts/alliances

Another area besides institutional reform that has typically been used as a route to foster cooperation between parties is that of pre-electoral alliances, pacts or, at the very least, some form of electoral assistance to other parties as a means of establishing channels of communication for future negotiations. There has been a long-established history of major British political parties engaging in such cooperation, from a local to a national level, particularly over the course of the early to mid-twentieth century.[42] Some discussions during the Callaghan Government did raise the possibility of helping parties such as the Liberals during a prospective 1978–79 election, a move which would potentially be useful in the event of another indecisive result. One example of this was Donoughue's meeting with Steel's assistant Archibald Kirkwood on 12 July 1978.[43] There were also indications of continued cooperation being raised even in the latter stages of the Lib–Lab Pact. Callaghan discussed the prospect of a 'hung parliament' and further minority government with Steel during several of their regular meetings. However, it does not appear that the Government sought to develop or coordinate pre-electoral alliances, pacts or special channels of communication with other parties. Any support offered to smaller parties, rather than serving as groundwork for future inter-party cooperation, would have been more likely aimed at preventing Conservative vote and seat gains from Liberals during an election, and, consequently, seeking to reduce the prospect of an indecisive outcome instead of preparing for one. Callaghan's discussions with Steel were as much bargaining tactics, attempts to prevent the Lib–Lab Pact from being ended early, or efforts to bring it to a peaceful conclusion, without causing political damage to the Government.[44] Although Callaghan had a relatively good working relationship with Steel, he remained unwilling publicly to accept another indecisive result and potential continuation of having to negotiate with other parties to construct a majority.

The Conservatives similarly did not seriously consider adopting pre-electoral agreements or pacts before the 1979 general election, partly because of the afore-mentioned adherence to a British majoritarian desire to win outright, borne out by opinion polls which consistently gave the Opposition a significant lead over the Government. One of the few notable instances of a prospective electoral interparty agreement being raised was in the aforementioned 'Hung Parliament Contingency', which considered 'a limited electoral pact' with the Liberals when contemplating possible conditions that would enable a post-electoral coalition. This option was, however, couched in terms of a possible future measure that might be adopted for 'the next but one General Election', after 1978–79. The paper was also generally discouraging in terms of an electoral pact's utility for the Conservatives, and ended on the note of practical concerns that 'There would, of course, be great difficulties in persuading Conservative Associations not to contest seats.'[45] The Conservatives had also previously given greater consideration to prospective electoral agreements with the Liberals during the 1974 minority government. A number of papers had been prepared at the time to study the implications of such a move, some of them actively advocating a pact. The party leadership, including Heath, had decided not to pursue this approach, fearing that it would be likely to reduce the prospect of a majority for any future Conservative Government.[46]

Groundwork for negotiations following an election

The possibility of a post-electoral minority government or coalition in other countries has, in some cases, led to political parties evolving tactics to prepare the groundwork for subsequent negotiations. One of these devices is that of setting out particular future policies or manifesto pledges in a format which more clearly distinguishes those whose adoption would be essential as part of any interparty agreement from those of a lesser importance which could be amended or shelved in potential negotiations. Examples of this were clearly evident in the UK general elections of 2010 and 2015. Even if the structuring of manifestos is not so explicitly in the shape of a negotiating position, commitments within a manifesto may still be framed vaguely to consult with other parties or to examine different possibilities in areas potentially of particular cross-party importance, such as constitutional reform.[47] The aforementioned convening of a Speaker's Conference had been a device used on several occasions during this period by the British Government to address certain issues of constitutional reform desired by different political parties.

However, there were no significant moves towards this approach in the final manifesto for Labour in either the election for October 1974, or in 1979, reflecting the continued long-established hostility towards interparty agreements. In the case of 1979, this position also represented an increasing loss of patience towards deal-making among leading government members, frustrated by their ongoing experiences of having to do political deals with smaller parties in return for the Government's day-to-day survival.[48]

The only visible adoption of this approach among the two main parties during the 1970s may be seen in the cited Conservative campaign for a government of national unity in October 1974. As part of this approach, the Conservative manifesto included a commitment to establish a Speaker's Conference to consider electoral reform. Even though such a measure could have helped in facilitating interparty cooperation, depending on a number of different factors, internal Conservative dialogues are quite clear that it was primarily intended as a tactical device to attract greater support from Liberal voters.[49]

The framing of the Conservatives' official discourse through the general election manifesto in 1979 also did not show any of the markers for potential negotiations that may be found in those of their counterparts abroad. It was suggested by opposition strategy-makers, including Patten, that in spite of the unlikelihood of an indecisive outcome, the Conservative manifesto should still contain a commitment to a Speaker's Conference on constitutional matters. The April 1978 paper on a 'Hung Parliament' similarly advocated a public commitment to a constitutional conference, as a means of gaining the support of additional voters, but also because 'it would give us [Conservatives] some room for manoeuvre after the election if we need to trade constitutional points with minor parties'.[50] A commitment of this nature would be very much in line with that promised in the Conservative October 1974 manifesto, and could have helped in the process of making an agreement with another party, judging that the Liberals, SNP and UUP were all likely to have had demands that could require significant constitutional changes.

The final wording in the 1979 manifesto was somewhat vague on this point, naming a number of constitutional matters as concerning those 'which we shall wish to discuss with all parties', rather than putting forward any specific commitment to a Speaker's Conference or other formal body. The tone of the section highlighting these issues focused around opposing the perceived unconstitutional role of industrial workers on strike during the winter, as well as decrying changes to the constitution 'for party political advantage'. Although the need for more action on the constitution was noted by the Shadow Cabinet in July 1978, references to unifying the nation were qualified as precluding interparty cooperation.[51] While the manifesto's avoidance of detailed commitments may have served as a useful basis for negotiations with other parties, it was conceived of by those framing the document purely as a reaction against too much detail in previous manifestoes from 1970 onwards, rather than as a preparation for a prospective minority government. Similarly, the avoidance of repeating anything resembling the October 1974 commitment on interparty cooperation, or even anything committing the Conservatives to examining wider constitutional reform, fitted very much with the party leadership's adherence to Britain's majoritarian political culture.

While the Government and Opposition publicly rejected any outcome short of an outright victory, their behind-the-scenes planning for a future minority government or coalition with the smaller parties was sometimes far more radical than publicly acknowledged. Limited debates within Labour focused around how Callaghan should respond to any indecisive result in terms of forming a new government and potential conditions for cooperation with the Liberals, SNP, UUP and/or SDLP. The Conservatives' multiple CRD papers on a 'hung parliament' considered everything from running a minority government to a full coalition with the UUP, as well as admittedly less likely outcomes, which might have included a Conservative–SNP coalition or a grand coalition with Labour.

However, clear hostility to the notion of interparty agreement remained strong within Labour and the Conservatives, and this work was, although significant, more sporadic and less extensive than that done by many of their European counterparts. Planning work was also not translated by the two main parties into measures typically adopted in other countries to facilitate better post-electoral interparty cooperation or coalition. Such measures, including modification of the parties' public discourse through manifestoes to signpost potential negotiating positions, or establishment of additional pre-electoral assistance or communication with other parties, were not significantly developed by either the Government or Opposition in 1970s Britain.

Having to address problems of potential minority or coalition government helped to shape the thinking of both main political parties after 1979 until the present day. These experiences provided a platform on which future leaders would build when faced with prospective political realignments, including the emergence of the Social Democrat Party in the 1980s. The examples of these years were also frequently invoked, particularly in the general elections of 1992 and 2015, when most forecasts incorrectly judged that the result would be indecisive. Campaign strategies and news headlines in the 2015 election were often dominated by discussions of support for minority governments or potential coalitions. The experiences of minority government and coalition politics in devolved parliaments after 1999, including those in Scotland and Wales following 2016, and, at a Westminster level between 2010 and 2015, and since June 2017, have reinforced the importance of strategy-making for parties with regard to participation in prospective minority and coalition governments. The extent to which parties in Britain have learned, or will learn, the lessons of their predecessors' experience in the 1970s will undoubtedly be the subject of much future debate.

In spite of the Callaghan Government's many successes in surviving without a majority in the House of Commons, they confronted their ultimate challenge in the no confidence vote in March 1979. While seemingly an isolated act, and, some would say, an inevitable conclusion, the navigation of this one vote by both main parties drew on and was conditioned by the strategies and experiences from the previous five years, as we shall see in Chapter 9.

Notes

1　CAC: THCR 2/1/6/194: Appendix E, 'The Hung Parliament', 12 April 1978.

2　Thorpe, *A History of the British Labour Party*, pp. 207–9; Coates (ed.), *What Went Wrong*, pp. 7–11, 28–32; Campbell, *Margaret Thatcher*, pp. 318–19; Seldon and Hickson (eds), *New Labour, Old Labour*, pp. 97, 321–2, 330; Cronin, *New Labour's Pasts*, pp. 195–6, 203–11; Morgan, *Britain since 1945*, pp. 221–2; Young, *One of Us*, p. 128; Hennessy and Seldon (eds), *Ruling Performance*, pp. 241–2; Särlvik and Crewe, *Decade of Dealignment*, pp. 20–2, 326–7; Whiteley, *The Labour Party in Crisis*, pp. 2–5, 148, 187; H. R. Penniman, *Britain at the Polls, 1979: A Study of the General Election* (Washington, DC: American Enterprise Institute, 1981).

3　Seldon and Hickson (eds), *New Labour, Old Labour*, pp. 96–7, 293; Moon, *Opinion Polls*, pp. 99–102; Särlvik and Crewe, *Decade of Dealignment*; Butler and Kavanagh, *The British General Election of 1979*.

4　CPA: CRD L/4/46/7, Inquest on the Election, 9 May 1979.

5　P. V. Warwick, 'Dissolvers, Disputers, and Defectors: The Terminators of Parliamentary Governments', *European Political Science Review*, 4:2 (2012), 263–81; Martin and Stevenson, 'The Conditional Impact of Incumbency on Government Formation', 503–18; Strøm, *Minority Government and Majority Rule*, pp. 78, 91, 237, 244; Herman and Pope, 'Minority Government in Western Democracies', 191–212.

6　A. Lijphart, *Patterns of Democracy: Government Forms and Performance in Thirty-Six Different Countries* (New Haven, CT: Yale University Press, 2nd edn, 2012), pp. 5–6, 9–12; Bergman, 'Formation Rules and Minority Governments', 60; G. B. Powell, *Contemporary*

Democracies: Participation, Stability, and Violence (Cambridge, MA: Harvard University Press, 1984), p. 143.

7 MS. Wilson, c. 1437, News Releases: S122/74, 7 June 1974; S128/74, 8 June 1974; PS67/74, 17 July 1974; 'Britain Will Win with Labour', General Election Manifesto, October 1974; Benn, *Against the Tide*, pp. 121, 154–5; Castle, *The Castle Diaries*, pp. 156–9; B. Brivati and R. Heffernan (eds), *The Labour Party: A Centenary History* (Houndmills: Palgrave Macmillan, 2000), p. 349,; Butler and Kavanagh, *The British General Election of October 1974*, pp. 56–9.

8 LHASC: CC Paper, 15 May 1974 'Party Strategy'; MS. Wilson, c. 1288, Letters between Wilson and Percy Clark, Director of Publicity, Labour Party, 2–12 July 1974; c. 1457, 'Issue Report on Coalitions'; Butler and Kavanagh, *The British General Election of October 1974*, p. 128.

9 CAC: DNGH 1/1/17, Bernard Donoughue to Prime Minister, PU/281, Chequer's Cabinet: 'Thoughts on the Government's Future Strategy', 2 June 1977; TNA: PREM 16/1621: 'Note for the Record – The Outcome of the Next General Election', 7 February 1978.

10 See Chapter 3: 1974: transitions to minority.

11 Callaghan Papers, Box 19, 2737: Lab/Elec: 78–9, David Lipsey to the Prime Minister, 2 May 1979.

12 Callaghan Papers, Box 19, 2737: Lab/Elec: 78–9, 'In the Event of Deadlock', 2 May 1979.

13 CAC: THCR 2/6/1/248, 'Stepping Stones Report', 14 November 1977; 'The Right Approach', Conservative Manifesto, 1976; Campbell, *Margaret Thatcher*, pp. 361–2; Ball and Seldon (eds), *Recovering Power*, p. 235.

14 CPA: SC 14, 26th Meeting, 12 May 1975; 27th Meeting, 13 May 1975.

15 CPA: CRD/D/7/21, Charles Bellaire, Memorandum: 'The Future Scene', 20 October 1978.

16 CAC: THCR/2/6/1/246, 'Some Thoughts on Strategy and Tactics', 11 November 1977.

17 CPA: SC 16, Covering Note from Chris Patten to Mrs Thatcher, 25 January 1978; 'Implementing our Strategy', 21 December 1977; THCR/2/6/1/233, [Extended Minutes] 51st Meeting, 30 January 1978.

18 CAC: THCR/2/1/1/38, Keith Joseph to Margaret Thatcher, 28 November 1977; THCR/2/1/1/39, Keith Joseph to Margaret Thatcher, 22 May 1978.

19 CPA: CCO 20/2/7, Various Letters, March–October 1974; LCC 1/3/4, 36th Meeting, 30 October 1974; CCO 20/7/21, Meetings, 17 September–9 October 1974; OG 54, Letter to Michael Fraser, 17 April 1974; OG 56/74/158; SC 12 (4), 3rd Meeting, 1 April 1974; (8), 7th Meeting, 1 July 1974; MF: Reel 95, 00082–7, Letter from Michael Fraser to Heath, 5 October 1974; 00202, Letter from Michael Fraser to Heath, 6 May 1974.

20 CAC: THCR 2/1/6/194: Appendix E, 'The Hung Parliament', 12 April 1978.

21 *Ibid.*; CPA: CRD/L/4/46/6, 'The Hung Parliament Contingency', 16 March 1978.

22 CPA: CRD/L/4/46/6, 'The Hung Parliament Contingency', 16 March 1978.

23 CAC: THCR 2/1/6/194: Appendix E, 'The Hung Parliament', 12 April 1978.

24 *Ibid.*

25 CPA: CRD/L/4/46/6, 'The Hung Parliament Contingency', 16 March 1978.

26 CAC: THCR 2/1/6/194: Appendix E, 'The Hung Parliament', 12 April 1978; CPA: CRD/L/4/46/6, 'The Hung Parliament Contingency', 16 March 1978.

27 CAC: THCR 2/1/6/194: Appendix E, 'The Hung Parliament', 12 April 1978.

28 CPA: CRD/L/4/46/6, 'The Hung Parliament Contingency', 16 March 1978.

29 CAC: THCR 2/1/6/194: Appendix E, 'The Hung Parliament', 12 April 1978.

30 CPA: CRD/L/4/46/6, 'The Hung Parliament Contingency', 16 March 1978.

31 CAC: HOSK 1/123, 'Stand by to Repel Coalition – Press-Gangs', 4 May 1978; Campbell, *Margaret Thatcher*, p. 328.

32 CAC: THCR 2/1/6/194: Appendix E, 'The Hung Parliament', 12 April 1978.

33 LSE: STEEL/A1, NEC Meeting, 24 June 1978.

34 Boulton and Jones, *Hung Together*, pp. 186–9, 193–5. Smaller party coalition partners may also sometimes threaten to collapse a government unless the leader resigns in a particular instance, or, if, when selecting a replacement, their preferred candidate is not selected. See W. P. Cross and A. Blais, *Politics at the Centre: The Selection and Removal of Party Leaders in the Anglo Parliamentary Democracies* (Oxford: Oxford University Press, 2012), pp. 30–1, 150–1.

35 LSE: STEEL/A1, David Steel Letter to Liberal Candidates, 8 June 1978.

36 LSE: STEEL/A1, NEC Meeting, 24 June 1978.

37 CPA: CRD/D/7/24, Memorandum from Peter Utley to Lord Thorneycroft, 12 January 1979; Campbell, *Margaret Thatcher*, pp. 421–3.

38 Loomes, *Party Strategies in Western Europe*, pp. 5–10, 30–40, 89–90; I. Stefuriuc, *Government Formation in Multi-Level Settings: Party Strategy and Institutional Constraints* (London: Palgrave Macmillan, 2013), pp. 1–33; B. E. Rasch, 'Why Minority Governments? Executive-Legislative Relations in the Nordic Countries', in T. Persson and M. Wiberg (eds), *Parliamentary Government in the Nordic Countries at a Crossroads: Coping with Challenges from Europeanisation and Presidentialisation* (Stockholm: Santérus Academic Press, 2011), pp. 9–17; Hazell and Paun (eds), *Making Minority Government Work*, pp. 56–9; S. N. Golder, *The Logic of Pre-Electoral Coalition Formation* (Ohio: Ohio State University Press, 2006), pp. 26–9; Strøm, *Minority Government and Majority Rule*, pp. 47, 224.

39 LHASC: HART 12/31, Reform of the House of Commons, April 1978.

40 TNA: CAB 128/62, 23rd Meeting, 23 June 1977.

41 LHASC: NEC Minutes, 'Report of Meeting with SDLP Representatives', 24 June 1976.

42 Oaten, *Coalition*, pp. 185–6; Müller and Strøm, *Coalition Government in Western Europe*, pp. 39, 47, 133, 174, 539; M. Laver (ed.), *Estimating the Policy Position of Political Actors* (London: Routledge, 2001), pp. 210–11; Searle, *Country before Party*.

43 Donoughue, *Downing Street Diary*, vol. 2, p. 347.

44 TNA: PREM 16/1794, 'Note of a Meeting Held in the Prime Minister's Room', 14 December 1977, 4.05 p.m.; 'Note of a Meeting Held in the Prime Minister's Room', 14 December 1977, at 19.30; 'Prime Minister's Meeting with Mr David Steel', 26 April [1978]; 16/2201, 'Note of a Meeting Held in the Prime Minister's Room', 24 May 1978; Donoughue, *Downing Street Diary*, vol. 2, pp. 307, 331, 341, 347.

45 CPA: CRD/L/4/46/6, 'The Hung Parliament Contingency', 16 March 1978.

46 CPA: CCO 20/2/7, Various Letters, March–October 1974; OG 54, Letter to Michael Fraser, 17 April 1974; LCC 1/3/4, 36th Meeting, 30 October 1974; MF: Reel 95, 00202, Letter from Michael Fraser to Heath, 6 May 1974.

47 See Chapter 6.

48 'The Labour Way is the Better Way, 1979', General Election Manifesto 1979; PREM 16/2214, 'Note of a Meeting Held in the Cabinet Room', 21 March 1979.

49 CPA: CCO 20/7/21, Meetings, 17 September–9 October 1974; SC 12 (8), 7th Meeting, 1 July 1974; Thatcher MSS: PREM 15/2069, 12.

50 October 1974 Conservative Party General Election Manifesto; CAC: THCR 2/1/6/194:

Appendix E, 'The Hung Parliament', 12 April 1978; 2/6/1/250: Covering Note, Chris Patten to Margaret Thatcher, 7 June 1978; More Thoughts on Strategy, 31 May 1978.

51 1979 Conservative Party General Election Manifesto; CPA: LCC 1/3/16, 215th Meeting, 12 July 1978; 216th Meeting, 19 July 1978.

9

Dissolving myths:
the day the Government fell

He [Callaghan] knew the Whips did not want an election now, nor did he, and we would continue to do our best to avoid a defeat, not least through the efforts of the Whips themselves. But he would make no bargains in order to do so. The Government would be able to stand on its record over the last three – indeed five – years, a record which had been made possible because of the Whips.[1]

This concluding statement from the minute of a meeting between Callaghan and all the Government whips on 21 March 1979 summarised the position taken by the leadership following a long discussion about what strategy to adopt. Although significant political uncertainty had arisen following the failure of the devolution referenda, this meeting occurred before it was known that same day that a no confidence motion would be tabled by the SNP. The underlying scenes of turmoil from the winter were still fresh in everyone's memory. Rubbish piling up in the snow, coffins left unburied and ambulance drivers on strike. Even although stark and haunting film clips of these scenes from what has become known as the 'Winter of Discontent' have been replayed many times in news broadcasts, it is still very difficult for us to appreciate the full psychological effect of the strikes that plagued members of the public and political leaders from late 1978 to the early months of 1979, particularly when combined with one of the coldest winters on record. Even where there have been debates over the actual as opposed to the televisual impact of the many different strikes, these events continued to have a significant effect on the subsequent political discourse, evident not least in the scenes featuring prominently in Conservative election broadcasts during the 1980s and 1990s.[2]

At the same time, however, this graphic portrayal of essential public services closing down has drawn attention away from the continued importance of events in Parliament. The Callaghan Government's defeat in a no confidence motion by 311 votes to 310 on 28 March 1979 represents perhaps one of the most dramatic moments of British parliamentary history in the late twentieth century. The myth that has arisen is, in effect, not only that of denying the importance of this vote, but the suggestion that the Government entered into it without any strategy, traumatised by tackling the terrible industrial disputes.

There were a number of individual instances where the Government could have gained the additional vote to avoid defeat, involving numerous devices, including, most notably, the honouring of a gentlemen's agreement between a Government and Opposition Whip always to find a pair if needed, signing one of the associated deals on a gas pipeline or gas price reduction for Northern Ireland, or getting an ambulance to bring in the Labour MP, Sir Alfred Broughton, who was seriously ill. The events surrounding the confidence vote itself were retold in a full-length BBC thirtieth anniversary documentary, *The Night the Government Fell (A Parliamentary Coup)*, which included interviews with participants from different parties. Texts considering the causes of the defeat have generally tended either to emphasise government mistakes over handling the failure of the devolution referenda, leading the SNP to oppose the Government in Parliament, or to suggest that the Government's fate was already sealed by the 'Winter of Discontent', and that the loss of the confidence vote was a foregone conclusion or did not have a significant effect in terms of the subsequent election.[3]

However, the holding of a no confidence vote in March 1979 and its subsequent loss were by no means certain. The vote was also significant in terms of what it highlighted about the British approach to minority government. The state of minority government led to Callaghan's defeat, but not only through the lack of votes. Ironically, the defeat also arose from the Government's experience as a minority over the course of the Parliament, conditioning the response of those formulating strategy. Additionally, the 'rational actors' from different parties did not behave in the way that contemporaries and most minority government theoreticians would have predicted. A particularly noticeable feature is how often notions of fair play, and the intense fears of being seen to 'cheat', were present in the dialogues of strategy-makers, including Callaghan.

This chapter will reconsider the no confidence vote in an effort to examine both main parties' strategy development in light of the British tradition of minority government. Accepting the risks of considering alternate history or counterfactual outcomes, it is worth highlighting some of the choices that were faced by the Government when handling the no confidence issue, to evaluate the potential calculations that may have influenced contemporary strategy-makers. Initially we will consider the Government's efforts to avoid the vote, the response of both the Government and Opposition, and the weighing up of formal approaches to other parties or individual initiatives to secure extra support. Finally, the chapter will examine how far the loss of the no confidence vote impacted on the subsequent election.

Avoiding the vote

The immediate trigger for the confidence vote was the outcome of the two referenda on devolution on 1 March 1979 and the Government's response. While a majority actually voted in favour in Scotland, the 40 per cent turnout threshold for Yes votes, added through Labour backbench rebellions in Parliament, was not met, requiring that the Government repeal the Act. The SNP threatened that they would table a vote of no confidence in the Government unless a vote was brought forward in the near future on the repeal of the Scotland Act and Labour committed to voting against the repeal, as a means of bringing forward the implementation of devolution.[4]

While it may be difficult to see how such a clear statement could be misinterpreted, contemporary perceptions among both the Government and opposition parties were that the result would not seriously threaten Callaghan's survival. The Conservatives were cautious about attempting any no confidence vote, considering the SNP's intermittent backing of the Government over the previous couple of years, and the fact that their own stance on devolution ran the risk of losing the support of some of their own members and the SNP MPs, as highlighted in correspondence between backbenchers and the party leadership. One such exchange in the weeks following the referenda involved Conservative MP Anthony Nelson, who warned Thatcher that any publicly hard-line stance against devolution would potentially not only alienate some Conservatives MPs but also 'lessen the possibility of obtaining SNP support on other matters in the remainder of this Parliament'.[5] The Conservative leadership clearly shared this concern, as is evident in their seeking repeal of the Devolution Acts, while also not discouraging the thought of a further negotiated compromise on devolution, fearful of taking action that would unnecessarily antagonise the smaller parties.

In line with the practices outlined in Chapters 4 and 5, the Government first sought in March 1979 to avoid any confidence vote, or, at the very least, to delay one. Some of the different attempts by the Government to deal with the issue of the Scotland Act's repeal in a way which would stave off SNP criticism have already been highlighted in contemporary reflections. The most famous of these methods was Foot's proposal to use a parliamentary technicality of voting against the repeal in order to keep the legislation, but not then implementing it, an initiative known variously within the Government as 'the Frankenstein solution' or 'the Frankenstein formula'. This course of action would leave open the prospect of revisiting devolution after a general election. Such a move was not accepted by Callaghan and others in the Government, who feared that this change in normal parliamentary practice would be perceived as 'cheating' and would not satisfy the SNP.[6] It would, however, appear that this unusual idea was not confined to the internal dialogue of a handful of strategy-makers, as similar concepts arose in discussion with other parties. Although the Liberals were no longer in any formal agreement with the Government, Callaghan met with Steel on 6 March 1979, five days after the devolution referenda but before any confidence motion was set down, in order to discuss the situation. Steel raised the thought of Parliament voting against the repeal but not implementing the legislation until after the election as being 'an attractive scenario, particularly since the Scottish Liberal Conference was taking place in two weeks' time'. Callaghan, however, did not directly answer this suggestion, delaying with the response that 'the Government did not wish to be rushed', and diverted the conversation by opening up the prospect of discussing ways of taking devolution forward.[7] Steel's rather optimistic suggestion here may appear difficult to explain against the outcome of the referenda, but came as part of a view that a sudden election was not inevitable. Even prior to the referenda, the Liberals did not think it likely that the SNP would bring down the Government if the result were to be negative. On 23 February, Steel reported to the Liberal NEC that he believed: 'the nationalists would probably not be prepared to vote against the Government while there was still a prospect of securing the enactment of the Scotland Bill'.[8] In the 6 March meeting, the Prime Minister's suggestion of Liberal support being crucial in preventing an early general election was, in several instances, rebuffed by the Liberal leader, who reiterated his view that the SNP would enable the Government's survival.[9]

In line with the sentiments of Callaghan and Steel's meeting, the Government's approach was very much one of playing for time, while stipulating that, although they would lay the repeal order, it would be for Parliament to decide upon it, the notion of all-party talks to resolve the issue became their focus. Such a view was shared by many of those formulating government strategy, including members of the Cabinet and those attending the Policy Unit meeting of 5 March.[10] At the 8 March Cabinet meeting, a week after the referenda, it was recognised that repealing the Act 'would have immediate consequences for survival of the Government'. In this meeting, Callaghan did raise the prospect of an amended Act being implemented, while the proposition put was for talks involving all parties to try to consider how to handle the outcome of the referenda. Although there was some suggestion of attempting to achieve a compromise, these talks were conceived of by the Government from the outset primarily as a tactical device, an attempt to expose differences of opinion between opposition parties, and to delay any no confidence motion. In the frank assessment of that Cabinet meeting, 'It had to be expected that interparty talks would be no more productive now than when attempted previously, but so long as they continued, the prospect remained of avoiding the Scottish National Party voting with the Opposition on any motion of confidence.'[11] Other parties were similarly seen as likely to desert the Government: 'It was nevertheless doubtful whether the Ulster Unionists and Plaid Cymru would be prepared to abstain on such a motion and the Liberal Party was committed to seeking an early General Election.'[12]

Several options were raised at this point. The previously mentioned solution of voting against the repeal order but not implementing the Act was put forward, with the suggestion that the SNP and Liberals 'would be found ready to support such a proposal'. The counter argument to this appears to have focused on the pressure to put forward immediately the repeal orders and the danger that, if they did not, then the Opposition would put down a censure or confidence motion on the issue and probably win. All-party talks were once again stressed at this point as providing a viable means of delaying requirement for government action. Another option was to avoid any such censure motion by the Government putting down its own confidence motion 'containing a continued commitment to Devolution'. The counter to this was being unable to ensure Liberal support and the probability that Labour backbenchers opposed to devolution would find such a move 'divisive' and potentially vote against it. Rather than firmly deciding on a course of action, Callaghan summed up the discussion by once again playing for time, hoping that a week later: 'some clearer assessment might be possible of the likely attitudes and intentions of the Scottish National Party and the Scottish Labour Party'.[13]

The inability to comprehend the reaction of some of the parties fuelled government hesitation. While in some ways the avoidance of a hasty reaction was not unreasonable, the perceived delay also only served to frustrate further the MPs of the SNP, and to increase suspicions that the Government intended to avoid tackling the devolution issue. As such, by the time of the next Cabinet meeting on 15 March, the SNP were insisting on debates on the repeal order being taken by 27 March 'and that the Government should commit themselves to the rejection of the Order'.[14] In this Cabinet, it was agreed to lay the repeal orders, but, instead of any firm commitment, to make a statement pressing for further reflection and an ad hoc forum for all-party talks. Although this time there was at least some suggestion of bipartisan consensus being reached, and that a time limit of four weeks should be set to avoid charges of delay, the device appears once again to have been aimed at ensuring that the opposition parties remained divided on the issue, and even to embarrass the Conservatives if, as expected, they refused to participate in the talks.

An even more detailed insight into the thinking and internal debates behind the government approach to the referenda outcome, and in terms of dealing with the no confidence vote itself, may be seen in the extensive minutes of a meeting between Callaghan and all the Government whips on 21 March 1979, occurring just before the SNP put down their no confidence motion.[15] Much has been made of the large number of Labour MPs, up to forty or even fifty, being prepared to rebel against the Government if it attempted to enforce a vote along SNP lines to prevent the repeal of devolution. It was suggested that, if the vote were made an issue of confidence, there would be a much smaller number of rebels, out of more than three hundred. Some whips challenged this as overly optimistic, but even a small number was unacceptable to Callaghan, whose own 'estimate [was] at least six Labour Scots members would vote against the Government if they were recommended a vote against the Orders, and that would mean a split party'. His mindset was very much in line with how earlier confidence votes had been handled, where even a modest loss of Labour MPs was taken to represent a grave challenge to the Government's authority. Others, including Assistant Whip James Marshall, supported quickly bringing a vote, MPs being bound by a 'three-line whip' to support the government line. Callaghan rejected this outright, making reference to a previous time in 1969 when he had set up the Government to vote against its own order, and subsequently had had to live with charges of 'gerrymandering'. Another suggestion focused on interparty cooperation, raised by Assistant Whip John Evans, proposing a constitutional conference on devolution as a means to retain support of the SNP. This was similarly ruled out by Callaghan as 'not compatible with setting a date with the votes on the Orders which would lead to an SNP censure motion'. In fact, throughout the meeting, Callaghan also took a very harsh line against interparty cooperation, talking of his frustrations with 'being blackmailed', and concluded the meeting with the sentiment that 'he would make no bargains'. Most of the whips appear to have endorsed such a line at this stage, which encouraged the notion that no firm date should be given as the SNP had stipulated. Indeed, Assistant Whip Ann Taylor suggested that, while a late election would be better, there was 'nothing wrong, however, with the Government being defeated while it was acting responsibly', a sentiment which would appear to have endorsed the notion of daring defeat, or even seeking it on this issue.

The Government's proposal of interparty talks but without a firm commitment to a date or rejection of the repeal order was insufficient. Thereafter, the SNP put down a no confidence motion on 22 March. Once this motion was tabled, followed quickly by a Conservative no confidence motion, the room for manoeuvre of the different parties in Parliament was significantly restricted, as parties had to back up their statements of intent in order to maintain their political credibility. There was the suggestion by some Labour MPs in the days immediately prior to 28 March that the Government should immediately announce a date for an election before holding the no confidence debate, thereby seeking to avoid having to face a parliamentary vote. It does not appear that this option was given any serious consideration by Callaghan, mindful of the 'Frankenstein formula' and other previous innovations to avoid parliamentary defeat which might have been perceived as 'cheating' by opposing parties and the electorate. Having failed to avoid the no confidence vote, the Government now faced the challenge of having to win it in order to survive.[16]

Confidence vote

Approach

Accounts of the vote and various attempts by the Government and individual Labour MPs to secure a majority will be looked at in the context of minority government and how both main parties approached the confidence vote.[17] It is worth bearing in mind not only the vote, but also how the methods employed to win it might have affected the Government's subsequent ability to manage Parliament. As indicated by Strøm, the survival of minority governments depends not only on their having the confidence of a legislature, but also effectiveness in terms of actually being able to pass legislation.[18]

In these counterfactual discussions, we should be wary that the importance of individual cases does not obscure the overall picture. Given that the vote was only lost by a margin of one, it may be tempting to suggest, for example, that the Government lost on 2 March, the day immediately after the devolution referenda, when Labour MP Thomas Swain died in a car crash. Such an argument, however, can become an endless exercise in speculation devoid of historical analysis, and, even if limited in scope, also runs the potential risk of unforeseen factors, not least, for example, that of not knowing how the potential interaction of members who were not present might have changed the votes of those who were.[19]

As for the prospect of a no confidence vote itself, the Government's approach would, at first glance, appear very much reactive, almost passive. Callaghan's sentiments in the whips' meeting would seemingly confirm other perceptions of contemporaries and commentators: feeling betrayed by the trade union strikes and hostile media commentary, he had grown tired of making deals to keep the Government in office, and was acting out of frustration rather than rational calculation. Ministers and MPs echoed these sentiments through public statements predicting the end of the Government or decrying talk of any deals.[20] At the same time, government advisers privately debated their approach prior to 28 March, some, including Donoughue and McNally, arguing that more should be done to prevent defeat in the vote.[21] However, while partly borne of frustration, there was still something of an underlying strategic rationale in Callaghan's thinking, not least along the lines of 'daring defeat', calculating (albeit incorrectly) that the smaller parties would not unite to bring down the Government, and that the political climate appeared to have shifted against deal-making. Although the Lib–Lab Pact had reflected a significant instance of interparty cooperation, it had still been a temporary and pragmatic step, with many both within and outside Parliament remaining hostile to further deals. The substantial pay settlements made during the 'Winter of Discontent' almost certainly fed into this notion, and hardened the government attitude against being seen to do deals with their political counterparts. Media outlets during this period variously characterised such potential interparty agreements in Parliament, particularly with reference to the Government, as a form of 'bribe' or 'cheating'.[22]

Deal or no deal – Plaid Cymru, Liberals, UUP, SDLP

The restrictions imposed by this political environment reduced the scope for deals, and implied that any such arrangements would have to be limited and disguised as far as possible. While interparty meetings were very much in evidence in the days prior to the confidence vote, these were often ad hoc, some lacking the participation or support of Callaghan, which had been crucial in delivering the Lib–Lab negotiations in 1977.[23]

Nevertheless, this is not to say that the Government did not give greater consideration to interparty cooperation, continuing to be mindful of the smaller parties and reticent about taking actions that would imperil their support. Meetings were also subsequently held which led to successfully negotiated outcomes in terms of informal interparty cooperation, although others did not. The Government's experience showed that they were in some ways more able to handle these negotiations than had been the case in previous years, although the persistence of negative views about deal-making limited the extent to which these could be implemented.

In the Cabinet meeting of 15 March, the importance of avoiding the quick repeal of the Wales Act on Devolution was stressed, 'as this would drive Plaid Cymru into supporting the Conservative Party', looking ahead to the possibility of any confidence vote.[24] Foot went on to obtain the support of the Plaid Cymru MPs in return for legislation to help those in the quarry industry suffering from the lung disease pneumoconiosis. The Government nevertheless sought to avoid the charge of a 'bribe' by presenting this as merely giving greater priority to something already announced in the Queen's Speech the previous autumn.[25]

While the UUP MPs were under pressure from their party to oppose the Government after the enactment of the bill increasing Northern Ireland's parliamentary representation on 15 March, their votes were not considered by either main party as guaranteed. When the Cabinet speculated on the likely support from smaller parties on 15 March, the UUP were seen as potentially pivotal in any vote, but 'it was not possible to forecast their likely attitude'.[26] Conservative Northern Ireland Spokesman Airey Neave, in a report to Thatcher during February, had warned that, even after passage of the bill increasing representation 'There seems to be no assurance however that [...] Enoch and his supporters will not make some deal with the Government.'[27] Any prospective deal was initially believed likely to include elements of tougher security policy and local government reform favourable to the Ulster Unionist position. While these aspects remained important, the main condition that actually emerged and became reported upon was more one of material benefits, in the form of funding the construction of a gas pipeline between England and Northern Ireland, at a cost of £100 million. Both main party leaderships publicly rejected this idea, not least because of the significant expense, as had the 21 March whips' meeting with Callaghan, where it had previously been raised. A subsequent watering down of the UUP position was the indication that they would be willing to sustain the Government in return for a reduction in gas prices in Northern Ireland, at a cost of around £10 million. Even prior to there being any no confidence motion, there was talk of the Government trying to do a deal with the UUP, and of Foot meeting with Powell, although it appears that Callaghan would not countenance acceptance of these demands. The votes of two UUP MPs were eventually gained in a last-minute deal by Cabinet Minister Roy Hattersley, in return for a written agreement on a special prices index for Northern Ireland.[28] Possible implementation of the pipeline was considered by the Opposition, including in a CRD paper by the then researcher, Michael Portillo, on 23 February. Portillo believed that it was possible the Government would agree to the pipeline, and advised keeping Conservative options open, recognising that 'If the Government does come out in favour, *it seems impossible in political terms for us to be clearly opposed.*'[29] The paper outlined how to attack the Government depending on their response. If a government commitment to the pipeline was only general, the paper advised pressing for 'explicit' details, while any commitment to legislation would be challenged as 'delaying the decision'. If the pipeline were rejected, the given response was to 'denounce the Government [...] and pledge to re-examine the question on coming to office'. At the same time, however, the paper suggested that Conservative backing of the pipeline would not, in itself, serve as a means to secure UUP support for the confidence vote: 'On balance, it seems unlikely that a very enthusiastic response would actually bring more Unionists into our lobby at some crucial time.'

While some meetings between the Government and the smaller parties were improvised, others given greater attention in terms of the preparation of briefings, witnessed, for example, in the thirteen-page memoranda prepared at Callaghan's request before his appointment to see Fitt on 15 March. Although the document did not represent a negotiating brief, it was couched in terms of seeking to address the SDLP's main concerns, including the allegations of a secret government pact with the UUP and hostility to the Government's particular implementation of policies in Northern Ireland.[30] Another concern was that of the Northern Ireland Secretary, Roy Mason, perceived as favouring the Ulster Unionists in the implementation of policy. There is some suggestion that Hattersley had apparently promised to Fitt that he would replace Mason as Northern Ireland Secretary after the general election in order to win over Fitt's support the day before the confidence vote, although it is difficult to substantiate this.[31] It is also difficult to tell whether this offer would have been acceptable, Fitt more likely requiring the immediate removal or announced removal of Mason at the very least. Such a move, if it had become public knowledge, may well have imperilled Hattersley's position in negotiating with the UUP, and pushed the remaining UUP members into opposing, not only on this issue, but also any subsequent legislation. No record was kept of Callaghan and Fitt's meeting, and it would appear that, whatever reassurances may have been given by other members, these were not sufficient, as Fitt subsequently abstained. During the no confidence debate, Fitt's speech conveyed one of the ironies in interparty cooperation brought about by the state of minority government. At the same time as severely criticising the Government's policies in Northern Ireland, Fitt also hoped that the Government would be re-elected 'with such a majority that never again will they have to rely on the votes of the Unionists in Northern Ireland'.[32] The Government's pursuit of interparty cooperation with the UUP from 1977 onwards in order to ensure their majority had thereby helped to lose the vote of a man who had very nearly been invited to join the Government to maintain its majority in April 1976.

While the Liberals would ultimately vote against the Government and appear not to have been amenable to making further deals in advance of the confidence vote, Callaghan's meeting with Steel on 6 March did also consider further Liberal cooperation with the Government in terms of any early election.[33] Callaghan 'raised the question of how far the Liberals could help in the Government's desire to put back the date of the election'. For Steel, 'the Liberals could not be counted upon in any matter except that of the constitution', in particular if the Government gave a firm commitment to preventing the repeal of devolution. In suggesting a possible way forward, Callaghan put it to Steel that such an option would only work 'if the Liberals supported them [the Government] in any votes of confidence, otherwise there would be a precipitate General Election'. Steel could not accept this, the Liberals already having made it clear that they wanted an early election, including through votes at the Liberal Party Conference. The then still recent experiences of, and hostility to, the Pact, and the Government's demonstrated inability to deliver Liberal priorities such as PR, also made it more difficult for Steel to offer deals in this situation.

The SNP

A deal with the SNP was considered unlikely by the Government, the nationalists having viewed the response to the devolution referenda as inadequate. The Government's reaction to the SNP appears to have been one of daring defeat, expressed through harsh public rhetoric. An often-cited jibe made by Callaghan during the debate itself was that the SNP voting against the Government was 'the first time in recorded history that turkeys have been known to vote for an early Christmas'.[34] This statement had even greater significance in the context of interparty cooperation, being used previously by Liberal MP David Penhaligon in March 1977, as a statement to his colleagues against entering into the Lib–Lab Pact.[35] Whether or not the use of the phrase represented a conscious imitation of this earlier sentiment is unclear. Nevertheless, Callaghan's statement was not only a warning for the SNP, but also a reflection of what the Government believed the SNP MPs' approach to be: divided, uncertain and irrational. In the previous confidence vote in 1978, the SNP Parliamentary Party had supported Labour. Callaghan at the time had suggested to the Cabinet that even without the SNP, 'who were known to be anxiously reconsidering their position', the Government was likely to win.[36]

Now, in March 1979, the assumption was, once again, that the SNP would not seek to bring down the Government. When Steel suggested to Callaghan during their 6 March meeting that SNP support could enable the Government's survival, Callaghan's response was to dismiss this idea as being 'no solution – the SNP were quite irrational'; he further stated that 'he would not enter into talks with the SNP on that issue [devolution]'.[37] The position of the SNP MPs also appeared to be changing from the Government's perspective on a daily basis, beginning with calls both for setting a definitive date that month for a vote on the Devolution Bills and the threat of a no confidence motion, but apparently subsequently dropping the requirement for setting a clear date. In the March meeting between Callaghan and the Labour whips, prior to the confidence motion being announced, the views were very much that the SNP did not want to commit what was perceived as electoral suicide, expressed through such sentiments as 'the SNP had put them-selves on the rack and were now trying to get off it' or 'the SNP were wavering'. Similar views were expressed in Cabinet, such as, 'The SNP were unpredictable and not necessarily united.' The Government's calculation, informed by these views was that, if pushed, the SNP would not vote against them, based both upon their previous voting behaviour during the Parliament and the fact that it was not rational for them to do so, as they were suffering from a low poll-rating and were unlikely to gain anything from a Conservative victory.[38] While the early March Cabinet meetings had sought to push the line of dialogue on devolution, the Cabinet meeting on 22 March, after the SNP had put down their no confidence motion, shows an increased toughening of this position, more along the lines of daring defeat, with the party perhaps even actively wanting to be defeated, with Callaghan's summary of the SNP being that 'if they chose to precipitate an elec-tion the Government would have a strong position on which to take their stand'.[39]

However, these calculations by the Government were mistaken. Firstly, they underestimated the strength of feeling among the SNP MPs as a result of the backlash for their support of the Government in the previous confidence vote. Secondly, they did not appreciate the extent to which efforts to delay any reaction to the referendum result would only further antagonise the SNP and would convey the idea that they were not being taken seriously by Labour. Finally, they did not fully recognise that once the SNP had announced their intentions to vote against the Government they felt compelled to follow through with them, even if it was on a Conservative no confidence motion.[40]

The Conservatives

Given the breakdown of cooperation with the Opposition which characterised the early months of the Callaghan Government, and the adversarial competition between Labour and the Conservatives, it is perhaps surprising that there was no similar breakdown towards the end of the Government. While the Opposition did seek to wear down the Callaghan Administration, there was no wholesale blocking of legislative business nor any attempt to defeat the Government on every piece of legislation. In part, this reflected a realistic recognition that it would not be possible to muster a majority along with the smaller parties against the Government on every bill, nor was it desirable to do so where legislation was in the interest of both main parties. Wholesale opposition was also recognised as being more likely to alienate some of the smaller parties, which were in agreement with the Government on particular areas. Even in the days preceding the possibility of a no confidence vote in March, the Shadow Cabinet continued to adopt a mixed strategy towards legislation, opposing some cases and abstaining in others. In several instances it was even decided that the Opposition would, in fact, support the Government against rebel Labour MPs. The 7 March meeting recorded that Conservatives 'should be prepared to vote with the Government against any revolts by their [Labour] backbenchers in these debates', on a report and motion concerning prevention of terror or, a week later, to 'vote with the Government' against any backbench Labour amendment on defence estimates.[41]

The Opposition were similarly reticent on devolution and the question of a no confidence vote. The Shadow Cabinet meeting of 5 March decided that the Opposition 'should not refer to any intention to table motions of confidence for the time being' nor to seek repeal of the Devolution Acts in the first instance, and should also 'carefully avoid making any further commitments'. When subsequently considering the possibility of a no confidence motion at the 21 March Shadow Cabinet meeting, it was decided that any motion should only be tabled if 'the SNP, the Liberals, and, if possible, the Welsh Nationalists gave firm assurances of support'. The meeting similarly emphasised the importance of opposition MPs communicating to Thatcher's office 'any reports they received as to the Government's intentions or the intentions of the minority parties'. Such caution reflected previous attempted no confidence motions in 1977 and 1978, the failure of which had damaged the credibility of the Opposition. Interestingly, the required assurances did not include the UUP, which may have partly reflected opposition considerations that, following passage of the bill increasing Northern Ireland representation and pressure from constituencies, their votes were more likely to be deployed against the Government. This is not to say that Ulster Unionist support was in any way assumed, meetings being held between the Opposition and the UUP in the days running up to the vote.[42] The assurances were also based on numerical calculations that the Conservatives made of the minimum votes required to give the opposition parties a majority on a no confidence vote.

While in some countries the loss of a confidence vote has led to an alternative coalition being formed in order to govern, as indeed remained a perhaps remote possibility in 2017, this option was not even considered by the leadership of the main parties in the aftermath of the Callaghan Government's defeat in 1979. As with the formation of the Government and the beginning of the Lib–Lab Pact, there was no question of any attempt to form an opposition coalition that would immediately enter power. Such a practice was unnecessary, British precedents favouring an election following the loss of a confidence vote, Parliament being near the end of its term and the Conservatives enjoying a substantial opinion poll lead.

Opposition preparations for the no confidence vote itself followed similar lines to previous instances, including the preparation of notes for the debate itself by the CRD, primarily couched in terms of providing statistics on the comparable economic situation in other countries and seeking to challenge the Government as having blocked previous Conservative attempts at all-party discussions on devolution.[43]

Following the Government's loss of the confidence vote, there were some concerns over the election date and the passage of a caretaker Budget. Nevertheless, this tacit cooperation between the Government and Opposition continued in terms of tidying up any remaining legislative arrangements, showing that, no matter how adversarial the contest may have become, the leadership on both sides remained willing to accept existing conventions of British governance, smoothing the transition to the normal *modus operandi* of an election campaign.[44]

Individuals

It is challenging to comment with regard to overall strategy from individual initiatives that would potentially have delivered the extra vote needed for the Callaghan Government to survive. It is also not possible here, within the scope of this book, to consider in detail all the rumoured individual cases, some of which are difficult to substantiate, including hints at peerages or some other form of government patronage.[45] Instead, it would be useful to examine briefly three of these individual cases, which relate directly to aspects of minority government strategy faced by the Callaghan Administration during the course of its previous three years in office.

One such initiative was the honouring of the pairing agreement between Harrison and his Conservative counterpart, Deputy Chief Whip Bernard Weatherill. This incident raised other issues that had come up during the early part of the minority government but not been dealt with, including aforementioned efforts to enable pairing for members who were unable to attend through illness.[46] At the same time as highlighting a functional, indeed constitutional, issue, the gentlemanly conduct of Weatherill offering to abstain himself in order to keep his word but Harrison refusing to accept such a political self-sacrifice by his counterpart illustrates something of the ad hoc nature of the British political tradition of handling minority government, where such instances of cooperation could exist even in the midst of a deeply divided and adversarial setting.

Similarly, there are challenges when considering the apparent government offer to Liberal MP Clement Freud, which was not acted upon, of obtaining his abstention by missing his train back from Liverpool, in return for the Government passing a version of his Private Member's Bill on Official Information.[47] The Government had opposed the legislation in the past, which undoubtedly presented an additional barrier, but did not, in of itself, necessarily make the attempt unworkable. Rather, what prevented success of this measure was the way in which it was approached, again indicating something of the negative side of the ad hoc nature of handling minority government. The contact with Freud was apparently made by Labour MP Chris Price, on behalf of the Chief Whip, through an unscheduled phone call while Freud was out campaigning in Liverpool for the upcoming parliamentary by-election. That this communication was only made in the final hours before the vote, contained no clear definition of what any legislation would actually look like and was in such a form as to lack the direct communication of any senior government figure, such as Callaghan or Foot, or even of a written assurance such as was given to the two UUP members, inevitably led Freud to question the credibility of the offer. Freud would also have approached the issue with the experiences of the Pact and the Government's failure to deliver Liberal priorities, including PR on direct elections, fresh in his mind. The covert nature of communications, reflecting the government desire to avoid acknowledging deals, would also potentially have set Freud against his party, which he was unwilling to countenance.[48] The Government's view of the bill was evident in Cabinet discussions on 15 March, before the no confidence vote had been announced, and showed no indication of attempting to enlist Freud's support. Indeed, criticism of the extensive nature of the legislation was scathing, albeit with some arguing for part of the bill being considered in a modified form for a subsequent Parliament. Callaghan's view in the meeting was uncompromising, suggesting that, through the Government submitting their own counterproposals, even if the legislation could not be defeated, 'the Government would be in a stronger position to hold back progress on the Bill'. Unlike minority governments elsewhere, the Callaghan Administration had not sought greater co-authorship or collaboration between government and opposition members on legislation. While there is no guarantee that such measures might have enabled the deal with Freud, the Government's continued majoritarian stance and handling of such offers certainly helped to restrict the possibility for successful cooperation with individuals from other parties in advance of the no confidence vote.[49]

The third difficult issue to consider here is that of Broughton, and the decision made not to bring him to Parliament by ambulance in order to vote, because of his serious ill health. This is perhaps the most widely recognised government decision on a measure relating to the actual night of the confidence vote itself, inspiring a speculative radio drama thirty years later centred on Broughton and the events of that evening.[50] When the whips were meeting after the vote, there were arguments over what could have been done differently so as to win, including on the point of bringing in Broughton, who had been willing to make the journey, even though his wife and doctor, fearing for his health, did not want him to go. Broughton had been brought in for previously tight votes, going against his doctor's advice, although on this occasion, as indicated by Philip Norton, his doctor threatened to go public 'if he were brought in for the vote'. Broughton was reportedly unhappy in the following days that he had not been able to go. He died five days later on 2 April 1979.[51]

While it is important to maintain a scholarly distance in any historical study, it is difficult with what was clearly as much an emotional and very human decision not to risk Broughton's frail health, even if it could save the Government. There are no formulae in minority government theory or in political strategy more generally that can claim to be fit to judge what the right decision would have been in this instance. Looking briefly at the hypothetical outcomes from a rather cold and strategic standpoint, Broughton's vote could have saved the Government that night, assuming that all others were cast the same way, but its use would also have extracted an added political price in terms of reliance on ill members, and would not have been available in subsequent controversial votes on repeal of the Devolution Acts and on the Budget.

Even in the event that the Government had been able to survive and to muster majorities to remain effective over the subsequent weeks, if Broughton had died while travelling to or from Westminster, it would almost certainly have been presented very negatively in the press, whether fairly or unfairly. This coverage would also have fed into opposition mantras of a dying government that was willing to sacrifice its own people in order to survive, both literally and figuratively. It would likely have been viewed by the electorate as a callous act on the part of the Labour leadership, and would have weighed heavily upon those who had taken the decision, including Callaghan. In discussion between the whips, one thought raised was the dreadful prospect of Broughton dying while within the precincts of the Palace of Westminster. While there was some thought of post-rationalising this possibility, that since commoners were not permitted to die in the Palace by law he would be regarded as having died in the ambulance or in the hospital, such a cold technicality was not shared by most members of the Government. Although there is some suggestion that Callaghan might have changed his mind at the last moment, it was too late to transport Broughton for the vote, even if this had been desirable. Although it had meant the end of his administration, Callaghan believed on reflection that, on the issue of Broughton at least, he had made the right decision.[52]

Confidence defeat and election result

Those within the Government who had sought to avoid defeat on 28 March feared the consequences of the vote on the subsequent electoral campaign.[53] It is very difficult to establish how much defeat in the confidence vote made a difference to the final electoral result for the Government, whether in terms of forcing the election earlier than had been intended by Callaghan, or in damaging Labour's electoral prospects through depressing morale and providing a powerful symbol of its parliamentary weakness.

With regard to electoral timing, it is impossible to say what the impact of the extra month or several months would have had. In the event that the confidence vote had been won, Callaghan may well have chosen June, September or October as opposed to May as an election date, following on from planning discussed in Chapter 7. It is unlikely that another no confidence motion would have been proposed by the Opposition in the months following March 1979 for fear of a further loss of credibility, unless they could have been assured that such a vote would succeed by a reasonable margin. It was more likely that Callaghan would have been able to choose to dissolve Parliament one or several months later, nearer the absolute deadline of the five-year parliamentary term. There were many within the Government, including the whips and those holding marginal constituencies, who preferred going on until autumn. Indeed, prior to the devolution referenda, Callaghan himself appeared to express such a preference for October.[54] While opinion poll changes during the campaign for the 1979 election were not as dramatic as those of June 2017, the polling situation during this period was nevertheless liable to change radically. Changes in opinion polls over the previous eight to ten months, oscillating between a Conservative lead of around three to eight, to a government lead of five to six in September, followed again by a Conservative lead of six to twenty-one, demonstrated to those in any doubt just how quickly the situation could be transformed. Another interesting point to note is that, although government polling support dropped during the early months of 1979, it never reached the low point experienced during the financial crisis and IMF loan in late 1976.[55] Some of the problems of the 'Winter of Discontent' would have perhaps lessened given more time, but there is no guarantee that an extra couple of months would have changed the underlying factors which led to a Conservative victory, whether in terms of the economic situation or frustration with the, in some cases continuing, industrial action.

The Government would have had the advantage of delivering a pre-election Budget that was more than merely a caretaker measure, but would still have had to secure parliamentary support for this and other legislation through negotiations with the smaller parties. The financial situation had also left limited room for politically advantageous Budget measures, an issue raised by Healey in Budget discussions with the Cabinet on 1 March. According to Donoughue,

Callaghan's preference for an October election would also appear to have changed to that of May over the days following 1 March, regardless of whether or not the Government won a prospective no confidence vote in Parliament.[56] This sentiment was partly borne out of Callaghan's frustration of dealing with the demands made by the other parties following the devolution referenda.

As for the effect of the confidence vote itself on the outcome, the opinion polls did not significantly change as a result of the defeat. Those published in the days immediately following 28 March showed a Conservative lead of between six and twenty-one points, largely in line with the eight- to twenty-point range in polls during February and early March. This trend is consistent even when considering the inaccuracies of polling already discussed, and even when discounting the eleven- to twenty-point Conservative leads perceived as overestimates, or polls deviating from the trend such as that showing a 0.7 per cent Labour lead on 28 April. Although the Conservatives won the election with a 5.2 per cent swing, the largest since 1945, and a comfortable 7 per cent lead over Labour, it does not appear that the loss of the confidence vote itself had a significant or lasting negative impact on the Government's poll ratings.[57]

It is more difficult to calculate the intangible effects of the confidence defeat on government members and their supporters. Undoubtedly the defeat further depressed the morale of Labour MPs and activists, but it could be suggested that it also helped to galvanise the campaign in terms of fighting the Conservatives. There is not scope here to discuss campaign strategy in full, but, whether or not surveys that differed widely from the trend are discounted, the polls do appear to have narrowed over the course of the campaign. The result has also understandably been judged against the losses suffered in 1979, or as part of a longer-term Labour decline, their percentage of the vote falling, as had been the case at every election since 1945 – the only exception being the landslide victory of 1966.[58] At the same time, the Government actually won slightly more votes overall in 1979, 11.52 million, than they had in the previous election, 11.45 million. Even though this rise in votes may be partly explained by a poorer turnout in 1974, despite losing fifty seats overall, Labour's performance did not represent a wholesale collapse in support. Although there were divisions within the party, these were more long-standing and do not appear to have been exacerbated by the confidence vote defeat itself. These divisions also did not manifest themselves as splits or the formation of new parties prior to the election, as would be the case with the loss of members to the SDP in the following parliament.[59]

Although, to some extent, the Callaghan Government was brought down by the events of the 'Winter of Discontent' and loss of the devolution referenda, both main parties did give greater strategic consideration than has previously been recognised as to how to approach the challenges of the no confidence vote in March 1979, whether in terms of either preserving or ousting the Government.

While attempting to avoid the vote, the Government's failure to do so and the loss of SNP support arose from miscalculations based upon previous experiences of dealing with the smaller parties during the course of Labour's Minority Government, and the misreading of SNP intentions. Although partly motivated by frustration with previous experiences of interparty deals, Callaghan continued to pursue what he considered to be a rational strategy, daring some of the opposition parties to defeat him, while simultaneously, albeit reluctantly in some cases, trying to facilitate deals that would enable the Government's survival. In some of these cases of deal-making, or the potential employment of a seriously ill member to ensure victory, there were prices which the government leadership, or individuals within the Government, were not willing to pay, whether for political or principled reasons. These possible initiatives reflected issues that had arisen but not been dealt with during Labour's Minority Government, whether in terms of cross-party cooperation or pairing of absent MPs.

The Opposition were cautious, given their previous unsuccessful experiences with confidence votes, and sought to ensure that they had sufficient support from the smaller parties before proceeding. Their reticence over issues such as the outcome of the devolution referenda also sought to avoid unnecessarily alienating the SNP, whose support they recognised as crucial in terms of winning against the Government.

The confidence vote signalled the end of three years of minority government under Callaghan, and the beginning of an election campaign that would result in Conservative Majority Governments for most of the next eighteen years, the exceptions being two brief periods of minority government under Major that are part of, but seldom recognised as distinct from, his embattled majority administration in 1992–97.

Notes

1 TNA: PREM 16/2214, 'Note of a Meeting Held in the Cabinet Room', 21 March 1979.
2 Heppell and Theakston (eds), *How Labour Governments Fall*, pp. 8, 14–60; Coates (ed.), *What Went Wrong*.
3 Sandbrook, *Seasons in the Sun*, pp. 765–81; Heppell and Theakston (eds), *How Labour Governments Fall*, pp. 127–8; Seldon and Hickson (eds), *New Labour, Old Labour*, pp. 197, 200–1; E. Shaw, *The Labour Party since 1979: Crisis and Transformation* (London: Routledge, 2002), p. 7; Hennessy, *The Prime Minister*, pp. 393–6; Callaghan, *Time and Chance*, pp. 558–63; BBC Documentary, *The Night the Government Fell*. For an alternative view regarding the inevitability of the 'Winter of Discontent' see Thorpe, *A History of the British Labour Party*, pp. 205–6. See Chapter 2.
4 TNA: CAB 128/65, 11th Meeting, 8 March 1979.
5 CAC: THCR 2/1/3/14, Correspondence between Anthony Nelson and Margaret Thatcher, 13–15 March 1979.
6 Ian Aitken, 'Callaghan Dilemma on Home Rule Acts', *Guardian* (16 March 1979); Morgan, *Michael Foot*, pp. 365–7; Callaghan, *Time and Chance*, pp. 559–60.

7   TNA: PREM 16/2201, Prime Minister's Meeting with Mr David Steel, 6 March 1979.
8   LSE: LIBERAL PARTY/1/10, Minutes of the Meeting of the National Executive Committee, 23 February 1979.
9   TNA: PREM 16/2201, Prime Minister's Meeting with Mr David Steel, 6 March 1979.
10 Donoughue, *Downing Street Diary*, vol. 2, p. 454.
11 TNA: CAB 128/65, 11th Meeting, 8 March 1979.
12 *Ibid*.
13 Donoughue, *Downing Street Diary*, vol. 2, p. 456.
14 TNA: CAB 128/65, 12th Meeting, 15 March 1979.
15 TNA: PREM 16/2214, 'Note of a Meeting in the Cabinet Room', 21 March 1979.
16 Ian Aitken and Ann Clwyd, 'Government Rejects Nationalist Pressure', *Guardian* (27 March 1979).
17 See, for example, Donoughue, *Downing Street Diary*, vol. 2, pp. 470–3; BBC Documentary, *The Night the Government Fell*; Callaghan, *Time and Chance*, pp. 562–3.
18 Strøm, *Minority Government and Majority Rule*, p. 5.
19 HC Hansard, vol. 963, col. 875 (5 March 1979).
20 Aitken and Clwyd, 'Government Rejects Nationalist Pressure'; Callaghan, *Time and Chance*, p. 562.
21 Donoughue, *Downing Street Diary*, vol. 2, pp. 469–71.
22 See Chapter 9: Avoiding the vote.
23 TNA: CAB 128/65, 11th Meeting, 8 March 1979; 12th Meeting, 15 March 1979.
24 TNA: CAB 128/65, 12th Meeting, 15 March 1979.
25 Donoughue, *Downing Street Diary*, vol. 2, pp. 466, 468; Callaghan, *Time and Chance*, pp. 558–63.
26 TNA: CAB 128/65, 12th Meeting, 15 March 1979.
27 CAC: THCR 2/1/3/14, The Situation in Northern Ireland, 8 February 1979.
28 TNA: PREM 16/2214, 'Note of a Meeting in the Cabinet Room', 21 March 1979; Adam Raphael, 'Only Two Votes in it', *Observer* (25 March 1979); Donoughue, *Downing Street Diary*, vol. 2, p. 461; BBC Documentary, *The Night the Government Fell*.
29 CPA: CRD/D/7/19, Gas Pipeline to Northern Ireland, 23 February 1979; emphasis in original.
30 TNA: PREM 16/2140, Assorted Correspondence and Briefing Notes, 14–19 March 1979.
31 Donoughue, *Downing Street Diary*, vol. 2, p. 469.
32 HC Hansard, vol. 965, cols 521–2 (28 March 1979); BBC Documentary, *The Night the Government Fell*.
33 TNA: PREM 16/2201, Prime Minister's Meeting with Mr David Steel, 6 March 1979.
34 HC Hansard, vol. 965, cols 471–2 (28 March 1979).
35 Michie and Hoggart, *The Pact*, p. 156.
36 TNA: CAB 128/64, 43rd Meeting, 14 December 1978.
37 TNA: PREM 16/2201, Prime Minister's Meeting with Mr David Steel, 6 March 1979. See Chapter 7.
38 TNA: PREM 16/2214, 'Note of a Meeting in the Cabinet Room', 21 March 1979; Ian Aitken, 'Callaghan Uses Delaying Tactics', *Guardian* (20 March 1979); Ian Aitken, 'Callaghan Sticks to Devolution as SNP Ponder Vote', *Guardian* (22 March 1979); Aitken and Clwyd, 'Government Rejects Nationalist Pressure'; Callaghan, *Time and Chance*, pp. 559–60.
39 TNA: CAB 128/65, 13th Meeting, 22 March 1979.

40 See Chapter 9: Confidence vote.

41 CPA: LCC 1/3/16, 231st Meeting, 31 January 1979; 236th Meeting, 7 March 1979; 237th Meeting, 14 March 1979; 238th Meeting, 21 March 1979.

42 CPA: LCC 1/3/16, 235th Meeting, 5 March 1979; 236th Meeting, 7 March 1979; Ian Aitken, 'Thatcher Action on Vote Urged', *Guardian* (15 March 1979); BBC Documentary, *The Night the Government Fell.*

43 CPA: CRD/B/23/5, No Confidence Debate, 27 March 1979.

44 CAC: THCR 2/6/2/118, Meetings between the Opposition and Civil Servants in a Pre-Electoral Period, 30 March 1979.

45 Donoughue, *Downing Street Diary*, vol. 2, pp. 476, 473; BBC Documentary, *The Night the Government Fell.*

46 Sandbrook, *Seasons in the Sun*, pp. 777–8; BBC Documentary, *The Night the Government Fell.*

47 Heppell and Theakston (eds), *How Labour Governments Fall*, p. 128.

48 See Chapter 5.

49 TNA: CAB 128/65, 12th Meeting, 15 March 1979; Benn, *Conflicts of Interest*, pp. 445–6, 472–3.

50 BBC Radio 4, *How are You Feeling, Alf?* (8 June 2009).

51 'Too-Ill MP "Upset"', *Guardian* (30 March 1979); Donoughue, *Downing Street Diary*, vol. 2, pp. 470, 473; Sandbrook, *Seasons in the Sun*, p. 777; Seldon and Hickson (eds), *New Labour, Old Labour*, pp. 200–1; BBC Documentary, *The Night the Government Fell.*

52 Callaghan, *Time and Chance*, p. 562; Donoughue, *Downing Street Diary*, vol. 2, p. 471; BBC Documentary, *The Night the Government Fell.*

53 Donoughue, *Downing Street Diary*, vol. 2, p. 469.

54 Donoughue, *Downing Street Diary*, vol. 2, pp. 452–3. See Chapter 7.

55 See Chapter 7.

56 TNA: CAB 128/65, 10th Meeting, 1 March 1979; Donoughue, *Downing Street Diary*, vol. 2, pp. 458–9.

57 See polls of NOP, Gallup/*Telegraph*, MORI, *Observer*, 1 February 1979 to 2 May 1979; F. Conley, *General Elections Today* (Manchester: Manchester University Press, 1994), pp. 97–9.

58 Conley, *General Elections Today*, pp. 97–9.

59 See Chapter 2: Wilson and Callaghan 1974–79.

10

Rewriting political mythology in 2017

> I worked in a minority government, I worked in the 1974 to 79 Labour Government, and if you're in that situation, then you have to compromise not only with your own side, but also with the other side as well, that's just the way the alchemy and the chemistry of Parliament works.[1]

This comment in the early hours of election night on 8 June 2017 by Jack Straw (who held a number of senior offices in Labour Governments between 1997 and 2010) epitomises how the experience of the 1970s has been assimilated by subsequent generations of decision-makers, and its critical importance in framing the approaches of both main parties to the hung parliament and newly formed Conservative Minority Government.

The previous chapters of this book have sought to reconsider Labour Governments and Conservative Oppositions during the minority governments of the 1970s. These administrations show the distinctively British tradition of minority government, firmly grounded within and inspired by its own historical majoritarian political culture, yet possessing a degree of pragmatic adaptation and development. The aspects examined also provide an alternative perspective on the established wider political science theory, and the experiences of minority governments internationally. This final chapter aims to look at the British experience of minority government after the 1970s. In this way, we may attempt to reconceptualise the place of Wilson and Callaghan's Minority Governments against the broader backdrop of recent British political history up to and including the aftermath of the general election of June 2017.

1979 to 2017

The year 2017 marked the formation of the first post-electoral minority government in Westminster since 1974. The manner in which this administration entered office demonstrates that Wilson and Callaghan's experiences, and the wider British tradition of minority government, continue to exert significant influence. Minority governments occurred during two brief periods in the 1990s at Westminster, a fact which had remained a relative lacuna in the media and scholarly commentary prior to the June 2017 election.[2] The creation of the devolved and distinctly more consensual legislatures of Scotland and Wales have led to new experiences of minority governance that, while partly influenced by Westminster, have developed their own traditions, which, in themselves, would constitute major studies. Even though the 2010 general election resulted in the Conservative–Liberal Democrat Coalition, this arose from exceptional economic and political circumstances which made a minority administration almost unviable, but was nevertheless informed by the experiences of their 1970s counterparts.

On losing their majority in November 1994, Major's Conservative Government faced some of the same questions as Callaghan in 1976, opposing MPs challenging the new 'minority government's' authority to implement policy, and arguing that opposition parties should hold the majority of seats on parliamentary committees. Indeed, these challenges were issued making specific reference to the Callaghan Government's experience.[3] The Major Government's response was also similar to its predecessors: a continued adherence to majoritarian principles and a public rhetoric of defiance that dismissed there being any alternative administration, while simultaneously engaging in political compromises where necessary (albeit with limited success).

Questions of interparty cooperation also formed an important part of this government, with Major compelled to rely upon the support of the UUP, particularly in the latter stages of 1996–97, while Labour engaged in informal agreements on electoral and constitutional matters with the Liberal Democrats.[4]

It is worth noting that there was only one defeat in each of the six-month periods when the Major Government lost its majority (November 1994–April 1995 and December 1996–May 1997), far fewer than the comparative of at least three to six defeats every six months under Callaghan, or the large number of summer defeats for Wilson in 1974. This seems especially ironic when considering the comparable embattled state of the Callaghan and Major Governments, which have tended to be cited in the same breath as exemplars of parliamentary weakness.[5] At the same time, however, Major's Administration was also in some ways more radical. The most obvious example of this was that it deliberately removed its own parliamentary majority and entered a state of minority government by withdrawing party membership from eight MPs in November 1994 (in response to rebellion over a vote on the European Communities (EC) Finance Bill), and only restored the Whip six months later. Confidence votes, rather more so than in Callaghan's experience, were employed by Major as a means to reverse actual policy defeats, including the adoption of the Protocol on Social Policy as a condition of the Maastricht Treaty in 1993. Major also more directly and publicly raised the prospect of an early general election in an effort to ensure the support from Conservative MPs.

Commentaries seeking to examine the foundations and antecedents of the 2010 UK coalition government have also looked at many historic forms of cross-party cooperation. Some of these considered more recent Conservative–Liberal Democrat cooperation at local council level, or the Conservatives and Liberal Democrats working together with Labour rebels to defeat the Brown Government in certain parliamentary votes, such as on the issue of Ghurkha settlement rights in 2009. Other more historic formative experiences of interparty cooperation have similarly been raised for the Liberals in particular: the Lib–Lab Pact of the 1970s; the Social Democrat Party of the 1980s; and the Blair–Ashdown Project of the 1990s.[6] However, while these influences were significant, the wider experience of the minority governments of the 1970s, and the distinctive British tradition of minority government, may be regarded as having had an equally profound impact. The 1970s minority governments provide perhaps one of the closest comparable situations to the post-2010 coalition and post-2017 minority government, serving as the early genesis of ideas that have helped to shape Britain's contemporary political situation.

Experiences of the Wilson and Callaghan Governments were also very much present during the coalition formation process in May 2010, whether in historical summaries of British experiences of minority and coalition government during media coverage of the campaign and negotiations, to some of the insights given into the discussions between coalition negotiators within the different political parties. When contemplating the possibility of minority or coalition government in 2007, Brown's political advisers first turned to examining the civil service files of Britain's previous minority government experiences in 1974 and thereafter, showing the continued influence of recent history on decision-making in the minds of those formulating strategy within Britain's political establishment.[7]

There will no doubt be, in the future, much more examination of the June 2017 election and Conservative Minority Government in the light of Britain's wider history and tradition of minority governance. At the time of writing, this government has been in office for several months, but there is still great uncertainty as to its operation and political future. There was much reference to the 1970s precedents by commentators during election night itself, although these were primarily summaries, focusing on the long-term unviability of minority governments.[8] It is too early to say what the long-term impact will be of the new arrangements for handling the exigencies of minority government, and, in some cases, there are details that will never be known. There will, no doubt, be other material that will not become apparent until after the Government has left office and key players may be interviewed, or until government and party files of the present administration are released after twenty to thirty years. However, although it is early to make comparisons between the May Minority Administration and that of her predecessors in the 1970s, the parallels and contrasts drawn in our summation may be a catalyst for future debate.

Wilson, Callaghan and May

Formation

In both 1923–24 and February 1974, the Conservatives lost their majorities in the elections and a Labour Minority Government was formed. These examples were cited in 2017, particularly the February 1974 example, which was invoked by commentator and former Labour Cabinet Minister Ed Balls, immediately following the announcement of the exit poll.[9] However, an important difference is that, in both these cases, the minority government was led by the party who had been in opposition before the election, whereas in June 2017 it was, in the first instance, a continuation of the incumbent government, the Conservatives.

We do not, at this stage, have the full details to determine the extent to which Labour or the Conservatives made any plans for a minority government in June 2017, although there were factors which might have limited any such planning. As with February 1974, the indecisive result was almost completely unexpected. However, the 1974 result occurred over forty-three years after the previous post-electoral hung parliament. By contrast, there were widespread media and opinion poll predictions of indecisive results in 2010 and 2015, parties (some more so than others) already having given more consideration as to how to respond strategically if there were no clear winner. This context, in addition to greater interparty cooperation at devolved levels, provided the parties in June 2017 with more political actors who had recent experience of hung parliaments and precedents to draw on. How far this advice was relevant to the particular situation, or was acted upon in June 2017, remains to be seen.

The Conservative/DUP negotiations in 2017 were, in some ways, more characteristic of those in the 1970s between Callaghan and the UUP. In 2010, publicly announced negotiating teams from both the Conservatives and Liberal Democrats were followed by crowds of reporters as they marched into and out of Whitehall buildings. By contrast, in June 2017, negotiations were mostly conducted behind closed doors, without public acknowledgement of their progress beyond general statements. At the same time, however, this was a very different type of arrangement from its 1970s counterpart, publicly acknowledged and symbolically publicised through stage-managed photo opportunities of DUP leaders outside No. 10 Downing Street, along with the formal signing of the Agreement.

It may have been suggested that a formal Conservative/DUP coalition in June 2017 would have provided a more stable government, and, at one stage in BBC coverage on Saturday 10 June, there was talk of all options being considered, including coalition.[10] However, it is unclear how seriously this possibility was actually being entertained, and the already adverse reaction to the idea from a number of Conservatives, including over the DUP's more socially conservative stance on several issues, made such a move politically too costly. This concern in some ways mirrored that of the rejection of Labour's coalition with the SDLP in the early stages of the Callaghan Government.

In the 2010 negotiations and during the 2015 election campaign, leaders and senior MPs from different parties made very public statements about 'red lines' and priorities for interparty discussions. By contrast, many statements from the government leadership in June 2017 echoed the 1970s approach of general intentions and political ideology, but not specifically setting out negotiating positions. May's short speech outside Downing Street after her audience with the Queen, in which she alluded to working with 'friends' in the DUP, contained very little detail, although sentiments on Brexit, security and fairness may have signalled particular priorities for discussion. Northern Ireland First Minister and DUP leader Arlene Foster's televised speech from Belfast later that day could be viewed in a similar light. Some further statements publicly re-emphasised broad negotiating goals, including Foster setting out in the *Belfast Telegraph* on 12 June what was described as her priorities of 'strengthening the Union, a good deal on Brexit, and getting "Stormont up and running again for the benefit of all"', but a lot of the detail in initial negotiations, including precise policy proposals, were conducted privately.[11]

That the Conservative Chief Whip Gavin Williamson travelled to Belfast in order to hold discussions with DUP Chief Whip Sir Jeffrey Donaldson on Saturday 10 June was a significant move on the part of the Conservatives. In contrast, previous interparty discussions during hung parliaments in the 1970s, 1990s and 2010 were all primarily conducted within Parliament or surrounding Whitehall buildings, including at No. 10. It is less clear the extent to which the decision to hold this meeting in Northern Ireland was intended as a gesture seeking to facilitate better negotiations, by meeting the DUP on their home territory, as opposed to being a method of avoiding publicity. It may even be, in the ad hoc nature of previous negotiations, something that simply emerged because of convenience or necessity, particularly at a time when there had not yet apparently been formal consultation of Conservative MPs as a whole. Nevertheless, this meeting would certainly appear to have facilitated the rapid movement towards announcement of the outline of a draft Confidence and Supply Agreement on the evening of Saturday 10 June.[12]

The speed at which announcements were made about a draft deal in June 2017 is striking. Rather than the five days before a coalition was formally confirmed in 2010, the time spent negotiating the Lib–Lab Pact in 1977 or the four days of failed coalition negotiations in February 1974, the broad shape of the Conservative/DUP deal as Confidence and Supply was already being publicly announced as agreed only a day after the last election result had been declared in June 2017. However, subsequent announcements suggest that this initial optimism was somewhat premature, with interparty talks continuing some two weeks after the election, and public announcements indicating that there were outstanding issues to resolve.[13] While possibly a result of miscommunication, it is also likely that the Conservative leadership wished to ensure that the architecture of an agreement was quickly put into place and publicised in order to reinforce their narrative of 'stable government'. The aim of this move would have been to avoid speculation that could harm the financial markets, to solidify the Government's position following the unexpectedly bad election result, and to buttress May's position as Prime Minister against both Labour's narrative of being ready to serve as a minority government, as well as the initiatives of those within the Conservatives who would potentially seek to remove her as leader. Unlike the Labour Minority Governments of 1924 and February 1974, the Conservatives in 2017, as the incumbent administration having lost seats, could not rely on any 'honeymoon' period in which opposition parties would be less inclined to vote down their major measures, such as the Queen's Speech. The perceived success of Labour's election campaign and popularity of Jeremy Corbyn as a leader presented further challenges for the Conservatives.

The media reporting of the prospective Conservative/DUP Confidence and Supply deal when it was first announced showed not only the immediate comparisons with the 1970s counterpart of the Pact, but also the way in which official narratives continue to rely on long-established understandings of the period. An example of this around half an hour after the outline deal was first publicly acknowledged on Saturday 10 June 2017 involved a newsreader on the BBC saying of Confidence and Supply that 'Last time it was used, according to the BBC Website, a very reliable source, was in the 1970s during the Lib–Lab Pact.'[14] This is in contrast to Kirkup's point that the Pact was not a typical Confidence and Supply arrangement, and our own analysis in Chapter 5 which challenges whether, in fact, it guaranteed either Confidence or Supply.

As with the Wilson Government, the Queen's Speech was a major confrontation and test of the new Conservative/DUP Government in 2017. While the 1974 Government feared that changing the date of the Speech would be a sign of weakness, public reporting of the decision on 12 June 2017 to delay the Speech should be seen in the context where opposition parties were almost guaranteed to vote against it, and where there were ongoing interparty negotiations to ensure a majority. Opposition parties seized on this delay as a sign of weakness, but it is difficult to see how the Conservative Minority Government could have taken the risk under the circumstances, as they wanted to try to avoid the fate of Baldwin being defeated by Parliament on the Queen's Speech in 1924. As pointed out in BBC coverage, there has been a longer interval between elections and the Speech in the past, as it was delivered twenty days after the election and coalition formation in 2010. The difference on that occasion, however, was that the date had been established prior to the election, in anticipation of interparty negotiations, rather than being delayed after the election by a government which needed more time to negotiate for their majority.[15] There were various efforts by the Government to justify the delay, including a reference to the quintessentially arcane British practice of the Speech being written on vellum and the ink taking days to dry. Regardless of how far this explanation was accepted by commentators, the delayed Speech was successfully passed with DUP support. It may be that the advance scheduling of a longer post-electoral time period in which to prepare the Queen's Speech becomes a standard fixture in Britain, if parties wish to allow time for the possible contingency of future indecisive results.

As the incumbent opposition, Labour's approach to prospective minority government following the June 2017 election was, in some ways, surprisingly close to that adopted by Wilson and the Shadow Cabinet in February 1974, publicly signalling a readiness to take office, opposing any deals with other parties and daring those others to defeat their prospective legislative programme if and when it was put forward. This was exemplified through the election night media coverage itself in the statements made in interviews by senior Labour MPs, including Shadow Foreign Secretary Emily Thornberry: 'we would put forward a Queen's Speech or Budget and call on other parties to support this [daring them to defeat us]. It would then be up to them [the smaller parties] to explain to their constituents why they voted it down.'[16]

However, the 2017 approach was even more assertive than in 1974, very publicly discussing how Labour could put forward an alternative Queen's Speech, even if the Conservatives remained in office. Similar ideas were originally proposed in discussion among Wilson's strategy-makers in 1974, but remained unimplemented after Heath chose to resign. Labour's February 1974 position was also somewhat different from June 2017. In the former case, they gained 20 seats and were the largest party with just over 301, whereas in the latter, they had gained 30 seats but, coming from a lower starting point, still came second at 262 to the Conservatives' 318 seats. The Conservatives proximity to having an overall majority in June 2017, having a clear lead in seats over Labour, and the number of opposition parties who would have had to join together would make it potentially much more challenging for a prospective Labour Minority Government to function than was the case in 1974.

In part, Labour's approach in June 2017 may be seen as the party positioning itself for a subsequent election. However, it may have been actively considering the possibility of replacing the Conservatives in office, seeking to use the institutional advantages to govern as a minority until such a time as there could reasonably be another early election. Comparable considerations to this from the 1970s could be Conservative discussions about a government of national unity, or the speculative assumptions by Callaghan's advisers about Labour needing to construct a government if Thatcher failed to form a Conservative minority or coalition administration after a 1978 or 1979 election. If, for any reason, the Conservative/DUP Government were to be defeated on a confidence issue in

2018 or thereafter, there may be speculation of an alternative administration being formed, rather than holding an immediate election. Such a government might potentially be couched in terms of Labour's position of daring other parties to defeat them. An alternative formula may be that of the 'progressive alliance' referred to by some of the smaller parties during and after the campaign, including the SNP. It is, however, short of exceptional circumstances, doubtful that Labour would accept the 'alliance' justification publicly, given their continued political opposition to these parties nationally.

While not being a totally inconceivable outcome, it is unlikely that this arrangement could function for long, even if other parties of the proposed Labour minority/'progressive alliance' continued to work together (the current divisions between them and hostility to formal interparty cooperation make this less likely). The only way to maintain this hypothetical Labour Administration would be if, daring other parties to defeat them, Labour were able to persuade Conservative MPs, as in March 1974, that any vote to bring down the Government would be detrimental to the Opposition in a subsequent election campaign. It should be noted that, even when successful, this approach was maintained for barely three months in 1974 before the Opposition felt sufficiently emboldened to vote down significant government measures.

Strategy-makers

The resignation of May's Co-Chiefs of Staff, Nick Timothy and Fiona Hill, the day after the election results were declared, signalled significant changes to those advising the Prime Minister. Their swiftly appointed replacement, Gavin Barwell, would appear to have been selected in order to mollify MPs who were highly critical of Timothy and Hill, given his diplomatic skills, honed through long-standing experience both as a minister and having worked for the Conservative Party Headquarters for seventeen years before becoming an MP. This is contrary to 1974 and 1976, where those advising the Prime Minister were retained following the formation of each minority government. However, there are instructive examples from both the 1970s and more recent history as to how strategy-making may change in the June 2017 Government.

The 2010 coalition involved significant new decision-making arrangements, including separate pre-Cabinet meetings of the respective parties, the full Cabinet consisting of both parties and the high-level 'Quad' meetings between David Cameron, Nick Clegg, George Osbourne and Danny Alexander. The 2017 Confidence and Supply arrangement did leave a number of bills to be negotiated on an issue-by-issue basis, in some ways institutionally resembling Callaghan's agreement with the UUP in 1977, but the Conservatives in 2017 created a new formalised structure for consultation, more in line with the Lib–Lab Pact. There are also established links between the Conservatives and

DUP which will continue to play a significant role, ranging from discussions held by whips to other informal connections. One connection that featured in news coverage following the June election was that of the champagne reception hosted by the DUP at the Conservative Conference in 2016. Although this may, as suggested by Foster, have partly arisen from a miscommunication about the scale of what they were offering to the conference, this sort of event may have helped in the personal side of building contacts between the parties. The Conservatives had already been looking to gain DUP support for Brexit in 2016–17, given their small overall majority and the likely divisiveness of the legislation involved.[17]

Existing institutions that work on political strategy will also have to adapt to minority government, informed by the 1970s and post-2010 experiences. Time in Cabinet and Shadow Cabinet discussions devoted to dealing with parliamentary affairs could, as in the 1970s, increase significantly. The advisers and research departments in the respective parties may also, as with their predecessors, gear their work towards dealing with specific aspects of the challenges posed by minority government. We do not know if there are periodic meetings between May and all Government whips, as had been the case with Callaghan, or a repetition of the 1970s meetings of all Government special advisers, although there may be a reaction against this, in light of how the latter's contributions to the June 2017 campaign are currently being viewed. Many potential alternative courses of action will likely be proposed, these 'roads not taken', as in the 1970s and since 2010, forming part of a wider strategic dialogue, and, in some cases, acting as precursors and precedents for subsequent administrations.

Both main parties in the 1970s were aware of something of the international instances of minority and coalition government, and were establishing greater contact with their counterparts at a transnational level during this period. However, these experiences did not generally feature as part of the main parties' rationale or internal strategic discourse, which were very much couched in terms of contemporary and nineteenth- and twentieth-century British experiences of minority and coalition government. It is conceivable that the main parties may increasingly draw on international exemplars in strategy-making, although, in 2017, public acknowledgement of such international experience was, as in the past, primarily to feature in the justification of particular policy ideas, rather than parliamentary practices of minority or coalition government.[18]

Managing Parliament

It may be some time before the actual implementation of the Conservative/DUP Agreement in June 2017 can be judged against its effectiveness in Parliament. Some of the issues which will be faced resonate with those of previous minority governments, particularly in parliamentary management. However, there have been institutional or political changes since 1979 which have altered how these challenges manifest themselves or may be navigated.

The composition of legislative committees along majoritarian lines had raised serious strategic issues in 1974 and 1976. Both the Wilson and Callaghan Governments clung to majoritarian principles, but subsequently accepted alterations to representation for new committees that reflected the changed parliamentary situation. Since the 1970s there have been a number of other reforms to the committee system, although public bill committees (known as standing committees until 2006) still fulfil the same functions of providing scrutiny and amendments to bills as legislative committees in the 1970s. These bodies of between sixteen and fifty MPs are formed to deal with specific pieces of legislation. They do have more powers to collect evidence and engage in public consultation regarding a bill than their predecessors, but are in other ways very similar.

The creation of select committees after the 1979 election was another significant change, responsible for scrutinising government departments and occasionally for considering legislation. Changes after the 2010 election led to both the chairs, and then members of the committees, being elected by secret ballot of all MPs (although chairmanships are pre-allocated to parties to reflect the balance of seats in the Commons). Negotiations for these still take place through the usual channels and the whips still play a significant role in the process.

However, unlike the 1970s minority governments, the June 2017 Government has already engaged in a radical change to committees. A controversial initiative adopted in September 2017 changed the rules so that the Government would automatically hold a majority on legislative committees with an odd number of members, and parity on those with even numbers, regardless of the composition of Parliament.[19] With support from the DUP, the Government was able to pass the measure through the Commons, although it remains to be seen what the long-term implications of this move will be. The policy is, in effect, as radical as that of an unimplemented change during Callaghan's Administration, of making committee composition reflect a bill's parliamentary majority rather than the political balance of the Commons. The same arguments that vetoed such a proposal in the 1970s are still valid concerns for the June 2017 Government, opposition MPs being pushed into more vociferous efforts to defeat legislation.

One other concern for the Government of 2017 may be that of the danger revealed by the 1976 incident over the vote on the Aircraft and Shipbuilding Industries Bill, where the Opposition's breaking off of cooperation with the Callaghan Minority Government led to significant disruption. Ending the pairing of MPs for votes was initially an ad hoc measure, although some Conservatives sought to turn it into a broader strategy. In an era where the legislative impasse of government shutdowns in the United States has become more commonplace, it remains to be seen if opposition parties in Britain adopt this confrontational approach. However, it should be re-emphasised that the 1976 incident also revealed the limits of this device of breaking cooperation in a wider strategic context, recognised by the Opposition as harming their own political position. The threat had a potent effect on Labour's approach to minority government in the late 1970s, but how far this would be successful in 2018 onwards is less certain. The success of any breaking of cooperation would probably depend on how competing narratives explaining the Opposition's action would evolve in the midst of rolling twenty-four-hour media coverage, and whether such a move could be construed of as a legitimate protest or as 'cheating', a concern shared by 1970s counterparts. The physical demands of such a move would also be shared by MPs on both sides, exacerbating problems of having to remain in attendance at Westminster because of the Government having no clear majority, removing even any published schedule about when upcoming votes would be tabled.

Opposition parties in 2018 and beyond may also continue to make use of parliamentary committees to deal with some of the challenging issues of minority government faced by their 1970s predecessors. Such committees have also been used in times of majority government, in some instances not opposing legislation in the Commons deliberately, with a view to amending it in committee, to avoid charges of being unnecessarily and visibly obstructive.[20] The handful of high-profile committee defeats in the late 1970s that are often referred to obscured the over 100 reversals suffered by Callaghan in legislative committees, and the even higher number of individual elements in bills that were modified or dropped in anticipation of such opposition. Although the Conservatives will, in theory, hold majorities on a number of these committees, or have DUP support on others, there are no guarantees all members will always support the Government, particularly given the divisive nature of issues such as Brexit.

Whipping arrangements are a particular challenge following June 2017, with features that are both similar but also distinctive from previous minority governments. Such technologies as mobile phones, email and instant messaging, have increased the communication power of the whips over that of their 1970s counterparts, but have also increased the ability for leaders and backbench MPs from all parties to organise against the Government for particular votes. There may well be rotas drawn up for large numbers of MPs to stay within the Westminster area for longer time periods, in addition to the need for fuller turnouts and longer sittings for any contentious measures.

There have already been examples of the June 2017 Government having to accept defeat, including Conservatives abstaining in early September when the DUP joined with Labour to back successful motions in favour of increasing NHS pay and against a rise in tuition fees. Another high profile defeat was inflicted on the Government by 11 Conservative backbenchers rebelling on an amendment to the European Union Withdrawal Bill in December 2017.[21]

If, in some cases, the DUP cannot be persuaded to vote for a measure, then they might still be convinced to assist the Government's passage of legislation by abstaining in that particular case. Similarly, there were votes in the 1970s which ended up relying on abstention of smaller parties in order to succeed. If a full turnout of Conservative MPs supporting any such measure could be ensured, DUP abstention could allow for it to be passed in the Commons with a slim majority of potentially up to three. This, however, would be very risky, and would be unlikely to be workable as a general approach, unless there are particularly tight whipping arrangements (potential internal Conservative divisions would make this very difficult to achieve) or if the Government would be willing to accept more defeats in Parliament or to frame legislation in a more cross-party format (both of which pose significant challenges in the present adversarial political context).

Alternatively, the Government of 2017 may seek to avoid defeat where possible by minimising or withdrawing prospective legislation. The legislative programme outlined on 21 June 2017 in the Queen's Speech, while in some cases potentially contentious, did not contain a number of controversial manifesto commitments. This was similarly the case with certain measures in the Wilson and Callaghan Governments, which avoided some defeats by not putting forward bills unlikely to be successful.[22] Contrary to the Callaghan Government judging that an eighteen-month or two-year parliamentary session would be badly received both within and outside Westminster, the June 2017 Queen's Speech set out an extended two-year timetable for legislation. Given the overarching issues surrounding Brexit negotiations this is potentially more justifiable, although it will still provide additional challenges for parliamentary management. It remains to be seen how far the June 2017 Government will adopt other measures either considered or enacted in the 1970s, using institutional mechanisms to ensure the passage of legislation, accepting defeats that occur but promising to reverse them in a future majority government, or even actively seeking defeat on certain issues for the tactical or strategic reasons of blaming opposition parties. It may well be that the timetabling of limited parliamentary business and increasing the length of recesses is also, as in the 1970s, used to provide the Conservative Minority Government with breathing space.

Some of these initiatives carry significant risks, as recognised when the Callaghan Government considered the possibility of engineering its own defeat on certain issues, either as a means to criticise the Opposition as obstructionist or even as an excuse for an early election. Ultimately, this initiative was viewed as a step too far in the late 1970s, contemporaries fearing that it would unnecessarily weaken the Government. Given the political context after June 2017 of an opposition party gaining electoral momentum and the likely Conservative caution following the loss of the Government's majority, there may not be the appetite to follow this course of action, unless it is viewed to hold some particular tactical advantage. The choice of issue could theoretically be a measure popular with government voters but guaranteed to be blocked by other political parties and not of such importance as to necessitate the Government's resignation if defeated. Nevertheless, the frequency of elections in recent years should make the issue of voter apathy, as in the 1970s, a significant concern for any political leaders contemplating this course of action.

At the same time, the definition and understanding of defeats may be modified in response to further experience of minority government. A number of defeats previously regarded as incompatible with a government surviving in the British system, such as over amendments to the Budget, were largely accepted during the 1970s, particularly during the Pact. At the time of writing, it remains to be seen if the same is possible in 2018 or thereafter without imperilling the survival of the Government. A critical battleground may well be the extent to which any further modifications to Brexit policy are accepted by the Conservative leadership, and by groups of backbench MPs who have particular political investment in leaving the EU.

If majorities can be ensured for confidence motions, then their selective use may bolster the Minority Conservative Administration, as had been the case both with Wilson and Callaghan. Contemporary strategy-makers would recall how both parties handled the no confidence vote in March 1979, which was lost through refusal to pay certain political prices and the misjudging of smaller parties including the SNP. Nevertheless, it is worth recognising that the approaches to this vote were conditioned by Labour and Conservative experiences of minority government over the previous three years, and that the outcome was also determined partly by opposition caution and a tactical approach to the issue.

As in the 1970s, there may theoretically be some use of the votes of MPs from different parties in 2018 or thereafter to pass different pieces of legislation, although, partly because of ideological divides, there are fewer potential options available. Alternative legislative majorities for different parts of the same bill was a concept viewed as too radical in the 1970s, concerns being raised that the political costs were too high and that relations with the smaller parties would be damaged.

Labour similarly have had to confront these issues as the Opposition from 2017, the Government potentially seeking to put forward measures that would either divide Labour MPs, or be difficult for them to vote against. Choosing what measures to oppose, what points to concede, how to avoid potential legislative traps, and how to present and justify all these decisions publicly, all factor into how the Opposition, and indeed the other parties, respond strategically to the challenges of minority government. Strategic deliberations by the opposition parties in the 1970s addressed these questions, while also seeking to frame legislation or amendments in a manner to gain smaller party support, and developing different responses to the media in the event of particular government legislation being either successfully passed or defeated.

As with previous governments of both majority and minority status, it is likely that there will continue to be amendments to or defeats of particular measures by the House of Lords. While it is possible that the Conservatives may consider use of the Parliament Act to push through legislation being blocked by the Lords, this move would likely be controversial and attract criticism not only from opposition parties but also backbench MPs. Use of the Act to force through legislation was considered in the early stages of the Callaghan Government, but never invoked, decision-makers recognising the political disadvantages and likely limited success of such an approach, which would force a potentially unsuccessful confrontation that could significantly weaken the Government.

Reform of the Lords to strengthen any minority government, another option contemplated but rejected in the 1970s, is equally unlikely to be applicable in 2018 onwards. Arguments are similar to those advanced nearly forty years ago, that is, not solving the contemporary minority government situation in the Commons and being unlikely to succeed when the Government has no majority to begin with. More unorthodox ideas considered during the Callaghan Government, such as putting the Devolution Bill to a nationwide referendum when its passage through Parliament appeared uncertain, were ultimately rejected as being innovations which would, once again, in themselves require a parliamentary majority, as well as setting dangerous precedents for future legislation. Some of this analysis seems remarkably prescient in light of the unexpected European referendum result in 2016. The Conservatives in the 1970s had similarly contemplated Lords reforms and the use of referenda to break national strikes, but did not enact these plans, reaching largely the same conclusions as their counterparts. Following the Brexit decision, any future minority or coalition government will, no doubt, think very carefully before choosing a referendum as a course of action to resolve a major political issue or to overcome legislative deadlock, mindful of the significant risks involved.

Pacts and interparty cooperation

In some respects, the Conservative Minority Government formed in June 2017 is in a weaker position than its 1970s counterparts in terms of prospective interparty cooperation. Although facing a number of challenges including Labour rebellions, Wilson and Callaghan both potentially had multiple options available to pass legislation, cooperating at different stages with parties including the Liberals, SNP, Plaid Cymru and UUP, in order to pass bills. By contrast, the DUP is the only party in the post-June 2017 Commons that would be willing to support a significant amount of potential Conservative legislation, and is also the only party willing to enter into any formal deal.

Lady Sylvia Hermon, an Independent Unionist MP from Northern Ireland, may also support the Conservative Minority Government on certain votes, but is unlikely to enter into any formal agreement or to be a guaranteed government supporter in Parliament, given that her original resignation from the UUP in 2010 was in response to their decision to formally ally themselves with the Conservatives. In any case, while the Government will probably seek to remain on reasonable terms where possible, Hermon's vote alone would not be sufficient to give the Government a majority, except as a replacement for a single MP.

Cooperation after June 2017 has been built on existing connections, in some cases involving more direct communication between party leaders and more meetings between key figures managing Parliament, including Conservative and DUP Chief Whips Julian Smith (since November 2017) and Donaldson. The Sunday 11 June 2017 reshuffle was designed not only to mollify May's opponents, but to put in place people who would facilitate cooperation with the DUP. One example of this may be seen in the appointment of Andrea Leadsom as Leader of the House of Commons, responsible for the Government's legislative programme. The move certainly appeared to signal the priority for Brexit as well as acting as a conciliatory move towards the Prime Minister's critics, given her position as May's main rival in the abortive Conservative Party leadership contest in 2016, and Leadsom's prominence in the Leave campaign in the referendum. However, Leadsom might have also been selected for this post as someone who would be more sympathetic to, and likely to have better relations with, the DUP. There is an interesting parallel here with Callaghan appointing Foot, as his main rival, to become Commons Leader in 1976. However, while Foot was instrumental in securing cooperation with different parties including the Liberals and UUP, Leadsom's appointment appears to have been much more focused on ensuring support from the Conservatives themselves and from the DUP. This is understandable as an approach, given the increased hostility of other parties to cooperating with the Conservatives, although it remains to be seen how far it affects the prospect of support from parties, such as the Liberal Democrats, who, while opposing any deals with the Conservatives, have suggested that they would consider particular legislation on its merits.[23]

The retention of James Brokenshire as Northern Ireland Secretary was similarly viewed as a move to ensure good working relations with the DUP.[24] There were some political challenges that arose from this latter appointment, particularly of the Conservatives endeavouring to be seen as neutral arbiters of efforts to restart power-sharing at Stormont, but simultaneously relying on DUP support at Westminster. Problems arising from the Callaghan Government's reliance on SDLP and later UUP support at Westminster in the 1970s, including that of Mason's perceived lack of neutrality in the Northern Ireland Office, had contributed to the withdrawal of SDLP support and the confidence vote defeat in 1979. Although there are no SDLP MPs in June 2017, and Brokenshire stepped down during a Cabinet reshuffle, questions over the Conservative Minority Government's political neutrality are still proving to be a significant stumbling block to the restarting and future operation of Stormont. An alternative in June 2017 might have been to appoint a more politically neutral figure to the Northern Ireland post, such as a cross-bench or independent peer, although this move would not necessarily have been accepted by the DUP, or indeed, by the Conservatives.

When facing prospective interparty cooperation, Labour and the Conservatives have increasingly had to contend with the interests of other groupings within their own parties, one of the potentially most influential in the future being that of MPs from Scotland and Wales. Ensuring that interparty cooperation did not harm existing internal consultations of MPs was something that both governments and oppositions had to be mindful of in the 1970s, particularly during the Pact. The public articulation of concerns about the prospective DUP deal by Scottish Conservative leader Ruth Davidson in June 2017 included requests to the Prime Minister to guarantee that any deal would not reverse lesbian, gay, bisexual, transgender and intersex (LGBTI) rights in Britain. The BBC reporting had echoes of the letter by Labour backbenchers to Callaghan in regard to giving undue influence to the Liberals during the Pact, a source close to Davidson emphasising that there were 'more' Scottish Conservative MPs than DUP MPs. May subsequently provided reassurance on these matters to the 1922 Committee meeting on 12 June 2017.

Although it is early at this stage to consider potential renewal and exit strategies, these will have to be kept in mind when managing Conservative/DUP cooperation. While such cooperation is ostensibly for the duration of the Parliament, there will be an interim review after some two years. The Pact's renewal in 1977, often taken for granted, showed greater strategic consideration by the Callaghan Government than the initial formation, from more detailed briefing papers and attempts to control the negotiating process, to discussion within bodies, such as the special June Strategy Cabinet meeting, about potential alternative forms of cooperation, including month-to-month renewal or a longer pact lasting into 1979.

Electoral timing and alternative governments

As the result was still emerging early on 9 June 2017, Andrew Marr's somewhat light-hearted response to David Dimbleby's question about history echoed what a number of MPs, peers and commentators have articulated about the prospects for another election following the June 2017 result:

> [I]t brings us back to February 1974, the last time we had a genuine hung parliament, and that of course led after the February Election to an October Election, so all of those people watching this and thinking I love elections, I want more elections, I want more of David Dimbleby again and again and again, this may be your year.[25]

Although minority governments have potentially less longevity than their majority counterparts, whether through being defeated in a no confidence vote or seeking an early election, there was no further election in 2017.It is equally possible that minority governments are able to survive for their term of office and to be re-elected with or without a majority, depending on the political context and how they are managed strategically, as was the case with the SNP Administration of 2007–11 in Scotland and the Labour Administration of 2011–16 in Wales. If the Conservative/DUP Agreement breaks down, or if there are other significant political developments, such as a new Conservative leader, another early election is still a possibility.

There is also always the potential for unknown and unexpected developments, referred to by Conservative Prime Minister Harold Macmillan as 'events dear boy, events'. The Grenfell tower block fire on 14 June 2017, and the subsequent political fallout, further damaged May's credibility as a leader capable of sustaining a minority government. The popular Latvian Prime Minister, Valdis Dombrovskis, unexpectedly resigned in 2013 after a supermarket collapsed in the capital city of Riga, taking responsibility for what he perceived to be a failure of the Government to ensure building safety. While May has not followed this example, the longer-term political impact of this disaster remains to be seen.

The Conservative/DUP Agreement in June 2017, based on Confidence and Supply, is not as formal as the 2010 coalition, nor does it have the same sizeable parliamentary majority. In some ways it resembles Callaghan's arrangements with the UUP, while in others it goes slightly beyond the Lib–Lab Pact. Unlike the Liberals or Liberal Democrats, the DUP, in the same position as their UUP counterparts in the 1970s, do not have to face the same electoral pressures of contesting seats in the whole of the UK, nor the prospect of their seats being taken by Labour or Conservative candidates. This could potentially make it easier for them to break off the Agreement if dissatisfied, while maintaining their parliamentary position. The Agreement may also face insurmountable challenges depending on developments in power-sharing at Stormont, or if there are subsequent breakdowns of cooperation over policy in Northern Ireland, such as the challenges already faced over Brexit and the question of the border. However, whether or not another general election is called, the different parties at Westminster will be aware of a number of factors which would make such a move a significant political gamble.

The most striking reason that party leaders may not want to hold an early election is the outcome of the June 2017 election itself, called early and expected to deliver a landslide majority, but leading to a second indecisive result in the space of three consecutive UK elections. This experience is likely to weigh heavily on future leaders considering an early election when it is politically expedient. Political history from the 1970s will likely further resonate with the situation following June 2017 and also factor into such calculations, examples including the early elections which led to Wilson's surprise defeat in 1970, Heath's in February 1974 and Wilson's narrow victory in October 1974, which opinion polls mistakenly forecast as a significant Labour majority. In his wider strategic dialogue in 1978, Callaghan refused to countenance an election if it were likely to produce another indecisive result (and at best, a further minority government).

The ongoing Brexit process could also discourage the potential uncertainty of another early election. While Wilson had called an early election in October 1974, and waited until he had a majority before approaching the EEC referendum question in 1975, May's triggering of Article 50 before the June 2017 election removes any equivalent option for delay. A further election may also open up more divisions within the main parties, and runs the risk either of increased instability in the financial markets or, even if this were to be avoided, the perception of market instability in media coverage.

There are, additionally, concerns irrespective of the immediate EU situation that may discourage early elections, including potential public apathy. In the space of three years, Britain had two general elections, a referendum on EU membership, the Scotland referendum on independence, elections to the Scottish Parliament and Welsh Assembly, EU elections and a number of local council elections. Future studies will investigate turnout by particular groups of voters as more detail becomes available, but the overall early trends may nevertheless be instructive. The June election of 2017 represented a higher turnout than any in the past twenty-five years (68.7%), but was not as high as previous postwar elections, including both elections in 1974 (78.8% and 72.8%). For the Conservatives in particular, there will likely be concern that turnout of their supporters is not guaranteed at a future early election, mirroring Wilson's fear of 'the big yawn' in 1974, or of the extensive calculations during his and Callaghan's Administrations regarding how factors including weather, holidays, economic indicators and sporting events would affect electoral timing. There have been a number of cases, both in Britain and abroad, where governments have called early elections seeking a greater majority, or have been compelled to hold another poll, following the inability to form a stable government, only to find that the outcome was not more decisive. Both British elections of 1910 produced a Liberal Minority Government with virtually identical numbers of seats, while the 1974 October election only gave Wilson a majority of three that, however effectively managed, was subsequently whittled away through by-elections and defections.[26]

The exhaustion of political parties and their resources may also militate against early elections in the near future. The 2015 election, EU referendum and devolved elections in 2016 occupied a significant amount of resources for British political parties in terms of money and manpower. Just as some of those advising Callaghan had considered wrong-footing opposing parties to waste their electoral resources in 1978, it could be, conversely, that the strain on other parties' resources and preparations had some influence on the Conservative choice of an election in June 2017. A number of news stories emerged in the early days of the campaign concerning the challenges of putting together electoral preparations, such as candidate selection, and of MPs from established parties individually appealing to their constituents for crowdfunded donations to support their local campaigns.[27]

The Fixed-Term Parliaments Act of 2011 has also removed the Prime Minister's power to call an election without parliamentary approval. While, as witnessed in April 2017, it may be possible for governments to vote to dissolve themselves, and difficult for opposition parties to prevent an election without appearing to support governments, this legislation has still created other added risks for a government seeking an early poll, the most tangible of which is the alternative government-in-waiting. Although oppositions parties in the 1970s did not consider an alternative administration, the public statements from Labour after the June 2017 election were couched much more in terms of forming a minority government if the Conservatives had failed. While a somewhat speculative scenario, it is not inconceivable that if, for whatever reason, the Conservative/ DUP Government lost a confidence vote, Labour could seek to form a minority government, rather than calling an election in the first instance. Such an administration could potentially dare other parties to defeat their legislation, including a newly created Conservative Opposition. Even if such an administration were only short term, and were challenged by greater numbers of opposing MPs, an opposition and other parties could well be mindful of the potential dangers of defeating the Government and forcing an election on an issue unfavourable to them, as had been the challenge for Heath in 1974.

Although the DUP may have some electoral insulation from breaking a deal, they are less likely to want to give up the present position of influence, having no guarantee of maintaining that influence after a subsequent early election. The DUP priorities have also already been identified more as financial and constitutional, rather than socially conservative. Contrary to their 1970s counterparts, the DUP elected in June 2017 can draw on their advance preparation for negotiations following the 2015 election, experience of governing in coalition in Northern Ireland and involvement in broader negotiations over the past few decades. In this respect, while undoubtedly being robust negotiators, both sides will actually be more experienced in the mechanics of interparty cooperation and in benefiting from the rewards of successful negotiations. As long as neither side puts the other in an impossible position, events in the UK or Northern Ireland do not conspire to undermine the Agreement and support of the wider parties towards the deal remains strong, then the rewards of a Conservative/DUP Government are likely to outweigh the costs for both, making it more likely that leaders on both sides will seek to ensure its survival.

Following the indecisive outcome in the 2010 election, there were similar widespread predictions of another election in the autumn, commentators believing that it was very unlikely that Conservative–Liberal Democrat negotiations would succeed, that a rainbow coalition with Labour would be unworkable and that no other options could produce a stable government. Even after the coalition was formed, many early commentaries predicted that it would not last for the full five-year Parliament. The coalition's success in remaining in office for five years was partly down to the efforts of party leaders and their strategy-makers in effective management, but was also a recognition by both sides that early forced termination could be disadvantageous electorally. Although the Lib–Lab Pact did not last nearly as long, similarly careful management by Callaghan, Steel and other strategy-makers in both parties, as well as awareness of potential hazards of breaking the agreement early, helped to ensure its continuation.

It would appear that prior to the June 2017 election there had been some preparations made by the parties for a possible snap poll, and it is likely that these will be given even greater consideration hereafter. In much the same way as their 1970s counterparts, both main parties will be calculating the best possible dates and trying to analyse the mindset of their opponents, as well as weighing up the effect of possible parliamentary defeats. These calculations may also include more assessments of the challenges imposed by opposition parties having to support any early dissolution under the fixed-term parliament legislation, such as the scenario of whether an alternative minority administration would be allowed to take office instead, as has sometimes been the case both in other countries and in nineteenth-century Britain.

Future minority and coalition governments

It is impossible to predict whether future general elections will deliver more indecisive results or a return to single-party majority governments. However, the indecisive outcomes in 2010 and June 2017, discussions of hung parliaments during election campaigns since 2010, and the presence of minority governments in Scotland and Wales after 2016, mean that parties are increasingly likely to recognise and make preparations for how they will respond to future indecisive results. Decision-makers in all these events have acted against the backdrop of history and the mythology that has grown up surrounding previous British minority experiences from the 1970s. Subsequent developments, including prospective political realignment with the Social Democrat Party/Alliance in the 1980s, and the seeming inability of Labour to achieve a breakthrough in the early 1990s, have also conditioned understandings of minority governance. The experience of the 1970s served as an important foundation for future approaches to questions of minority and coalition faced up until and including the present, both through the participants who had held high political office during the period and as exemplars used by commentators, political scientists and historians.

Since 2010, we have increasingly seen election campaigns in which Labour and the Conservatives have in some ways subtly accommodated the potential for an indecisive result, particularly in highlighting their political priorities for (unstated) prospective negotiations, but have also maintained their adherence to a majoritarian political culture of publicly aiming for outright victory. This majoritarian view is particularly evident in the increasing use of ideas about prospective coalitions or interparty agreements as arguments to criticise political opponents. For Labour, this has manifested itself in leaflets against the Liberal Democrats' cooperation with the Conservatives when they were part of the 2010 coalition, or through references to SNP–Conservative cooperation during the 2007–11 SNP Minority Government in Scotland. The Conservatives have used striking anti-coalition imagery, from picturing Labour leader Ed Miliband in the then recently former First Minister Alex Salmond's pocket in 2015 to May's often-cited line from April to June 2017, warning against the opposing parties forming a 'coalition of chaos'. Ironically, both these images have subsequently been used against the Conservatives, 'coalition of chaos' becoming Labour's slogan to criticise the Conservative/DUP deal and cartoons emerging of May in the pocket of a stereotypical portrayal of a DUP politician vested in regalia from the Orange Order. The statements used in 2017 echo Wilson's dismissal of Heath's national unity government policy as a 'con-trick' in 1974, but they have become far more central to campaign messages than was the case in the 1970s. It is possible that such attacks will continue to be used, although, the Conservatives' inability to win a majority in June 2017, and the boomerang effect of their own statements, may counsel party strategy-makers and those managing future election campaigns against this type of vituperative slogan.

In institutional terms, the 1970s governments did not make significant concessions towards long-term reform that would be more conducive to the operation of future minority or coalition governments, whether in terms of all-party committee representation or electoral reform along PR lines – facing the prospect of significant internal divisions within their own ranks over such issues, and still viewing majority government as ultimately the only realistic objective to be pursued. It would seem likely from Labour and the Conservatives' continued stance of seeking outright victory, and moves away from formalised coalitions by all parties at a UK level after 2015, that the main parties will remain firmly anchored in a majoritarian political culture for the foreseeable future, and will not seek institutional changes better to facilitate future minority or coalition governments, unless there is a radical shift in opinion within either party's leadership.

The increased online organisation of tactical voting in 2017, and withdrawal of some parliamentary candidates from both sides of the political spectrum, raises the possibility for new forms of local electoral pacts or agreements which may resemble or sharply differ from those considered during the 1970s, and those subsequently implemented in such cases as Labour and the Liberal Democrats in 1997. At the same time, however, the continued majoritarian discourse after the June 2017 election would suggest that neither main party will likely formally endorse such agreements at a UK level, unless there is a radical change in their approach to elections. Just as their 1970s counterparts had concluded, the main justification against this remains that it would likely end the prospect of future majoritarian governance.

Formal planning for minority government and different forms of interparty agreements or coalitions is another area that may well receive greater attention from parties in the future, even if only conducted as hypothetical exercises, or by trusted advisers on an ad hoc basis. While publicly denying any considerations other than victory, the 1970s experiences show how parties went about examining questions from the pre-selection of potential coalition partners to the setting out of possible negotiating positions, and the secret planning discussed in Chapter 8. While the CRD papers in the late 1970s advanced competing visions and different practical approaches to government formation that were very much products of their time, they also show strategy-makers coming to terms with unfamiliar political scenarios not far removed from situations between 2010 and 2017. The notions put forward in these Conservative documents, whether of some form of coalition government with the UUP or of the more radical ideas of an agreement with the SNP or grand coalition with Labour, show some of the antecedents of those approaching minority and coalition politics in 2010, 2015 and 2017, having to consider previously unthinkable political options in the climate of indecisive electoral results.

It is possible that the future political culture and *modus operandi* for parties in Britain may further change in response to minority and coalition government, whether to accommodate other forms of pre-electoral or post-electoral cooperation, or, alternatively, to endorse measures that would ensure a continued adherence to majoritarian politics and engage in the poker game of daring opponents to defeat them. In the future, the election of party leaders may include more questions about how they would handle questions of minority or coalition government, and there may be further internal institutional reforms to ensure clear approaches to negotiations and the greater consultation of wider party decision-making bodies or memberships prior to the adopting of any informal or formal deals.

Equally, of course, it may be that the experiences of minority government since 2017 do not lead to as many lasting changes, in much the same way that detailed memories of the Wilson and Callaghan Governments of the 1970s were swept aside from political consciousness by the subsequent decades of Conservative and then Labour Governments with significant majorities. Similarly, following the end of the coalition in 2015, there was little high-profile public reference, in the context of a new Parliament with a Conservative majority, to the previous five years of formal interparty cooperation, beyond instances of historical reference to policies that had been enacted.

Britain and the world of minority government

New comparisons of historical and contemporary minority government in Britain and elsewhere may be able to build on the approach in this book, considering not only the governments themselves, but also the unique challenges faced by those opposing them. In studying these administrations, the investigation of areas not previously given the same attention, including electoral timing and the extent to which parties plan for future minority and coalition governments, may offer new insights into party strategy-making and the transformation of political culture. Considering where ideas or inspiration are drawn from in formulating strategies, whether domestic or international, may further our understanding of the dissemination of political ideas globally and of historical analogies employed in this strategy-making process. Combining such analysis with empirical case studies whose unusual features may challenge or qualify existing theoretical frameworks also offers the opportunity to re-evaluate minority governance as both a national and global phenomenon.

The Wilson and Callaghan Minority Governments saw both main parties adopting some of the techniques used by governments and oppositions facing indecisive election results around the world. In their rationale and the carrying out of their strategies, both considered, and in some cases made use of, radical alternative courses of action, from the breaking of parliamentary cooperation as a strategy to deliberately seeking defeats or even exploring formalised interparty coalitions. Nevertheless, both Labour and the Conservatives remained firmly anchored within and built upon a distinctly British tradition of minority government, seeking to justify internal strategic dialogues through appeal to parliamentary precedents or, where necessary, pragmatic innovation grounded in existing majoritarian principles. Within wider minority government theory, the British experience of the late 1970s affirms some long-established precepts about the operation of parties in a national Parliament without a legislative majority, but, at the same time, provides a unique case study challenging dominant ideas and their theoretical bases. The experiences and actions of these decision-makers helped to lay the foundations for British political parties up to the post-2010 coalition and 2017 minority governments.

These historic experiences continue to play an important role in the minds of current strategy-makers in Britain's political parties, as they grapple with considerations of how to approach the working of the Conservative Minority Government of June 2017 and prospective future minority or coalition governments, in an increasingly uncertain political future.

Notes

1 *BBC Election Night* (8 June 2017).
2 *BBC Election Night* (9 June 2017).
3 HC Hansard: vol. 250; cols 1073–4 (29 November 1994); cols 1222–4 (30 November 1994); cols 1327 (1 December 1994); vol. 251, cols 196–8, 282–3 (6 December 1994); cols 431–4, 436–9 (7 December 1994); cols 490–2 (8 December 1994).
4 Walker, *A History of the Ulster Unionist Party*, pp. 244–6, 254.
5 Crowson, *The Conservative Party and European Integration*, p. 61; D. Baker, A. Gamble and S. Ludlam, 'The Parliamentary Siege of Maastricht 1993: Conservative Divisions and British Ratification', *Parliamentary Affairs*, 47:1 (1994), 37–60; D. Baker, A. Gamble and S. Ludlam, 'Whips or Scorpions? The Maastricht Vote and the Conservative Party', *Parliamentary Affairs*, 46:2 (1993), 151–66.
6 See, for example, BBC1 feature on the Callaghan Government, *The Andrew Marr Show* (26 April 2015).
7 David Muir Speaker Series: 'Downing Street and the Realities of Power', University of Glasgow, 9 March 2012. See Chapter 1.
8 *BBC Election Night* (8–9 June 2017).
9 *ITV Election Night* (8 June 2017).
10 *BBC News* (10 June 2017).
11 Suzanne Breen, 'DUP Chief Foster Vows to Forge Best Deal for Northern Ireland Ahead of Talks with May' *Belfast Telegraph* (12 June 2017); *BBC News* (9–12 June 2017).
12 *BBC News* (10 June 2017).
13 *BBC News* (20 June 2017).
14 *Ibid.*
15 *BBC News* (12 June 2017; 6 May 2010).
16 *BBC Election Night* (8–9 June 2017).
17 *BBC News* (9–12 June 2017).
18 For example, Conservative General Election Manifesto 2010.
19 *BBC News* (8–12 September 2017).
20 See Chapter 4: Daring defeat.
21 Rowena Mason, Deputy Political Editor, and Henry McDonald, Ireland Correspondent, 'May Suffers Humiliation as DUP Backs Labour on NHS Pay and Tuition Fees', *Guardian* (13 September 2017).
22 *BBC News* (21 June 2017).
23 *BBC Election Night* (8–9 June 2017); *BBC News* (11 June 2017).
24 *BBC News* (11 June 2017).
25 *BBC Election Night* (9 June 2017).
26 See Chapter 7.
27 *BBC News* (19–21, 28 April, 1–2 May 2017). See Chapter 7.

Bibliography

Primary sources

Conservative Party Archive
(Bodleian Library, Oxford)

Hansard
(Parliamentary Archives, London)

Labour History Archive Study Centre
(New People's Museum, Manchester)

Liberal Party Archive
(London School of Economics)

Papers of the Prime Minister
(The National Archives, Kew, London)

Parliamentary Briefing Papers
(House of Commons, London)

The Cabinet Archives
(The National Archives, Kew, London)

Newspapers

Belfast Telegraph
Daily Mail
Guardian
Observer
The Sunday Times
The Times

Private papers

Papers of Professor Brian Abel-Smith
(London School of Economics)

Papers of Baron James Callaghan
(Bodleian Library, Oxford)

Papers of Baron Bernard Donoughue
(Churchill Archive Centre, Cambridge)

Papers of Sir Michael Fraser
(Bodleian Library, Oxford)

Papers of Lord Hailsham
(Churchill Archive Centre, Cambridge)

Papers of Judith Hart
(New People's Museum, Manchester)

Papers of Sir John Hoskyns
(Churchill Archive Centre, Cambridge)

Papers of Enoch Powell
(Churchill Archive Centre, Cambridge)

Papers of Jo Richardson
(New People's Museum, Manchester)

Papers of Lord David Steel
(London School of Economics)

Papers of Baroness Margaret Thatcher
(Margaret Thatcher Foundation and Churchill Archive Centre, Cambridge)

Papers of Baron Harold Wilson
(Bodleian Library, Oxford)

Diaries

Benn, T., *Against the Tide: Diaries 1973–1976* (London: Hutchinson, 1989).
Benn, T., *Conflicts of Interest: Diaries, 1977–80* (London: Arrow Books, 1991).
Castle, B., *The Castle Diaries 1974–1976* (London: Weidenfeld & Nicolson, 1980).
Donoughue, B., *Downing Street Diary: With James Callaghan in No. 10*, vol. 2 (London: Jonathan Cape, 2008).
Donoughue, B., *Downing Street Diary: With Harold Wilson in No. 10*, vol. 1 (London: Pimlico, 2006).

TV/Radio programmes

BBC Documentary, *Five Days that Changed Britain* (10 January 2011).
BBC Documentary, *The Night the Government Fell (A Parliamentary Coup)* (31 May 2009).
BBC Election Night (8–9 June 2017).
BBC News.

BBC Radio 4, *How are You Feeling, Alf?* (8 June 2009).
BBC Radio 4, *Today Programme* (26 February 2015).
BBC1 feature on the Callaghan Government, *The Andrew Marr Show* (26 April 2015).
ITV Election Night (8–9 June 2017).

Public lectures/panels

David Muir Speaker Series: 'Downing Street and the Realities of Power', University of
Glasgow, 9 March 2012.

Articles

Baker, D., Gamble, A., and Ludlam, S., 'The Parliamentary Siege of Maastricht 1993:
Conservative Divisions and British Ratification', *Parliamentary Affairs*, 47:1 (1994),
37–60.

Baker, D., Gamble, A., and Ludlam, S., 'Whips or Scorpions? The Maastricht Vote and the
Conservative Party', *Parliamentary Affairs*, 46:2 (1993), 151–66.

Bale, T., 'The Black Widow Effect: Why Britain's Conservative–Liberal Democrat
Coalition Might Have an Unhappy Ending', *Parliamentary Affairs*, 65:2 (2012),
323–37.

Beattie, A., 'British Coalition Government Revisited', *Government and Opposition*, 2:1
(1966), 3–34.

Beavan, J., 'The Westminster Scene', *The Political Quarterly*, 47:2 (1976), 203–14.

Bergman, T., 'Formation Rules and Minority Governments', *European Journal of Political
Research*, 23 (1993), 55–66.

Birch, A. H., 'Britain's Impending Constitutional Dilemmas', *Parliamentary Affairs*, 37:1
(1984), 97–101.

Blackburn, R., Fox, R., Gay, O., and Maer, L., 'Who Governs? Forming a Coalition or a
Minority Government in the Event of a Hung Parliament', Hansard Society: Study of
Parliament Group (2010), 1–23.

Blick, A., and Wilks-Heeg, S., 'Governing without Majorities: Coming to Terms with
Balanced Parliaments in UK Politics', *Democratic Audit General Election Briefing*, 1
(2010), 1–10.

Bogdanor, V., 'The Constitution and the Party System in the Twentieth Century',
Parliamentary Affairs, 57:4 (2004), 717–33.

Bräuninger, T., and Debus, M., 'Legislative Agenda Setting in Parliamentary Democracies',
European Journal of Political Research, 48:6 (2009), 821–8.

Burton, I., and Drewry, G., 'Public Legislation: A Survey of the Session 1974', *Parliamentary
Affairs*, 29:2 (1976), 155–89.

Burton, I., and Drewry, G., 'Public Legislation: A Survey of the Sessions 1977/8 and
1978/9', *Parliamentary Affairs*, 33:1 (1979), 173–209.

Cairney, P., 'Coalition and Minority Government in Scotland: Lessons for the United
Kingdom?', *The Political Quarterly*, 82:2 (2011), 261–9.

Dufresne, Y., and Nevitte, N., 'Why do Publics Support Minority Governments? Three
Tests', *Parliamentary Affairs*, 67:4 (2014), 825–40.

Dutton, D., 'Anticipating "the Project": Lib–Lab Relations in the Era of Jo Grimond', *Contemporary British History*, 20:1 (2006), 101–17.

Gamble, A., 'Austerity as Statecraft', *Parliamentary Affairs*, 68:1 (2015), 42–57.

Geller-Schwartz, L., 'Minority Government Reconsidered', *Journal of Canadian Studies*, 14:2 (1979), 67–79.

Green-Pedersen, C., 'Minority Governments and Party Politics: The Political and Institutional Background to the "Danish Miracle"', *Journal of Public Policy*, 21:1 (2001), 53–70.

Hay, C., 'The Winter of Discontent Thirty Years On', *The Political Quarterly*, 80:4 (2009), 545–52.

Herman, V., and Pope, J., 'Minority Government in Western Democracies', *British Journal of Political Science*, 3:2 (1973), 192–212.

Heyton, R., 'Conservative Party Statecraft and the Politics of Coalition', *Parliamentary Affairs*, 67:1 (2013), 6–24.

Landes, R. G., 'The Canadian General Election of 1980', *Parliamentary Affairs*, 34:1 (1981), 95–109.

Levy, R., 'The Search for a Rational Strategy: The Scottish National Party and Devolution 1974–79', *Political Studies*, 34:2 (1986), 236–48.

Ludlam, S., 'The Gnomes of Washington: Four Myths of the 1976 IMF Crisis', *Political Studies*, 40:4 (1992), 713–27.

Lundberg, T. C., 'Politics is Still an Adversarial Business: Minority Government and Mixed-Member Proportional Representation in Scotland and in New Zealand', *British Journal of Politics and International Relations*, 15:4 (2013), 609–25.

Lundberg, T. C., 'Tensions between Constituency and Regional Members of the Scottish Parliament under Mixed-Member Proportional Representation: A Failure of the New Politics', *Parliamentary Affairs*, 67:2 (2014), 351–70.

Lyon, V., 'Minority Government in Ontario, 1975–81: An Assessment', *Canadian Journal of Political Science/Revue canadienne de science politique*, 17:4 (1984), 685–705.

Marsh, I., 'Liberal Priorities, the Lib–Lab Pact and the Requirements for Policy Influence', *Parliamentary Affairs*, 43:3 (1990), 292–321.

Martin, L. W., and Stevenson, R. T., 'The Conditional Impact of Incumbency on Government Formation', *American Political Science Review*, 104:3 (2010), 503–18.

Martin, L. W., and Vanberg, G., 'Wasting Time? The Impact of Ideology and Size on Delay in Coalition Formation', *British Journal of Political Science*, 33:2 (2003), 323–32.

Moury, C., and Timmermans, A., 'Inter-Party Conflict Management in Coalition Governments: Analyzing the Role of Coalition Agreements in Belgium, Germany, Italy and the Netherlands', *Politics and Governance*, 1:2 (2013), 117–31.

Paun, A., and Hazell, R., 'Hung Parliaments and the Challenge for Westminster and Whitehall: How to Make Minority and Multiparty Governance Work', *The Political Quarterly*, 81:2 (2010), 213–27.

Quinn, T., Bara, J., and Bartle, J., 'The UK Coalition Agreement of 2010: Who Won?', *Journal of Elections, Public Opinion and Parties*, 21:2 (2011), 304–9.

Rasmussen, J., 'Constitutional Aspects of Government Formation in a Hung Parliament', *Parliamentary Affairs*, 40:2 (1987), 139–53.

Redvaldsen, D., '"Today is the Dawn": The Labour Party and the 1929 General Election', *Parliamentary History*, 29:3 (2010), 395–415.

Rodgers, W., 'Government under Stress: Britain's Winter of Discontent 1979', *The Political Quarterly*, 55:2 (1984), 171–9.

Rogers, C., 'The Economic Consequences of a Hung Parliament: Lessons from February 1974', *The Political Quarterly*, 81:4 (2010), 501–10.

Strøm, K., 'Minority Governments in Parliamentary Democracies: The Rationality of Nonwinning Cabinet Solutions', *Comparative Political Studies*, 17:2 (1984), 199–227.

Taylor, M., and Laver, M., 'Government Coalitions in Western Europe', *European Journal of Political Research*, 1:3 (1973), 205–48.

Tomlinson, J., 'British Government and Popular Understanding of Inflation in the Mid-1970s', *Economic History Review*, 67:3 (2014), 750–68.

Warwick, P. V., 'Dissolvers, Disputers, and Defectors: The Terminators of Parliamentary Governments', *European Political Science Review*, 4:2 (2012), 263–81.

Books

Adelman, P., *The Rise of the Labour Party 1880–1945* (New York: Longman, 2nd edn, 1986).

Aitken, J., *Margaret Thatcher: Power and Personality* (A&C Black, 2013).

Andeweg, R. B., De Winter, L., and Dumont, P. (eds), *Puzzles of Government Formation: Coalition Theory and Deviant Cases* (London: Routledge, 2011).

Arter, D., *Democracy in Scandinavia: Consensual, Majoritarian or Mixed?* (Manchester: Manchester University Press, 2006).

Artis, M., and Cobham, D. (eds), *Labour's Economic Policies 1974–1979* (Manchester: Manchester University Press, 1991).

Axelrod, R., *Conflict of Interest: A Theory of Divergent Goals with Applications to Politics* (Chicago: Markham, 1970).

Bagehot, W., *The English Constitution* (Brighton: Sussex Academic Press, 1997).

Ball, S., 'The Conservatives in Opposition, 1906–1979: A Comparative Analysis', in Garnett, M., and Lynch, P. (eds), *The Conservatives in Crisis* (Manchester: Manchester University Press, 2003), pp. 7–28.

Ball, S. (ed.), *The Conservative Party since 1945* (Manchester: Manchester University Press, 1998).

Ball, S., and Seldon, A. (eds), *Recovering Power: The Conservatives in Opposition since 1867* (Houndmills: Palgrave Macmillan, 2005).

Barnett, J., *Inside the Treasury* (London: André Deutsch Limited, 1982).

Bartram, P., *David Steel: His Life and Politics* (London: W. H. Allen, 1981).

Beckett, A., *When the Lights Went Out: What Really Happened to Britain in the Seventies* (London: Faber & Faber Ltd., 2009).

Beech, M., and Lee, S. (eds), *The Cameron-Clegg Government: Coalition Politics in an Age of Austerity* (Houndmills: Palgrave Macmillan, 2011).

Behrens, R., *The Conservative Party from Heath to Thatcher: Policies and Politics, 1974–1979* (Farnborough: Saxon House, 1980).

Bell, P., *The Labour Party in Opposition, 1970–1974* (London: Routledge, 2004).

Berger, S., *The British Labour Party and the German Social Democrats, 1900–1931* (Oxford: Oxford University Press, 1994).

Bergman, T., *Constitutional Rules and Party Goals in Coalition Formation: An Analysis of Winning Minority Governments in Sweden* (Umeå: Umeå University, 1995).

Bickerton, J., and Gagnon, A. (eds), *Canadian Politics* (Plymouth: University of Toronto Press, 5th edn, 2009).

Blake, R., *The Conservative Party: From Peel to Major* (London: Arrow Books, 1998).

Bogdanor, V., *Coalition Government in Western Europe* (London: Heinemann, 1983).

Bogdanor, V., *Multi-Party Politics and the Constitution* (Cambridge: Cambridge University Press, 1983).

Bogdanor, V., *The People and the Party System: The Referendum and Electoral Reform in British Politics* (Cambridge: Cambridge University Press, 1981).

Boston, J., Levine, S., McLeay, E., and Roberts, N. S. (eds), *From Campaign to Coalition: New Zealand's First Election under Proportional Representation* (Wellington: Dunmore Press, 1997).

Boston, J., Church, S., Levine, S., McLeay, E., and Roberts, N., *New Zealand Votes: The General Election of 2002* (Wellington: Victoria University Press, 2003).

Boulton, A., and Jones, J., *Hung Together: The Cameron–Clegg Coalition* (London: Simon & Schuster, 2012).

Brand, J., *British Parliamentary Parties: Policy and Power* (Oxford: Oxford University Press, 1992).

Brazier, A., and Kalitowski, S. (eds), *No Overall Control?* (London: Hansard Society, 2008).

Brivati, B. and Heffernan, R. (eds), *The Labour Party: A Centenary History* (Houndmills: Palgrave Macmillan, 2000).

Butler, D., *Governing without a Majority: Dilemmas for Hung Parliaments in Britain* (London: Collins, 1983).

Butler, D., and Kavanagh, D., *The British General Election of 1979* (London: Macmillan, 1980).

Butler, D., and Kavanagh, D., *The British General Election of October 1974* (London: Macmillan, 1975).

Butler, D., and Kavanagh, D., *The British General Election of February 1974* (London: Macmillan, 1974).

Callaghan, J., *Time and Chance* (London: HarperCollins, 1987).

Campbell, J., *Edward Heath: A Biography* (London: Jonathan Cape, 1993).

Campbell, J., *Margaret Thatcher: Grocer's Daughter to Iron Lady* (London: Vintage, 2009).

Cannon, J., *The Fox–North Coalition: Crisis of the Constitution 1782–4* (Cambridge: Cambridge University Press, 1969).

Cerny, K. H., *Germany at the Polls: The Bundestag Elections of the 1980s* (Durham, NC: Duke University Press, 1990).

Cheibub, J. A., *Presidentialism, Parliamentarism, and Democracy* (Cambridge: Cambridge University Press, 2007).

Childs, D., *Britain since 1939: Progress and Decline* (Houndmills: Palgrave Macmillan, 1995).

Clemens, C., and Saalfeld, T. (eds), *The German General Election of 2005: Voters, Parties and Grand Coalition Politics* (London: Routledge, 2013).

Coates, K. (ed.), *What Went Wrong: Explaining the Fall of the Labour Government* (Nottingham: Spokesman Books, 1979).

Conley, F., *General Elections Today* (Manchester: Manchester University Press, 1994).

Cook, C., *A Short History of the Liberal Party: The Road Back to Power* (Houndmills: Palgrave Macmillan, 2010).

Cowley, P., *The Rebels: How Blair Mislaid His Majority* (London: Politico's, 2005).

Crines, A. S., and Hickson, K. (eds), *Harold Wilson: The Unprincipled Prime Minister? Reappraising Harold Wilson* (London: Biteback Publishing, 2016).

Cronin, J. E., *New Labour's Pasts: The Labour Party and its Discontents* (Harlow: Pearson Education, 2004).

Cross, W. P., and Blais, A., *Politics at the Centre: The Selection and Removal of Party Leaders in the Anglo Parliamentary Democracies* (Oxford: Oxford University Press, 2012).

Crowcroft, R., *Attlee's War: World War II and the Making of a Labour Leader* (London: I.B.Tauris & Co., 2011).

Crowson, N. J., *The Conservative Party and European Integration since 1945: At the Heart of Europe* (London: Routledge, 2006).

Diamond, P., *New Labour's Old Roots: Revisionist Thinkers in Labour's History, 1931–97* (Exeter: Imprint Academic, 2004).

Dietze, G., *America's Political Dilemma: From Limited to Unlimited Democracy* (London: University Press of America, 1985).

Donoughue, B., *Prime Minister: The Conduct of Policy under Harold Wilson and James Callaghan* (London: Jonathan Cape, 1987).

Douglas, R., *Liberals: A History of the Liberal and Liberal Democratic Parties* (London: Hambledon & London, 2005).

Dutton, D., *A History of the Liberal Party since 1900* (Houndmills: Palgrave Macmillan, 2013).

Elgie, R., *Semi-Presidentialism: Sub Types and Democratic Performance* (Oxford: Oxford University Press, 2011).

Evans, E. J., *Thatcher and Thatcherism* (London: Routledge, 1997).

Field, B. N., *Why Minority Governments Work: Multilevel Territorial Politics in Spain* (Houndmills: Palgrave Macmillan, 2016).

Giannetti, D., and Ineoit, K. (eds), *Intra-Party Politics and Coalition Governments* (London: Routledge, 2008).

Golder, S. N., *The Logic of Pre-Electoral Coalition Formation* (Ohio: Ohio State University Press, 2006).

Gould, P., 'The Land that Labour Forgot', in Chadwick, A., *The New Labour Reader* (Cambridge: Polity Press, 2003), pp. 39–42.

Hassan, G., *The Modern SNP: From Protest to Power* (Edinburgh: Edinburgh University Press, 2010).

Hayter, D., *Fightback! Labour's Traditional Right in the 1970s and 1980s* (Manchester: Manchester University Press, 2005).

Hazell, R., and Paun, A. (eds), *Making Minority Government Work: Hung Parliaments and the Challenges for Westminster and Whitehall* (London: UCL Constitution Unit, 2009).

Hazell, R., and Yong, B., *The Politics of Coalition: How the Conservative–Liberal Democrat Government Works* (Oxford: Hart Publishing, 2012).

Hazell, R., Donnelly, K., and Smith, N., *Report of the Commission on the Conduct of Referendums* (London: UCL Constitution Unit, 1996).

Healey, D., *The Time of My Life* (London: Penguin Books, 1990).

Hennessy, P., *Distilling the Frenzy: Writing the History of One's Own Times* (London: Biteback Publishing, 2013).

Hennessy, P., *The Prime Minister: The Office and its Holders since 1945* (London: Penguin Books, 2001).

Heppell, T. (ed.), *Leaders of the Opposition: From Churchill to Cameron* (Houndmills: Palgrave Macmillan, 2012).

Heppell, T., and Seawright, D., *Cameron and the Conservatives: The Transition to Coalition Government* (London: Palgrave Macmillan, 2012).

Hickson, K., *The IMF Crisis of 1976 and British Politics* (London: I.B.Tauris & Co., 2005).

Hoffman, J. D., *The Conservative Party in Opposition: 1945–51* (London: MacGibbon & Kee, 1964).

Holmes, M., *The Labour Government, 1974–79: Political Aims and Economic Reality* (London: Macmillan, 1985).

Jefferys, K. (ed.), *Labour Forces: From Ernest Bevin to Gordon Brown* (London: I.B.Tauris & Co., 2002).

Jefferys, K., *The Labour Party since 1945* (London: Macmillan, 2002).

Jenkins, R., *A Life at the Centre* (London: Politico's Publishing, 2006).

Kaarbo, J., *Coalition Politics and Cabinet Decision Making: A Comparative Analysis of Foreign Policy Choices* (Ann Arbor, MI: University of Michigan Press, 2012).

Kirkup, J., *The Lib–Lab Pact: A Parliamentary Agreement, 1977–78* (Houndmills: Palgrave Macmillan, 2016).

Laver, M. (ed.), *Estimating the Policy Position of Political Actors* (London: Routledge, 2001).

Laver, M., and Schofield, N., *Multiparty Government: The Politics of Coalition in Europe* (Oxford: Oxford University Press, 1998).

Laver, M., and Shepsle, K. A., *Making and Breaking Governments: Cabinets and Legislatures in Parliamentary Democracies* (Cambridge: Cambridge University Press, 1996).

Leach, S., *The Changing Role of Local Politics in Britain* (Bristol: The Policy Press, 2006).

Lijphart, A., *Patterns of Democracy: Government Forms and Performance in Thirty-Six Different Countries* (New Haven, CT: Yale University Press, 2nd edn, 2012).

Loomes, G., *Party Strategies in Western Europe: Party Competition and Electoral Outcomes* (London: Routledge, 2013).

Lyman, R. W., *The First Labour Government, 1924* (London: Chapman & Hall, 1957).

Lynch, P., *SNP: The History of the Scottish National Party* (Welsh Academic Publishing, 2nd edn, 2013).

McAllister, L., *Plaid Cymru: The Emergence of a Political Party* (Bridgend: Seren Books, 2001).

McDonald, A. (ed.), *Reinventing Britain: Constitutional Change under New Labour* (London: University of California Press, 2007).

McKibbin, R., *The Evolution of the Labour Party 1910–1924* (Oxford: Oxford University Press, 1974).

Martin-López, T., *The Winter of Discontent: Myth, Memory and History* (Liverpool: Liverpool University Press, 2014).

Mershon, C., *The Costs of Coalition* (Stanford, CA: Stanford University Press, 2002).

Michie, A., and Hoggart, S., *The Pact: The Inside Story of the Lib–Lab Government, 1977–8* (London: Quartet Books, 1978).

Minogue, M. (ed.), *Documents on Contemporary British Government*, vol. 1: *British Government and Constitutional Change* (Cambridge: Cambridge University Press, 1977).

Moon, N., *Opinion Polls: History, Theory and Practice* (Manchester: Manchester University Press, 1999).

Moore, C., *Margaret Thatcher: The Authorised Biography*, vol. 1: *Not For Turning* (London: Allen Lane, 2013).

Morgan, A., *Harold Wilson* (London: Pluto Press, 1992).

Morgan, K. O., *Britain since 1945: The People's Peace* (Oxford: Oxford University Press, 2001).

Morgan, K. O., *Callaghan: A Life* (Oxford: Oxford University Press, 1997).

Morgan, K. O., *Michael Foot: A Life* (London: HarperCollins, 2007).

Moury, C., *Coalition Government and Party Mandate: How Coalition Agreements Constrain Ministerial Action* (London: Routledge, 2013).

Müller, W. C., and Strøm, K. (eds), *Coalition Governments in Western Europe* (Oxford: Oxford University Press, 2000).

Müller, W. C., and Strøm, K., *Policy, Office, or Votes? How Political Parties in Western Europe Make Hard Decisions* (Cambridge: Cambridge University Press, 1999).

Nikolenyi, C., *Minority Governments in India: The Puzzle of Elusive Majorities* (Abingdon: Routledge, 2010).

Norton, P., *Dissension in the House of Commons: 1974–1979* (Oxford: Oxford University Press, 1980).

Oaten, M., *Coalition: The Politics and Personalities of Coalition Government from 1850* (Petersfield: Harriman House, 2007).

Osmond, J., *Crossing the Rubicon: Coalition Politics Welsh Style* (Cardiff: Institute of Welsh Affairs, 2007).

Otte, T. G., and Black, J. (eds), *Coalition Government in British Politics: From Glorious Revolution to Cameron–Clegg* (London: Social Affairs Unit, 2011).

Paun, A., *United We Stand? Coalition Government in the UK* (London: Constitution Unit, 2010).

Penniman, H. R., *Britain at the Polls, 1979: A Study of the General Election* (Washington, DC: American Enterprise Institute, 1981).

Perkin, H. J., *The Third Revolution: Professional Elites in the Modern World* (London: Routledge, 1996).

Powell, D., *British Politics, 1910–1935: The Crisis of the Party System* (Abingdon: Routledge, 2004).

Powell, G. B., *Contemporary Democracies: Participation, Stability, and Violence* (Cambridge, MA: Harvard University Press, 1984).

Prosser, B., and Denniss, R., *Minority Policy: Rethinking Governance when Parliament Matters* (Melbourne: Melbourne University Publishing, 2015).

Pugh, M., *Speak for Britain! A New History of the Labour Party* (London: Vintage, 2011).

Rasch, B. E., 'Why Minority Governments? Executive-Legislative Relations in the Nordic Countries', in Persson, T., and Wiberg, M. (eds), *Parliamentary Government in the Nordic Countries at a Crossroads: Coping with Challenges from Europeanisation and Presidentialisation* (Stockholm: Santérus Academic Press, 2011), pp. 1–31.

Rasch, B. E., and Tsebelis, G. (eds), *The Role of Governments in Legislative Agenda Setting* (London: Routledge, 2013).

Redvaldsen, D., *The Labour Party in Britain and Norway: Elections and the Pursuit of Power between the World Wars* (London: I.B.Tauris & Co., 2011).

Reitan, E. A., *The Thatcher Revolution: Margaret Thatcher, John Major, Tony Blair, and the Transformation of Modern Britain, 1979–2001* (Oxford: Rowman & Littlefield, 2003).

Riker, W., *The Theory of Political Coalitions* (New Haven, CT: Yale University Press, 1962).

Rogers, R., and Walters, R., *How Parliament Works* (London: Routledge, 6th edn, 2013).

Rose, P., 'The Wilson–Callaghan Government of 1974–79: By-elections (Eventually) Bring Down a Government', in Cook, C., and Ramsden, J. (eds), *By-elections in British Politics* (London: Routledge, 1997), pp. 215–27.

Rosen, G., *Old Labour to New: The Dreams that Inspired, the Battles that Divided* (London: Politico's, 2005).

Russell, A., and Fieldhouse, E., *Neither Left nor Right? The Liberal Democrats and the Electorate* (Manchester: Manchester University Press, 2005).

Russell, P., *Two Cheers for Minority Government: The Evolution of Canadian Parliamentary Democracy* (Toronto: Emond Montgomery, 2008).

Sandbrook, D., *Seasons in the Sun: The Battle for Britain, 1974–1979* (London: Penguin UK, 2012).

Särlvik, B., and Crewe, I., *Decade of Dealignment: The Conservative Victory of 1979 and Electoral Trends in the 1970s* (Cambridge: Cambridge University Press, 1983).

Searle, G. R., *Country before Party: Coalition and the Idea of 'National Government' in Modern Britain, 1885–1987* (London: Longman, 1995).

Seldon, A. (ed.), *UK Political Parties since 1945* (Hemel Hempstead: Philip Allan, 1990).

Seldon, A., and Hickson, K. (eds), *New Labour, Old Labour: The Wilson and Callaghan Governments* (London: Routledge, 2004).

Seldon, A., Finn, M., and Thomas, I. (eds), *The Coalition Effect, 2010–2015* (Cambridge: Cambridge University Press, 2015).

Setälä, M., and Schiller, T. (eds), *Referendums and Representative Democracy: Responsiveness, Accountability and Deliberation* (London: Routledge, 2009).

Shaw, E., *The Labour Party since 1979: Crisis and Transformation* (London: Routledge, 2002).

Shepherd, J., 'The Fall of the Callaghan Government, 1979', in Heppell, T., and Theakston,

K. (eds), *How Labour Governments Fall: From Ramsay Macdonald to Gordon Brown* (London: Palgrave Macmillan, 2013), pp. 113–41.

Shepherd, J., and Laybourn, K., *Britain's First Labour Government* (Houndmills: Palgrave Macmillan, 2006).

Shepherd, J., Davis, J., and Wrigley, C. (eds), *Britain's Second Labour Government: A Reappraisal* (Manchester: Manchester University Press, 2011).

Simms, M., and Wanna, J., *Julia 2010: The Caretaker Election* (Canberra: ANU E Press, 2012).

Smith, A., *Election Timing* (Cambridge: Cambridge University Press, 2004).

Stacey, F., *British Government 1966–1975: Years of Reform* (Oxford: Oxford University Press, 1975).

Steel, D., *A House Divided: The Lib–Lab Pact and the Future of British Politics* (London: Weidenfeld & Nicolson, 1980).

Stefuriuc, I., *Government Formation in Multi-Level Settings: Party Strategy and Institutional Constraints* (London: Palgrave Macmillan, 2013).

Stevenson, J., *Third Party Politics since 1945: Liberals, Alliance and Liberal Democrats* (Oxford: Blackwell Publishers, 1993).

Strøm, K., *Minority Government and Majority Rule* (Cambridge: Cambridge University Press, 1990).

Strøm, K., Müller, W. C., and Bergman, T. (eds), *Delegation and Accountability in Parliamentary Democracies* (Oxford: Oxford University Press, 2006).

Tanner, D., Thane, P., and Tiratsoo, N., *Labour's First Century* (Cambridge: Cambridge University Press, 2000).

Thatcher, M., *The Path to Power* (London: HarperCollins, 1995).

Thorpe, A., *The British General Election of 1931* (Oxford: Oxford University Press, 1991).

Thorpe, A., *A History of the British Labour Party* (London: Palgrave Macmillan, 4th edn, 2015).

Thorpe, A., *Parties at War: Political Organisation in Second World War Britain* (Oxford: Oxford University Press, 2009).

Tierney, S., *Constitutional Referendums: The Theory and Practice of Republican Deliberation* (Oxford: Oxford University Press, 2012).

Torrance, D., *David Steel: Rising Hope to Elder Statesman* (London: Biteback Publishing, 2012).

Tsebelis, G., *Veto Players: How Political Institutions Work* (Princeton, NJ: Princeton University Press, 2011).

Turpin, C., and Tomkins, A., *British Government and the Constitution: Text and Materials* (Cambridge: Cambridge University Press, 2007).

Vowles, J., Aimer, P., Karp, J., Banducci, S. and Miller, R. (eds), *Voters' Veto: The 2002 Election in New Zealand and the Consolidation of Minority Government* (Auckland: Auckland University Press, 2004).

Walker, G., *A History of the Ulster Unionist Party: Protest, Pragmatism and Pessimism* (Manchester: Manchester University Press, 2004).

Walter, D., *Strange Rebirth of Liberal England* (London: Politico's, 2003).

Warde, A., *Consensus and Beyond: The Development of Labour Party Strategy since the Second World War* (Manchester: Manchester University Press, 1982).

Whitehead, P., 'The Labour Governments: 1974-1979', in Hennessy, P., and Seldon, A. (eds), *Ruling Performance: British Governments from Attlee to Thatcher* (Oxford: Basil Blackwell, 1989), pp. 241-273.

Whitehead, P., *The Writing on the Wall: Britain in the Seventies* (London: Joseph, 1985).

Whitelaw, W., *The Whitelaw Memoirs* (London: Aurum Press, 1989).

Whiteley, P., *The Labour Party in Crisis* (London: Methuen & Co., 1983).

Williamson, P., *National Crisis and National Government: British Politics, the Economy and Empire, 1926-1932* (Cambridge: Cambridge University Press, 2003).

Wilson, G., *SNP: The Turbulent Years 1960-1990* (Stirling: Scots Independent, 2009).

Wilson, H., *Final Term: The Labour Government 1974-1976* (London: Weidenfeld & Nicolson, 1979).

Worley, M., *The Foundations of the British Labour Party: Identities, Cultures and Perspectives, 1900-39* (Farnham: Ashgate Publishing, 2009).

Young, H., *One of Us: A Biography of Margaret Thatcher* (London: Macmillan, 1989).

Ziegler, P., *Edward Heath: The Authorised Biography* (London: HarperCollins, 2010).

Index